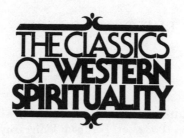

THE CLASSICS
OF WESTERN
SPIRITUALITY

Augustine of Hippo
Selected Writings

TRANSLATION AND INTRODUCTION BY
MARY T. CLARK

PREFACE BY
GOULVEN MADEC

PAULIST PRESS
NEW YORK • RAMSEY • TORONTO

Cover Art:
KEVIN F. NOVACK, C.S.P. is a free-lance artist who is assigned at the St. Thomas More Newman Center of Ohio State University.

Library of Congress
Catalog Card Number: 84-60736

ISBN: 0-8091-2573-0 (paper)
0-8091-0348-6 (cloth)

Published by Paulist Press
545 Island Road, Ramsey, N.J. 07446

Printed and bound in the United States of America

CONTENTS

CONTENTS

Editor of this Volume

MARY T. CLARK is a Religious of the Sacred Heart and professor of philosophy at Manhattanville College. For many years she chaired the Department of Philosophy there and has been visiting professor at Villanova University, Fordham University, the University of San Francisco, and the University of Santa Clara. After graduating from Manhattanville College she completed her doctoral studies at Fordham University and was a postdoctoral Fellow at Yale University.

Augustinian scholars are familiar with her *Augustine, Philosopher of Freedom* and *Augustinian Personalism* as well as her translation of the Trinitarian treatises of Marius Victorinus in the Fathers of the Church series. She is also the author-editor of *An Aquinas Reader* and the *Problem of Freedom*.

Widely known as a lecturer, Sister Clark delivered several papers at the International Patristic Conferences held at Oxford and gave the St. Augustine Lecture at Villanova University in 1969. Her articles have appeared in *Downside Review, Religious Education, Revue des Etudes Augustiniennes, International Philosophical Quarterly*, and *Augustinian Studies*.

Sister Clark is past president of the American Catholic Philosophical Association, treasurer of the Society for Medieval and Renaissance Philosophy, and a member of the executive committee of the Society of Christian Philosophers and of the Conference of Philosophical Societies. She is on the advisory board of *Dionysius* and *Logos*, and on the editorial board of *Faith and Reason*, the journal of the Society of Christian Philosophers.

Author of the Preface

GOULVEN MADEC was born in 1930 in Brittany (France). He studied theology in Rome, classics and philosophy in Paris—the Sorbonne and the Institut Catholique.

Madec received his Doctor of Letters with his work *Saint Ambrose and Philosophy* and his Doctor of Philosophy with his translation of and commentary on the *De Magistro* and *De libero arbitrio* of Augustine, and numerous articles on Augustinian doctrine. He has also edited the *De divina prae destinatione* of John Scotus Eriguena in the *Corpus Christianorum*.

For twenty-five years he has been a member of the Institut d'Etudes Augustiniennes in Paris. He is professor of the History of Patristic Philosophy at the Institut Catholique of Paris and research professor at the National Center of Scientific Research.

To
JAMES D. CLARK, O.S.A.
My beloved brother
who died January 4, 1982
while this book was being written
on St. Augustine
whom Father Clark cherished
and
imitated
by preaching the Christian Message
effectively
because he, like his father Augustine,
loved Christ.

Preface

> *May hymns and weeping ascend in*
> *your sight from the hearts of my*
> *brethren, your censers.*
> *—Confessions, X.4.5*

In 1986 we will celebrate the sixteenth centenary of the conversion of St. Augustine. This work of Mary T. Clark comes just in time for many people to prepare for the celebration of this event. It would be a pity indeed if the festivities were limited to a few congresses or colloquia for scholars. It would, moreover, be contrary to the spirit of Augustine, for as a shepherd of souls he did not favor the intellectual elite. F. Van der Meer expressed it well:

> The best was not good enough for him, and even when he was speaking to *rudes* and *idiotae* he kept nothing back. What he gave out amongst them was that by which he himself lived: "To give you all bread which you can touch and see, that is something which I cannot do", he once said at a distribution of alms on the anniversary of his consecration, "but this word is your portion. I give you the nourishment on which I myself subsist. I am your fellow servant, not the father of your household". It was wholly alien to Augustine to seek to achieve some higher *gnosis* for himself and to preach some kind of vulgarized religion to his people. He knew no ranks in the school of God. . . . He has no hesitation in broaching problems which are solved indirectly or by implication in Scripture but are not explicitly stated or treated here.

One recalls, for instance, the explanations in his sermons of how we draw near to God, not "in a spatial sense, moving as it were from point to point, but by becoming like unto him", or of how we can reach God with the sharp inner insight of the spirit and become happy in that contemplation, or his remarks on the incorporeal and transcendent nature of God, on the relations between the three divine persons, on aspects of Christology, on the Holy Ghost as the soul of the Church, or on the illumination which God grants to the soul so that she is enabled to gain knowledge. He speaks of all this quite freely and in such simple terms that the unlearned can follow him.[1]

Augustine's spirituality is nothing else than the ideal of the Christian life. There is a danger of making a mistake if one looks only for what is original and peculiar to him. After his conversion to the Christian faith Augustine wished to be only one of the *fidelis;* he sought first of all to understand what he believed.[2] After returning to Thagaste, he shared the fruits of his meditation and prayer with those present and absent, with some by conferences, with others by his books.[3] As a priest and later as bishop, he exerted himself for the "defense and illustration" of Christian truth, as he conceived it. And he still wants simple readers with fraternal attitudes who are ready to share the fruit of his confessions.[4]

But the spirituality of Augustine certainly is marked by his experience as a convert and by his own doctrinal personality. In fact, he has interpreted his own spiritual journey as identified with biblical man: with Adam the sinner renewed and saved in Jesus Christ; with David, with the prodigal son, with Paul. And that is why so many Christian readers, such as Teresa of Avila,[5] can identify with the author of the *Confessions* for all time, whatever the cultural differences. The spirit of Augustine breathes where

---

1. F. Van der Meer, *Augustine the Bishop* (New York: Sheed and Ward, 1961), pp. 433, 435.
2. Cf. Augustine, *Contra Academicos*, III.20.43.
3. Possidius de Calama. *Vita s. Augustini*, 3.
4. Augustine, *Confessions*, X.4.5–6.
5. Cf. *Introduction*, below.

it wills and its influence is as varied as it is multiple. Nevertheless one can say that his contribution to Christian spirituality applies both to the personal realm by the themes of conversion, of interiority, of the reflection of the mind upon itself and on God; and to the realm of community, of the Church, the total Christ, the two cities, and last but not least with the ideal of religious life in common: *anima una et cor unum*.

At the time of his conversion, Augustine, while reading the *Libri platonicorum*, received a "liberating shock," says P. Henry.[6] These books directed him toward an interiority in which the mind finds itself while going beyond itself in order to meet God, its foundation, Absolute Being. On several occasions Augustine recognized his indebtedness to Neoplatonism. Consequently certain people find reasons for maintaining that this dependence with respect to philosophy compromises his understanding of the Christian faith; but Mary Clark insists rightly on the differences.[7] The God of Augustine is not the One of Plotinus. As E. R. Dodd said most aptly: "Plotinus never gossiped with the One as Augustine gossiped in the *Confessions*."[8] When P. Alfaric affirmed that Augustine in 386 was converted morally as well as intellectually to Neoplatonism rather than to the Gospel,[9] he was gravely mistaken as to the importance of Augustine's decision to be baptized. It is true that the *Confessions* do not emphasize this point,[10] but reading the account of Marius Victorinus's conversion will be sufficient to make it clear that becoming a Christian did not necessarily go along with being an intellectual Neoplatonist. It was not enough to recognize Neoplatonic principles in John's Prologue; one had to "enter the Church of Christ" and "confess Christ before men without blushing at the mysterious humility of the Word."[11]

It is also true that the conversion of Augustine was not limited to the decision to be baptized. It was also a commitment to a life of asceticism and contemplation, which the reading of the *Hortensius* of Cicero made him desire.[12] This meant renouncing

---

6. P. Henry, *Plotin et l'occident* (Louvain, 1934), p. 78.
7. Cf. *Introduction*, below.
8. E. R. Dodd, *Hibbert Journal* 26 (1927–1928); 471.
9. P. Alfaric, *L'evolution intellectuelle de S. Augustin* (Paris, 1918), p. 399.
10. Cf. *Confessions*, IX.6.14.
11. Ibid., VIII.2.3.
12. Cf. *Introduction*, below.

false goods—pleasure, riches, glory—and seeking happiness through the love of that Wisdom which is God, the only good. This eudemonism is itself suspect in the eyes of some people. Recently it was maintained that Augustine falsified the Christian idea of love by confining it in the schema *frui-uti*.[13] There can be no doubt that the Augustinian ideal is certainly generous and disinterested love. However, it requires being able to practice it, that is, stripping oneself of egotism, of a possessive love, and uniting oneself to God, the universal Good, pure generosity, the Principle of all generosity. For there are two loves: one that is holy and one that is impure; one that is social, the other private; one that is mindful of the common good in view of the heavenly society, the other that reduces even the common good to private property with a view to arrogant domination.[14] And these loves are rivals in the heart of man as in the story of the two cities.[15]

Certainly Augustine, in his reflection, made free use of various philosophical themes that he judged, rightly or wrongly, in harmony with Christian teaching; but these themes were included in a train of thought that was specifically Christian, Christic. Indeed, the thought of Augustine is developed entirely in the framework of the theme of the two Adams. Before sin, in paradise, God refreshed man by an interior spring; man had no need to receive words from without; he drank of the spring itself—the Truth that came forth from the intimacy of his being. Pride destroyed this regime of interiority. Man turned away from God; he cast out his intimate being, thus drying up the interior spring. Henceforth he has need of the rain that falls from the clouds, that is, from Revelation, from the teaching of God formulated in human language by the Prophets and uniquely by Christ the Incarnate Word.[16] The Word became man in order to meet man in his actual condition, in the regime of exteriority, the consequence of original sin; in order to bring him back to the regime of interiority and to restore the mind to the image of God. "There is only one teacher: incorruptible Truth, the only interior teacher, who has become the exterior teacher in order to recall exterior

---

13. Cf. J. Brechthen, *Augustinus doctor caritatis* (Meisenheim am Glan: Hain, 1975).
14. Cf. Augustine, *De Genesi ad litteram*, XI.15.20.
15. Cf. Introduction to the *City of God*, below.
16. Cf. Augustine, *De Genesi Contra Manichaeos*, II.4.5–5.6.

realities to interior realities. He took the form of a slave and he deigned to show himself as lowly to those who were fallen low so that his sublimity could be known by those who are rising."[17] Christ, the Mediator, is the way to the Fatherland: Listen to the Lord, "I am the way, the truth, and the life" (Jn 14:6). If you seek the truth, follow the way, for the way is also the truth; it is where you are going; it is the means by which you go. It is through Christ that you come to Christ. How do we come to Christ by Christ? To Christ God by Christ man; by the Word made flesh to the Word which was in the beginning with God; by what men have eaten to what the angels eat each day. It is in fact what was written: "He gave them the bread of heaven; man ate the bread of angels" (Ps 77:24–25). "What is the bread of angels?" "In the beginning was the Word and the Word was with God and the Word was God" (Jn 1:1). How did man eat the bread of angels? "And the Word was made flesh and dwelt amongst us" (Jn 1:14).[18]

The humility of God makes up for the pride of man. The bread of angels has adapted itself to the present condition of humanity; it has become the milk of babes. It is like the mother who nourishes herself with bread and changes it into milk for her child.

> In the Church, those who are united to the Truth speak the Truth by which all things were made (cf. Jn 1:2). The Truth is the Word made flesh and his dwelling among us. The Truth is Christ born of God, one from one, the only and coeternal Son. Truth is in the form of a slave; Truth is born of the Virgin Mary, Truth is in the passion, the crucifixion, resurrection and ascension. It is alway the Truth that the little one can grasp and that the little one cannot grasp. Truth in the bread and the milk, in the bread of the mighty and the milk of little ones; for it is the same bread which passes through the flesh to become milk.[19]

---

17. Cf. Augustine, *Contra epistolam Manichaei quam vocant fundamenti*, 36, 41; cf. Introduction, below.

18. Augustine, *Tractatus in Johannis evangelium*, XIII.4.

19. Augustine, *Enarratio in psalmum*, 33.s.1,6.

God wants to nourish us with milk not in order to keep us at the stage of childhood, but so that nourished by milk we may arrive at solid food, the bread of angels, the Word of God. "Our milk is the humble Christ, our food is the same Christ equal to the Father. He nourishes you with milk, in order to fill you with bread."[20] Need I develop further this doctrine of spiritual growth which is purely Pauline in inspiration?[21]

To anyone seeking a formula to sum up Augustinian spirituality I would like to propose the famous sentence from the *Confessions*, VII.10,16: "I am the food of grown men. Grow and you shall feed upon me. You will not change me into yourself, but you will be changed into me." Moreover, it corresponds perfectly with the theological axiom "believe that you may understand," according to which faith has to overflow into the intelligence. We understand, I hope, that every work by Augustine is essentially spiritual, like those of the other Fathers of the Church; at least that could be claimed if his works were not concerned with controversy. Nonetheless the works of Augustine abound in spiritual riches, and Mary T. Clark had to make some difficult choices. One is tempted to collect many small quotations into an anthology so as to satisfy by its literary quality the aesthetic sense of the readers rather than to select quotations because of the spiritual aspirations expressed. For my part I would like to congratulate Mary T. Clark for having resisted that temptation and for presenting works or at least whole books. It must be recognized that some of these writings—but also the sermons and letters—are the spiritual exercises that Augustine produced and that readers experience with him in their meditation in order to progress in the spiritual life.

---

20. Augustine, *Tractatus in epistulam Johannis*, III.1.
21. Cf. 1 Cor 3:2.

Foreword

This volume offers translations of some writings of St. Augustine of Hippo that reveal the character and the depth of his spirituality. His spirituality is Trinitarian. His religious experience centered on the Divine Persons to which the New Testament witnessed. In the *Confessions* we see his religious experience developing and in *On the Trinity* he reflects on the foundations of this spirituality.

In the *Confessions* Books VII–X the reader sees Augustine responding to the human vocation to return to God by becoming authentically personal, returning to the self, the source of those actions, intellectual and voluntary, which make existence personal. Gradually he integrated all the bodily, emotional, and intellectual levels of human existence within his love for the Triune God. This process of re-formation to the image of God was a conversion that continued all his life. He was then able to declare that the glory and responsibility and dignity of personal existence is its capacity for God. The fulfillment of this capacity is re-formation to the image of God by the grace of Christ and by human freedom. This is the essential process of Augustinian spiritual life as it is of Christian life.

In Augustine's dialogue *The Happy Life*, the Wisdom of the Father is discovered as the spiritual sun illuminating the mind and uniting the soul by God's Spirit with the Source of that Truth which brings happiness.

In his *Homilies on the Psalms* 119–122 Augustine calls on Christ as the Interior Master to open the minds of the faithful to the spiritual understanding of Scripture. Chanting these "songs of the steps," the faithful can ascend from the valley of tears that Christ has sanctified with his sufferings only by opening their hearts to the love of God to be transformed. Their own love or longing for

God is made effective by the Gift of charity, the Gift of the Holy Spirit, who impels the faithful toward the peace of the Mystical Jerusalem or City of God. In these homilies Augustine teaches that it is love that gives vitality to Christianity and to prayer.

In his *Homilies on the Gospel of St. John* Augustine emphasizes the role of love in binding the faithful to Christ. Christ is the seed of Abraham, and to be part of Christ is to belong to the Covenant of Faith. The mystery of the Incarnate Word is bound up with the mystery of the Church and the Sacraments and with Christ's universal Lordship. Through this Word of God persons are both created and re-created.

In his *Homily on the First Epistle of St. John* he warns that even those who believe in God can become practical heretics if they do not love their neighbors. Only by fraternal love does one come to the knowledge of God that is life in the Trinity.

In *On the Trinity* he shows the Christian how to ascend from contemplating the image of the Trinity in the soul to the contemplation of Trinitarian life. He speaks of the presence of God in the memory, understanding, and will.

In the treatise *On Seeing God* Augustine tries to reconcile the Scriptural statement that Moses spoke to God face-to-face with the statement in Matthew 5:8: "No man has seen God at any time." In the process we learn that the vision of God as He is belongs only to hearts that are cleansed; God is seen with the eyes of the mind by the pure of heart.

In the treatise *On the Presence of God* we learn of God's dwelling in each one as in many temples and in all together as in one temple. In this temple Christ dwells as in a body of which He is the Head. The Communion of Saints is this Temple of God. This is the special dwelling place of God; but as God the Creator He is present everywhere, and in His human body He is somewhere in heaven.

In the *City of God* the theme of the Communion of Saints is expanded, and so our volume ends where it began—on a discussion of the experience of human sufferings and the hope of happiness: that longing for God in sorrow and in joy portrayed in the *Confessions* and in *The Happy Life*. The vestige of God in every good thing calls us to appreciate it and yet transcend it by allowing the infinite longing of the human heart to seek true happiness in the Infinite God. Such happiness is visible only to the eyes of faith and is a gift of God to whom one prays for happiness. Here, too, we see the social aspect of Augustinian spirituality, the love of God uniting people into the City of God.

Finally, in the *Rule of St. Augustine* it is clear how very close to Vatican II orientations is the Augustine who authored the first monastic rule in the West, since this Rule promotes interpersonal unity through mutual love as the Christian environment that enables all to remain "intent upon God." Charity and contemplation purify the heart for the seeing of God and He takes up his dwelling in each temple and in the Monastery as in one temple of God. The evangelical inspiration of this Rule is the Acts of the Apostles 4:32, where we read: "The whole group of believers were united, heart and soul."

To follow the *Rule of St. Augustine* is to make a spiritual ascent to that Beauty which is God, the Splendor of Truth, the Source of happiness. The monastery is intended to be the paradigm of all Christian life, namely, a "living in freedom under grace." I am grateful to T. J. Van Bavel, O.S.A., for the use of his headings in the *Rule of St. Augustine*. My translation is based on the Latin text in the critical edition made by L. Verheijen, O.S.A.

In all these translations I have modernized the punctuation to adapt it to English usage, and where English and French translations exist I have been assisted by the numerous versions I was able to consult and compare.

I now wish to express gratitude to Richard Payne, the inaugurator of the Classics of Western Spirituality, who suggested that I select and translate those writings of Augustine most likely to let us participate in the spirituality of this great saint. To Dr. John Farina, the associate editor of the Paulist Press, who has assumed the editorial tasks related to the Classics, I express sincere appreciation for his professional advice and careful supervision. The early interest and continued encouragement of Ewert Cousins, director of the Spirituality Program at Fordham University and consultant for this series, have been influential in the completion of this work.

I received welcome and helpful advice on sections of the Introduction from colleagues—Peter Brown, Peter Manchester, Robert Crouse—when it was first being formulated. And I am grateful to Margaret Williams, R.S.C.J., my former teacher, for her generous editorial assistance.

FOREWORD

My final word of gratitude is expressed to all those Augustinian scholars from whom I have learned at conferences in Oxford and in America and by reading their books and articles throughout many years. They are too numerous to list and yet to them the twentieth century owes an ever greater knowledge of Augustine of Hippo, a saint for all times, a medieval bishop and a modern thinker whose wisdom is needed by an age like ours when the human spirit is thirsting for truth to guide its love. Finally, with you I thank God for Augustine.

Introduction

THE SPIRITUALITY OF ST. AUGUSTINE

The purpose of this volume is to make the spirituality of St. Augustine of Hippo available to people of the twentieth century, some of whom have forgotten that Augustine's *Confessions* was once *the* classic of the spiritual life in the Western world. That is why there will be no direct attempt to trace the genesis and the evolution of Augustinian spirituality. Instead, the Augustinian tradition in spirituality, which was the common heritage of the Christian laity and of many religious orders in medieval and modern times, can be found represented in the necessarily selective number of writings reproduced in this volume.

In this Introduction I focus on Augustine's religious consciousness in its living relationship with the objects of his Christian faith. This presupposes dogmatic theology, on which this spirituality is based, and of which he is one of the earliest architects. Many excellent books, however, have already treated Augustine the theologian; here we encounter Augustine as guide to the spiritual life. Spirituality is also very closely allied to moral theology, because spirituality is concerned with human acts, very specifically with those human acts that refer explicitly and immediately to God, above all, prayer and everything connected with prayer in the ascetical and mystical life, that is, religious exercises as well as religious experiences.

As Louis Bouyer has so well shown in his monumental studies of the spiritual life, the variety of spiritualities is traceable to the uniqueness of individual vocations and of individual personalities, this very uniqueness causing "variations in the concrete application of the Gospel to a human life."[1] That is why Augus-

---

1. Louis Bouyer, *The Spirituality of the New Testament and the Fathers* (New York: The Seabury Press, 1963), p. xi.

tinian spirituality, which has often been called a spirituality of conversion, can never be understood apart from St. Augustine's *Confessions*, where he reveals his own personality and his unique call from God.

Christian spirituality, as we know, existed from the time of Christ's encounter with His first disciples, who responded to His creative power of transforming them by His words and actions into children of God, images of this Divine Son who exists as generous love.

This is the spirituality Augustine discovered in the Scriptures and interpreted by the reflection of his classically educated mind, which was forced to respond to the challenges of heretics. This spirituality, derived from the Scriptures and made public in the Liturgy, had been lived and discussed for two centuries before Neoplatonism appeared on the scene. The Word of God was the source of this Christian spirituality, which was referred to by the Greek Fathers as a *gnosis*, an understanding, as far as possible, of the Mystery, "an interiorized comprehension of the Scriptures causing us to attain the very heart of the design of God as it is realized in Christ."[2]

This Christian *gnosis* was what St. Paul called true wisdom, an awareness of the Divine Plan discoverable in Scripture and in history. Very early in his career Augustine experienced the call to wisdom, and he instinctively felt that this was a call to Christ. He discovered that the role of the Logos was to win us from ignorance and to lead us to the light of wisdom expressed in the Divine Law. Later he became convinced that wisdom cannot thrive without faith, hope, and charity. In his first completed work, *The Happy Life*, he concluded that happiness is found in a perfect knowledge of God, the Truth. But Monica, his Christian mother, reminded all present that this perfect knowledge is obtained by a "well-founded faith, a joyful hope, and an ardent love."[3] It took many years for Augustine's notional assent to this remark to become real assent.

As Clement of Alexandria once said: "Christian *gnosis* be-

---

2. Ibid., p. 295.
3. Augustine, *The Happy Life*, I.4.35.

comes firmly founded through charity."[4] Faith working through love allows one to be nourished by the truths of faith and this increases the exercise of charity. Faith comes with baptism and it leads to intimacy with God, an intimacy that grows with understanding. The early Greek Fathers spoke of the presence and growth of the Logos in the soul. This is the basis of Christian mystical experience. The human spirit is given a participation in the Divinity, which permits friendship with God, communion and communication by prayer and loving action. For the Christian who shares in the being of God, this union leads to a gradual liberation from the body, not in any sense of separation or denunciation, but of a liberation from all sensible things and actions that interfere with unitive prayer. The motivation for this mystical life as well as for the monastic life, which was formed to liberate the Christian from all bodily interference, was evangelical. The Gospel promoted union with God and sacrifice.

Although Christians were encouraged to say yes to life, the following of a crucified Christ whose kingdom was not of this world entailed the acceptance of the Cross as life-giving. Christian asceticism was not, therefore, a condemnation of the world. It was primarily a choice for union with Christ begun in baptism. The Christian dialectic, like that of Christ, was triadic: dying–rising–giving the Spirit of Love. The disciples who received the Spirit understood what God had revealed through the Prophets and his Son. One of the first to express what he understood was St. Paul, whose discipleship began by a sudden conversion. An early theologian, he recognized Grace to be the gift of a new Life, a new Being, the Life of the Risen Christ entered into by baptism through the gift of the Spirit. This Spirit is the Spirit of Christ, who raised Jesus from the dead. We are "in Christ Jesus," according to St. Paul, and that is why Christ's Resurrection is ours. This is an early discussion of Christian mystical life (where the mystical life is not understood as an "extraordinary" experience), a union without confusion, which calls Christians to allow the realization of the presence of God to flood their consciousness.

Martyrdom had ensured a direct and immediate union with God; monastic asceticism later replaced it as a means for promot-

---

4. Clement, *Stromata*, VI.9.78, quoted in Bouyer, *Spirituality*, p. 272.

ing union in this life. The pleasurable life was seen as a possible temptation to forsake the reality of the Gospel, the Good News of a God-man whose treasure was in heaven, namely, the Trinity. Only charity admitted one to life in the Trinity. The ascetic life was chosen by Christians to enable them to dominate those passions that might threaten charity.

Whereas it is true that Augustine's reading of the books of the Platonists enabled him to understand philosophically the spirituality of God that was presupposed in the Scriptures, he has told us that they sent him back to the Scriptures. There he began to learn, first from St. Paul and later from St. John, the great differences between Platonic philosophy and the true philosophy of Christianity. The charity and humility of Christ made the great difference. For Plotinus the soul sought to regain its intellectuality in order to resemble the One. For Augustine the soul must seek to love rightly and generously in order to resemble the Blessed Trinity. He found Christian perfection explained in the Gospel as "becoming children of God" who resemble Him by an ever greater growth in wisdom. This wisdom is an awareness that God is Love and that he opens Himself only to those who by his Gift of the Spirit dwelling in their hearts live the life of love in spirit and in truth as did the Son.

The fact that Augustine was influenced by the fourth-century culture of the late Roman Empire to express his spiritual insights through philosophical language and through images drawn from Neoplatonic writings should not blind us to the evangelical origin of his spirituality. We should adopt as a working principle that if an Augustinian insight can be equally well derived from Scripture or from Christian theology or from Platonism/Neoplatonism, there is no justification, in the absence of parallel literary evidence, to conclude that it had been learned only from philosophical writings. This is the case even when the insight under discussion is defended philosophically.

Meditation on the Scriptures in the light of the Logos-made-flesh formed the mind of St. Paul, and also that of St. Augustine. Consider their completely new view of the world as a reality where human freedom encounters divine freedom in the life of the human spirit called to resurrection through baptism in Christ. This new risen life, in the likeness of the Son entered into here and now by faith and baptism, was described by St. Paul in the

INTRODUCTION

following passage. Augustine, who wrote commentaries on the Pauline epistles, was deeply affected by this passage:

> So, then, my brothers, there is no necessity for us to obey our unspiritual selves or to live unspiritual lives. If you do live in that way you are doomed to die; but if by the Spirit you put an end to the misdeeds of the body you will live.
>
> Everyone moved by the Spirit is a son of God. The Spirit you received is not the spirit of slaves bringing fear into your lives again; it is the spirit of sons, and it makes us cry out, "Abba, Father!" The Spirit himself and our spirit bear united witness that we are children of God. And if we are children we are heirs as well: heirs of God and coheirs with Christ, sharing his sufferings so as to share his glory.
>
> I think that what we suffer in this life can never be compared to the glory as yet unrevealed, which is waiting for us. The whole creation is eagerly waiting for God to reveal His sons. It was not for any fault on the part of creation that it was made unable to attain its purpose, it was made so by God; but creation still retains the hope of being freed, like us, from its slavery to decadence, to enjoy the same freedom and glory as the children of God. From the beginning till now the entire creation, as we know, has been groaning in one great act of giving birth; and not only creation, but all of us who possess the first-fruits of the Spirit, we too groan inwardly as we wait for our bodies to be set free. For we must be content to hope that we shall be saved—our salvation is not in sight, we should not have to be hoping for it if it were—but, as I say, we must hope to be saved since we are not saved yet—it is something we must wait for with patience.
>
> The Spirit too comes to us in our weakness. For when we cannot choose words in order to pray properly, the Spirit expresses our plea in a way that could never be put into words, and God who knows everything in our hearts knows perfectly well what He means, and that the pleas of the saints expressed by the Spirit are according to the mind of God.

INTRODUCTION

We know that by turning everything to their good God cooperates with all those who love Him, with all those that he has called according to his purpose. They are the ones he chose specially long ago and intended to become the images of his Son, so that his Son might be the eldest of many brothers. He called those he intended for this; those he called he justified, and with those he justified he shared his glory.

Nothing therefore can come between us and the love of Christ, even if we are troubled or worried, or being persecuted, or lacking food or clothes, or being threatened or even attacked. As scripture promised: "For your sake we are being massacred daily, and reckoned as sheep for the slaughter." These are trials through which we triumph, by the power of him who loved us.

For I am certain of this: neither death nor life, no angel, no prince, nothing that exists, nothing still to come, not any power, or height or depth, nor any created thing, can ever come between us and the love of God made visible in Christ Jesus our Lord.[5]

It was clear to Paul and became gradually clear to Augustine that the spiritual life was that lived by Christ on earth, a life of truth and love that was rooted in the Trinity.

Augustinian spirituality centers on the Divine Trinity revealed in the New Testament and understood as far as possible by reflection on its image in the human soul—the memory, understanding, and will converted to God the Father in the light of the Word and under the influence of the Holy Spirit. Although the early Christians read about the Trinity in Scripture and could discover the Father, Son, and Spirit revealing themselves through their salvific actions, the piety of Christians tended to focus on Father and Son, and up until the fourth century the word "God" was generally used to mean the "Father." Only in A.D. 325, under attack from the Arians, was the consubstantiality of the Son declared a dogma at Nicaea. After Athanasius, the theologian who did most to defend the dogma of the Trinity was Marius Victor-

---

5. Rom 8.

inus,[6] who worked out the first metaphysical exposition of the consubstantiality of Father, Son, and Holy Spirit. His very vigorous statement of the Spirit as consubstantial with the Father and Son was not a widely prevalent position before this. One can also see from the hymns authored by Marius Victorinus that the Spirit was not as present in his own personal piety as were the Father and Son.

Augustine, however, developed a Trinitarian spirituality in which the Trinity to which the New Testament centrally witnessed became a reality in his religious consciousness. We see Augustine in dialogue with Father, Son, and Spirit throughout the *Confessions*.

Augustine's Experience

Since the *Confessions* were begun in A.D. 397, more than ten years after Augustine's conversion, it was inevitable that he should record there the religious understanding not yet possessed in 386. He naturally evaluated many of his youthful actions in the light of his more mature understanding of the Christian faith. That is the significance of the Scriptural quotations generously scattered throughout this work. Although he made a distinct effort to speak frankly of his actions and attitudes in the days before his baptism, his faith only later enabled him to realize what God was doing to draw him to Himself through the people, the actions, and the circumstances that were part of his life.

The *Confessions* open with an expression of hope that the God who is everywhere may be responsive to Augustine's prayer for God to come within his soul to save him by enabling him to fulfill the great commandment to love God. This began the dialogue with God that unites all parts of the *Confessions*.

The content of the prayer is significant. Augustine praised and thanked God for the providence, conversion, and illumination that had brought his soul's journey to a happy ending. When he declared: "You have made us to be *toward* Yourself, O Lord, and our hearts are restless until they rest in You,"[7] he was declaring creation to be a call to union with God, a conviction he only dimly

---

6. Marius Victorinus, *Theological Treatises on the Trinity*, trans. M. T. Clark (Washington, D.C.: Catholic University Press, 1981).

7. Augustine, *Confessions*, I.1 (hereafter *Conf.*).

INTRODUCTION

experienced as a youth but one that was reinforced by his reading of St. Paul and St. John. The discussion of conversion as the soul's journey to God used the language of *reditus*[8] at times to indicate introversion in contrast to preoccupation with the sensible world, more often to indicate Godlikeness or that primary state of graced perfection to which the soul yearns to return.

In the first six books of the *Confessions* he relates how he had sought God outside himself by means of his bodily senses. In the seventh book he explains how the Platonists had taught him to go from the exterior to the interior, the "better part," and how he had attempted, like the Platonists, to use his intellect to see God, trying to take himself from his own interior to the superior, or God.

> I was admonished by all this to return to my own self, and, with you to guide me, I entered into the innermost part of myself, and I was able to do this because you were my helper. I entered and I saw with my soul's eye (such as it was) an unchangeable light shining above this light of my soul and above my mind. It was not the ordinary light which is visible to all flesh, nor something of the same sort, only bigger, as though it might be our ordinary light shining much more brightly and filling everything with its greatness. No, it was not like that; it was different, entirely different from anything of the kind. Nor was it above my mind as oil floats on water or as the heaven is above the earth. It was higher than I, because it made me, and I was lower because I was made by it. He who knows truth knows that light, and he who knows that light knows eternity. Love knows it. O eternal truth and true love and beloved eternity! You are my God; to you I sigh by day and by night. And when I first knew you, you raised me up so that I could see that there was something to see and that I still lacked the ability to see it. And you beat back the weakness of my sight, blazing upon me with your rays, and I trembled in love and in dread, and I found that I was far distant from you, in a

---

8. Cf. R. D. Crouse, "*Recurrens in te unum:* The Pattern of St. Augustine's *Confessions,*" Studia Patristica XIV (Berlin, 1976).

region of total unlikeness, as if I were hearing your voice from on high saying: "I am the food of grown men. Grow and you shall feed upon me. And you will not, as with the food of the body, change me into yourself, but you will be changed into me!"[9]

We see that Augustine was drawn to God by natural desire. He ascended from the body to sense power and from sense power to intellectual judgment by which he acknowledged the eternity of Truth above his changing mind. "And then in a flash of a trembling glance, my mind arrived at That Which Is."[10] He was torn away by the weight of his sins, bad habits that enchained him and made him fall back, through weakness. He tried to find a way of gaining the strength needed for enjoying God but could not find it until he

embraced that Mediator betwixt God and men, the man Christ Jesus, who is over all, God blessed for evermore, calling to him and saying: I am the way, the truth, and the life, and mingling with our flesh that food which I lacked the strength to take; for the Word was made flesh, so that Your Wisdom by which you created all things, might give its milk to our infancy.[11]

But he did not immediately embrace the Creator because at that time (A.D. 385) he thought of Christ simply as a man of the very highest wisdom.[12] Whereas the Platonists had enabled him to understand the immateriality of God, St. Paul[13] admonished him to follow Christ, the only way to the Father. Through the word and/or the actions of Christians, that is, through Monica, Ambrose, Simplicianus, Ponticianus and the two Roman civil servants, Anthony, Victorinus, Paul, through such Christians Augustine had been awakened to the reality of the kingdom of God, which is not of this world.

When Augustine finally understood that Christ in the Scrip-

---

9. *Conf.* VII.10.
10. Ibid., VII.17.
11. Ibid., VII.18.
12. Ibid., VII.19.
13. Rom 13:13.

INTRODUCTION

tures was witnessing to His divine Father and to the Holy Spirit, and when he learned from Genesis that man was made to the image and likeness of the Trinity, he discovered the glory and the responsibility and the dignity of personal existence. Human dignity, he learned, was not based on man's unlikeness to the beast but on man's possible likeness to God through deification. To be a human person is to be *capax Dei*. This capacity is actualized through the Son but it refers to the Trinity. If the soul was made to the image of the Son of God, as St. Paul taught, then in fact it was made to the image of the Trinity, since Christ had said: "I and the Father are one." And the Spirit sent by Christ was spoken of as "My Spirit."

The conversion Augustine experienced was a re-formation to the image of the Trinity through the gifts of faith and love. This interior re-formation is a divine work surpassing human power. Throughout the *Confessions* we follow this re-formation as it engaged his consciousness and consent. In later years he was to teach that this image of the Son can be remade in the human person only by the Trinity who originally made man to the image of God in holiness and justice. The Trinity re-forms persons not only to intimacy with themselves but to Christian community as well, a community of faith and charity. "And in making all things you did not make them out of Yourself in your own likeness (which is the exemplary form of all things) but out of nothing, in a formless unlikeness to Yourself, which afterwards might be formed by your likeness, *returning to You*, the One, according to its appointed capacity in the measure given by You to each being in its own kind."[14]

This movement of return toward the One is initiated by the Word of God, who in receiving all in love from the Father returns all in love. Love is the special name of the Spirit, Augustine wrote in a later work, but since God is Love and God is Trinity, the Father is Love as is the Son. As love, the Father is the principle of creation and providence; as love, the Word is the principle of conversion and illumination, and the Spirit as the principle of love is the principle of *return* to the Father. Loving intimacy with the Trinity is true contemplative wisdom, and wisdom is the true and only image of God, a dynamic process of involvement in God,

---

14. *Conf.* XII.28.38.

society, and the world through love. Wisdom, the most active of all active things, reaches from end to end mightily. Through intimacy with the divine Persons the soul attains likeness to Wisdom and shares in divine creative and providential action, illuminating and loving action. Augustine experienced the Christians of his day participating in such action.

To understand the soul's movement toward union with God recorded in the *Confessions* we need to be aware of Augustine's ladder of being or hierarchy of natures: above the soul, which as life-giving is called *anima* and as intellectual, *animus*, there is *mens* or mind, receiving its spiritual substance "from above," as *spiritus*. Below the soul there is *sensus*, and below *sensus* there is *corpus*. The conversion described by Augustine in the first part of the Confessions was from *sensus* to *mens*, from one level of the soul's life to another as he became aware of his philosophical capacities through reading Cicero's *Hortensius* and the books of the Platonists. Later, through the gifts of faith and love, came that conversion to God which unified his various levels of human existence by healing the division in his heart. At last he could declare: "And now, my soul, I say to you that you are my better part; you animate the whole bulk of the body, giving it life—a thing which no body can do for another body. But your God is for you, also, the life of your life."[15]

To try to enjoy that divine life Augustine by thought ascended above the summit of his soul. He ascended beyond the life-force, beyond the force of perception to "the fields and spacious palaces of memory, where lie the treasures of innumerable images of all kinds of things brought in by the senses."[16] In his memory was all that he had learned from the liberal sciences. He remembered not only how he had learned them but how he felt when he did. The multiplicity within the memory symbolized for him human life as a "life variously manifold and quite immeasurable."[17]

He ascended beyond this memory-force and drew near to the Light above, to God who transcends the memory. Because God is Truth, and the mind participates in truth, to remember what we

15. Ibid., X.6.
16. Ibid., X.8.
17. Ibid., X.17.

have learned is to find God in our memory or mind. He is not the mind but the God of the mind. And so Augustine met God in his memory, listened to Him and loved Him, confessing:

> Late it was that I loved You, beauty so ancient and so new, late I loved You! And look, You were within me and I was outside, and there I sought for you and in my ugliness I plunged into the beauties that you have made. You were with me and I was not with you. Those outer beauties kept me from you, yet if they had not been in you, they would not have existed at all. You called, you cried out, you shattered my deafness: you flashed, you shone, you scattered my blindness: you breathed fragrance, and I drew in my breath and I pant for you! I tasted and I am hungry and thirsty: you touched me, and I burned for your peace.[18]

In Book X Augustine revealed the state of his soul at the time of writing. He spoke of the variety of his life-forms, his life-levels still in need of an ever greater personal unity if they were to reflect their Exemplar: One God in Threeness. The unity he needed has to be given from above, from God, who presides above the memory to illuminate the mind. He confessed: "Only in You, when my scattered parts are gathered, do I find a stable place for my mind."[19] He admitted that after being a priest and a bishop he had not yet arrived at that perfect unity to which, as images of God, we are called. He spoke of this unity, this wholeheartedness in loving God above all things, as the result of true prayer and asceticism.

> When in my whole self I shall cling to you united, I shall find no sorrow anywhere, no labor; wholly alive will my life be all full of you. Those whom you fill, you raise up. And now, since I am not yet full of You, I am a burden to myself.[20]

---

18. Ibid., X.27.
19. Ibid., X.40.
20. Ibid., X.28.

INTRODUCTION

Image of the Trinity

In his book *On the Trinity* Augustine worked out the theology of that Trinitarian God of whom his religious experience had made him increasingly conscious. First there had been the experience of Truth and then there came the experiential knowledge of God through love. This experience of love was an experience of the Spirit but also of the entire Trinity.

Because he studied the Trinity in the cultural climate of the Arian claim of the Son's inequality with the Father, Augustine's Trinitarian theory, unlike that of the Greek Fathers, stressed the unity of the Divine Substance rather than the distinction of the Divine Persons. He spoke of the Trinity as one single divine Nature subsisting in three Persons having the same nature. At first the Greek Fathers had used the word "God" only of the Father whereas for Augustine "God" signified the Godhead, referring implicitly to all the Persons. He attributed to all three Persons indistinctly all external divine activities, but some divine actions were appropriated to each divine Person, whereas the Greek Fathers tended to emphasize the distinct role of each Person in a community of action.

The divine unity was safeguarded by the status of the Persons as mutual relations of the Divine Essence itself. Unlike Aristotelian accidents, the relations do not add perfections to God but constitute something beyond the perfection of the essence alone. In later theology they were called "subsistent relations." This means that to be the Divine Being is to be related as Father, Son, and Holy Spirit are related.

Although Augustine learned much about the Trinity from Gregory Nazianzen, Hilary of Poitier, Ambrose, and other Fathers of the Church, his understanding of the Trinity as "imaged" in the human soul was truly original. And since the Trinity is central to Augustinian spirituality, this spirituality can be distinguished rather sharply from that of the Greek Fathers, who studied directly the Mystery of God in Christ.[21] The influence of his later reading of the Greek Fathers led Augustine to deal more fully with the divine relations within the Trinity itself. But he was fascinated with the mystery of the human self, which he tried to fathom in the light of the Trinity. This reflexive and anthropo-

---

21. Bouyer, *Spirituality*, pp. 467–94.

15

centric orientation contributed to Western Christianity a valid interest in human experience. It also promoted the interiorization of Christianity, which ensured that for centuries the Church would be marked by the mystical element of religion accented by Baron Von Hugel as of supreme importance for authentic religion.

Because of the universal influence of Augustinian spirituality with its emphasis on the self, it has been said that the Latin West was deprived of Greek spirituality's direct approach to the Christian Mystery, a *gnosis* set forth at Alexandria and developed by the Greek Fathers of the Church.[22] Christians in the West, it was said, tended to see asceticism as the implication of Augustinian introspection instead of as the actualization of the baptismal union with Christ crucified, which it really is. Augustine also rejected the Alexandrian identification of the image with the divine Word according to which man was created, a position his Western predecessor, Marius Victorinus, had accepted. For Augustine, man was made to the image of the Trinity because Scripture described him as made "to *our* image."

Although there was more emphasis in the East on the Incarnate Christ than is found with Augustine, his encounter with the Trinity in the depths of the human soul did not prevent an interest in history and the temporal world, as the above criticism might suggest. The mind that becomes conscious of itself as an image of God does not cease to be aware of the objective world it judges and to which it relates itself. Augustine's interest did not remain within the mind alone but focused on the ceaseless task of judging the realities that belong to the human world. The norm of judgment is the Interior Word, but realities are in need of this judgment. The greater temptation is to remain with the visible realities and the dogmatic formulas rather than to experience the invisible reality of the self as image of God, whose Trinitarian life can be enjoyed. Such enjoyment implies the sharing of the external missions of the divine Persons as well. Although the Greek Fathers focused on the Mystery that is Christ and his Cross seen as "fulfilling the Scriptures," Augustine's concern with interiority was a concern with the Mystery of Christ living in us, which he recognized as opening us to Trinitarian life.

---

22. Ibid.

INTRODUCTION

It is undeniable that the whole thrust of his work *On the Trinity* is to contemplate the Trinity within the human soul. When the soul's capacity for God is actualized, whoever sees the Christian's life of love can find there a mirror of the Trinity. But the true love of neighbor is grounded in the love of God, and in this interior life of love Augustine discovered the image of the Trinity:

> Now this trinity of the mind is God's image, not because the mind remembers, understands, and loves itself, but because it has the power also to remember, understand, and love its Maker. And it is in so doing that it attains wisdom. If it does not do so, the memory, understanding, and love of itself is no more than an act of folly. Let the mind then remember its God in whose image it was made, let it understand and love him. In a word, let it worship the Uncreated God who created it with the *capacity for himself,* and in whom it is able to be made partaker. For this cause it is written: "Behold the worship of God is Wisdom" (Jb 28:28). Wisdom will be the mind's not by its own illumination, but by partaking in that Supreme Light; and only when it enters eternity will it reign in bliss.[23]

From this text and others it is clear that Augustinian "memory" is not entirely identifiable either with Platonic reminiscence or with the Aristotelian-Thomist conception of sense or intellectual memory as a storehouse of past images or concepts. It has the functions of Aristotelian memory but is not limited to those functions. To think naturally or spontaneously of things implicitly known is to remember, according to Augustine. God transcends the memory but is present within it, close to the light that enlightens the memory. Although not identified with it, He is its immediate principle, so that by this light, which is His highest work in natural man, He somehow touches man even when the latter is far from Him in the region of unlikeness. Moreover, in Book XII of

---

23. Augustine, *On the Trinity*, XIV.12.15. Cf. R. D. Crouse, "St. Augustine's Theory of Personality," in *Neoplatonism and Christian Thought* (London: Variorum, 1981) (hereafter *Trin.*).

INTRODUCTION

On the Trinity Augustine explicitly rejected Plato's theory of recollection and said:

> But we ought rather to believe that the nature of the
> intellectual mind is so formed as to see those things
> which, according to the disposition of the Creator, are
> subjoined to intelligible things in the natural order, in a
> sort of incorporeal light of its own kind, as the eye of the
> flesh sees the things that lie about it in this corporeal
> light, of which light it is made to be receptive and to
> which it is adapted.[24]

Although, like Aristotle, he spoke of the memory as a treasure house of the knowledge of those things acquired through itself, through the senses and through the testimonies of others, he referred to a "principal memory," a "latent memory" very much like a subconsciousness or superconsciousness in which the memory of God is present.

> For we usually say that we understand what we have
> found to be true by thinking of it, and this indeed we
> again leave in our memory. But there is a more profound
> depth of our memory, where we also find those contents
> which we think of for the first time, and where the inner
> word is begotten which does not belong to the language
> of any nation, as it were, knowledge of knowledge, vision
> of vision, and understanding of understanding, for the
> understanding which appears in thought comes from the
> understanding which already existed in the memory but
> was latent there.[25]

It is not God in the past but God in the present who is remembered. The memory as the presence of truth and the origin of knowledge was underscored when Augustine said that the intellectual memory has a likeness to the Father, the Unbegotten who begets. How does knowledge of God belong to the memory

---

24. *Trin.*, XII.15.24.
25. Ibid., XIV.11.14.

even when one does not think of it? The memory is father to the mind, united by the will's love. "That is not unreasonably to be called memory, by which the mind is present to itself, so that it can be understood by its own thought, and both can be joined together by the love of itself."[26] Because man was made by God as a capacity for God there is in him an unthematized basic knowledge, an unconscious force that activates the psychic longings of man until he raises this knowledge to consciousness. Not by its own light but by a participation in the highest light is the soul wise. This is the creative "umbilical cord" that is never severed; its reality is in everyone's memory. God is remembered not in the past but in the present; there is no need to posit the preexistence of the human soul. The memory like the Father begets all true knowledge; the begetting is by love, and the knowledge leads to love. This image doctrine, the final one in his theology of the Trinity, is not to be interpreted as a psychological analogy; all his early analogies are but prelude to the true image, the reality of actual intimacy with the Trinity through the gift of the Spirit activating the will to remember God, to understand Him, and to love Him in Himself, in His image, man, and in His Mystical Christ, the Christian community. This presence of God in the human memory is discussed by Augustine in his interpretation of St. Paul's words: "And indeed 'He is not far from anyone of us,' as the Apostle says, and then adds: 'In Him we live and move and have our being.' "[27]

"To be without Him without Whom he cannot exist" is then the great misery of man. "For undoubtedly he is not without Him in whom he is, and yet if he does not remember him or love him, he is not with him."[28] Far from being merely a storehouse, the memory holds the possibility for knowing God; it is the natural capacity for knowing God, a capacity actualized only by the conversion of the will touched by grace. So it is that Augustine recalled that "Among other things the ninth Psalm says: 'Let the wicked be turned to hell, all the nations that *forget* God.' "[29] Later, the twenty-first Psalm declares:

---

26. Ibid.
27. Acts 17:27–28; *Trin.*, XIV.12.16.
28. *Trin.*, XIV.12.16.
29. Ps 9:18.

'All the ends of the earth shall be *reminded* and shall be *returned* to the Lord.'[30] In cleaving to the Lord, its desires will be satisfied with good things, whose image it is; and that nothing may henceforth injure it, it will be the secret of His face,[31] so filled with His abundance that it will never find delight in committing sin. But now when it sees itself, it does not see anything unchangeable.[32]

Not recollection of the past but remembering God so that, being mindful of Him, one loves Him: such is the significance of Augustine's statement: "And He is whole everywhere, and on that account it lives, moves, and has its being in Him, and therefore it can *remember* Him."[33] Augustinian memory provides the experience of truth, available to all human beings. "But it is reminded that it should turn to the Lord as to that light by which it was touched in some way, even when it was turned away from Him. For hence it is that even the godless think of eternity, and rightly condemn and rightly praise many things in the moral conduct of men."[34] Such rules of conduct cannot come from changeable minds and so they must derive from unchangeable Truth, to which men naturally have access. The very common experience of guilt and remorse testifies to this contact with the "holiness of truth."[35]

Memory wherein God arouses mindfulness of Himself is a participation in divine wisdom, which understands and loves itself. Since creation was not necessary and since God is Love, there must be in God a plurality. But since man is not a threesome and yet love is the way that God's image in mankind is made bright and beautiful, there seems to be a necessity for community, life in common characterized by the unity of love. Augustine teaches that man's love for God has to extend to his fellowmen so as to build a City of God, a Christian fellowship, a communion of saints. "Love, then, which is from God and is God, is properly the

---

30. Ps 21:28.
31. Ps 30:21.
32. *Trin.*, XIV.12.16.
33. Acts 17:28; *Trin.*, XIV.15.21.
34. *Trin.*, XIV.15.21.
35. Ibid.

Holy Spirit through whom the Charity of God is poured forth in our hearts, through which the Holy Trinity dwells in us."[36]

The image, according to the Apostle,[37] is a mirror that more or less perfectly reflects God. But inasmuch as the image is located in the intellectual acts of remembering, understanding, willing, there is no suggestion here of a material image like a picture but rather of a similar activity directed to God the Trinity under the influence of the Trinity. There will come the day of transformation unto the "same image from glory to glory, as, through the Spirit of the Lord."[38] This is interpreted by Augustine to signify spiritual progress, for he says: "This is what takes place in those who are making progress steadily day by day."[39] That is why he prayed: "May I remember you, understand you, and love you. Increase these gifts in me, until you have reformed me completely."[40]

Plotinus: Comparison and Contrast

It is probable that Augustine was led through the writings of the Neoplatonists Plotinus and Porphyry, translated from Greek into Latin by the Roman rhetorician Marius Victorinus, to recognize the sensible world and the human soul as the reflection of intelligible light and beauty. In Plotinian philosophy the way to the knowledge of God was by likeness to him, based on the assumption that like is known by like. If generation from the One resulted in a certain degradation or unlikeness to the One, this unlikeness was rooted in multiplicity. In the case of man, the multiplicity was not only ontological but psychological as well; man was preoccupied with the many and experienced dispersion, fragmentation, alienation. To become like the One, the soul was to strive for unity. The way to unity is to be present to mind, which by identifying itself with *Nous*, the second Hypostasis, is raised to the intelligible world where conversion to the One occurs. It is strictly by transcending and not only by negating thought, how-

---

36. I Cor 13:12; *Trin.* XV.18.32.
37. I Cor 13:12.
38. 2 Cor 3:18.
39. *Trin.*, XIV.17.23.
40. Ibid., XV.28.51.

ever, that one arrives at that which is beyond thought. Neoplatonic ecstasy follows on the most intense activity of thought.[41]

Augustine was also, as we have noted, directed to his interiority by Plotinus. After going from the exterior to the interior, Plotinus had asked: "This centre of the soul, is it what we are seeking? Must one not think rather of something else toward which converge all the centres?" And he answered this question by saying: "By our own centre we are attached to Him as to the centre of all things and it is there that we find our rest."[42]

The reality symbolized by spatial expressions like "within" and "above" is psychological and metaphysical-religious: Leaving the exterior for the interior is purifying the self from the multiplicity of things that have attached themselves to the soul to weigh it down; and leaving the interior for the superior is uniting oneself to one's Source. The soul is a wanderer, midway between the temporal and eternal, able to choose the level on which it lives, giving attention to its own body or acting as providence with All-Soul, or united to Intellect (*Nous*), poised for becoming oned with the One or Good.

The Augustinian spirituality of *metanoia* or conversion seems to have much in common with the Plotinian spirituality of coming from the One and returning to the One, but there are at least four crucial points of difference. These are found in their doctrines of God, of the soul, of the image, and of the way of conversion.

First of all, if the One is Plotinus's God, then his God is not trinitarian as is the God of Christianity revealed in Scripture and believed in by Augustine. Augustine's God-the-Trinity is not derived from Greek philosophy but from Scripture and from reflection on intellectual experience, illuminated by Scripture. This is explicitly stated in his work *On the Trinity*, the only book he himself decided to write without pressure by circumstances or by polemic.

Second, Augustine makes use of the Platonic notion of participation in the divine ideas as the basis of likeness to God in all nature. But Augustine identifies the likeness in which all things participate with the Son of God, his perfect Image. Although all

---

41. Plotinus, *The Enneads*, V.9.7 and 11; VI.7.34 (hereafter *Enn.*).
42. *Enn.*, VI.9.8; cf. *Enn.* IV.6.3; IV.9; VI.4.4; II.1.5. Augustine, *Epistle* 140.2.3.

things are vestiges of God, He created only one species according to the Image, His Son. This species is man: male and female completing the species. Christ is the perfect Image, equal to God, while man is an imperfect image, not equal to God but approaching Him by likeness. This likeness is effected through wisdom, the understanding of faith exercised in love, and the fullest possible likeness is in the risen life of glory.[43] The creature made to the image of God comes directly from God and between this image and God no other nature intervenes. It has an immediate tendency toward God as its Exemplar-Principle because it not only participates in being and life but has the capacity for wisdom. All creatures are like God in some respect because they are created through the Word of God, but only those intellectual creatures who are made *ad ipsum* ("toward him") are images of God. The capacity for conversion is found in the image's intellectual dynamism and in the presence of God. The journey to God is by way of becoming a more perfect image of God the Trinity. God's perfect Image, His Son, is the only way to this.

The image theme is to be found in the *Enneads* of Plotinus. But Augustine's use of it is different in an important respect. For Plotinus the *Nous* or Intellectual Principle proceeds directly from the One as an image of it and when it turns and contemplates the One, it becomes the One's likeness but only as an inferior copy. As an image it also generates All-Soul, which again is inferior to *Nous* and to the One. Only by contemplating its source does Soul produce its own images. The final generation is Matter, which is only a very faint vestige of the One. To attain likeness to its source every image must generate a copy of itself, which Plotinus speaks of as an illuminating process.[44]

So we see that inferiority is considered essential to the Plotinian image although Augustine shows that there can be equality between the Image and the Exemplar when the Image is perfect. Instead of the Plotinian dynamism of return to the One, there is for Augustine a dynamism of return to the Trinity, and here the Word's relation to the Father becomes exemplary. Although for Plotinus both *Nous* and Soul are imperfect copies of the One, they

---

43. Augustine, *On the Spirit and the Letter*, 22.37–24.42; *Homilies on St. John's Gospel*, 40.9; *On True Religion*, 45.81; *On the Trinity*, VI.10.11.

44. *Enn.*, I.6.8; Augustine, *Unfinished Book on Genesis*, 16.59–60.

seem more applicable to Augustine's intellectual creature, man, made to the image of God as an imperfect image. Yet for Plotinus both *Nous* and Soul are divine and can naturally recover likeness by returning to the One whereas for Augustine man is formed by God to his likeness but created out of nothing. The tendency to nonbeing is in tension with the tendency to God. To return to God, man needs God's help illuminating and strengthening his will. Augustine does not seem to take up and use Plotinus's teaching that every image naturally produces another image. Augustine's doctrine of society as the expression of love seems to be derived from meditation on St. John's Gospel and Epistle. Unlike Plotinus, he also uses the image of God in man as a source of affirmative knowledge of God and as a means of contact with God.[45]

The third crucial point that differentiates Augustinian from Plotinian spirituality is the soul's Trinitarian function: the soul, not as image of the *Nous* or of the One, but of the Trinity. The only way that unity and equality can come to the actions of remembering, understanding, and loving is for them to be converted to God above the memory. God's love for us manifested in the actions of Christ and given through the Spirit arouses the love that unifies one's personal actions of remembering, understanding, and willing God. Because of this unification man is able to integrate his various life-levels in one life "toward" God. This leads to the final crucial difference.

Fourth, conversion is mediated not by the internal Word or *Nous* as understood but by the Incarnate Word in whom we believe:

> What shall wretched man do? Who shall deliver him from the body of this death, but only Your Grace, through Jesus Christ our Lord, whom you have begotten co-eternal and formed in the beginning of Your ways, in whom the prince of this world found nothing worthy of death, yet killed Him, and the handwriting, which was against us, was blotted out. None of this is to be found in the books of the Platonists.[46]

---

45. *Trin.*, XV.23.44; *Epistle* 92.3.
46. *Conf.*, VII.21.

INTRODUCTION

At the end of the tenth book of the *Confessions* Augustine acknowledged that after many years of being a Christian, after ordination to the priesthood and consecration as a bishop, he still needed to be renewed and reconciled with God. Many people, he said, attempt reconciliation by their own powers or seek a wrong mediator.

> But the true Mediator whom in your secret mercy you have shown to men and have sent Him so that they, by His example, might learn humility, that Mediator between God and man, the Man Christ Jesus, appeared between mortal sinners and the immortal Just One: mortal with men, just with God; so that, because the wages of justice are life and peace, He might, by a justice conjoined with God, make void the death of those sinners who were justified by Him; for He was willing to let that death be common both to Him and to them. He was revealed to the holy men of old so that they might be saved through faith in His passion that was to come, just as we may be saved through faith in His passion now that it is in the past. For insofar as He is man, He is mediator; but insofar as He is the Word, He is not midway between God and man; for He is equal to God, both God with God, and together one God.[47]

Ascent to the Supreme

In speaking of dialectic as mediating his union with the One, Plotinus used the language of ascent: "What is the art, what is the method, what is the practice which leads us where we must go? Where must one go? It is to the Good and to the First Principle. This is what we pose as agreed upon and demonstrated in a thousand ways; and the demonstrations given of it are also the means of rising to it."[48]

The Platonic structure of Augustine's many theories of ascents to the Absolute is well documented by Augustine himself.[49] The ecstasies at Milan and Ostia are faithful to the moments of

---

47. *Conf.*, X.43.
48. *Enn.*, I.3.1.
49. *Conf.*, VII.17.23.

ascent as structured by Plotinus: Consider only the statement from *Ennead* I.6.7: "In order to attain to the Good, we must mount up to the supernal regions" where we shall be "ravished with delight."

Augustine's earliest enumeration of the Ascent to God is elaborated in his work *De Quantitate Animae* (A.D. 388), in which he discusses the seven steps of soul energy leading to union with God. They are *animatio* (the soul animating the body), *sensus* (the soul perceiving sensible things), *ars* (the soul as source of artistic skills), *virtus* (the soul directing itself toward good things), *tranquillitas* (the soul stabilized), *ingressio* (the soul fixing its attention above), and *contemplatio* (the soul serenely gazing on Truth). This work is of special interest as containing his earliest mystical theory but he included a wide variety of structures for ascent in later writings. In the *Confessions* he described his own experiences as those of the Prodigal Son returning to the Father. In the Gospel he had read of the young man who "entered into himself." He found that the Plotinian schema of introversion and ascent coincided with the actions of the Prodigal Son. This strengthened and maintained the Augustinian *redite ad cor*.[50] Moreover, the "steps of ascent" are not to be understood spatially but psychologically, as ever higher awakenings of the self, and they are to be understood metaphysically as an evolution toward unity. Ascent is more aptly expressed as a convergence of soul energies in conversion to God.

Descent of Christ

We have noted that the apparent similarity of the conversion theme to Neoplatonic thought conceals a drastic dissimilarity in respect to how conversion is effected. With a decisiveness to be taken seriously, Augustine says: "But I did not find in the books of the Platonists: 'He came unto His own, and His own received Him not; but as many as received Him, to them He gave power to become the sons of God, as many as believed in His name.' "[51]

Indeed, he did not find in the Platonic books that "the Word was made flesh and dwelt amongst us," nor

---

50. Augustine, *On Christian Doctrine*, 1.77–8.88; *City of God*, VII.10.16; VIII.5; IX.10.
51. *Conf.*, VII.9.

that He emptied himself, taking the form of a servant, being made in the likeness of men, and found in fashion as a man, humbled Himself and became obedient unto death, even the death of the Cross: wherefore God hath exalted Him from the dead, and gave Him a name above every name, that at the name of Jesus every knee should bow, of things in heaven, and things on earth, and things under the earth; and that every tongue should confess that the Lord Jesus Christ is in the glory of God the Father.[52]

Although Augustine was admonished by the Platonic books to forsake the many for the One, to withdraw into himself and contemplate the Light above his mind, all such effort proved futile and left him disintegrated. His early conviction, expressed on reading the *Hortensius,* that without Christ there can be no wisdom was reinforced on reading the books of the Platonists who seemed to disregard man's need for healing, the need for a savior better and more powerful than man himself.

Through reading Scripture, especially St. Paul, Augustine's personal experience of fallibility in the intellectual and moral order was illuminated, and he began to declare the priority of faith to understanding, the priority of grace to virtuous action.

In the process of answering questions raised by Simplicianus he made his first clear declaration of faith's priority. Previously, writing on Paul's Epistle to the Romans, he had said: "If we believe, it is our work; but if we do good, this is the work of the one who gives the Spirit to believers."[53] When he wrote Question 66.3–5 of the *Eighty-Three Questions* he was of the opinion that God does not grant mercy if good will has not preceded the gift of His grace. By greater attention to the teaching of St. Paul (Rom 9:29), he recognized his false opinion after deep reflection on his own life in the light of the Epistle to the Romans and its commentators. He saw that the initiative for faith, as that for good works, comes from God. Faith is a revelation from God and precedes all good works.

His early position on the priority of the will to faith implied

---

52. Ibid.
53. Augustine, *Commentary on St. Paul's Epistle to the Romans*, 60.

that the hidden merits of certain people brought them the gift of faith. At last in the *To Simplicianus*[54] he clearly taught that doing good works must be preceded by grace. Although not denying his former statement that free choice is indispensable for any moral action, he affirmed that free choice is not sufficient to act justly. Assuredly, free choice can be used to pray to God for the grace needed, but this prayer is itself inspired by grace so that the prayer becomes efficacious. The prayer is a declaration that one wants to do what God has commanded but that one is expecting help from the one who has commanded. The grace given allows one both to pray and to love efficaciously, for the "God who made us without ourselves will not save us without ourselves."[55] So God does not constrain us to believe or to do good works; he invites us in a way that disposes us to consent without compelling us. Augustine speaks of the will as "prepared by the Lord" to consent.

Triadic Schema of Freedom

To assess the depth of Augustinian spirituality is to undertake a study of St. Paul's influence on Augustine's view of human freedom. Commenting on Romans 5:12–13, he learned from Paul that there are three progressive stages in the present life of human beings. The first stage is man's natural birth in a carnal condition since Adam's sin. This stage is before the Law and consists in the ignorance of one's sin and the abandonment to sensual pleasures. The second stage is under the Law when a man knows that what he does is evil but the weight of habit inhibits him from doing otherwise, and as yet there is no assistance from faith. The third stage is the stage of Grace, when "we confide ourselves absolutely to our Liberator, attributing nothing to our merits. Surrendering ourselves affectionately to His Mercy we do not let ourselves be overcome by the delights of bad habits drawing us into sin. Still tempted by their allure, we do not, however, yield to them."[56]

Then there is the state of man after death, when "there is absolutely nothing in man which resists the Spirit but all is

---

54. Augustine, *To Simplicianus, on Various Questions*, I.1.14; II.2.2; II.2.3 (hereafter *To Simpl.*).
55. Augustine, *Sermon*, 169.11.13.
56. *To Simpl.* 66.3.

harmoniously unified and coordinated in a stable peace."[57] "That state will be realized when the mortal body will be vivified, 'when this corruptible flesh will put on incorruption, when this mortal flesh will put on immortality.' "[58] This is the condition of the risen person. "But if the Spirit of him who raised Jesus from the dead dwells in you, then he who raised Jesus Christ from the dead will also bring to life your mortal bodies because of his Spirit who dwells in you."[59]

After having discussed this risen state Augustine described it as a state of freedom, the liberty of the children of God. He wrote: "But the text: 'Even the creature will be freed from the yoke of death and admitted to the liberty of the glory of the children of God,'[60] seems to signify that we, we are not creatures, but children of God in whose liberty of glory the creature will be liberated from slavery. 'For we know that all creation groans and travails in pain until now.' "[61] This freedom of the children of God also characterized Adam and Eve except that in Paradise there was the possibility of losing that liberty by the free choice of an apparent good that was incompatible with continued adherence to God, the Absolute Good.

Although Augustine did not mention paradisal freedom among the three stages described as prior to the Law, under the Law, under Grace, he often spoke of it during the Pelagian controversy as a graced liberty that was lost through personal sin. His frequent references to this lost liberty (*libertas*) led some of his hearers to conclude too hastily that he had eliminated free choice from human nature. On the contrary, he distinguished between free choice (*liberum arbitrium*) and freedom (*libertas*) as between a capacity for spiritual freedom and actual spiritual freedom.[62] The capacity for free choice remained but the liberty to love God was lost through disobedience to God, and could be restored only by God himself. This restoration took place through Christ, who reformed the will of man, strengthening it with charity through the

57. Ibid. 66.7.
58. 1 Cor 15.54–55.
59. Rom 8:11.
60. Rom 8:21.
61. Rom 8:22.
62. M. T. Clark, *Augustine, Philosopher of Freedom* (New York: Desclee, 1959).

gift of His Spirit, thus making possible progress toward eternal peace.

The stages of freedom are correlated with the three stages in the life of man. In the first stage, before the Law, there is abundant use of free choice, choosing to do wrong with delight because of ignorance of what is sinful. This is the stage described in the first few books of the *Confessions*—it was a life of sensuality and license, and there was no remorse at the time because in his unbaptized state Augustine had not meditated on the Law.

In the second stage of freedom, under the Law, one uses free choice to gratify oneself but with reluctance and regret. Through reading Scripture and listening to Monica and Ambrose and other exemplary Christians, Augustine began to measure his deeds against the Law of God. Making heroic efforts to do what was right without wholly wanting to do so, he found all his efforts futile.

In the third stage of freedom, under Grace, one gladly does what is right, both wanting to do it and doing it with God's help. In this stage freedom is experienced as wholeheartedness, a delight in doing good. This is the period of constant growth in spiritual liberty: Free choice is used rightly and with delight. It is especially in Book X of the *Confessions* that Augustine describes this third stage of freedom. Through grace God has established Augustine's will in Himself. And so Augustine experienced a certain stability, the stability of faith; however, not that of eternity. Temptations are not absent from the children of God, even those endowed with His glorious liberty of loving within the Trinitarian life and sharing that goodness with others. Augustine spoke there of his own temptations from the "lust of the flesh, the lust of the eyes, and the ambitions of the world." He opened to the Lord the present state of his soul "in this kind of evil, rejoicing with trembling in your gifts and grieving for my imperfection and hoping that you will perfect your mercies in me till I reach that fullness of peace which both my inward and my outer self will have with you when death shall be swallowed up in victory."[63]

This evolution in freedom through the various stages on earth to the complete freedom of the risen life is a constant motif in the spirituality of St. Augustine. It requires an education in that love

---

63. *Conf.*, X.30.

which unifies the heart, making it whole. Maturity in freedom is reached by the authentic human person who is mindful of God, understanding and loving Him. In making man to be "toward" His own Image, God who is Love intended that man should image that love, the love uniting the Three.

If the true freedom of the mature person depends both on willing according to truth and on loving what he wills, the deeper one's participation in God, the greater one's freedom. To be truly free by oneself in isolation from others is an impossible metaphysical task in any order—before or after Adam's sin. Adam, who knew he was both creature and friend of God, was asked to keep his freedom by way of humility, an abiding in truth. When Adam withdrew from truth, he defied his metaphysical status as participated being, participated truth, participated freedom. On his own he sought an absolute independence. Slavery by way of pride, which is untruth, became the lot of his heirs, with free will a diminished power. Man continued to desire the good with his will and was able to choose to sin, but unable of himself to act righteously for eternal life.

To free man for loving God there came one who humbled Himself and became obedient even unto death. Just as creation was a Trinitarian act, so was conversion or salvation. "It is only from God the Father, through Jesus Christ, with the Holy Spirit, that men have the love of God through which they come to God."[64] That is why mature freedom cannot be gained without Christ, who, as Mediator, reorients man to God. The Father "draws" man to Him by showing Christ His Son, Wisdom Incarnate, the generous healer of souls, the Truth that makes man free. The more conscious the person becomes that Christ is Incarnate Love, the more spontaneously the will responds to His attraction. The law of pleasure that rules the physiological phases of life is not altogether absent from the psychological plane. If Grace is a participation in the divine nature, does it not bring with it divine tendencies, a delight in the Lord?

Grace makes it not difficult to do what one ought to do. If the choice of evil is a deviation from the will's natural tendency to the good, the choice of the good is the continuation of creation in harmony with the wisdom of God. For this, man opens himself to

---

64. Augustine, *Against Julian*, IV.3.33.

INTRODUCTION

the Transcendent Good, loving the Good for itself, taking neither himself nor any created good as an absolute—this is the point of departure for spiritual liberty, a positive power of attachment to the Absolute Good, with a negative concomitant of detachment from the relative. In loving God, man makes God's will his own, and by thus doing his own will, he does more easily what he ought to do. Augustine expressed this psychological experience when he said: "Love and do as you please."[65] "With the Holy Spirit, by whose Gift we are justified, we take delight in this, that we sin not,—and that is freedom; without the Spirit we take delight in sin, and that is slavery."[66]

So we see that for Augustine growth in freedom is personal growth, the harmonious development of the psychological powers of memory, understanding, and will through their attention to God, triune, to whom they are dynamically related and from whom they receive unity. This call to freedom qualifies personal existence, marking its likeness to God and its unlikeness to animals. Love is the key to this personal freedom "My love is my weight; by it I am carried wherever I am carried."[67] Love as the unitive force is the force of conversion. By graced freedom one becomes Godlike.

Augustine refused to let go of either free choice or grace as necessary for the return to God. While he emphasized free choice in writing against the Manichees and emphasized grace in writing against the Pelagians, his Christian anthropology includes both.

> We, however, on our side affirm that the human will is so divinely aided in the pursuit of righteousness that (in addition to the free choice with which man was created, and in addition to the teaching by which he is instructed how he ought to live), he receives the Holy Spirit, by whom there is formed in his mind a delight in, and a love of, that supreme and unchangeable good which is God, even now while he is still "walking by faith" and not yet "by sight"; in order that by this gift to him of the down payment, as it were, of the free gift, he may conceive an

---

65. Augustine, *Homilies on St. John's Epistles,* VII.8.
66. *On the Spirit and the Letter,* 16.
67. *Conf.,* XIII.9.

ardent desire to cleave to his Maker, and may burn to enter upon the participation in that true light, that he may be approved by Him to whom he owes his existence. A man's free will, indeed, avails for nothing except to sin, if he knows not the way of truth; and even after his duty and his proper aim shall begin to become known to him, unless he also take delight in and feel a love for it, he neither does his duty, nor sets about it, nor lives rightly. Now, in order that such a course may engage our affections, "God's love is shed abroad in our hearts," not through the free will which arises from ourselves, but "through the Holy Spirit who is given to us."[68]

Therefore we see that the greater the truth the greater the freedom. Christianity opened a new way to truth, chiefly the way of love. Augustine said: "We pilgrims make our way by faith and hope, and strive to reach our end by love."[69] He distinguished false freedom from true freedom, egotistical love from personal love. "Indeed, the truth of the Christians is incomparably more beautiful than Helen of the Greeks. For the former, our martyrs fought more valiantly against this Sodom than those famous heroes fought for the latter against Troy."[70]

In the final analysis, love is the key to the freedom and the unity and the peace of the world. The person who loves according to truth and is really free achieves that unity with God, unity within self, and unity with others which is the prelude to the Eternal Peace of the risen life where there is perfect freedom or spiritual liberty. Love builds the City of God where freedom flourishes because it is made up of persons in loving relation to God. To frustrate the person's capacity for relating to God is the only way to allow for everlasting slavery, to allow death its victory. Just as the intellect is purified by the gift of faith in Christ to know God as Trinity, so the work of the Spirit is re-formation of human freedom by the gift of charity.

No discussion of Augustine's views on freedom can ignore the fact that he has been interpreted by some readers as upholding

---

68. *On the Spirit and the Letter,* 3.
69. Augustine, *Epistle,* 55.
70. Augustine, *Epistle* 40.

a theory of predestination, which cannot be reconciled with the existence of human responsibility. Theories of predestination incompatible with free will have always been condemned by the Church whether or not they put themselves forward under the authority of St. Augustine. According to many Augustinian scholars, however, he has consistently upheld human responsibility for cooperation with the divine Will in the work of salvation.

Eugene Portalié[71] quotes Augustine as having said in his work *On Genesis against the Manicheans:* "All men can be saved, if they wish it."[72] When Augustine referred to this passage in his *Retractations* after having written the work *On the Gift of Perseverance,* he commented: "It is absolutely true that all men can do this, if they wish, but their will is prepared by the Lord."[73] He first interpreted this preparation as, in some sense, exterior, as when he said to Simplicianus: "Whomever he has mercy on he calls in such a way as he knows to be appropriate for him that he not spurn the Caller."[74] Later he interpreted this preparation to be a series of actual graces given interiorly to the will to enable it to have faith in Christ, to love God and neighbor through good works, and to persevere in faith and love until death. Yet he still spoke of this interior grace as preparing the will and still gave to the human will the power of cooperation with the divine will. In his last volume, the *Incomplete Work against Julian,* he said: "Man can will good, but his will is prepared by the Lord."[75] Portalié notes that in his sermons Augustine not only said: "Not knowing whether you are predestined, struggle as if you were," and added: "It depends on you to become one of the elect." "You have received the power to take your place on the right hand of the Lord, that is, to become a son of God." "It is now in your power . . . to choose which of these two [elect or reprobate] you wish to be . . . choose while there is time."[76]

We need to ask: Did Augustine conceive his teaching on

---

71. Eugene Portalié, *A Guide to the Thought of St. Augustine* (Chicago: Henry Regnery Company, 1960), pp. 177–229. For an opposing opinion, see J. P. Burns, *The Development of Augustine's Doctrine of Operative Grace* (Paris: Etudes Augustiniennes, 1980).

72. Augustine, *On Genesis against the Manicheans,* 3.6.

73. Augustine, *Retractations,* 10.2.

74. *To Simpl.* I.2.13.

75. Augustine, *Incomplete Work against Julian.* II.6.

76. Augustine, *Homilies on Ps.* 120.11.

predestination as contrary to human responsibility or did he conceive it as only contrary to the autonomy of the human will with regard to salvation? Are we saved by God or by ourselves? He said that we are saved by God but not without ourselves. The existence of the "reprobate" shows only that without our consent God will not save us. In his late work *On the Gift of Perseverance* he said: "By this teaching of predestination only that most pernicious error is overthrown whereby it is said that the grace of Christ is given according to our merits."[77] The fact is that God saves even those who have no merits if they consent. The Augustinian position is strong on mercy. It allows for deathbed conversions among those who have previously led lives out of harmony with God's expressed will. His position never included any predestination to sin. In speaking of the lists of the elect as already closed, he referred to God's foreknowledge of how men will respond to His call to faith and charity. But in his work *On Free Choice* he argued forcefully for the compatibility between God's knowledge (called foreknowledge only from the human point of view) and human freedom. God's sovereignty signifies that it is God who offers salvation. Those who accept it and persevere are those who want salvation coming to them through the grace of Christ. Because God does not eliminate human responsibility, there are some who do not will to be saved through the grace of Christ and they are among the reprobate. If God's sovereignty were really absolute to the point of eliminating human responsibility, then all persons would be saved since it is inconceivable that God does not wish this and Christian tradition teaches that He does.

Indeed, Augustine explicitly stated: "Who are the elect? You, if you wish."[78] And: "Are you not attracted? Pray that you may be."[79] "It is prepared for others. Become like others [in wanting it] and it is prepared for you."[80]

Augustine as Mystic

The question of whether Augustine was a mystic is one that has led to so many opposing answers that the question cannot be considered a closed one. The most comprehensive treatment of the

---

77. Augustine, *On the Gift of Perseverance*, 17.42.
78. *Homilies on Ps.* 73.5.
79. *Homilies on St. John's Gospel*, tr. 124.
80. *Homilies on Ps.* 126.4.

question is found in the report by M. André Mandouze at the International Augustinian Congress in Paris in 1954.[81] There one finds the opposing positions.

Dom Cuthbert Butler in his 1922 book *Western Mysticism* called Augustine the prince of mystics while Portalié saw "in the admirable fusion of a profound intellectualism with an enlightened mysticism ... the characteristic trait of Augustine." Agreeing with Butler was P. Fulbert Cayré, who declared that Augustine was certainly a mystic whose loving approach to God was suffused with intellectualism. On the other hand, P. de la Taille criticized Butler's position and that of Cayré by expressing grave doubts that Augustine had experienced the states of "spiritual marriage." Paul Henry in his work *La Vision d'Ostie* taught that the mystical element of religion noted by F. von Hugel in *The Life and Works of St. Catherine of Genoa,* namely, the aspiration to God and things divine, was the supreme principle of explanation of his work and teaching. For him Augustine was a mystic, however, only in the broad sense of that word. Charles Boyer defended the mysticism of Augustine in the strict sense. But R. P. Cavallera maintained against Boyer that although the pages of the *Confessions* are religious, they do not describe "infused contemplation," since it is impossible to discover in his religious experience "the character of passivity essential to every mystical state."

Nevertheless, Endre von Ivanka emphasized the continuity for Augustine between natural knowledge and mystical knowledge: from the one same tendency toward God knowledge arises from man's intellectual nature, from grace, and from the light of glory as different degrees of participation.

In 1936 P. E. Hendrikx denied that Augustine was a mystic if "mystical" has the strict technical sense connoting the infusion of the gift of contemplation with a specific feeling of passivity leading to "divine nuptials." He agreed with Joseph Geyser against Johannes Hessen whose thorough knowledge of Plotinus enabled him to interpret the Augustinian experience more adequately. Hendrikx would only call Augustine a mystic if one takes the word "mystic" in its general meaning as fervor with the nuance of "religious fervor" that the word "enthusiasm" adds.

---

81. Augustinus Magister III. *Congrès International Augustinien* (Paris: Etudes Augustiniennes, 1954).

INTRODUCTION

But Olphé-Gaillard, writing in the *Dictionary of Spirituality*,[82] accepted on the authority of J. Maréchal that Augustine was a mystic. His serene, radiant mysticism impregnates the Plotinian dialectic he inherited.

From the extensive controversy reported by Mandouze it is clear that the disagreement hinges on a prior disagreement as to what constitutes a mystical experience. In this controversy there is a tendency to speak of the mystical in the strict sense and in the large sense of the term. Yet it is futile to enlarge the field of the mystical to the point of confusing it with spirituality, and it is just as futile to reduce the field of the mystical by magnifying the conditions of infusion, passivity over against immediacy and intuition. Mandouze expressed the hope that the Augustinian case would provoke theologians to revise their theoretical definitions. A definition of the mystical should not be formulated by studying a limited number of mystics in modern times and in certain cultures, often taking St. John of the Cross as the paradigm. Any definition of the mystical should be applicable to the mystics of all times and cultures, including those of the Patristic period when subtle theological distinctions were not made in the description of religious experience.

There is a trend today to look suspiciously on the intellectual aspect of the Augustinian ascents as being too Platonic, a trend showing very little confidence that the philosophical mode of approaching God is intended by Him as being both a human and a religious approach. Olphé-Gaillard rightly asked: "Does an intellectual intuition obtained by a Plotinian mode of ascent exclude a strictly infused mode of spiritual experience, or indeed was Augustine able to realize within the framework of Neoplatonic dialectic the highest kind of supernatural contemplation?"

Boyer was convinced that every ascent to God according to the Augustinian method ends with an act of infused contemplation. What puzzled Boyer was the statements of the opponents that infused contemplation was lacking in the Augustinian experience. He exclaimed: "How can they claim to know the inner state of another?" As for his own claim, he is merely saying that Augustine has described a certain contact with God, and when that truly takes place, it does so through special divine grace.

---

82. *Dictionnaire de spiritualité* II, col. 1911–1921.

INTRODUCTION

Cayré was in agreement when he affirmed that whereas the *City of God* and *On the Trinity* are the works of a mystic, the *Confessions* is a properly mystical work.

In any attempt to formulate an adequate definition of the mystical experience, a contact with God that is deep and satisfying, transforming and fruitful in charity, takes precedence over other factors. The mystic describes an experience that he frequently calls ineffable, so he is describing only that part of it that he can know and he is not describing how it is accomplished; but if it really is accomplished, whether or not there is human preparation and purification for it, it is still only God who can give Himself. One ought not to stand on the sidelines and say that God may give Himself only to Christians. This means that the discussion of whether Augustine's ascents to God were Plotinian or Christian is beside the point if Plotinus himself by God's power enjoyed the ecstasy he described.

In his later life, after meditating on the Gospels and Epistles, Augustine recognized explicitly Christian forms of union with God, sharing with St. Paul his Christ-Mysticism and his Community-Mysticism, the intimacy of Christ with his mystical members. P. Rondet spoke of it in these words:

> Augustinian mysticism, like Pauline mysticism, gives to Christ a large place, greater than the Savior occupies in his theology, which is not Christocentric. The mysticism of Augustine is that of a man of action, of a man engaged by vocation in the apostolic tasks of pastor, preacher, controversialist. No ecstasy, no ravishment, but a perpetual presence of God which could indeed be the form of the highest union with Christ and the other persons of the Trinity.[83]

Then there is the mystical aspect of his Image doctrine: As an image man is related to God the Trinity so that self-knowledge can engage him in that contact with God through the Trinitarian acts of remembering, understanding, and loving God when the capacity for God is realized through God's gift of Himself.

Some theologians have maintained that the mystical experi-

---

83. *Recherches de Sciences Religieuses* XLI (1953): 290–291.

ence is the normal culmination of Christian life. It is the full development of the theological virtues and the gifts of the Holy Spirit insofar as charity establishes the connaturality or likeness of the soul to God by which union is achieved. Since wisdom is the actuality of Trinitarian life, the wisdom of the mystics is a participation in divine wisdom.

Essentially, mystical experience is an intuitive and responsive act of the mind caused by charity, an act of the will, aroused by the experience of being loved and resulting in the experience of wisdom, an experimental affective awareness of God's touch. Contemplation or mystical experience is therefore both intellectual and affective, with love having a certain priority. As intellectual, it is a graced intuition of God as Being, Truth, Goodness. As affective, it is a tasting of God (*sapientia*), a knowledge through love. In Psalm 109 Augustine links mystical experience to the forgiving love of God. Charity is the soul's beauty bestowed by transcendent Beauty and manifested most fully in the life of Christ. If Christ's love of the Father manifested itself in a constant love of neighbor, so must the mystic's love, which has as its first fruit the transformation into Christ, the re-formation of the Image of God in the soul, and as its second fruit the realization of the community of faith and love.

Was the experience of Augustine at Ostia with his mother, Monica, leaning in a window looking onto a garden, a mystical one? They were speaking of the joys of eternal life.

> Then, with our affections burning still more strongly, toward the Selfsame, we raised ourselves higher and step by step passed over all material things, even the heaven itself from which sun and moon and stars shine down upon the earth. And still we went upward, meditating and speaking and looking with wonder at your works, and we came to our own souls, and we went beyond our souls to reach that region of never-failing plenty where Thou feedest Israel forever with the food of truth and where life is that Wisdom by whom all these things are made, both what is past and what is to come. But Wisdom herself is not made; she is as she has been and will be forever; or rather, there is no place in her for "to have been" or "to be going to be"; one can only say "to be"

since she is eternal and "have been" and "going to be" are not eternal. And as we talked, yearning toward this Wisdom, we did with the whole strength of our hearts' impulse just lightly come into touch with her, and we sighed and left behind there the first fruits of the Spirit.[84]

Many have noted in this description the structure of Neoplatonic ecstasy and the presence of the Holy Spirit with His gifts of union and transformation. Nor is this an isolated experience. Years lateer when in Book X of the *Confessions* he recorded his present state of soul, he referred to frequent experiences as foretastes of eternal life:

And in all these things which I contemplate as I am consulting You I find no secure place for my soul except in You, and in You I pray that what is scattered in me may be brought together so that nothing of me may depart from You. And *sometimes* working within me You admit me to a state of feeling quite unlike any I am used to, a kind of sweet delight which if it were made permanent in me would be something not of this world, not of this life.[85]

It has proven misleading to some that Augustine does not radically separate the philosophic way to the discovery of truth and of God from the mystical approach to the contemplation of God. He accented the dynamism of the human spirit as a drive for the Absolute, the presence of God in the human mind. The desire to know and to love is a basic urge toward absolute truth and goodness or God, a desire made powerful and efficacious by grace. The spirit's natural contact with God is the foundation for the life of faith. God's presence in the mind was the prethematic experience of Augustine as described in the *Confessions* and analyzed in *On the Trinity*. In his early philosophical dialogues he reasoned to God's presence there by an analysis of truth as illumination: an intuition of the regulating truths of the intellectual and moral life

---

84. *Conf.*, IX.10.
85. Ibid., X.40.

insofar as they manifest the perfect Truth on which the mind in its knowing action depends, providing an indirect intuition of God.

For persons made to be "toward God," resting in God is authentic happiness. This does not imply devaluation of the temporal order or of earthly values. Augustine said: "Am I not to love what God has made?"[86] The answer is yes, but not to find one's complete happiness in them. All self-denial is to restore the "order of love" within persons so that God's world can be rightly loved and enthusiastically loved. The heart's yearning for God is profound prayer experienced by all. This aspiration to God does not remove one from time and history, for, as Augustine learned, the eternal is in the temporal as the source of its beauty that leads to God.

Although his early religious experiences were markedly intellectual, through faith in Revelation he understood the implications of graced orientation to Christ, who led him into the Trinitarian experience of life, wisdom, love—the fulfillment of all the basic human longings.

When we speak of Augustine as a mystic we are referring to the experiential aspect of his Christian life, his experience as a "spiritual" man. As a Pauline term this word "spiritual" should not be interpreted merely Platonically. It signifies the proper unity between Christian doctrine and life, between theology and piety. The word "mystical," we have noted, was in Christian use before the origin of Neoplatonism and it did not signify the "extraordinary." It was used to convey the mystery of Christ, who communicates to us the divine reality, and it was used to refer to the hidden spiritual reality of the Sacraments. Origen spoke of Christ as "our guide in mystical and ineffable contemplation."[87]

As Augustine deepened his theology of the Incarnation, he experienced union with God through Christ as head of the Mystical Body, the vine and the branches. One might almost say that as he became the Doctor of Grace, his spirituality, which included the consciousness of grace as friendship with God, became a mystical spirituality. If charity is common to our experience both here and hereafter, then the life of intimate union with the Trini-

---

86. *Homilies on St. John's Epistles* 2.15.
87. Origen, *Commentary on John* XIII.24, quoted in Bouyer, *Spirituality*, p. 410.

ty has already begun. Yet to have Christian love the heart has to be purified of pride, greed, egoism of every sort. Asceticism is the purification of the heart from all that interferes with a sincere and generous love of neighbor. This purification prepares for the "seeing of God." Augustine taught that only those monasteries ordered for the promotion of love are justified as Christian institutions. Pastoral action provided the asceticism in his life of charity, a life motivated by the mystical aspiration to see God. This mystical spirituality is not introversion as a flight from the world. In this apostolic life there is concern for the self and for the other. Some have misunderstood Augustine's statement that "the love of God to the contempt of self built the City of God." In *On the Trinity* he says that love of God is not a contempt for the true self inasmuch as it is love of the very Love from which all life and true love proceed.

Augustinian Spirituality: Conclusion

We have seen that the essential process of the spiritual life for Augustine is the re-formation of the Image of God in the human person by the grace of Christ and human freedom. Transformed into a friend of God the soul enters into union with him not merely as creature with Creator but as friend with Friend. God offers this grace of friendship to all through Christ, the universal way. This is typical of all forms of Christian spirituality, which differs from other kinds by the centrality of Christ, whose signs are humility and love. Christ is present in the Church in Word and Sacrament. The ecclesial community is the beginning of the pilgrimage toward unity in the total risen Christ. This unity of minds and hearts is nourished by the Eucharistic bread and wine and manifested in charity toward all. Since God is Love, we enter by charity, the Spirit's gift, into the intimacy of Trinitarian life, the fulfillment of the deepest longings of mankind for life, wisdom, and love.

The Augustinian emphasis on love is an admission of the social dimension of human existence. In his Letter 130 he speaks of friendship as a necessity of life; indeed, no one can be truly known except through friendship. Only in the risen Christ does friendship withstand death. Friendship not only liberates persons to be themselves but is the very goal of human existence. Thus spiritual life is not a solitary affair: The common love of truth unites people, and the common love of Christ unites all Christians.

After studying St. Paul and St. John, Augustine took the position that faith in Christ implies community in the Church, and the Church aims at the unity of all mankind.[88] It is important to see that Augustinian spirituality is not in opposition to matter but is a requirement that matter be used in the service of love to unify people. It is opposed to naturalism but not to nature, and only because the fruit of naturalism is an individualism that divides people from one another.

When one takes Pentecost seriously, the Church is Christ, a City of Love mystically raised up by the Holy Spirit's acceptance by people. It is clear that, as Augustine has shown, the experience aspect of faith cannot be separated from the interpretation of Scripture present in Christian dogmas. Christology is related to Trinitarian theology and the theology of the Church, the Sacraments, the Holy Spirit, and Eschatology. Christology became for Augustine the substitution for the circular movement of Plotinian generation. Christ came into the world in order to return to the Father with us. In moral theology we learn of the human vocation to conversion in Christ and the moral obligations that follow. In Christian spirituality we learn of the Christian experience in reference to the structure and laws of the Christian's personal development. Augustine's spirituality, like that of all Catholic Christians, was developed by meditating on the Christ, the Word by which God calls all to Himself. It is made known in Scripture and made present in the Church through the liturgy and Sacraments.

Within this Christian spirituality the dominant characteristics of Augustinian spirituality are a thirst for God, a delight in searching for Him, joy in the Truth, willing submission to God's sovereignty, commitment to contemplation, responsiveness to the neighbor's need, activity in the Church's worship and work, unity with all in charity. The harmony that results from the legitimate tensions of these characteristics is fully described in Book XIX of *The City of God*, which is presented in this volume. There we hear that no man must be so committed to contemplation as to ignore

---

88. *Homilies on St. John's Gospel* 32.8.

the needs of his neighbor, nor so absorbed in action that he forgets the contemplation of God. The *caritas veritatis* (love of truth) must give way to the *necessitas caritatis* (necessity of charity).

Why this primacy of charity? Augustine teaches that no one comes to the truth except through love.[89] And in reflecting deeply on St. John's words he has recognized the love quality of interpersonal relationships as another image of the Trinity. Fraternal love is a participation in the unity of God, in his intimate life; that intimate life is the life of Trinitarian relationships of love. Through rightly ordered love, the love of generosity, human persons participate in the Trinitarian mystery and enjoy a foretaste of eternal life: the communion of Saints, the City of God.[90]

The primacy of charity is a call to community where there can be a constant and common search for truth. The deepest understanding of the Church is that which sees its reality as a community of the faithful united by their common love of Christ. The role of religious monasteries is to witness to the possibility of true community by manifesting, as far as possible to human frailty, the actuality of community. All Augustinian congregations are intended to be schools of charity. This is their common goal; it is also the way to attain it. Community life, according to Augustine, is genuine to the extent that all are intent on God; God gives himself, however, only to those who love one another. This spirituality of Christian community is a friendship in Christ that liberates and develops all that is best in human persons. Such is Augustine's view of the primary aspect of evangelical life: the fulfillment of Christ's prayer "that all may be one, as you Father are in me, and I in you."[91]

Augustine tells us today as in his own day that "only they live together in harmony in whom the charity of Christ is perfectly found."[92] And with the eyes of faith we may recognize God in his world when we understand man as God's sacred symbol—an image of the Triune God in the human soul and in personal relationships. And this is because the God manifested in Christ is the God who is Love.

By contact with the very words of Augustine every genera-

---

89. Augustine, *Against Faustus*, 32.18.
90. Augustine, *Sermon on the Creed*, 2.4.
91. Jn. 17:21.
92. Augustine, *Homilies on Ps.*, 132.12.

tion has the possibility of experiencing the vitality of Augustinian spirituality. For this purpose ten selections from his voluminous writings are presented in this book. To experience their vitality, however, is to read them prayerfully, opening one's heart to the Interior Master who alone can ensure that their vitality is actualized. Augustine himself said:

> We can admonish by the sound of our voice; but unless there is One who teaches interiorly, the sound we make is futile. . . . Let Him therefore speak to you interiorly, in that place where no one can enter, for you can have someone at your side, but no one can enter into your heart. Or rather, let there be no one in your heart—let Christ be in your heart.[93]

> Enter then into your heart, and if you have faith, you will find Christ there. There He speaks to you. I, the preacher, must raise my voice, but He instructs you effectively in silence. I speak in sounding words; He speaks within by inspiring a holy fear. It is for Him, then, to sow my words in your hearts. . . . Because faith and Christ are in your hearts, He will teach you what I want to communicate to you through the sound of my words.[94]

Life and Times

If you were to travel to Souk-Ahras in Algeria on the border of Tunisia you would be in the area where Augustine was born in the town of Thagaste in A.D. 354. There in the fourth century you would have heard Latin, Punic, and perhaps certain dialects spoken.

Augustine's life was spent in North Africa, then in Italy, and finally in Africa again, where he died as bishop of Hippo in A.D. 430. More specifically, he lived out his life successively in Thagaste, Madaura, Carthage, Rome, Milan, Rome, Thagaste, and Hippo. Thagaste was an agricultural village but his father, Patricius, was a middle-class Roman town councillor (*municeps*). A

---

93. *Homilies on St. John's Epistle*, 3.13.
94. Augustine, *Sermon*, 102.2.

pagan all his life, he was baptized at death in A.D. 370. Augustine had one sister and two brothers. Like most early Christians, he was not baptized at birth, although he had a Christian mother, Monica. After attending primary school at Thagaste, he went at age eleven to school at Madaura, twenty miles south of Thagaste, for classical studies. At sixteen he took, as they would say today, a leave of absence while his father sought to borrow money to send him for higher studies. His excessive leisure led him into excessive license. At seventeen he went to Carthage for rhetoric, his expenses paid by Romanianus, his father's friend.

Of the Carthage experience Augustine was to say: "I became to myself the barren land." Carthage was an advanced and dissipated city and he was affected by the environment. He took a concubine to whom he was loyal for all of fifteen years, and when he was eighteen they had a son whom they called Adeodatus, whose natural brilliance was evident and whose life ended when he was seventeen. When not in class, Augustine patronized the theater, and this screened him from reality. At nineteen he read Cicero's *Hortensius,* an invitation to philosophy, that is, to search for wisdom. He became aware that rhetoric could never substitute for having something worth saying about man's ultimate concern.

Although this reading stimulated his search for wisdom, the absence of the name of Christ in Cicero's work convinced him that Cicero could not provide the wisdom he praised. In the fervor of this early eagerness he met some Manichees who boasted that their Christian truths were demonstrable by reason. This coupled with their praise of Christ attracted Augustine, who had an almost instinctive conviction of the centrality of Christ in any search for wisdom. The Manichees also defended the New Testament by repudiating the Old, and this pleased him since he had always been repelled by Old Testament stories of scandalous actions. Moreover, by positing two principles of good and evil at war in the world, the Manichees accounted for his own tensions and he welcomed being absolved from any personal guilt. Thus began his nine-year immersion in Manichaeism. During this time he taught rhetoric for one year at Thagaste and for eight years at Carthage.

It was not long, however, before Augustine had to face some doctrinal difficulties as well as dilemmas regarding natural science. The Manichees could not answer his questions but they promised that Faustus, a traveling Manichaean bishop, would know all. Faustus proved not to know the answers. This led Augustine to lose confidence in Manichaeism and to look elsewhere.

In A.D. 383 he left Carthage for Rome to find better-disciplined pupils, and there he was exposed to the skeptical opinions of the New Academy. For a time he accepted their unusual position that only probable truth was attainable. Discovering that his Roman students could not be relied on for tuition payment, he applied for the position of Public Orator for Milan and received it with the help of Manichaen friends. In the autumn of 384 he moved to Milan.

For ten years Ambrose had been bishop of Milan. A provincial governor before his conversion, he was philosophically cultured and knew Origen's works well. Because he was eloquent, Augustine attended church to hear him. From Ambrose he learned far more than good oratory. He learned to appreciate the Old Testament, to recognize the contradictions in the positing of ontological principles of good and evil, and to discover how his free will was involved in his own evil.

Augustine had a tendency to think of God as material, and this prevented him from completely accepting all that Ambrose said of God. In 386, when reading some books of the Platonists, he learned that there was spiritual reality, and his mental block was removed. He also learned to seek unity above. Once again the absence of the name of Christ, this time from the Platonic writings, sent him to St. Paul's Epistles in search of the full meaning of wisdom and above all of the Way to wisdom.

During this period he attempted to make an intellectual ascent to God and to achieve his own moral purification. His concubine was sent back to Africa by Monica. A concubine was of a lower class and there could not be full legal marriage with her. Roman law required marriage partners to be of equal status. His concubine was not returned to Africa, therefore, because of moral scruples but because the ambitious Augustine was preparing for an advantageous marriage. In the meantime he took another mistress, and his last state was worse than his first. It was a time of intense struggle between the two wills in Augustine, the self-indulgent will and the Good-directed will, his experience of his divided self. In Ambrose he had recognized that unity of will, that integration of personal levels which he so much needed. This integration in others made them his exemplars, exerting on him a powerful attraction. These persons were Simplicianus, the assistant priest to Ambrose; Marius Victorinus, the great Roman rhetor and translator of Neoplatonic writings whose conversion to Christianity a generation before had been related by Simplicianus; St. Anthony, whose commitment to Christ was made known by Ponticianus; and two Roman civil servants who became monks in response to reading Anthony's life story, a fact he heard of from Ponticianus.

It was in August of A.D. 386 that the tumult in his heart arose from comparing these living examples of mature Christians with his own indecision and disintegration. He fled to the garden and, seeking direction from God, opened St. Paul's epistle to the Romans 13:13 where he read: "Let us walk becomingly as in the day, not in reveling and drunkenness, not in debauchery and wantonness, not in strife and jealousy. But put on the Lord Jesus Christ, and as for the flesh, take no thought of its lusts." He was thereupon given the grace to will wholly what he was commanded and in this conversion to his God he was unified.

At the end of August he settled at Cassiciacum, fifty miles from Milan, and in the fall he resigned his post and began to compose his early Dialogues, more or less faithful reproductions of his efforts to educate his disciples—Alypius, Evagrius, Trygetius, Licentius, Adeodatus. Monica was an important participant in the discussions, often deferred to by her son for her Christian convictions.

In 387 at the end of winter he returned to Milan to give in his name for baptism and to take instructions from Ambrose. In April at the Paschal vigil Augustine, Adeodatus, and Alypius were baptized. In the autumn the group left Milan for the Roman seaport of Ostia to proceed to Africa, where they planned to live as a contemplative community. There at Ostia Monica and Augustine shared the religious or mystical experience described in Book IX of the *Confessions*. There also Monica fell sick and died, and there her son buried her. Since ships were not to sail for Africa for more than a year, he was detained at Rome where he wrote two important books: *On the Morals of the Manichees* and *On the Morals of the Catholic Church*.

By 388, however, Augustine was following a monastic style of life at Thagaste but in 391, on visiting Hippo, he was seen by

INTRODUCTION

Bishop Valerius in church and was taken for ordination to the priesthood—a method that was customary in those days. He became an assistant to Bishop Valerius after persuading him to agree to the continuation of a community life. For Augustine the contemplative life was to be chosen and yet the active life was to be led whenever pastoral needs constrained the cleric to leave the monastery. When Bishop Valerius died in 395 Augustine became bishop of Hippo and continued to live in the community that became the training ground for the secular clergy and gave ten future bishops to Africa. In addition to his episcopal community, he set up monasteries elsewhere for men and some for women. In all of these, intellectual work as well as manual work was required. The main requirements were charity, asceticism, chastity, poverty, with an emphasis on ministry. They were apostolic communities where the order of the day was readily sacrificed to the needs of the ministry.

During his forty years in the See of Hippo Augustine presided at the daily Liturgy and preached several times a week and often daily to his own congregation. He often preached before the Council of African Bishops at Carthage, presided over by Bishop Aurelius, his friend. Alypius became bishop of Thagaste. Augustine's days were filled with instructing converts and giving spiritual direction by word and letter as well as organizing good works to care for the poor, administering Church lands, and acting as judge in the bishop's court. Throughout this busy ministry he remained a contemplative and a writer. His contemplation illuminated his preaching and his writing influenced not only his contemporaries but people of future times.

Four major polemics engaged his attention: against the Manichees (387–400), against the Donatists (400–412), against the Pelagians (412–430), against the pagans.

Manichaeism can be traced to the Persian prophet Mani, who was born in Babylonia around A.D. 216. It was a gnostic religion seeking salvation through understanding certain books of the New Testament. In man, whose life was determined by astrological conditions at birth, the principle of evil warred against God, the principle of good, and both were material principles: darkness and light.

The Donatists were the followers of Donatus, who repudiated the episcopal consecration of Caecilianus in 312 to the See of

INTRODUCTION

Carthage because he had reportedly compromised his Christianity during the Diocletian persecution. They declared that any unworthiness of the minister of sacraments eliminated their efficacy, and therefore rebaptized Catholics who joined the Donatist group, which, in fact, comprised the majority of the African Church. This African schism engaged Augustine's attention for a long time. After trying every peaceful means to end the schism he finally accepted the offer of Roman power to do so.

The Pelagian heresy originated with the monk Pelagius, who came from the British Isles to Rome in A.D. 410. To his way of thinking he converted Coelestius, a lawyer, and influenced Julian, bishop of Eclanum. The heresy consisted in attributing to the human will alone the power to act virtuously so as to merit heaven: Grace is simply God's gift of human nature to man and it can also facilitate man's virtue. Augustine taught, on the contrary, that God gives grace to enable a person to will and to do those actions that will merit eternal life, that is, divine life. The Pelagians took the position that God's grace was helpful but not necessary and that the heirs of Adam were not stained with original sin. Coelestius was condemned by an African Council in 412 and eventually Pope Zosimus condemned both Pelagius and Coelestius. Bishop Julian sided with the followers of Pelagius, and it was to Julian that Augustine addressed much of his anti-Pelagian writings. In 539 the Council of Orange sustained the position of Augustine but not his extreme literal statements on predestination. But semi-Pelagianism has survived as a recurrent mentality in Christianity.

As Augustine's life drew to a close the controversies were continuing. In the end of his life he was arguing against Arianism and semi-Arianism and against the pagans who blamed Christianity for the fall of Rome in A.D. 410. Although Arianism and semi-Arianism had been condemned at the Council of Constantinople in 381, many of the barbarians had been converted into Arian Christianity and these made their way to Africa. Augustine died in A.D. as the Vandals were besieging the city of Hippo.

Works

Augustine left his legacy of thought to the world in 113 books of varying lengths, in 218 letters, and in about 800 sermons. He began by writing *Dialogues* at Cassiciacum after having undergone the influence of Christian Neoplatonism. In addition to his controversial works against the Manichees, the Donatists, and the Pelagians, he also wrote:

- theological works like *On the Trinity*
- educational works like *On Christian Doctrine* and *On Catechesis*
- exegetical works like his five commentaries on *Genesis*, his commentaries on the Psalms, on the Gospels, on the Epistles, and his Concordance of the Gospels
- moral treatises like *The Morals of the Catholic Faith, On Lying, On Fasting, On Virginity, On the Goodness of Marriage*

The *Confessions* contain his biography, his spirituality, and the main traits of his theological thought. *The City of God* is a masterly reflection on the history of the world, a history divided into two parts by the Incarnation of Christ. It is also an inspired analysis of the destiny of mankind: salvation through Jesus Christ.

It is worth noting that among the letters of Augustine there are doctrinal and spiritual treatises, and in his sermons we encounter again not only his exegesis but also his direction of souls toward a Biblical and Trinitarian spirituality.

In A.D. 426 he reread his books to evaluate them and to criticize them in the light of his mature faith. This review allows us to have an exact chronological list of his works with awareness of what occasioned these writings. Letters and sermons are excluded. In the Introduction to these *Retractations,* he said: "For, whoever will read my little works in the order in which they were written will perhaps discover how much progress I made in writing. To enable the reader to do this, I shall take care in this work, to inform him as to this order, as far as I can."

Influence

It is impossible to estimate the vast influence of Augustine as a spiritual guide on the countless persons who have read the *Confessions.* Next to the Bible, it has been the most widely read book in the world. Augustine of the *Confessions* has helped to form Christian mystics in all historical periods. St. Teresa of Avila, who said of the *Confessions:* "I saw myself described there," admitted to being nourished on this spirituality. This spirituality has been more precisely influential through the many religious orders that follow the *Rule of St. Augustine* or an adaptation of it. The Rule is reproduced in this volume.

Although monasticism is popularly associated with Cassian in Egypt and the Desert Fathers, the African monks inspired by St. Augustine's Rule became foundation stones of Western monasticism long before the time of St. Benedict. The Augustinian Rule was accepted in the twelfth century by the Canons Regular, the Premonstratensians, and later by the Dominicans, who followed the same ascetical ideals of Augustine, whereas the Canons of St. Victor, notably Hugh, Richard, and Adam, carried on his humanism and mysticism. The Order of the Hermits of St. Augustine (now called the Order of St. Augustine) was founded in 1256 by Alexander IV to federate the small groups of hermits, chiefly Tuscan, who were the survivors of the original Augustinian impetus to asceticism. Through Cardinal Berulle there was founded in 1613 the Oratory of France, a society of apostolic and studious priests whom the cardinal wished to animate with the spirit of St. Augustine.

The nineteenth century saw a rebirth of religious life through the foundation of many religious orders inspired by Augustine's spirituality or given his Rule to follow. In the middle of the century the Augustinians of the Assumption were brought by Father d'Alzon under the Rule of St. Augustine.

The encyclicals of Pius XI in 1930 and of Pius XII in 1954 announced to the twentieth century what Pope Celestine had solemnly said in A.D. 431:

> The life and merits of Augustine, of sainted memory, always preserved him in our communion, so that he was never tainted with any suspicion of evil. We remember him as a man of such great wisdom that he was always counted by my predecessors as one of the greatest teachers.[95]

---

95. Celestine, Letter 21.

INTRODUCTION

And in 1973 Paul VI said:

> What a great Saint you have in St. Augustine of Hippo! We ourselves are a devoted follower of his, always very enthusiastic and sure that we will never consult a page of his writings without profit, without finding a penetrating and striking word. Really you should know that we too have this program, this proposal of taking nourishment every now and then from this source of the spiritual life which seems to us always to soar to greater heights and to be unique in the school of the Church; unique for its richness, unique for its clarity of thought, unique for its depth of human experience, unique for its modernity!
>
> If St. Augustine were alive today, he would speak as he spoke a thousand and more years ago. Why? Because he really personifies a humanity that believes, that loves Christ and our beloved God.[96]

---

96. Paul VI, Rome: *Acta O.S.A.* XVII (1973): 11–12.

INTRODUCTION

The translations in this volume are based on the following Latin texts:

Corpus Christianorum, vol. 27 *(Confessions)*

Corpus Christianorum, vol. 29 *(The Happy Life)*

Corpus Christianorum, vol. 40 *(Homilies on the Psalms)*

Corpus Christianorum, vol. 36 *(Homilies on the Gospel of St. John)*

Patrologia Latina, Migne, vol. 35 *(Homily on the First Epistle of St. John)*

Corpus Christianorum, vols. 50 & 50A *(On the Trinity)*

Patrologia Latina, Migne, vol. 33, cols. 596–622 *(On Seeing God)*

Corpus Scriptorum Ecclesiasticorum Latinorum, vol. 57 *(On the Presence of God)*

Corpus Christianorum, vol. 48 *(The City of God)*

L. Verheijen, O.S.A. *La règle de saint Augustin* (Paris: Etudes Augustiniennes, 1967; critical text of *Rule of St. Augustine;* pp. 417–437)

Augustine of Hippo

CONFESSIONS

Introductory Note. Shortly after Augustine became bishop he was asked by Paulinus of Nola to write his confessions. In his Retractations, *the review of his writings 427, Augustine wrote: "The thirteen books of my* Confessions, *dealing with my evil and good deeds, give praise to the just and good God, and also awaken man's mind and heart to Him" (*Ret., *2.6).*

The first nine books describe how God awakened Augustine's own mind and heart to Himself. In them he shows how Divine Providence worked in the events of the first thirty-three years of his life to open him to God. The tenth book reveals the spiritual state of Augustine after his conversion and at the time he was writing this book. It is a gloriously frank self-examination wherein the struggle and conflict of Christian life is squarely faced with the confidence given by grace and hope. Not the misery of man but the mercy of God is the theme of this book. The last three books relate to eschatology, which Augustine develops more fully in the last four books of The City of God. *These final books of the* Confessions *represent his meditations on Scripture leading to personal reflections on time and eternity, creation and reconciliation, transfiguration and the restoration of all things in the Word of God through whom they were created.*

In the first book of the Confessions *Augustine's great religious discovery was: "You have made us to be 'toward' you, and our heart is restless until it rests in you." The peace that comes from rest in God is strongly desired and leads to prayer, God's gift to those who acknowledge their need for Him, their spiritual restlessness. This happiness of repose arrives fully only in the Heavenly Jerusalem to those who have opened their wounds to the healing power of Christ, the "humble Physician."*

Here we present Books VII to X. Book VII records Augustine's intellectual conversion through the reading of Platonic books. Book VIII vividly describes the moral influ-

ence of fervent Christians on Augustine, the tale of the unexpected conversion of Victorinus, and Augustine's sudden moral conversion. In Book IX a son describes the influence of a Christian mother and recalls the ecstasy at Ostia of mother and son. In Book X Augustine explains his motivation for writing the Confessions *and makes a penetrating analysis of memory, which will be an appropriate foundation for his Image doctrine in* On the Trinity. *After a prayer of confidence to God, he confesses the temptations to which he is still subject from the lust of the flesh, the lust of the eyes, and the pride of life. But he also admits to moments of experiencing God that "if made permanent would be hard to distinguish from the life to come."*

His hope, however, is firmly placed not in these transitory religious experiences but rather in Christ the Mediator.

Book Seven

But now my wicked and sinful youth was over and I was growing into manhood. The older I became, the baser was my vanity. I could not conceive of any substance other than what I was used to seeing through bodily eyes. But I did not think of you, O God, in the shape of a human body. From the moment I began to learn any wisdom, I always avoided that; and I rejoiced to have found this same idea in the faith of our spiritual Mother, your Catholic Church. But it did not occur to me how else I should think of you. And I, but a man, and such a man, tried to think of you as the sovereign and only true God; that you are incorruptible, inviolable, unchangeable, I believed with all the powers of my soul. For, not knowing whence and how, yet I plainly saw and was certain that whatever can be corrupted is worse than that which cannot be corrupted, and whatever cannot be injured, without a doubt, I prefer to what can be injured, and whatever suffers no change is better than that which can be changed. My heart violently cried out against all my imaginings, and with this one truth I tried to beat back the hovering crowd of impurities from my mental vision. And they were scarcely dispersed when in the twinkling of an eye they surrounded me again, forcing themselves on my sight and overclouding it, so that although I did not think that you had the form of a human body, yet I was constrained to imagine you as something bodily extended through space, whether infused in the world or diffused through the infinite space outside the world. I even imagined this of that incorruptible, inviolable, unchangeable being which I preferred to corruptible, violable, and changeable things. For, whatever I abstracted from such spaces seemed to me to be nothing, not emptiness but absolute nothingness. For if a body were removed from a place and the place remains completely empty of any body, either earthly, or watery, or airy, or heavenly, it will still be an empty place, a space—occupying nothingness.

I was so gross of mind (for I could not even clearly discern myself) that whatever was not spatially extended, either diffused or condensed or swollen out or having some such qualities or being capable of them, I thought to be a mere nothing. My mind was looking for the images like those my eyes were accustomed to see. I did not realize that the mental act by which I formed these images was itself not a material image and yet it could not have formed images unless it were itself something, and something great. So also I conceived of you, O Life of my life, as penetrating the whole mass of the world, and outside it diffused in every direction without end so that the earth should have you, the heaven should have you, all things should have you, and that they should be bounded by you, but you were boundless. For just as the body of the air above the earth does not prevent the sun's light from passing through it, the light which penetrates not by breaking or cutting it but simply by filling it completely, so I thought that the body not only of the heaven and the air and the sea, but also of the earth was penetrable by you and easily penetrable in all its parts, great and small, to receive your presence, while your secret inspiration ruled inwardly and outwardly all the things you had created. So I conjectured, because I could not think of anything else; yet this was false. For in this way a greater part of the earth would contain a greater part of you, and a lesser part, less of you, and so all things would be so filled with you that an elephant's body would hold more of you than a sparrow's, simply because it is larger and occupies more room; and so piece by piece you would make yourself present to all parts of the world, greater parts to large things, small parts to small things. But it is not this way. But not yet had you enlightened my darkness.

2

Against those deceived deceivers and loquacious mutes, since your word did not sound from them, that argument sufficed which long ago at Carthage had been proposed by Nebridius, and which forcibly struck those of us who heard it. According to the Manichaean Creed, there is a nation of darkness set up as an opposing substance to you. What would it have done to you, Nebridius asked, if you had refused to struggle against it? If they answered that it would have injured you, then you would be subject to injury and corruption. But if they said that it could not have harmed you, then there would be no cause for fighting against it. But it was supposed to be the result of such fighting that some part or member of you, some offspring of your substance, was mingled with those contrary powers, those natures not created by you, and was so far corrupted by them and changed for the worse as to fall from beatitude into misery and to need help to be delivered and cleansed. This offspring of your substance was the human soul.

In its condition of slavery and contamination and corruption it was to be assisted by your Word, which was free, pure, and entire. But that Word was itself corruptible because it was the offspring of the same substance as the soul. And so if they affirmed you, in your real nature, that is, in your substance by which you exist, to be incorruptible, then all these notions of theirs must be false and execrable. But if they called you corruptible, that would obviously be false and to be abominated. This argument of Nebridius, then, was sufficient against the Manichees and I should have wholly vomited them up from my overcharged stomach inasmuch as they had no way of escape without the most horrible blasphemy of heart and tongue in thinking and speaking of you in this way.

3

But I as yet, although I both said and thought most firmly that you, O Lord, true God, who made not only our souls but also our bodies, and not only souls and bodies but all things and everything, were not to be corrupted nor changed in any way at all, yet I did not understand clearly and without difficulty the cause of evil. Nevertheless whatever the cause might be, I realized that no explanation was possible which would force me to believe the immutable God to be mutable, lest I become what I am seeking, namely, the cause of evil. And so I sought it peacefully and was certain that what the Manichees said was not true. With my whole heart I renounced them because I saw that in their inquiries into the origin of evil they were full of evil themselves insofar as they preferred to believe that your substance could suffer evil rather than that their substance could do evil.

Whereupon I tried to understand what I had heard, that free

will is the cause of our doing evil, and your just judgment the cause of our suffering evil, and I was not able clearly to discern this. Trying therefore to draw my mind's eye out of that abyss, I was again plunged into it; and as often as I tried, so often was I plunged back. But this raised me a little toward your light because I now was just as certain that I had a will as that I had a life. So when I willed to do or not to do something, I was very certain that I and no other did will and not will, and there was the cause of my sin, as I now perceived. But what I did unwillingly, that I seemed to suffer rather than to do, that I judged to be not a fault but a punishment. Since I knew you to be just, I readily admitted to not being unjustly punished. But I inquired again: "Who made me? Did not my God who is not only good but goodness itself? How then could it be that I should will evil and refuse my assent to good so that it would be just for me to be punished? Who placed in me and engrafted into me this plant of bitterness, since I was wholly made by my most loving God? If the devil is responsible, where did the devil come from? And if he himself by his own perverse will turned from a good angel into a devil, whence came that bad will in him to make him a devil, inasmuch as he had been made wholly angel by that most good Creator? By these thoughts I was again cast down and overwhelmed, but I was not brought down to the hell of that error where no one confesses unto you, and where it is held that you suffer evil rather than that man does evil.

4

So I tried to find out other truths as I had already discovered that what was incorruptible was better than the corruptible. For no soul ever has been or ever will be able to conceive of anything better than you, who are the highest and best good. But since most truly and certainly that which is incorruptible is preferred to that which is corruptible (just as I now preferred it) I might have been able to reach by thought something better than my God except for the fact that you are incorruptible. When, therefore, I saw that the incorruptible is to be preferred to the corruptible, then I ought to have sought you, and to have gone on to discover where evil is, that is, discovered the origin of corruption itself by which your substance can in no way be affected. For in no way can corruption affect our God, neither by will, nor by necessity, nor by chance, since He Himself is God and what He wills is good, and He himself is goodness; but to be corrupted is not good. Nor are you forced unwillingly to anything, because your will is not greater than your power. But it would be greater if you were greater than yourself. For the will and power of God are alike God Himself. What chance can befall you, you who know all things? There is nothing existing except as the result of your knowing it. Why, however, should I speak further as to why that substance which is God is not corruptible when, if this were the case, it would not be God?

5

I sought the origin of evil, and I sought it badly, and I did not see the evil in my very mode of inquiry. I set before the sight of my spirit the whole creation, whatever in it was visible (such as the sea, the earth, the air, the stars, the trees, and mortal creatures) and whatever was invisible (such as the firmament of the heaven above and all the angels and spiritual beings there), yet even those I imagined to be bodies, each in its imagined place. And I thought of your creation as one great mass, distinguished according to the kind of bodies in it, whether indeed they really were bodies or only such bodies as I imagined spirits to be. I conceived of this mass as enormous, not the size it actually was, of which I was unaware, but as huge as seemed necessary and on every side finite. And I thought of you, Lord, surrounding it on every side and penetrating it, but as altogether unlimited. It was as though your Being were a sea, infinite and immeasurable everywhere, yet still only a sea which had within it a huge sponge but nevertheless finite. This sponge would in all its parts be filled with the immeasurable sea. So I thought of your creation as finite and filled utterly with you, the infinite, and I said: "Here is God, and here is what God has created; and God is good and most mightily and incomparably better than all these; but being good, He created them good; and behold how He surrounds them and fills them."

Where, then, is evil, and what is its origin, and how has it crept into the creation? What is its root, and what is its seed? Or, is it nothing at all? Why then do we fear and beware of that which is nothing? Or, if our fear is groundless, our fear itself is evil, for by it the soul is driven and tormented for no reason. And so much the greater evil is that fear if there is nothing to fear; yet we do fear.

Therefore, either there is evil which we fear or our fearing is evil. Therefore, from where does evil come since God is good and created all things good? The greater and highest Good created these lesser goods, but Creator and Creation are alike good.

Where, then, did evil arise? Was there some evil matter out of which He made this creation and did God shape and form it, yet still leave in it something which He did not change into good? But why? Was He who was omnipotent unable to change matter wholly so that nothing evil remained in it? Indeed, why did He choose to use such material for making anything? Would he not prefer with this same omnipotence to cause it not to exist at all? Could it exist against His will? Or, if that evil matter was eternal, why did He so long suffer it to exist through infinite time and then much later was pleased to make something out of it? Or, if He suddenly wanted to do something, would not the omnipotent prefer to act in such a way that this evil matter should cease to exist, and that He alone should be the whole, true, highest, and infinite Good? Or, since it was not good that He who was good should make and establish something not good, why did He not remove and reduce to nothing the material that was evil and then provide good matter from which to create all things? For He would not be omnipotent if He could not create something good unless assisted by that matter which He himself had not created.

Such thoughts I pondered in my miserable heart, weighed down with growing anxieties concerning the fear of death and my failure to find the truth. Yet the faith professed in the Catholic Church of your Christ, our Lord and Savior, firmly dwelt in my heart, though indeed in many aspects unperfected as yet and swerving from the norm of doctrine. Nevertheless, my mind did not relinquish it, but daily drank of it more deeply.

6

By now also I had rejected those deceitful divinations and impious follies of the astrologers. Let your mercies, from the very depths of my soul also make confession to you, my God! For this was entirely due to you. Who else calls us back from the death that all error is except that life that knows no death, and the wisdom which itself needing no light enlightens darkened minds, that wisdom by which the whole world even to the trees' fluttering leaves is governed? You cured my obstinacy when I struggled with Vindicianus, that sharp old man, and with Nebridius, that great-souled youth: the former vehemently affirming, the latter often with some doubt saying that there was no art of knowing the future, but that men's conjectures often had the help of fortune and that by speaking much, something future was often mentioned by chance, those speaking scarcely aware but stumbling now and then upon what was true by not remaining silent. You then provided a friend for me who was a fairly frequent consulter of the astrologers. He was not thoroughly skilled in the art but, as I said, he pursued it with some curiosity. He did know something, however, which he said he had heard from his father but he did not know how useful this information was for the rejection of any belief in their art. This man, Firminus by name, well educated and trained in rhetoric, consulted me as a dear friend about various matters concerning his worldly ambitions, desiring to learn how I thought his constellations, as the astrologers called them, stood in the matter. I had now begun to incline toward Nebridius's opinion, yet, while remaining uncertain, did not refuse to conjecture and to tell him how things seemed to me. I added, however, that I was almost persuaded that the whole affair was a ridiculous waste of time. Then he told me that his father had been very curious about such books and that he had a friend also searching them. These with joint study and dialogue were eagerly into this nonsense with the same burning zeal so that they would observe the moments of the birth of the young of those dumb creatures kept in their homes, and they observed the position of the heavens at those moments by way of getting experience in the art.

And he said that he had heard from his father that when his mother was pregnant with him, Firminus, a certain maidservant of his father's friend was also pregnant. Of this her master was not unaware for he was careful by diligent examination to have such knowledge even of his dogs. The friends had numbered the days and hours and even the smallest parts of the hours, the one for his wife and the other for his servant with most careful observation. And it happened that both women brought forth their child at the same instant so they were forced to cast the very same horoscope, even to the exact second for both children, the one for his son, the other for his servant. As soon as the women began to labor, each man notified the other what was happening in his own house and had messengers ready to send to each other as soon as either became aware of the child's being born, a fact they could learn instantly in their own household. And my friend said that the messengers sent from each one met on the way at a point equally distant from both houses, so that neither one of the calculators could observe any other position of the stars, or any moment of time different from the other. Yet Firminus, born to riches in his parents' home, had one of life's brighter careers, grew in wealth and was raised to positions of honor, whereas the servant was not released from his burdensome conditions and continued to serve his masters. So Firminus who knew him told me.

When I heard and believed these things—because Firminus was a reliable man—all my former resistance disappeared. First of all, I tried to recall Firminus from that curiosity by telling him that if I had to consult his stars to give him a true forecast of the future, I certainly ought to have seen in them that his parents were eminent persons among their neighbors, and that he had been descended from a noble family in his own city, that he was born free and had a good and liberal education. But if that servant born under the same constellations had consulted me as to his forecast, I ought to have seen in the stars I consulted (which were exactly the same as those under which Firminus was born) that his family was low-born, his condition servile, and in every other respect he had a completely different lot in life from that of Firminus. Consequently, after consulting the same stars, I must, if I were to speak truthfully, assert different things in the two cases (for if I were to predict the same fortunes it would be a falsehood). So I concluded most certainly that whatever was truly said from consulting these constellations was not said by art but by chance, and whatever was said falsely was not because of unskilled art but because of bad luck.

With this approach to the matter I began to reflect more deeply into the same kind of argument lest one of those fools who traded in astrology and whom I desired to challenge and refute as ridiculous might so oppose me as to suggest that either Firminus or his father had falsely informed me. So I considered the situations of those who are born twins. Most of them emerge from the womb so close to each other that the small interval of time involved (however much influence in nature they contend it has) cannot be estimated by human observation so as to put into the records what the astrologer has to inspect in order to proclaim the truth. Of course it will not be the truth. After observing the same records, an astrologer would have had to predict the same fortunes for Esau and Jacob, but in fact, the same things did not happen to them. Therefore, he would either have had to foretell falsely or if he had foretold truly, then he would have had to see different things in the same horoscope. Not therefore by art, but by chance would he have spoken truly. For you, O Lord, the most just ruler of the universe, can so act by your secret influence so that, while neither he who consults nor he who is consulted knows what is being done, yet when a man consults he hears out of the abyss of your just judgment what he should hear, given the hidden merits of souls. Let no man say to you: What is this or why is this? He must not say it, he must not say such things. For he is a man.

7

And so, my helper, you had freed me from those chains. But I still asked: What is the origin of evil? And I could find no answer. Yet with all the ebb and flow of my thought you did not permit me to be carried away from the faith, a faith by which I believed that you existed, that your substance was unchangeable, that you cared for men and would judge them, that in Christ, your son, our Lord, and in the Holy Scriptures commended by the authority of your Catholic Church you had established the way of men's salvation that they might attain that life which is to come after this death.

With these convictions safely and irremovably settled in my mind, I was still inflamed to learn the origin of evil. What agonies I endured, what groans, my God, came from my heart in its labor! And you were listening although I knew it not. And when in silence I vehemently inquired, the silent contrition of my soul was a strong cry to your mercy. You know how much I suffered, and no man knew it. For how little it was that my tongue uttered of it in the ears of even my closest friends! Did they hear the tumult of my soul for which I had neither time nor tongue to express? Yet all of it reached your hearing, all the roaring and groaning of my heart, and my desire was before you (Ps 38:9), and the light of my own eyes was not with me. For that light was inward, but I was outside. That was not in space, but my mind was attentive to those things which were in space, and I could find there no place for rest, and the things of space did not attract me so that I could say: "It is enough and all is well"; nor did they allow me to return where I might find well-being and sufficiency. For to these things I was superior, but inferior to you. You are my true joy, and I am subject to you, and you have made subject to me the things below me that you have created. This was the right order and the middle way of my salvation that I might remain in your image and so in you should rule over my body. But when I rose up proudly against you and "ran against my Lord with the thick neck of my shield" (Jb 15:26), then these inferior things became greater than I and pressed me under so that I could neither loosen their hold nor so much as breathe. On all sides wherever I looked they surrounded me, massed thick, and whenever I tried to think, the images of corporeal things barred me from turning back toward the truth as if saying: "Where are you going, you unworthy and unclean creature?" All these things had grown out of my wound because you humble the proud like one wounded. And through my swollenness (Ps 89:10) I was separated from you, as though my cheeks had swelled out and closed my eyes.

8

But you, O Lord, abide forever, and you are not angry with us forever since you are merciful to dust and ashes, and it was pleasing in your sight to reform my deformity. And you kept stirring me with your secret good to make me restless until you should become clear to the gaze of my soul. Through the secret hand of your healing my swelling subsided, and from day to day the troubled and darkened sight of my mind gained strength by the stinging ointment of wholesome sorrow.

9

And, first of all, wanting to show me how "you resist the proud, but give grace to the humble" (Jas 4:6) and how greatly your mercy, the way of humility, is shown to men in that the Word was made flesh and dwelt among men, you procured for me through a certain man, extraordinarily conceited, some books of the Platonists translated from Greek into Latin. And there I read although not in the very words, the fact, proved by all kinds of reasons, that "in the beginning was the Word, and the Word was with God and the Word was God: the same was in the beginning with God. All things were made through him, and without him was made nothing. In that which was made is life, and the life was the light of men. And the light shone in the darkness, and darkness did not comprehend it." And that the soul of man, although it "gives testimony to the light," yet it is "not itself the light," but the Word, God Himself, "is the true light which illumines every man coming into this world"; and that He was "in this world, and the world was made by Him, and the world knew Him not." But that "He came unto his own, and His own received Him not, but as many as received him, to them he gave the power to become Sons of God, as many as believed in his name" (Jn 1:1–12)—this I did not read there.

Likewise in those books I read that God the Word was "born not of flesh, nor of blood, nor of the will of man, nor of the will of the flesh, but that he was born of God." But "that the Word was made flesh and dwelt among us," I did not read there. Indeed I discovered in those writings expressed in many different ways that "the Son who was in the form of the Father did not think it robbery to be equal to God" (Phil 2:6) because by nature He is the same; but that "He emptied himself, taking the form of a servant (Phil 2:7) made in the likeness of man (Phil 2:8) and was found in the human condition and humbled himself and became obedient unto death, even the death of the Cross: wherefore God raised him from death and gave him a name above every name (Phil 2:9), that at the name of Jesus every knee (Phil 2:10) among those in heaven, on earth, under the earth shall bow and every tongue shall confess that Jesus the Lord is in the Glory of God the Father" (Phil 2:11): Those books have not all this in them. But that your only-begotten Son, co-eternal with you, was before all times and remains beyond all times unchangeable, and that "of His fullness souls receive" the power to become happy; and that by participation in the wisdom remaining in them, they are renewed, that they may be wise: This is there. But that He in due time died for the wicked, and that "you did not spare your only Son but handed Him over for us all" (Rom 8:32)—that is not there. "For you have hidden these things from the wise, and you have revealed them to the little ones, that those laboring and heavily burdened might come unto Him and He might refresh them because He is meek and humble of heart, and He directs the meek in judgment, and He teaches the humble His ways, seeing our humility and our labor and forgiving all our sins" (Mt 11:28). But those exalted to the elevation of a sublimer learning do not hear him saying: "Learn of me because I am meek and humble of heart, and you will find rest for your souls" (Mt 11:29). And "if they know God, they do not glorify him as God or give thanks, but wax vain in their thoughts, and their foolish heart is darkened and asserting that they are wise, they become fools" (Rom 1:21–22).

And there I also read that they had "changed the glory of your incorruptible nature" (Rom 1:23) into idols and various images, into the likeness of the image of corruptible man, and of birds, beasts, and serpents; indeed, into that Egyptian food for which Esau (Gn 25) sold his birthright since that firstborn people worshiped the head of a four-footed beast instead of you, in their heart turning toward Egypt and bowing your image, their own soul, before the image of a "calf which eats hay" (Ps 106–20). These things I found there; but I did not nourish myself with them. For it pleased you, O Lord, to remove the reproach of inferiority from Jacob, that the elder brother should serve the younger, and you have called the Gentiles into your inheritance. And I myself came to you from the Gentiles; and I focused on that gold which you willed your people to take from Egypt (Ex 3:22), since it was yours, wherever it was. And to the Athenians you said through your apostle that "in you we live and move and have our being as also some of their own writers had said" (Acts 17:28), and surely these books were from Athens. But I did not focus upon the idols of Egypt which "they served with your gold, those who changed the truth of God into a lie and worshiped and served the creature rather than the Creator" (Rom 1:25).

10

And being admonished by all this to return to myself, I entered into my inmost part, with you as leader, and I was able to do so because you were my helper. I entered within and saw, with my soul's eye (such as it was), an unchangeable light. It was shining above the eye of my soul and above my mind, not that ordinary light visible to all flesh nor something of the same kind, only greater as though it might be our ordinary light shining more brightly and with its greatness filling all things. Your light was not that kind but another kind, utterly different from all these.

Nor was it above my mind as oil is above the water it floats on, nor as the sky is above earth; it was higher than my soul because it made me, and I was below because I was made by it. Whoever knows truth knows that Light, and whoever knows it, knows eternity. Charity knows it. O eternal Truth and true Love and beloved Eternity! You are my God, to you I sigh day and night. And when I first knew you, you lifted me up so that I might see that there was something to see but that I was not yet the man to see it. And you beat back the weakness of my gaze, shining on me too strongly, and I trembled with love and dread. And I knew myself to be far from you in the region of unlikeness, as if I heard your voice from on high: "I am the food of strong men; grow and you will feed on me; nor will you change me like ordinary food into your flesh, but you will be changed into me." And I learned that "for iniquity you have rebuked man, you made my soul to waste away like a moth" (Ps 39:11), and I said: "Is truth therefore nothing at all, since it is neither diffused through infinite spaces nor through finite ones?" And you cried from afar: "I am who am" (Ex. 3) and I heard, as one hears in the heart, and from that moment there was no reason for me to doubt. I would more easily doubt that I lived than doubt that there truth existed: which is "clearly seen, being understood by the things that are made" (Rom 1:20).

11

And I reflected upon the other things which are inferior to you, and perceived that they neither have being wholly nor are they wholly nonbeing. They have being certainly because they are from you, and yet they have nonbeing because they are not what you are. For that truly is which remains unchangeable. "It is good then for me to hold fast to God" (Ps 73:28) because, if I do not abide in Him, neither can I abide in myself. But He remaining in Himself renews all things; and "you are my God, since you need none of my goods" (Ps 16:2)

12

And it became clear to me that those things which are subject to corruption are good. They would not be subject to corruption if they were the highest good or not good at all. For, if they were the highest good, they would be incorruptible, but if they were not good at all, there would not be anything in them to be corrupted. For corruption harms, and unless goodness in a thing were diminished, corruption would not harm. Either, therefore, corruption does no harm at all, which cannot be the case, or, which is quite certain, all things which are corrupted are deprived of something good in them. But if things are deprived of all goodness, they will have no being at all. For if they continue to exist and can no longer be corrupted, they will be better than before, because they will be permanently beyond the reach of corruption. And what is more monstrous than to say that those things which have lost all goodness have become better? If they were deprived of all goodness, they would be altogether nothing. Therefore, as long as they are, they are good. Therefore, all things which exist are good, and that evil the origin of which I sought is not a substance because, if it were a substance, it would be good. For either it would be an incorruptible substance, that is, the highest good, or it would be a corruptible substance which, unless it were good, would not be corruptible. Therefore I saw and clearly realized that all things you have made are good, and there are certainly no substances which you have not made. And since all things which you have made are not equal, they have an individual existence and also exist as part of a whole. They are good individually and likewise are altogether very good since God "made all things very good" (Gn 1:31)

13

To you, then, nothing at all is evil. This is true not only of you but of your whole creation, because there is nothing outside it to break in and corrupt the order which you have imposed on things. But in parts of creation because things clash with one another, they are thought evil; but those same things agree with other things and are good, and in themselves they are good. All these things which do not harmonize with one another are suitable to the lower part of reality which we call earth, which has the cloudy and windy sky suitable for it. And God forbid that I should ever say, "These things ought not to be," because if I saw only these things, certainly I would desire better, but even for these alone I ought to praise you: Since these things of earth show that you ought to be praised; "dragons and all abysses, fire, hail, snow, ice and stormy wind which fulfill your word; mountains and all hills, fruitful trees, and all cedars; beasts and all cattle; creeping things and flying fowls; kings of the earth and all people; princes and all judges of the land; young men and maidens; old men and children, let them praise your name" (Ps 148:1–12). Since even in heaven they praise you, praise you, our God, in the heights all your angels, all your hosts, sun and moon, all the stars and light, the heaven of heavens and the waters above the heavens, praise your name: I did not now desire better because I was thinking of them all, and I embraced the better judgment that certainly the higher things are better than the lower things, but all things together are better than the higher ones by themselves.

14

There is no sanity in those to whom any one of your creatures is displeasing just as there was no sanity in me when many things which you have made displeased me. And because my soul did not dare to be displeased by my God, I was unwilling to admit that whatever did displease it was yours. Thus, my soul moved to the error of two substances, and was restless and speaking perversely. And next it went back again and fashioned for itself a God to fill the infinite distances of all space, and it imagined this God to be you and had placed it in its own heart so that once again it became the temple of its own idol, a temple abominable to you. But you, unknown to me, laid your kindly hand upon my head and covered up my eyes lest they see vanity, and then I relaxed a little from myself, and sleep fell upon my madness. And I awakened in you and saw that you were infinite in a different way, and this sight was not derived from the eyes of flesh.

15

And I observed other things and discerned that they owe their being to you, and that all finite things are in you, but differently, not as in space but because you are and hold all things in the hand of your truth and all things are true insofar as they exist; nor is falsehood anything except that something is thought to exist when it does not. And I observed that all things harmonized not only with their places but also with their times; and that you, who alone are eternal, did not begin to work after countless ages, because all ages, both past and future, could neither go nor come unless you are permanently present and working.

16

I knew from experience that there is nothing unusual in the fact that bread which is uneatable by a sick person is pleasurable to a healthy one or that good eyes love the light and poor eyes hate it. Your justice also displeases the wicked; but displeasing also are vipers and reptiles which you created good and suited to the lower parts of your creation, to which indeed the wicked themselves are well suited, insofar as they are unlike you, although they become suited to the higher parts insofar as they become more like you. And I inquired what wickedness was and I found that it was not a substance but a swerving of the will from the highest substance, you, O God, toward lower things, casting away what is most inward to it and swelling greedily for outward things.

17

And I marveled to discover that finally I loved you and not a phantom instead of you. But I did not remain in the enjoyment of my God; I was ravished to you by your beauty, and yet soon by my own weight I was torn away from you and fell back groaning toward these lower things. And this weight was carnal habit. But the memory of you remained with me, and I knew without any doubt that it was you to whom I should cleave, but I knew also that I was not yet able to do so: for "the corruptible body weighs down the soul, and the earthly dwelling weighs down the mind which muses on many things" (Wis 9:15). And I was most certain that "your invisible works are clearly seen from the creation of the world, being understood through the things that are made. So too are your eternal power and Godhead" (Rom 1:20). For, wondering how I recognized the beauty of bodies, whether heavenly or earthly, and by what criterion I might rightly judge concerning mutable things and say: "This ought to be so, that ought not to be so," wondering, therefore, what was the source of my judgment when I did thus judge, I had discovered the unchangeable and true eternity of truth above my changing mind. And so, by degrees passing from bodies to the soul which uses the body for its perceiving and from this to the soul's interior power, to which the bodily senses present exterior things, as indeed the beasts are able to do, from there I passed to the reasoning power to which whatever is received from bodily senses is referred for judgment. This also finding itself mutable in me awakened itself to its own understanding and withdrawing my thought from its usual ways, removing it from the confused crowd of phantasms so that it might discover what light suffused it, without any doubt cried aloud that the unchangeable was to be preferred to the changeable and that it had come to know the unchangeable itself; for if it had not arrived at some knowledge of the unchangeable, it could in no way have preferred it with certainty to the changeable. And then in the flash of a trembling glance my mind arrived at that which is. Now indeed I saw your "invisible things, understood through those things which are made" (Rom 1:20). But I could not fix my eye long upon them; in my weakness I felt myself falling back and returning again to my old habits, bearing with me nothing but an affectionate memory of it and a desire for something of which I had sensed the fragrance but which I was not yet strong enough to eat.

18

And I sought a way of gaining the strength necessary for enjoying you, and I could not find it until I embraced that "Mediator between God and Man, the Man Jesus Christ, who is over all, blessed forevermore" (1 Tm 1:51; Rom 9:5), calling to me and saying: "I am the Way, the truth and the Life" (Jn 14:6), and who united with our flesh that Food which I lacked the strength to take. For the "Word was made flesh" (Jn 1:14) that by your wisdom, through which you created all things, He might give its milk to our infancy. For I was not humble enough to hold the humble Jesus as my God, nor did I know what lesson was taught by His weakness. For your Word, the eternal truth, exalted above the highest parts of your creation, raises to itself those who are cast down. He built for Himself here below a humble dwelling out of your clay through which He might bring down from themselves and bring up to Himself those who were to be made subject, healing the swollenness of their pride and nourishing their love so that instead of progressing in self-confidence they should put on weakness seeing the deity in the weakness it had put on by sharing the tunic of our skin (Gn 3:21), and being at last weary, they might cast themselves upon His humanity and rise again in its rising.

19

But I did not think this way at this time. I thought of my Lord Christ as a man of excellent wisdom, whom no one could equal; and I saw His miraculous birth from a virgin (with the example it gave of how to despise temporal things for the sake of obtaining immortality), as a mark of divine care for us which certainly merited for Him complete authority as our master. But what mystery was contained in "the Word was made flesh" I could scarcely conjecture. All I learned from those things written of Him—that He ate, and drank, slept, walked, rejoiced and sorrowed and discoursed—made me believe that His flesh had only become united with your Word by means of a human soul and a human mind. Everyone knows this who knows the unchangeableness of your Word which I myself now knew, as well as I could, nor did I have the least doubt of it. For at one time to move the members of the body through the will, at another time not to move them; at one time to be stirred by some affection, at another time not to be affected; at one time to utter wise opinions through words, at another time to keep silence: These are marks of a soul and mind that are mutable. If these things were falsely written of Him, all the rest would run the risk of being a lie, and there would be no sure faith in Scripture left for mankind. And so because true things have been written there, I acknowledged in Christ a complete man: not just the body of man or with a body and soul of a man and not merely a man's mind but altogether man and I thought He was to be preferred to all others not as the very Truth in person but because of the great excellence of His human nature and His more perfect participation in wisdom.

As for Alypius, he thought that Catholic belief in a God clothed in flesh meant that in Christ were God and flesh but no soul. He thought that they did not believe Him to have a human mind. And since he was well persuaded that those actions recorded of Christ could not be done except by a vital and rational creature, he moved toward the Christian Faith the more slowly.

But when he learned that this was the error of the Apollinarian heretics, he was better pleased with the Catholic faith and approved. But I confess that I only learned much later that it was in this sentence, "The Word was made flesh," that Catholic truth was distinguished from the heresy of Photinus. Indeed the refuting of heresies greatly clarifies what your Church believes and what sound doctrine is. "For there must be heresies so that what is approved may be manifest among the weak" (cf. 1 Cor 11:19; Rom 14:1).

20

But then, having read those books of the Platonists, where I was admonished to seek incorporeal truth, I beheld your "invisible things understood through the things that are made" (Rom 1:20); and driven back, I perceived that, although through the darkness of my mind I was not allowed to contemplate, I was certain that you are infinite, yet not in the sense of being diffused throughout finite or infinite space, that you truly are, and are always the same, varying in no part and by no motion, and indeed that all other things are from you, because of this one very strong evidence, that they exist. Indeed I was certain of these things, yet too weak to enjoy you. I talked on as if I were learned, but unless I had sought the way to you in Christ, our Savior, I would have come not to instruction but to destruction. For I had begun to want to seem wise, and this indeed was the fullness of my punishment; and I did not weep for my condition, but was badly puffed up with knowledge. Where was that charity building upon the foundation of humility which is Christ Jesus? Or when would these books have taught me that? Yet I believe you wished me to come upon those books before I studied your Scriptures that it might be impressed on my memory how I was affected by them so that afterward when I was made responsive to you by your books and my wounds healed by the care of your fingers I might discern the difference between presumption and confession, between those who see what the goal is but do not see the way and those who see the way leading to that country of blessedness, which is there not only to be seen but also to be dwelt in. For if I had been first informed in your holy Scriptures and you had grown sweet to me through their familiar use, and I had later come upon these books of the Platonists, they might have swept me away from the solid ground of piety; or if I had persisted in that healthy disposition which I imbibed from Scripture I might perhaps have thought that one was able to acquire it from those books if one studied only them.

21

And so most avidly I seized the most venerable writings of Your Spirit and above all, of the Apostle Paul. And there disappeared those questions in which he seemed to me sometimes to contradict himself, and in which the text of his discourse did not agree with the testimonies of the Law and the Prophets. In that pure eloquence I saw one face and I learned "to exult with trembling" (Ps 2:11). I found that whatever truth I had read in the Platonists was said here with praise of your grace: that he who sees should not "glory as if he had not received" (1 Cor 4:7) not only what he sees but even the power to see. "For what has he that he has not received?" I found too that one is not only instructed so as to see you, who are ever the same, but also so as to grow strong enough to take hold of you; and whoever is far off and unable to see you may yet walk along the road by which he will arrive and see you and lay hold on you. For, "although a man be delighted with the Law of God according to the interior man" (Rom 7:22), what shall he do about that "other law in his members, fighting against the law of his mind and leading him captive in the law of sin which is in his members?" (Rom 7:23). For "you are just, O Lord, but we have sinned and committed iniquity and have acted wickedly" (Dn 9:5), and your hand has grown heavy upon us, and we were justly handed over to that ancient sinner, the ruler of death, because he persuaded our will to become like his will whereby he did not stand in your truth. "What shall wretched man do? Who shall deliver him from the body of this death except your grace through Jesus Christ our Lord whom you have begotten co-eternal and brought forth in the beginning of your ways: in whom the prince of this world found nothing worthy of death" (Rom 7:24, Prv 8:22) and yet killed him; and the "handwriting which was against us was wiped out" (Col 2:14)? Those writings of the Platonists tell nothing of this. Those pages show nothing of the faith and look of pity, the tears of confession, "your sacrifice, a troubled spirit, a contrite and humble heart" (Ps 51), the salvation of your people, "the espoused city, the promise of the Holy Spirit, the chalice of our redemption." In them no one sings: "Shall not my soul be submitted to God? For from Him comes my salvation. For He is my God and my salvation, my defense; I shall never more be moved" (Ps 62:1–2). No one there hears Him calling: "Come to me, you who labor" (Mt 11:28). They disdain learning from Him because "He is meek and humble of heart (Mt 11:29). For these things you have hidden from the wise and prudent and you have revealed them to the little ones" (Mt 11:25). For it is one thing from a wooded mountain top to see the land of peace (Dt 32:49) and not find the way to it, and vainly struggle through impassable roads, beset roundabout by deceitful fugitive deserters under their leader, the "Lion and the Dragon": and it is quite another thing to hold to the way leading there, a road built and guarded by the care of the heavenly Commander where none of those who deserted the heavenly army are plundering on the road; for they avoid it like the plague. Marvelously these truths engraved themselves in my heart when I read that "least of your Apostles" and looked upon your works and trembled.

Book Eight

My God, let me remember you with gratitude, and confess your mercies to me. Let my bones be penetrated with your love and exclaim: "Lord, who is like unto you? You have broken my bonds: I shall offer you a sacrifice of praise" (Ps 86:8). And how you have broken them I shall narrate, and upon hearing this all those who adore you will say: Blessed be the Lord both in heaven and on earth; great and wonderful is His name. Your words had become deeply rooted in my heart and I was "surrounded on all sides by you" (Jb 1:10). I was now certain of your eternal life, although I saw it "through a glass darkly" (1 Cor 13:12), as it were; yet all my doubt concerning incorruptible substance, from which all other substance came, was removed, nor did I desire to be more certain of you but to stand more firmly in you.

As for my own temporal life all things were tottering, and "my heart had to be purged from old leaven" (1 Cor 5:7). The way, the Savior Himself, delighted me, but I was still unwilling to enter His narrow way. But you inspired me and it seemed good to me to go to Simplicianus, who seemed to me to be your good servant, and in him your grace shone forth. I had also heard that from his youth he had lived devoutly for you; now he was grown old; and it seemed to me that from a long life of steadfastly following your way he must have experienced much and learned much. And he truly had. Hence after disclosing to him my troubles, I wished him to suggest from his experience and learning the most appropriate way for someone with my sentiments to begin to follow you.

For I saw the Church full; and one went this way, and

another that way. But it was displeasing to me that I acted like a worldling, and it was greatly burdensome to me now that the hope of honor and of money no longer inflamed my desires as it formerly did to help me endure such a heavy bondage. For those hopes no longer delighted me when compared with the sweetness and beauty of your house, which I loved. But I was still strongly bound to a woman; nor did the Apostle forbid me to marry (1 Cor 7:8), although he exhorted to a better state, greatly desirous as he was that all men should be as he himself was. But I, weaker than he, chose the softer place; and on that account my life was in confusion because I languished and pined away with growing anxieties, because there were many things I was unwilling to suffer but had to put up with for the sake of living with a wife, a way of life to which I was bound. I had heard from the mouth of Truth itself that "there were some eunuchs who had made themselves such on account of the Kingdom of Heaven; but, he said, let whoever can take this, take it" (Mt 19:12). Certainly "all those men are vain in whom there is no knowledge of God, and who could not from those things which are good discover Him who is" (2 Wis 13:1). But I was no longer in that vanity: I had transcended it, and by the common witness of all your creation I had discovered you, our Creator, and your Word, God with you, and with you one God, through whom you had created all things. There is also another kind of impiety, that of those who "knowing God, did not glorify Him as God or give thanks" (Rom 1:21). Among these also I had fallen, but your right hand sustained me and removing me placed me where I might improve. Because you have said to man: "Behold the fear of the Lord is wisdom," and: "Be unwilling to seem wise because those calling themselves wise become fools" (Jb 28:28; Prv 3:7). But I had now found the "pearl of great price" (Mt 13:46) and should have sold all that I had and bought it but I hesitated.

2

Therefore I went to Simplicianus, who had fathered Bishop Ambrose into your grace and whom he truly loved as his own father. To him I told the winding ways of my error. But when I revealed that I had read certain books of the Platonists which Victorinus, once a Rhetor of the City of Rome (who, I heard, had died a Christian), had translated into Latin, he congratulated me for not having fallen upon the writings of other philosophers full of "fallacies and deceptions, according to the rudiments of this world" (Col 2:8), whereas in these writings, God and His Word are everywhere implied. Next, to exhort me to Christ's humility, "hidden from the wise and revealed to little ones" (Mt 11:25), he recalled Victorinus himself whom, when he was at Rome, he knew very intimately, and concerning whom he told me this story which I shall not pass over in silence. For it entails great praise of your grace, which should be confessed to you, to learn that this most learned old man, very skilled in all the liberal sciences; one who had read and considered carefully so many opinions of the philosophers; a teacher of so many noble senators, who because of the unusual brilliance of his teaching had both deserved and received a statue in the Roman Forum (which citizens of this world consider an honor)—up to old age he had worshiped idols and joined in those sacrilegious rites which were the fashion with almost all the Roman nobility, who had inflamed the people with their enthusiasm for Osiris and the dog Anubis and that monstrous brood of deity which once took arms and fought in arms against Minerva, Neptune, Venus—gods which Rome had once conquered and whom she now adored. And for all these years old Victorinus with his thundering eloquence had been the defender of these gods; yet he did not blush to become the child of your Christ, an infant at your font, submitting his neck to the yoke of humility and submitting his forehead to the scandal of the Cross.

O Lord, Lord, you "who have lowered the heavens and descended, touched the mountains and they smoked" (Ps 144:5), by what means did you make your way into the heart of that man? He read, as Simplicianus said, the holy Scriptures and he most studiously investigated and searched through all the Christian writings and said to Simplicianus not publicly but privately as friend to friend: "I should like you to know that I am now a Christian." And Simplicianus answered: "I shall not believe nor shall I count you as a Christian unless I see you in the Church of Christ." But, smiling, Victorinus said: "Do walls therefore make Christians?" And he often repeated that he was a Christian, and Simplicianus just as often answered in the same way, and Victorinus would make the same retort about "the walls." For he feared

to offend his friends who were important people and devil-wor-
shipers: From the height of their Babylonian dignity, as from the
height of the cedars of Lebanon, which the Lord had not yet
brought down, he thought a storm of ill-will would fall upon him.
But when by reading and desire he had gained strength, he grew
afraid that Christ might deny him before His angels if he feared to
confess Christ before men. He saw himself guilty of a great crime
by being ashamed of the Sacraments of the humility of your Word
while not having been ashamed of the sacrilegious rites of those
proud devils whom as a proud follower he had worshiped. So he
turned his pride against what was vain and became humble toward the truth. Suddenly, without warning he said to the surprised Simplicianus: "Let us go to the church: I want to be made a
Christian." And Simplicianus, overcome with joy, went along
with him. When he was instructed in the first Sacraments, he gave
his name as one who wished to be reborn through baptism. Rome
marveled and the church rejoiced. The proud "saw and were
indignant, they gnashed their teeth and pined away with grief";
but you, Lord God, were the hope of your servant and he "did not
look back at vanities and lying follies" (Ps 39:5).

Finally, when the hour had arrived for his profession of faith
in a set formula from a platform in the sight of the faithful people,
as was the custom at Rome for those about to come to your grace,
Simplicianus told me that the priests had offered Victorinus the
opportunity of making his profession in private as the custom was
with those who seemed likely to be frightened or embarrassed by
the public ceremony. But he chose rather to profess his salvation
in the sight of the church congregation. For there had been no
salvation in the rhetoric that he taught and yet he had professed it
publicly. How much less therefore should he fear your meek flock
in proclaiming your Word, he who did not fear proclaiming his
own words before the crowds of madmen? And so when he
ascended the platform to make his profession, all who knew him
(and was there anyone who did not?) whispered his name to one
another with glad murmurs. From the lips of the rejoicing congregation sounded the whisper: "Victorinus, Victorinus." Quickly
they spoke with exultation when they saw him, and quickly they
became silent so that they might hear him. He proclaimed aloud
the true faith with glorious confidence, and they all wished to

draw him within their very hearts. Indeed they did take him to their hearts by their love and rejoicing: These were the hands by which they clasped him.

3

O loving God, what in man makes him rejoice more over the salvation of a soul that has been despaired of, of one delivered from a major danger, than if there had always been hope for him or if the danger had been less great? Indeed even you, merciful Father, "rejoice more over a penitent than over ninety-nine just persons who have no need of repentance" (Lk 15:7). And it is with great joy also that we heard how the lost sheep was brought home again upon the shoulders of the exultant shepherd, and how the lost coin was replaced in your treasury, her neighbors rejoicing with the woman who found it. And the joy experienced at your church Liturgy brings tears as we hear read the parable of the younger son who was dead and brought back to life, who had been lost and was found (Lk 15:11–32). Indeed you rejoice over us as also over your angels who are steadfast in holy charity. For you are always the same because you know in the same manner all those realities which themselves neither are always existent nor always the same.

What is it in the soul, I again ask, that makes it more delighted to have found or regained those things which it loved than if it had always possessed them? There are many other examples of this; indeed the evidence everywhere proclaims that this is so. The general triumphs as a conqueror, but he would not have conquered unless he had fought, and the greater danger there was in battle, so much the more rejoicing is there in the triumph. The storm tosses the sailors and threatens shipwreck; everyone grows pale at the approach of death: But the sky and sea grow tranquil and as they have exceedingly feared, they exceedingly rejoice. A dear friend is sick, and his pulse reveals that he is in danger. All who want him healthy are likewise sympathetically sick with him: He recovers, although not yet walking with his former strength; and there is more joy than there was previously when he was well and perfectly able to walk. We procure the very pleasures of our human life by way of pain, not only unexpected pain and contrary to our wills but even unpleasantness planned and willingly accepted. There is no pleasure in eating and drinking unless the vexation of hunger and thirst precedes it. Drunkards eat certain salty things to bring about an uncomfortable dryness which makes for delight when this thirst is quenched. It was also customary that engaged girls be not immediately given over lest the husband, for not having sighed after her, esteem her less.

This is the case in pleasures that are foul and disgraceful as well as in pleasures that are permitted and lawful. We notice this in sincere and honorable friendship and also in the case of him who was dead and was brought back to life, was lost and was found. Everywhere the greater joy is preceded by the greater pain. Why is this, O Lord my God, since you are for yourself eternal joy, you yourself are joy and those around you find their joy forever in you? Why is it that this portion of the universe alternates between need and fulfillment, between discord and harmony? Is this their lot and have you given a certain proportion to them, when from the highest heavens to the lowest parts of the earth, from the beginning to the end of time, from the angel to the worm, from the first movement to the last, you settled all the varieties of good and all your just works each in its proper place, all accomplished in their due seasons? Alas for me, how high you are in what is the highest things, how deep in what is deepest. And from us you never depart, yet we with difficulty return to you.

4

Come, O Lord, stir us up and call us back, kindle and clasp us, be fragrant to us, draw us to your loveliness. Let us love, let us run! Do not many, from a deeper pit of blindness than Victorinus, return to you and are illuminated by light which "they who receive also receive the power to become your sons" (Jn 1:12)? But if they are less well known among the people those who know them also rejoice less. For when many rejoice together, the joy of each one is fuller because they warm themselves at one another's flame. Finally, because they are known by many they guide many to salvation and are sure to be followed by many. Even those preceding them on the same way feel great joy, and not only for them. Far be it that in your tabernacle the persons of the rich should be more welcome than the poor, or the noble before the common people, since you have chosen the weak things of this world to confound the mighty, and "you have chosen the base and contemptible things and those things which are not but should be to bring to nought the things which are" (1 Cor 1:27). You spoke those words by the tongue of the "least" of your Apostles. Yet, when Paulus the Proconsul had his pride overcome by the spiritual warfare of the Apostle and was put under the easy yoke of Christ, now made a humble subject of the Great King, he also desired to be called Paul instead of Saul, which was his previous name—as a sign of so great a victory. For the enemy is more overcome in that victory of a man over whom he had greater hold and by whom he held many others. But he had more hold on the proud by reason of their nobility and of many more through them by reason of their authority.

Therefore the heart of Victorinus was all the more welcome because the devil had held it as an invincible fortress, and the tongue of Victorinus because it was a strong keen weapon by which the devil had slain many. It was right for your sons to rejoice very specially because our King had bound the strong man and because they saw his "vessels taken from him and cleansed to become serviceable in your honor and become useful to the Lord unto every good work" (Mt 12:29; 2 Tm 2:21).

5

As soon as your man Simplicianus had told the story of Victorinus, I was on fire to imitate him, and this, of course, was why he had told it. He added that at the time of the Emperor Julian, when a law was made to forbid Christians from teaching literature and rhetoric, that he obeying this law chose rather to give up his wordy school than to forsake your Word, by which you make eloquent even the tongues of infants. He seemed to me not only brave but fortunate because he had the opportunity to devote all his time to you. I was also sighing for that opportunity, fettered as I was not by another's irons but by the iron bondage of my own will. The enemy held my will and made a chain out of it and bound me with it. From a perverse will came lust, and slavery to lust became a habit, and the unresisted habit became a necessity. These interconnected links—which I have called a chain—held me fast in a hard bondage. And the new will, which had begun to be mine, for worshiping you in freedom and enjoying you, O God, the only certain sweetness, was not yet able to overcome my old will, hardened by age. So my two wills, one old, the other new, one carnal, the other spiritual, conflicted and by their discord laid waste my soul.

Thus I came to understand by way of personal experience what I had read, how the "flesh lusts against the spirit, and the spirit against the flesh" (Gal 5:17). I no doubt was on both sides, but I was more myself on that side which I approved of for myself than when I was on that of which I disapproved for myself. For I myself was no longer on the latter side, because for the most part I suffered against my will rather than did it willingly. Yet habit had grown stronger against me by my own help because I had come willingly where I was unwilling now to be. And who then can rightly complain when just punishment overtakes the sinner? And I no longer had that excuse by which it seemed to me that I could not forsake the world to follow you because the knowledge of truth was for me uncertain. By now I was quite certain. But I was still tied down to earth and refused to accept service in your army. I was as much afraid of being freed from what hindered my going to you as I should have feared whatever might hinder this. So I was as pleasantly weighed down by the baggage of this world as one often is in sleep. And the thoughts by which I meditated on you were like the struggles of someone desirous to get up and yet overcome by a deep sleep, falling back again into it. There is no one who wishes to sleep always since according to everyone's sound judgment it is better to be awake; nevertheless a man postpones shaking off his drowsiness when there is a heavy sluggishness in his body, and although it displeases him he willingly settles in to another doze although he knows the time for rising has come. In like manner I was certain that it was better for me to commit myself to your love rather than to yield to my sensuality; but although the former course was pleasing and convincing, the latter delighted my body and held it in bondage. For I had now no excuse when you called: "Arise, you who sleep and rise up from the dead and Christ will enlighten you" (Eph 5:14); and whereas on all sides you showed me that you spoke truly, I, convinced of the truth, had no answer except for the slow and sleepy words: bye and bye, see, I come soon. But "bye and bye" had no ending and my "soon" went on forever. In vain "I delighted in your law according to the inner man, when another law in my members rebelled against the law of my mind, and led me captive in the law of sin which was in my members" (Rom 7:22). For the law of sin is the violence of habit by which the mind is drawn and held even against its will, deserving this by having willingly slid into the habit. Therefore, "who then should deliver wretched me from the body of this death except your grace through Jesus Christ our Lord?" (Rom 7:24–25).

6

And how you delivered me from the chains of my desire for sex by which I was so closely bound and from the servitude to worldly affairs, I shall declare and confess to your name, O Lord, my Helper and my Redeemer. As I led my usual life, anxiety grew greater and greater, and every day I sighed to you. I visited your church as much as I was allowed by my business, under the burden of which I groaned. Alypius was now with me, at leisure from his law work after the third time as Assessor, awaiting clients to whom he might sell his counsel, as I used to sell the power of speaking if such power can be taught. Nebridius, however, as an act of friendship had agreed to lecture under Verecundus, a great friend of ours, a citizen and elementary-school master of Milan who eagerly wanted Nebridius's assistance and by the right of friendship even demanded from one of our group the faithful aid which he greatly needed. Nebridius was not drawn to this by any desire of profit—for he could have done better for himself by teaching literature, if he pleased—but as a good and gentle friend he was too kindly a man to turn down our request. But he did it very discreetly, desirous of being unknown to persons of worldly reputation, avoiding all disturbance of mind, for he wished to have a free mind and as many hours of leisure as possible to seek or read or hear truths concerning wisdom.

Therefore on a certain day—I do not recall why Nebridius was absent—behold there came to our house, to me and Alypius, a certain Ponticianus, our fellow-citizen, an African, holder of an important office at the court of the Emperor. He had something or other he wanted from us, and we sat down to talk about it. Nearby was a game table and he happened to notice the book lying there; he took it, opened it and found it to be the Apostle Paul, certainly contrary to what he expected to find; for he thought it would be one of those books I wore myself out teaching. Smiling then and gazing closely at me, he expressed pleasure as well as surprise that I had this book and only this book at my side. For he was a Christian and a faithful one, and often prostrated himself before you, our God, in church in daily prayers, and many times daily. I indicated to him that I was greatly concerned with those Scriptures. Then he began to tell the story of Anthony the monk of Egypt, whose name was esteemed among your servants although we had not until then heard of him. When he discovered this, he talked about him all the more, eager to make known so great a man to those who knew him not, and very much marveling at our ignorance. But Alypius and I were amazed to hear of your wonderful works, done in the true faith and in the Catholic Church so recently, indeed, practically in our own time and witnessed to by so many. We all marveled—we, that such great things were done, he, that we had never heard of them before.

He went on to speak of the great groups living in monasteries, of their way of life which was full of the sweet fragrance of you and of the fruitful deserts in the wilderness of which we knew nothing. There was actually a monastery at Milan, outside the city walls. It was full of good brethren and was under Ambrose's direction, and we had never heard of it. He continued to speak and we listened intently. Then he began to say that he and three other comrades—I know not when—at Treves when the emperor was busy with circus chariot races, went walking in the gardens near the city walls; and it so happened that they separated into two groups, one walking with him and the other two going off by themselves. But as these two were wandering up and down, they stumbled by chance upon a certain small house where dwelt some of your servants, "poor in spirit, of which is the Kingdom of Heaven" (Mt 5:5) and they found there a book in which was written the Life of Anthony. One of the two began to read it, to marvel and be inflamed, and while reading to ponder on his own living of such a life and forsaking his military pursuits, serving you. For these two men were both officials in the emperor's civil service. Then suddenly filled with holy love, and a sober shame, angry with himself, he looked at his friend and said: "Tell me, I beg you, for what post of honor are we striving with all our labors? What are we seeking? Why are we serving the State? Can our hopes in court rise higher than to become the emperor's friends? And is not such a place insecure and full of danger? And through how many dangers must we go to arrive at a greater danger? And how long will it take to get there? But if I want, I can be the friend of God now, this moment." He said this and perplexed in the labor of a new life to which he was giving birth he looked again at the book. He read on and was inwardly changed where you alone could see; and his mind was emptied of worldly affairs, as was soon made evident. For while he read and the waves of his heart rose and fell, he expressed his self-anger, saw the better way, and chose it for himself. And having become yours, he said to his friend: "Now I have torn myself from those hopes of ours, and have decided to serve God; and this—from this moment in this place I shall undertake. If you are unwilling to imitate me, do not dissuade me." The other answered that he would remain his companion in so great a service for so great a prize. And both, now yours, built a spiritual tower at the only adequate cost, that of leaving all things and following you.

Then Ponticianus and the one with him who had walked through other parts of the garden seeking for their friends came upon them and warned that they should return because the day was ending. But they declared to them their resolutions and purpose and told them how that will had arisen in them and was now fixed, and they begged their friends, if they would not join them, not to interfere with their purpose. Ponticianus and his friend, though not changed from their former state, nevertheless wept, for themselves, as he told us, piously wishing them well and recommending themselves to their prayers; and with their hearts still turned toward earthly things, they returned to the court. But the other two, with their hearts fixed on heaven, remained in that cottage. And both of them were to be married; when their fiancées heard what had happened, they also dedicated their virginity to you.

7

This was the story Ponticianus told. But you, O Lord, while he was speaking turned me around to face myself, taking me from behind my back, where I had placed myself when I was reluctant to see myself; and you set me in front of my own face that I might see how deformed, how crooked and sordid, stained and ulcerous I was. I saw and I was horrified and found no way to flee from myself. And if I tried to turn away my gaze from myself, he continued to relate this story. And you set me in front of myself and thrust me before my own eyes so that I might discover my iniquity and hate it. I was aware of it, but I pretended to be unaware. I deliberately looked the other way and dropped it from my mind.

Then indeed the more ardently I loved those young men as I heard of their determination to win health for their souls by giving themselves totally to your healing, the more bitterly I hated myself in comparison with them: Since I had already squandered so many years—about twelve—since my nineteenth year, when, having read Cicero's *Hortensius*, I was first stirred up to study wisdom, and I was still postponing the contempt of earthly happiness and the inquiry into that of which not only the finding but even the search should have been preferred before the already found treasures and kingdoms of this world and before all bodily pleasures readily available. But I, wretched young man that I was, even more wretched in my early youth, had begged chastity from you and had said: "Give me chastity and continence but not yet." For I feared that you would hear me too soon and too soon deliver me from my disease of concupiscence which I wrongly desired to have satisfied rather than extinguished. And I had gone along evil ways, following a sacrilegious superstition through the wicked ways of Manichaeism not because I was convinced by it but because I preferred it to the Christian teachings into which I did not inquire in a religious spirit but merely opposed in a spirit of malice.

I had thought that the reason I postponed from day to day forsaking worldly hope to follow you was only because there did not seem any certain goal to which to direct my course. But now the day had come when I stood naked in my own sight and when my own conscience accused me: "Why is my voice not heard?" Surely you are the man who used to say that for an uncertain truth you could not cast off the baggage of vanity. Behold there is now certainty and that burden still weighs upon you. Others have received wings to liberate their shoulders from the load, others who have neither worn themselves out searching nor spent more than ten years considering it. So I was being gnawed at inside and vehemently confused with horrible shame while Ponticianus went on with his story. But when he finished both his speech and his business, he went his way and I retired into myself; nor did I leave anything unsaid against myself. With what lashes of accusations did I not scourge my soul so that it might follow me trying to follow you? My soul hung back. It refused to follow and yet found no excuse for not following. All its arguments had already been used and refuted. There remained only trembling silence, for it feared as very death the cessation of that habit of which it was wasting away unto death.

8

Then in the midst of the great tempest of my inner dwelling, a tempest which I had so vigorously excited against my own soul in the chamber of my heart, wild both in mind and countenance, I rushed upon Alypius, exclaiming: "What is wrong with us? What is this which you have heard? The unlearned rise up and take heaven by violence, and we with all our learning, behold, how we wallow in flesh and blood! Because they have preceded, does it shame us to follow or is it not a shame not to follow them?" Some such words I said and in my rage I broke away from him while, astonished, he said nothing, gazing after me. For I did not sound like myself.

My forehead, my cheeks, my eyes, my flesh, the tone of my voice, expressed my mind more than the words I uttered. There was a garden attached to our house which we used as we did the whole house, for the master of the house did not live there. There the tempest in my breast drove me, there where no one would impede the fierce suit which I had brought against myself until it could be settled—in what way you knew but I did not. But there I was, going mad on my way to sanity, dying on my way to life; aware how evil I was, unaware of how much better I was to be in a little while. Therefore, I withdrew into the garden and Alypius followed close after me. For I was no less in privacy when he was near. And how could he forsake me in such a state? We sat down as far from the house as we could. My mind was frantic, I was boiling with indignation at myself for not going over to your law and your covenant, O my God, where all my bones cried out that I should be, extolling it to the skies. And the way there is not by ship or chariot or on foot. The distance is not as great as I had come from the house to that place where we were now sitting. For to go there and to arrive fully required nothing other than the will to go, but to will strongly and totally, not to turn and twist a half-wounded will this way and that with one part rising up and struggling with the other part that would keep to the earth.

Finally in the torment of my irresolution I made many movements with my body which sometimes men want to make and cannot, if either they have not the limbs to make them or if those limbs be bound with cords, weakened by infirmity, or in some way hindered. If I pulled at my hair, beat my forehead, locked my fingers together, if I clasped my knee within my hand, all this I did because I willed to do it. But I might have willed it and not have done it, if the movement of my limbs had not followed the dictates of my will. Therefore, I did many things when the will was not identical with the power; and I did not do that which would have far more pleased me, which soon after, when I should have the will, I should have the power to do because when I willed, I should will it wholly. For there the power was one with the will, and the very willing was the doing. Yet it was not done and the body more easily obeyed the slighest wish of the mind that the limbs should immediately move than my mind obeyed itself so as to carry out its own great will which could be accomplished simply by willing.

9

How explain this absurdity? What is the cause of it? Let your mercy enlighten me so that I might ask whether the answer lies in the mysterious punishment that has come upon men and in some deeply hidden damage in the sons of Adam. Why this absurdity? And how explain it? The mind commands the body, and is immediately obeyed; the mind commands itself and is resisted. The mind commands the hand to move and the readiness is so great that the commanding is scarcely distinguishable from the doing. Yet the mind is mind whereas the hand is body. The mind commands the mind to will, the mind is itself, but it does not obey. Why this absurdity? And what is its cause? I say that the mind commands itself to will; it would not give the command unless it willed; yet it does not do what it commands. The reason is that it does not wholly will: Therefore it does not wholly command. It commands insofar as it wills, and it disobeys the command insofar as it does not will. The will is commanding itself to be a will, commanding itself, not another. But it does not wholly give the command; therefore that is not done which it commanded. For if the will were wholly itself, a unity, it would not command itself to will because it would already will. It is therefore no absurdity, partly to will, partly not to will, but it is only a sickness of soul to be so weighed down by habit that even when supported by truth it cannot totally rise up. And so there are two wills in us because neither of them is whole, and one has what the other lacks.

10

Let them vanish from your sight, O God, as they do vanish, these vain babblers and seducers of the mind who because they have noticed that there are two wills in the act of deliberating conclude that there are in us two minds of two different natures—one good, the other evil. They themselves are truly evil when they believe these evil opinions, and these same men could be good if they were to realize the truth and consent to the truth so that your apostle may say to them: "Once upon a time you were darkness, but now you are light in the Lord" (Eph 5:8). But these people want to be light not in the Lord but in themselves when they think that the nature of the soul is what God is. Thus they have become deeper darkness since they withdrew further from you in horrid arrogance, from you, the "true Light, enlightening every man coming into this world" (Jn 1:9). Take care what you say and blush for shame: "Draw near to Him and be enlightened and your faces shall not blush for shame" (Ps 34:5). As for me, when I deliberated about serving the Lord my God as I long meant to do, it was I who willed it, I who was unwilling. It was always the same I. I neither willed wholly nor was wholly unwilling. Therefore I struggled with myself and was torn apart by myself. This tearing apart took place against my will, yet this did not prove that I had a second mind of a different nature; but it was merely the punishment suffered by my own mind. Thus I did not cause it but the "sin dwells in me," and since I am a son of Adam, I was suffering from his freely committed sin.

For if there are as many contrary natures in man as there are conflicting wills, there would not only have to be two natures but many more. If a man should deliberate with himself as to whether he should go to the Manichaean Center or to the theater, the Manichees will exclaim: "Notice the two natures, a good one leads here, another evil one leads away. For how explain this hesitation of the wills thwarting each other?" But I say that both wills are evil, the one that leads a man to the Manichees and the one that leads him to the theater instead. But they believe that the will by which one comes to them is good. Suppose then one of us should deliberate and through the opposition of his two wills be undecided whether he should go to the theater or to our church, will not the Manichees be troubled as to what to answer? For either they must confess, which they will not want to do, that the will which leads to our church is good just as the will is good which leads men who have received and are bound by their sacraments to their church; or else they must suppose that in one man there are two evil natures and two evil wills in conflict; and then what they are wont to say will not be true: that there is one good and one evil will. Or else they will have to be converted to the truth and no longer deny that when anyone deliberates there is just one soul pulled in different directions by different desires.

Let them no longer say, therefore, that when they perceive two conflicting wills in one man the conflict is between two opposing minds of two opposing substances, from two opposing principles, one good, the other evil. For you, O God of truth, refute them and convict them of error, as in the situation where both wills are evil when, for example, a man deliberates whether he should kill a man by poison or by the sword, whether he should seize this or that part of another man's property when he cannot seize both, whether he should squander his money on pleasure or hoard it like a miser or whether he should go to the games or to the theater if both were to be shown the same day. I add also a third possibility, whether he should rob another's house if the opportunity arose; and I add a fourth, whether he should commit adultery if the chance occurs at the same time. If all these concurred at the same moment and all were equally desired and yet cannot all be simultaneously done, then they truly tear apart the mind among four opposing wills or even more than four when one considers the variety of things which are desirable: Yet the Manichees do not hold such a multitude of different substances. So it is also with good wills. For I ask them whether it is good to take delight in reading the Apostle, and whether it is good to be delighted by the serenity of a Psalm, and good to discuss the Gospel? To each of these they will answer: "It is good." Suppose then these things all equally delight us at the same moment, are not these different wills dividing the heart of man as we deliberate which of these we should choose? All these wills are good and yet they struggle with one another until one is chosen, and then the whole will which was divided into many is unified. So also when eternity delights the higher faculties, and the pleasure of some temporal good holds the lower ones, it is the one same soul which is willing both but not either one with its whole will. And it is therefore torn apart and deeply distressed when truth gives priority to the one way and habit keeps one to the other way.

11

Thus was I heartsick and tortured, accusing myself more bitterly than usual, turning and twisting myself in my chain so that it might be totally broken, for what still held me was so small a thing. But, although small, it still held me. And you, O Lord, stood in the secret places of my soul, by a severe mercy redoubling my lashes of fear and shame, lest I should give way again and lest that small and tender tie which still remained should not be broken but renew its strength and bind me more strongly than ever before. For I was saying within myself: "Behold let it be done now, let it be done now," and with this word I came to a decision. Now I almost did it, and I did not do it; but neither did I slip back to the beginning but stood still to regain my breath. And again I tried, and I was very nearly there; I was almost touching it and grasping it, and then I was not there; I was not touching it, I was not grasping it. I hesitated to die to death and to live to life; inveterate evil had more power over me than the novelty of good; and as that very moment in which I was to become different drew nearer and nearer, it struck me with more and more horror. But I was not forced back nor turned away but held in suspense between the two.

Trifles of all trifles and vanities of vanities, my former mistresses held me back, plucking at my garment of flesh and softly murmuring: "Are you dismissing us?" and "From this moment shall we never more accompany you?" and "From this moment will you never be allowed to do this or that?" And My God, what was it, what was it they suggested in those words, "this and that?" In your mercy keep such things from the soul of your servant! How filthy, how sordid were the things they were suggesting!

And now I only half heard them nor were they freely contradicting me so openly; it was as if they were muttering behind my back, stealthingly jerking my sleeve as I left so that I should turn and look at them. Yet they held me back as I delayed tearing myself away and shaking them off and taking the great step in the direction where I was called. Violence of habit said to me: "Do you think that you can live without them?" But by now it spoke very faintly. In the direction toward which I had turned my face and still trembled to take the final step, I could see the chaste dignity of Continence, serene and calm, cheerful, without wickedness, honestly entreating me to come to her without hesitating, extending her holy hands to receive and embrace me, hands full of multitudes of good examples. With her were many young men and maidens, many youths of all ages, serious widows and women grown old in virginity and in them all Continence herself, not barren but "a fruitful mother of children" (Ps 113:9), her joys by you, O Lord, her spouse. She smiled at me, and there was encouragement in her smile as though she were saying: "Can you not do what these men and women have done? Or do you think that their power is in themselves and not in the Lord their God? The Lord their God gave me to them. Why do you stand upon yourself and therefore not stand at all? Cast yourself upon Him, do not be afraid; He will not withdraw and let you fall; cast yourself fearlessly upon Him. He will receive you and heal you."

And I blushed for shame because I still heard the muttering of those vanities and still hung back hesitantly. And again it was as if she said: "Stop your ears against those unclean members of yours, so that they may be mortified. They tell you of delights, but not of such delights as the law of the Lord your God tells" (Col 3:5). This controversy raging in my heart was about nothing but myself against myself. But Alypius stayed beside me, silently waiting to see how my unusual agitation would end.

12

When from my secret depths my searching thought had dragged up and set before the sight of my heart my total misery, a storm arose within me, bringing with it a great downfall of tears. And so that I might give way to my tears I left Alypius—solitude seemed more suitable for the business of weeping—and withdrew further so that even his presence might not embarrass me. That is how I felt, and he realized it. Doubtless I had said something or other and he felt the weight of my tears in the sound of my voice, and so I left him. But he, amazed, remained there where we were sitting. I flung myself down on the ground somehow under a fig tree and gave way to tears; they streamed and flooded from my eyes, "an acceptable sacrifice to you," and I kept saying to you, perhaps not in these words but with this meaning: "And you, O Lord, how long? How long, Lord; will you be angry forever? Remember not our former iniquities" (Ps 6:3, 79:5). For I felt that they still held me fast. In misery I exclaimed: "How long, how long shall I continue to say: 'tomorrow and tomorrow'? Why not now? Why not this very hour put an end to my uncleanness?"

This I said, weeping, in the most bitter contrition of my heart. And suddenly I heard a voice from a neighboring house in a singing tune saying and often repeating, in the voice of a boy or girl: "Take and read, take and read." Immediately I stopped weeping, and I began to think intently as to whether the singing of words like these was part of any children's game, and I could not remember ever hearing anything like it before. I checked the force of my tears and rose to my feet, interpreting it as nothing other than a divine command to open the book and read the first passage to be found. For I had heard of Anthony that he happened to enter when the Gospel was being read, and as though the words were spoken directly to himself he accepted the admonition: "Go, sell all that you have and give to the poor, and you shall have treasure in heaven, and come, follow me" (Mt 19:21), and by such an oracle he had been immediately converted to you.

So I eagerly returned to that place where Alypius was sitting, for there I had left the book of the Apostle when I stood up. I snatched the book, opened and read in silence the passage which first met my eye: "Not in rioting and drunkenness, not in chambering and wantonness, not in strife and envying: but put you on the Lord Jesus Christ, and make not provision for the flesh in concupiscence" (Rom 13:13). I did not want to read further, there was no need to. For as soon as I reached the end of this sentence, it was as though my heart was filled with a light of confidence and all the shadows of my doubts were swept away.

Before shutting the book, I put my finger or some other marker in the place; with a calm face I told Alypius what had happened. And he in turn told me what was going on in himself, which I knew nothing about. He asked to see what I had read; I showed it, and he looked further than I had read, and I was unaware of the words which followed. They were these: "Him that is weak in the faith, receive" (Rom 14:1). He applied this to himself and told me so. By this admonition he was strengthened; calmly and without hesitation he joined me in a purpose and resolution so good and so right for his character which had always been very much better than mine.

Next we go inside to mother and tell her. How she rejoices! We related to her how everything happened; she exulted and gloried and was now blessing you who are able to do above that which we ask or conceive, because she recognized that with regard to me you have given her so much more than she used to beg for when she wept so pitifully before you. For you converted me to you so that I no longer sought a wife nor any other worldly hope. I was now standing on that rule of faith just as so many years before you had shown me to her in a vision. And you had changed her mourning into joy, a joy much richer than she had wanted and much dearer and purer than she looked for by having grandchildren of my flesh.

Book Nine

"O Lord, I am Your servant; I am Your servant and the son of Your handmaid: You have broken my bonds. I will offer to You the sacrifice of praise" (Ps 115:16–17). Let my heart and my tongue praise you, and let all my bones say, "O Lord, who is like unto You?" Let them speak, and You answer me and say unto my soul, "I am Your salvation" (Ps 34:10). Who am I and what am I? What evil have I not done in my acts, or, if not in my acts, in my words, or if not in my words, then in my will? But you, O Lord, are good and merciful, and you looked helpfully upon the depth of my death, and from the bottom of my heart you emptied out the sea of corruption with your right hand. And this was what your hand did: I was able totally to turn from what I willed and to will what you willed. But where was my free choice for so long a time, and from what profound and secret hiding place was my free will suddenly called forth at the moment in which I bowed my neck under your "easy yoke" and my shoulders under your "light burden," O Christ Jesus, my Helper and my Redeemer (Ps 12:15)? How sweet it suddenly became for me to be without the sweetness of trifling things! And how glad I was to give up the things that I had been so afraid to lose! For you cast them out, O true and highest Sweetness, and you entered into me to take their place, sweeter than all pleasure, though not to flesh or blood; brighter than all light, but more hidden within than any secret thing; higher than all honor but not for those highly conceited. Now my mind was free of those gripping cares of ambition, of acquisition, of wallowing in filth and scratching the itch of lust. And I was conversing like a child to you, to my Brightness, my Wealth, and my Salvation, my Lord God.

2

And in your sight I resolved that I would withdraw not suddenly but slowly my tongue's service from the market places of eloquence; no longer should my young students (who were meditating not so much on your law and your peace as on absurd deceptions and wordy skirmishes) buy from my mouth weapons for their own madness. Fortunately there were only a few more days before the vintage vacation. So I resolved to endure them so that I might retire in the usual manner. Having been ransomed by you, I could not return to be put up for sale. Therefore, our plan was known to you, but not known to me, except to our own friends. Among ourselves we had agreed not to spread the news, although, as we were ascending from the "valley of tears" and singing that "song of the steps," you had given us "sharp arrows" and "destroying coals" (Ps 120) against the deceitful tongues of people who, pretending to advise, would try to thwart us and by loving us would consume us, as people do with their food.

You had pierced our hearts with the arrow of your love, and we carried about with us your words like arrows thrust deeply in our flesh; heaped up in the recesses of our thought were the examples of your servants whose darkness you had turned to light and whose death to life so that our heavy slothfulness that might have dragged us once again down to the depths was utterly burned up and consumed. We were so much on fire that every gust of opposition from a deceitful tongue far from extinguishing the fire only made it burn more brightly. Yet because of your name which you have made blessed throughout the earth there would doubtless be those who would praise our resolution and vows, and I thought it would seem like ostentation if, instead of waiting for the oncoming vacation, I should resign beforehand from a public profession well known to all. All faces would turn toward me and upon what I have done, namely, that I had not wished to wait for the vintage season, although so near, and many would say that I wanted to make myself seem important. And how would it benefit me to have people thinking and talking about my intentions and reviling our good (Rom 14:16)?

Furthermore, that summer my lungs began to give way as a result of overwork in teaching. It was difficult to breathe; pains in the chest testified to the lesions so that I had to resist speaking too loud or too long. At first I was greatly troubled since I was being practically forced by necessity to give up the burden of teaching or, if I could possibly be cured and made well again, to give it up for the present time. But now my will in its fullness had risen up and was determined to "be still and see that you are God" (Ps 45:11). From this moment I began actually to be pleased that in this illness also I had a very genuine excuse to soften the injured feeling of those parents who, for the sake of their children, wanted me never to resign at all. Filled, then, with such joy, I endured the interval of time, about twenty days, I believe, which was still to pass, yet they were rendered tolerable only by fortitude. For the desire for sensible goods which used to enable me to bear the heavy work had left me, and I should have been overburdened had not patience come to replace it. Some of your servants, my brethren, may say that I sinned in this, because, with my heart fully set on your service, I went on holding for one hour the chair of falsehood. I do not dispute this. But have you not, most merciful Lord, also pardoned and remitted this sin along with other terrible and deadly sins in the holy water of baptism?

3

Verecundus was tormented with anxiety because of the good we had found. He saw that by reason of his own chains, by which he was tightly bound, he was to be forced to lose our companionship. He was not yet a Christian, although his wife was. She, however, was a chain which clung to him more tightly than all the rest, preventing him from setting forth on the journey on which we had started. For he said that he would not be a Christian in any other way except the way that was impossible to him. Nevertheless, he kindly offered us the use of his house as long as we would remain there. You, O Lord, will reward him "in the resurrection of the just" (Lk 14:14) because you have already awarded him their lot. This happened in our absence; we were already at Rome when Verecundus became ill, of a bodily sickness; during his sickness he became a baptized Christian and then departed from this life. So "you had mercy not on him only but on us also" (Ps 125:3), for we would have been tortured with intolerable pain whenever we thought of this kindness received from our friend if we knew that we could not count him as one of your flock. We thank you, our

God. We are yours; Your inspirations and consolation affirm this. Faithful to your promises, you will repay Verecundus for his country house at Cassiciacum, where far from the turmoils of the world we rested in you, with the loveliness of your paradise ever fresh and green; for you have forgiven him his sins upon earth and placed him above the earth in that fragrant mountain, your mountain, that mountain of abundance.

Verecundus was therefore very much worried, but Nebridius altogther joyful. He too was not yet a Christian and in the past he had fallen into that pit of deadly error, believing the flesh of your Son, who is the Truth, to be but a phantasm. But rising above this error he was, although he had not yet received the Sacraments of your Church, a most ardent searcher after truth. Not long after our conversion and rebirth through your baptism, you took him from this fleshy life; by then he also was a baptized Christian, serving you in perfect chastity and continence among his own people in Africa, and having converted his whole household to the Christian faith. Now he lives "in the bosom of Abraham" (Lk 16:22). Whatever that is, whatever is signified by this bosom of Abraham, there my Nebridius lives, my sweet friend, but your adopted son, no longer a freedman: There he lives in a place concerning which he often questioned me, a poor ignorant man. Now he no longer places his ear at my mouth but places his spiritual mouth at your fountain and drinks his full of all the wisdom he desires, endlessly happy. Nor do I think that he is so inebriated with that wisdom as to forget me, since you, O Lord, of whom he drinks, are mindful of us. This is the way we were, comforting Verecundus, saddened by our conversion, but in unbroken friendship urging him to fidelity to his own state of life, the married life. But we waited for Nebridius to follow us. He was so close to us that he could have done so, and he was just about to do it when those days of waiting came to an end. Long and many they seemed to me because of my love for leisurely freedom in order to sing to you from the depths of my being: "My heart has said unto You, I have sought your face; your face, O Lord, will I seek" (Ps 26:8).

4

The day arrived when I was actually to be freed from the profession of rhetoric, from which in my thoughts I was already free. So it was done. You rescued my tongue as you had already delivered my heart from it. I blessed you, rejoicing, and with all my friends set off to the country house. My writing was now wholly in your service but during this breathing space still smacked of the school of pride. My books exist to witness with their record of discussions either with my friends present there or with you when I was alone with you; and there are my letters to show what correspondence I had with Nebridius while he was away. But when shall I get time to bring back in memory all your great acts of goodness to us, especially at that time, since I must hasten to tell of even greater matters?

For my memory recalls them, and it pleases me, O Lord, to confess to you by what inward spurs you completely subdued me, and how you leveled me down, "making low the mountains and hills of my thoughts, making straight what was crooked, and plain what was rough" (Is 40:4). And I remember how you also made Alypius, that brother of my heart, subject to the name of your only-begotten Son, our Lord and Savior Jesus Christ, which at first Alypius considered unfitting to be mentioned in our writings. For he wanted them to exude the odor of the lofty cedars of the schools, which the Lord has already broken, rather than that of the herbs of the Church, which are protection against the serpents.

My God, how I poured out my heart to you as I read the Psalms of David, those songs of faith, those songs of piety which admit of no pride of spirit! I, still uninitiated in your true love, spent my vacation in the country house with Alypius, a catechumen like myself, and with my mother who, in that close association with us, was womanly in her dress but virile in her faith, mature in her serenity, motherly in her love, Christian in her piety. How I cried aloud to you in those Psalms! How they inflamed me toward you! How I burned to utter them aloud, if possible, to the whole world against the pride of mankind! But they are already sung throughout the world, nor can "any hide himself from your heat" (Ps 18:7). With what strong and bitter grief I was enraged against the Manichees! Yet I also pitied them for their ignorance of those medicinal Sacraments and for raging insanely against the antidote which might have made them sane. I wished that they might be near me—without my knowing that they were there—and could see my face and hear my words when in that period of leisure I read the Fourth Psalm so that they could see how that Psalm affected me! "When I called, the God of my righteousness heard me; in tribulation you enlarged me. Have mercy upon me, O Lord, and hear my prayer" (Ps 4:2). Would that they could have heard me without my knowing that they heard, lest they think that on their account I spoke as I spoke when reciting these words: and in fact if I realized that I was being seen by them and overheard, I would not have said what I said or in the way that I said it; nor, if I had said these same things would they have understood how I was speaking with myself and to myself in front of you out of the intimate feelings of my soul.

I trembled with fear, and at the same time I was on fire with hope and with exaltation in your mercy, O Father. And all these emotions were expressed in my eyes and in my voice when your Holy Spirit turned to us and said: "O you sons of men, how long will you be dull of heart? Why do you love vanity so much and seek after lying" (Ps 4:3)? For I had loved vanity and had sought after lying. "And you, O Lord," had already "exalted your Holy One, raising Him from the dead, and setting Him at your right hand," whence "from on high" He should send His "promise, the Comforter, the Spirit of Truth" (Lk 24:45–50; Acts 2:29–34). And already He had sent Him and I knew it not. He had sent Him because He was already exalted, having risen from the dead and ascended into heaven. For since the "Spirit was not yet given, because Jesus was not yet glorified," and the Prophet exclaims: "How long?" He cries aloud: "Know this." And I, so long ignorant, have loved vanity and sought after lying.

And so I listened and trembled, for they were spoken to such as I remember myself to have been. For in those phantasms which I had taken for truth there were both vanity and lying. And in my grief at the remembrance of it I cried aloud many things earnestly and strongly. I wish that those who still love vanity and seek after lying could have heard me. Perhaps they would have been troubled and vomited up their poison. And you would have forgiven them when they cried to you. For it was by a true death in the flesh that He died for us who now "intercedes unto you for us" (Rom 8:34).

I also read: "Be angry and sin not" (Ps 4:5; Eph 4:2). And how I was moved, my God, I who had already learned to be angry with myself; for it was not that some other nature belonging to the race of darkness committed the sin in me, as the Manichees believe, who are not angry with themselves and who "treasure up wrath against the day of wrath and of the revelation of your just judgment" (Rom 2:5).

The good I now sought was not in the things outside me to be seen by the eye of flesh under the sun. For those finding their joys in things outside easily become vain and waste themselves on visible and temporal things and, with their minds starving, go licking at images. Oh, that they would weary from want of nourishment and say: "Who will show us good things?" (Ps 4:6). Then we should say and they would hear, "The light of Your countenance is sealed upon us, O Lord" (Ps 4:6–7). For we are not ourselves "that light which enlightens every man" (Jn 1:9) but we are enlightened by you so that "having been once darkness, we may be light in you" (Eph 5:8). If only they could see Eternal Light inside themselves! I had seen it and I was frantic that I could not make them see it even were they to ask: "Who shall show us good things?" For the heart they would bring me would be in their eyes, eyes that looked everywhere but at you. For there, there in the place where I had been angry with myself inside, in my room, there where I had been pricked, where I had made my sacrifice, offering up my old self and beginning the plan for my renewal, with my hope set on you—there it was that you began to grow sweet to me and to "put gladness in my heart" (Ps 4:7). I cried out as I read this with my outward eye and inwardly recognized its truth. Nor did I wish that my earthly goods be multiplied: In these one wastes and is wasted by time, whereas in your eternal simplicity I had other corn and wine and oil.

With a deep cry from my heart I called out the following verse: "Oh, in peace, Oh, in the Selfsame!" Oh, why did he say: "I will grow drowsy and take my sleep" (Ps 4:9)? For who shall stand against us when "that saying comes to pass which is written, death is swallowed up in victory" (1 Cor 15:54)? And you supremely are the Selfsame, you who do not change, and in you is that rest in which all labor is forgotten, since there is no other beside you, nor are we to seek for those many other things which are not what you are. But you, O Lord, alone have "made me dwell in hope" (Ps 4:8). I read and was set on fire. What could be done, I wondered, with those deaf and dead men of whom I myself had been a pestilent member, a bitter and blind critic of Scriptures which are all honeyed with the honey of heaven and all luminous with your light: And now I was fretting my heart out over the enemies of these same Scriptures.

When shall I recall the whole story of those vacation days? Nor have I forgotten, nor will I pass over in silence how bitter was the scourge with which you afflicted me, and the marvelous swiftness of your mercy. At that time you tormented me with a toothache, and when it became so aggravated that I could no longer speak, it came into my heart to ask all my friends who were present to pray for me to you, the God of all health. This I wrote on wax, giving it to them to read. As soon as we had gone down on our knees in all simplicity, the pain left. But what pain was it? And how did it go? I was terrified, I admit, my Lord and my God; for in all my life I had never experienced anything like it. And so in the depths of me I experienced the power of your command and, rejoicing in faith, I praised your name. But this faith did not put me at ease about my past sins, since these had not yet been forgiven by your baptism.

5

When the vintage vacation ended I gave the people of Milan notice that they must provide someone else to sell the art of words to their students, because I had chosen to serve you and because I was no longer able to continue my profession on account of the pain in my chest and my difficulty in breathing. In a letter I also told your bishop, the holy Ambrose, of my past errors and my present purpose, that he might advise me which of your Scriptures I had best read to prepare myself and become more fit to receive so great a grace. He told me to read the prophet Isaiah because, I believe, he foretells the Gospel and the calling of the Gentiles more clearly than the other writers. But in fact, not understanding my first reading of this book, and thinking that all the rest would be like that, I put it aside intending to return to it when I should be more practiced in the Lord's way of speaking.

6

Then when the appropriate time came for me to submit my name, we left the country and returned to Milan. Alypius also had decided to be born again in you at the same time, for he was already clothed in that humility which befits your Sacraments, and he had so subdued and mastered his own body that, showing the most extraordinary fortitude, he could go barefooted over the icy soil of Italy. We also took with us the young Adeodatus, the son of my flesh, begotten by me in my sin. You had made him well. He was barely fifteen, but he showed more intelligence than many serious and learned men. In saying this I am but acknowledging to you your own gifts, my Lord my God, Creator of all and full of power to reform our deformities: for I myself had no part in that boy but the sin. That he was reared by us in your teaching was because you and no other had inspired us, I do but acknowledge to you your own gifts. There is a book of mine called *De Magistro;* it is a dialogue between him and me. You know, O God, that all the ideas which are put into the mouth of the other person in the dialogue were truly his, when he was in his sixteenth year. Many other remarkable qualities of his I also experienced. His talent filled me with awe. And who but you could be the maker of such wonders? You took his life early from this earth, and without anxiety I think of him, for there is nothing in his boyhood or youth or indeed as a man to cause me to fear for him. We associated him with us as our contemporary in your grace, to be educated in your studies. So we were baptized, and all anxiety over our past life vanished. Nor in those days could I ever have enough of the wonderful sweetness of meditating upon the depth of your design for the salvation of mankind. What tears I shed in your hymns and canticles! How deeply I was moved by the voices of your sweet-singing Church! Those voices flowed into my ears, and the truth was distilled into my heart, which overflowed with my passionate devotion. Tears ran from my eyes, and I was happy in those tears.

7

The Church of Milan had only lately begun practicing this kind of consolation and exaltation, to the great enthusiasm of the brethren singing together with heart and voice. It was only a year or so ago that Justina, the mother of the boy emperor Valentinian, was persecuting your servant Ambrose on behalf of her own heresy: for she had been led astray by the Arians. The devoted people had remained day and night in the church prepared to die with their bishop, your servant. There my mother, your hand-maid bearing a great part of the trouble and vigil, had lived in prayer. I myself, though not yet warmed by the fire of your spirit, was stirred by the state of excitement and alarm in the city. Then began the practice of singing hymns and Psalms in the manner of the Eastern Churches, lest the people grow faint from sorrow. The custom has continued from that day to this and has been imitated by many, in fact, by almost all of your congregations in other parts of the world.

At that time you revealed to your bishop Ambrose in a vision the place where the bodies of the martyrs Gervasius and Protasius lay hidden. You had for so many years concealed them uncorrupted in your secret treasury from which you might produce them at the proper moment to check the fury of a woman, even though an empress. When they were discovered and unearthed, they were brought with due honor to Ambrose's basilica. Not only were people tormented by unclean spirits cured when these demons acknowledged their presence, but also a certain man who had been blind for many years and as a well-known citizen of Milan asked and was told why the people were shouting with joy. He jumped up and asked his guide to lead him to the place. When he arrived he begged to be allowed to touch with his handkerchief the bier on which were lying the "saints whose death is precious in Your sight" (Ps 115:15). He did this, placed the handkerchief upon his eyes, and immediately his eyes were opened. The news spread abroad. Your praises were fervent and glowing. And Justina was restrained from the insanity of persecution even though her mind was not brought back to the sanity of belief.

Thanks be to you, My God! From where and to where have you led my memory that it should confess to you these great things which I had completely forgotten? Yet even then, "when the odor of the ointments was so sweet smelling" (Cant 1:2–3), I did not "run after you." And so I wept all the more at the singing of your hymns, as one who had once sighed for you and now breathed you in as far as there can be any breath of air in this house of grass (cf. Is 40:6).

8

You, who make "men of kindred minds to dwell in one house" (Ps 67:7), led Evodius, a young man from our town, to join us. He had been in the government service, had been converted to you and baptized before us, had resigned from his official post and became active in your service. We were together, intending to remain together in our devout purpose. We sought for some place where we might more usefully serve you and therefore we started back to Africa. And when we had come as far as Ostia on the Tiber my mother died.

I pass over many things because I am in much haste. Accept my confessions and my thanksgiving, O my God, for innumerable things of which I do not speak. But I shall not pass over whatever my soul brings forth about that servant of yours who brought me forth, giving me birth in the flesh to this temporal light, and in her heart to light eternal. Not of her gifts do I speak but of your gifts in her. For she did not make herself nor did she bring herself up. You created her nor did her father and mother know what kind of being was to come forth from them. The rod of your Christ, the discipline of your only-begotten Son educated her in your fear, in a faithful household worthy to belong to your church. Yet she used to speak not so much of her mother's care in training her as of the care of an elderly woman servant who had carried her father on her back as a baby, as small children are often carried about on the backs of the grown-up girls. Because of this service and on account of her age and excellent behavior this servant was greatly respected by her master and mistress in this Christian household. Consequently, she had charge of the daughters of the family, one she fulfilled most conscientiously; in restraining the children when necessary she acted sternly and with a holy severity, and in teaching them she manifested sound prudence. For example, except at the times they were fed—and very temperately—at their parent's table, she would not even let them drink water however thirsty they might be, thus guarding against the formation of a bad habit, saying very sensibly: "Now you are drinking water because you are not allowed to have wine. But when you become married and become mistress of your stores and cellars, water will not be good enough for you, but you will have this habit of drinking." By this advice and by the authority she exercised, she brought under control the greediness from which children suffer and disciplined the girls' thirst to a proper moderation so that they no longer wanted what they ought not to have.

Nevertheless, as your servant [Monica] confided in me, her son, there did come upon my mother an inclination toward wine.

For when, as the custom was, she as a good sober girl was told by her parents to go and draw some wine from the barrel, she would hold the cup under the tap and then before pouring the cup into the decanter, she would sip a little, just wetting her lips, since she did not like the taste and could not take more. Indeed, she did this not out of any craving for wine, but rather from the excess of childhood's high spirits, which tend to break loose in ridiculous impulses and which in our childhood years are usually kept under restraint by the sobering influence of elders. And so, adding to that daily drop a little more from day to day—for he "who despises small things shall fall little by little" (Eccl 19:1) she fell into the habit, so that greedily she would gulp down cups almost full of wine. Where then was that wise old woman with her stern prohibition? Was there anything strong enough to deal with a hidden disease unless your healing powers, O Lord, watched over us? Mother, father, and nurses may not be there, but you are there, you who made us, you who call us, you who also use those placed over us to do some good for the salvation of our souls. What did you do, then, O my God? How did you cure her? How did you make her healthy? Did you not from another soul bring forth a harsh and cutting taunt, as if bringing forth a surgeon's knife from your secret store, and with one blow amputate that corruption? For a maidservant with whom she usually went to the cellar one day fell into a quarrel with her small mistress when no one else chanced to be about, and hurled at her the most biting insult possible, calling her a drunkard. My mother was pierced to the quick, saw her fault in its true wickedness, and instantly condemned it and gave it up. Just as the flatteries of a friend will pervert so the insults of an enemy will sometimes correct. Nor do you, O God, reward men for what you do through them but according to what they themselves intended. For that maid being in a temper wanted to hurt her young mistress, not to cure her, for she did it when no one else was there, either because of the time and place where the quarrel started, or because she feared that the elders would be angry that she had not mentioned it sooner. But you, O Lord, Ruler of heavenly and earthly things, who turn to your own purposes the very depths of the torrents as they run and order the turbulence of the flow of time, brought health to one soul by means of the unhealthiness of another, showing us that if someone is improved by any word of ours, we must not attribute this to our own power, even if we intended this result to occur.

9

She was educated, therefore, in a modest sober way, being rather made obedient to her parents by you than to you by her parents. And when she reached marriageable age, she was given to a husband whom she served "as her lord" (cf. Eph 5:21). She tried to win him to you, preaching you to him by her behavior in which you had made her beautiful to her husband, reverently lovable and admirable in his sight. So she tolerated his infidelities and never had a jealous scene with her husband about them. She awaited your mercy upon him, that he might grow chaste through faith in you. Although an extremely kind man by nature, he was, in fact, also very hot-tempered. But my mother knew that an angry husband must not be opposed, not in deed nor even in word. Only when he had calmed down and had become quiet, when she saw an opportunity, she would explain her actions, if perchance he had been aroused to anger unreasonably. Indeed there were many wives with much milder husbands who bore the marks of beatings, even in the form of facial disfigurement, and coming together to talk they would complain of their husbands' behavior. Yet my mother, speaking lightly but seriously, warned them that the fault was in their tongues. They had all heard, she said, the marriage contract read out to them and from that day they should regard it as a legal instrument by which they became servants; so, mindful of their station, they should not set themselves up against their masters. And they were often amazed, knowing how violent a husband she had to live with, that it had never been heard of, nor had there been any evidence to show that Patricius had ever beaten his wife or that there had been a family quarrel that had lasted as much as a single day. And when her friends asked her intimately how she managed it, she told them her rule, which was as I have just related. Those who followed it found it good and thanked her; those who did not went on being bullied and beaten.

She also won over her mother-in-law by the respect shown her and by unfailing patience and mildness when her mother-in-law had begun by being angry because of the whispers of malicious servants. Her mother-in-law ended by going to her son telling him of the tales the servants had gossiped about to destroy the family peace between herself and her daughter-in-law, and asking him to punish them for it. So he, out of obedience to his mother and in the interest of household order and peace among the womenfolk, had those servants whose names she had given him beaten. To which she added the promise that anyone must expect a similar reward from her if they tried to please her by speaking ill of her daughter-in-law. None dared after that to do so, and after that they lived together in the sweetness of mutual good will.

This great gift also, O my God, my mercy, you gave to your good servant in whose womb you created me, that she showed herself, whenever possible, a peacemaker between people quarreling and minds at discord. She might hear very many bitter things said on both sides, and this outpouring of swelling and undigested malice is very likely to occur when a woman talks to a present friend about an absent enemy; on such occasions hatred is expressed in crude and bitter terms. But my mother would never report to one woman what had been said about her by another except insofar as what had been said might help to reconcile the two. I might consider this a small virtue if I had not had the sad experience of knowing innumerable people who, through some horrible infection of sin, not only tell others who are angry what their enemies said about them in anger, but actually add things which never were said. Whereas ordinary humanity would seem to require not merely restraining from exciting or increasing wrath among men by evil tongues, but that we endeavor to extinguish anger by speaking kindly. This is what my mother did, and you were the master who, deep in the school of her heart, taught her this lesson.

Finally, toward the end of his earthly life, she won her husband over to you, and now that he was a believer she no longer had to lament the things she had to tolerate when he was not yet a believer. She was also the servant of your servants. Whoever knew her praised many things in her, and honored and loved you, because they felt your presence in her heart, through the fruitful evidence of her saintly manner of life. She had been the wife of one husband, had requited her parents, had governed her house piously, was well reported of for good works; she had "brought up her children" as often "travailing in birth of them" as she saw them straying away from you (1 Tm 5:9; Gal 4:19).

Finally, Lord, of all of us—since by your gift we are allowed to speak—who before her death were living together after receiving the grace of baptism, she took as much care as though she were the mother of us all, and served us as though she were the daughter of us all.

10

The day was now approaching on which she was to depart this life—the day you knew though we did not—it came about, as, I believe, by your secret arrangement that she and I stood alone leaning in a window which looked onto the garden inside the house where we were staying, at Ostia on the Tiber where, apart from the group, we were resting for the sea voyage after the weariness of our long journey by land. There we conversed, she and I alone, very sweetly, and "forgetting the things that were behind and straining forward to those ahead" (Phil 3:13), we were discussing in the presence of Truth, which you are, what the eternal life of the saints would be like, "which eye has not seen nor ear heard, nor has it entered into the heart of man" (1 Cor 2:9). But with the mouth of our heart we also panted for the supernal streams from your fountain, the fountain of life which is with you (Ps 35:10) so that if some drops of that fountain, according to our capacity, were to be sprinkled over us, we might somehow be able to think of such high matters.

And our discourse arrived at this point, that the greatest pleasure of the bodily senses, in the brightest corporeal light whatsoever, seemed to us not worthy of comparison with the joy of that eternal life, unworthy of being even mentioned. Then with our affections burning still more strongly toward the Selfsame we advanced step by step through the various levels of bodily things, up to the sky itself from which the sun and moon and stars shine upon this earth. And higher still we ascended, by thinking inwardly and speaking and marveling at your works, and we came to our own minds and transcended them to reach that region of unfailing abundance where you feed Israel forever on the food of truth (Ez 34:13). There, life is wisdom by whom all these things come into being, both those which have been and those which will be. And wisdom itself is not made; it is as it has ever been, and so it shall be forever: Indeed, "has ever been" and "shall be forever" do not pertain to it, but it simply is, for it is eternal; whereas "to have been" and "to be going to be" are not eternal. And while we were speaking and panting for wisdom, we did with the whole impulse of the heart slightly touch it. We sighed and left behind "the first fruits of the Spirit" (Rom 8:23) which were bound there, and returned to the sound of our own tongue where the spoken word has both beginning and ending. How is it like your word, our Lord, "remaining ageless in Itself and renewing all things" (Wis 7:27)? We said therefore: If to any man the uproar of the flesh grew silent, silent the images of earth and sea and air; and if the heavens also grew silent and the very soul grew silent to itself, and by not thinking of self ascended beyond self; if all dreams and imagined revelations grew silent, and every tongue and every sign and if everything created to pass away were completely silent —since if one hears them, they all say this: We did not make ourselves, but He who abides forever made us. Suppose that, having said this and directed our attention to Him who made them, they also were to become hushed and He Himself alone were to speak, not by their voice but in His own, and we were to hear His Word, not through any tongue of flesh or voice of an angel or sound of thunder or involved allegory, but that we might hear Him whom in all these things we love, might hear Him in Himself without them, just as a moment ago we two, as it were, rose beyond ourselves and in a flash of thought touched the Eternal Wisdom abiding over all. If this were to continue and other quite different visions disappear, leaving only this one to ravish and absorb and enclose its beholder in inward joys so that life might forever be such as that one moment of understanding for which we had been sighing, would not this surely be: "Enter into the joy of Your Lord" (Mt 25:21)? But when shall it be? Perhaps when "we shall all rise again" and "shall not all be changed" (1 Cor 15)?

Such thoughts I uttered although not in this way or in these words. Yet, O Lord, you know that on that day when we talked of these things this world with all its delights seemed worthless to us, even as we were speaking of it. Then my mother said: "Son, as for me, I no longer take delight in anything in this life. What I am doing here now, and why I am here I do not know, now that I have nothing else to hope for in this world. There was only one reason why I wanted to remain a little longer in this life, that I should see you a Catholic Christian before I died. This God has granted me superabundantly, for I see you as His servant to the contempt of all worldly happiness. What am I doing here?"

11

What I answered to this I do not clearly remember; within five days or not much longer she fell into a fever. And in that sickness she one day fainted away and for the moment lost consciousness. We ran to her, but she quickly regained consciousness, and seeing my brother and me standing by her, she said to us, as though seeking an answer to some question, "Where am I?" Then gazing intently upon us as we stood speechless in our grief, she said: "Bury your mother here." I was silent and restrained my weeping; but my brother said something about hoping that she would have the good fortune to die in her own country and not in a foreign land. But when she heard this, she looked anxious and gave him a reproachful look because he still relished earthly things. Then she looked into my face and said: "See how he talks." Soon she said to both of us: "You may lay this body of mine anywhere: Do not worry at all about that. All I ask you is this: that wherever you may be, You will remember me at the altar of the Lord." And when she had expressed this wish in such words as she could, she fell silent as the agony of her sickness grew stronger upon her.

But as I considered your gifts, O invisible God, which you have placed into the hearts of your faithful and which have produced such wonderful fruit, I rejoiced and gave thanks to you, recalling that I knew how worried and anxious she had always been about the question of her burial. She had already provided herself and prepared a tomb close to that of her husband. Since they had lived together in such harmony, she had wished—so little is the human mind capable of grasping things divine—that it should be granted her as an addition to her happiness and to have it spoken of among men, that after her pilgrimage across the sea the earthly part of both man and wife should lie covered under the same earth. Just when this vain desire began to leave her heart through the plenitude of your goodness, I did not know; but I was pleased and surprised that it had now vanished, although in that conversation of ours together in the window, when she said: "What am I still doing here?" she had shown no desire to die in her own country. Furthermore, I later heard that when we were at Ostia, she spoke one day to some of my friends, as a mother speaking to her children, of the contempt of this life and of the good of death. I was not there at the time. They marveled at such strength of a woman—but it was you who had given it to her— and inquired whether she was not afraid to leave her body so far from her own city. "Nothing," she said, "is far from God, and I do not fear that he will not know at the end of the world from what place He is to raise me up." And so on the ninth day of her illness, in the fifty-sixth year of life and the thirty-third of mine, that religious and holy soul was released from the body.

12

I closed her eyes; and an immense wave of sorrow flooded my heart and would have overflowed in tears. But my eyes under the mind's strong constraint seemed to pump that fountain dry, and in that struggle it was agony for me. Then as soon as she had breathed her last, the boy Adeodatus broke out in lamentation until, constrained by all of us, he grew silent. But in this very deed the childish element in me which was breaking out in tears was checked and silenced by the manlier voice of my mind. For we felt that it was not appropriate that her funeral should be marked with moaning and weeping and lamentation, because these are the ways people grieve for an utter wretchedness in death or a kind of total extinction. But she had not died miserably nor did she wholly die. Of this we had good reason to be certain from the evidence of her way of living and from her "unfeigned faith" (1 Tm 1:5).

What was it then that grieved my heart so deeply except the freshness of the wound, in finding the custom I had so loved of living with her suddenly snapped short? I rejoiced in the testimony she gave me in the very last days of her illness when, as I was doing what service I could for her, she spoke so affectionately to me, calling me her good and dutiful son, with such great love, she told me that she had never once heard me say a word to her that was hard or bitter. And yet, my God, who made us, what comparison was there between the honor I showed her and the service she rendered me?

Because I had now lost the great comfort of her, my soul was wounded and my very life torn asunder, for it had been one life made up of hers and mine together. So when the boy was quieted from weeping, Evodius took up the Psalter and began to chant—with the whole house making the responses—the Psalm "Mercy and judgment I will sing to You, O Lord" (Ps 101:1). And when it was known what we were doing, many brethren and religious women gathered. And while those whose function it was made arrangements for the burial, I with some of my friends who thought I should not be left alone found another part of the house where we could properly be, and there I spoke to them on such subjects as I thought appropriate for the occasion. So I was using truth as a kind of balm to relieve my torment, a torment known to you but unknown to the others. They listened closely to me and thought that I lacked all feeling of grief. But in your ears where none could hear me, I rebuked the tenderness of my feeling, and suppressed the flow of guilt. It yielded a little, then gathered strength and again swept back on me though not with any outburst of tears or change of facial expression. But I well knew what I was crushing down in my heart. I was ashamed that those human feelings could be so strong in me—though it belongs to the due order and the lot of our earthly condition that these things should be—and I felt a new grief at my grief and so was afflicted with a twofold sorrow.

When the body was carried to the grave, we went and returned without tears. During the prayers we poured forth to you when the sacrifice of our redemption was offered for her—while the body, as customary there, lay by the grave before it was actually buried—during those prayers I did not weep. Yet all that day I was heavy with hidden grief and in my troubled mind I begged you, as best I could, to heal my sorrow; but you did not, impressing, I think, upon my memory by this one experience how strong is the bond of all custom even when that soul now feeds upon no deceiving word. It seemed to me that I should go to bathe myself because I had heard that the word for bath—which the Greeks called *balneum*—was derived from the Greek *balaneion* because it drives anxiety from the mind. And this also I confess to your mercy, O Father of orphans, that I bathed and was the same man after as before. The bitterness of grief had not sweated out of my heart. Then I fell asleep and awakened to find that my grief was much relieved. And as I lay alone in bed I remembered those true verses of your Ambrose: for it is you who are

> Creator Thou of everything
> Director of the circling poles
> Clothing the day in lovely light
> Giving night the grace of sleep
> That peace may fall on loosened limbs
> To make them strong for work again
> To raise and soothe the tired mind
> And free the anxious from their care.

Then little by little I began to recover my former feelings about your handmaid, her devout and holy behavior in regard to you, her saintly kindness and benevolence toward us, of which I was suddenly deprived. And I found solace in weeping in your sight both about her and for her, about myself and for myself. So I allowed the tears which I had been holding back to fall, and I let them flow as they would, making them a pillow for my heart, and my heart rested on them, since only your ears were there, not those of some man who would have scornfully misunderstood my tears. And now, O Lord, I am confessing this to you in writing. Anyone who cares can read what I have written and interpret it as he likes, and if he finds it is sinful that I wept during this small portion of an hour for my mother, now dead and lost to my sight, who had wept so many years for me that I should live ever in your sight, let him not despise me but rather, if he is a man of great charity, let him weep for my sins to you, the Father of all the brethren of your Christ.

13

Now that my heart is healed of that wound, in which one might criticize the element of bodily emotion, I pour forth to you, our God, on behalf of your handmaid tears of a very different kind, those which flow from a broken spirit from the thought of the perils that exist for every soul that dies in Adam. Although she after having been made alive in Christ and when still not freed from the flesh so lived that in her faith and her actions your name was praised, yet I dare not say that from the time of her rebirth in baptism no word came from her mouth contrary to your commandment. It was said by Truth, your Son: "Whosoever shall say to his brother, you fool, shall be in danger of hell fire" (Mt 5:22); and it would fare badly with any man, however praiseworthy his life, if you were to lay aside your mercy before examining it. But because you do not look too rigorously into our sins, we have hope and confidence of a place with you. Yet if a man recounts before you the merits he truly has, he is only telling you of your gifts to him. If only men would recognize that they are men, so "that he that glories, would glory in the Lord" (2 Cor 10:17).

And so, O my Praise and my Life, O God of my heart, leaving aside for the time her good deeds for which I joyfully thank you, I now pray to you for my mother's sins. Hear me, through Him who is the remedy of our wounds, who hung upon the cross, and now "sitting at your right hand, intercedes to you for us" (Rom 8:34). I know that she dealt mercifully and from her heart forgave those "who trespassed against her" (Mt 6:12). Do you also forgive her such trespasses as she may have been guilty of in all the years since her baptism, forgive them, O Lord, forgive them, I beseech you: "Enter not into judgment with her. Let your mercy be exalted above your justice," because your words are true, and "you have promised mercy unto the merciful" (Mt 5:7). That they should be merciful is your gift "who wilt have mercy on whom you wilt have mercy, and compassion on whom you have had compassion" (Rom 9:12).

And I believe that you have already done what I am now asking, but accept, O Lord, the "free offerings of my mouth" (Ps 118:208). For on that day when her death was so near, she was not concerned that her body should be richly adorned for burial or embalmed in spices; she did not desire a special monument, nor was she anxious to be buried in her own country. These things she did not command us, but only desired to be remembered at your altar which she had served without so much as missing a day on which she knew that the holy victim was offered, "by whom the handwriting that was against us is blotted out" (Col 2:14), by which the enemy was overcome who, reckoning up our sins and seeking what there was to lay to our charge, "found nothing in Him" (Jn 14:30) in whom we are conquerors. Who shall restore to Him His innocent blood? Who shall return to Him the price by which He purchased us and so take us from Him? To this sacrament of our redemption your handmaid had bound her soul by the bond of faith. Let none wrest her from your protection; let neither "the lion nor the dragon" (Ps 90:13) bar her way by force or by wiles. For she will not answer that she owes nothing lest she be convicted and seized by that cunning accuser. She will answer that her debts have been remitted by Him to whom no one can repay the price which He, owing nothing, paid for us.

Let her, therefore, rest in peace with her husband, before or after whom she had no other, whom she obeyed, "with patience bringing forth fruit" for you, so that she might win him for you also. And inspire, my Lord and my God, inspire your servants, my brethren, yours sons, my masters, those whom I serve with heart and voice and pen, so that as many as shall read this may remember at your altar Monica, your servant, with Patricius her husband, through whose flesh you introduced me into this life, though how I know not. May they with holy affection remember those who were my parents in this transitory light, who are my brethren under you, our Father, in our Catholic Mother, and my fellow citizens in the eternal Jerusalem which your people sigh after in their pilgrimage from the beginning of their journey until their return, so that what my mother in her extremity asked of me may be fulfilled for her more fully through my confessions by the prayers of many rather than through my prayers alone.

Book Ten

Let me know you, who knows me, "let me know even as I am known" (1 Cor 13:12). O you, the power of my soul, enter into it and adapt it to yourself so that you may have and possess it without spot or wrinkle. This is my hope; therefore I speak and in that hope I rejoice when my joy is sound. As for the other things of this life, the more we weep for them the less they deserve being wept for, and the less we weep for them the more we ought to weep. For, behold, you have loved truth, since he "who does the truth comes to the light" (Jn 3:21). I want to do this in my heart before you in confession, and in my writings before many witnesses.

2

And certainly from you, O lord, before whose eyes the depth of the human conscience is laid bare, what in me could be hidden although I were unwilling to confess it to you? I could not then be hiding myself from you, but you from myself. But now when my groaning witnesses to my displeasure with myself you shine out on me and you are pleasing to me, loved and desired so that I am ashamed of myself and renounce myself and choose you and, except in you, can please neither you nor myself. Whatever I am, therefore, O Lord, is laid bare before you. And the benefit I derive from confessing to you, I have stated. Nor do I confess with bodily words and speech but with words of the soul and the clamor of my thoughts which your ear understands.

For when I am wicked, to confess to you is to be displeased with myself; but when I am good to confess to you is not to attribute this goodness to myself: since you, O Lord, bless the just, but first you convert him from ungodliness to justice. And so my confession, O my God, is made in your sight silently and not silently. For although it makes no noise, it cries aloud in my heart. For if what I say to men is right, you have first heard it from me but anything you hear from me you yourself have first said it to me.

3

Why should men hear my confessions as if they would heal all my infirmities? They are a race very curious about the lives of others, very slothful in improving their own. Why should they wish to hear from me what I am when they are unwilling to hear from you what they are? And when from me they hear my account of myself, how do they know that I speak truly seeing that "no man knows what is in man but the spirit of man which is in him" (1 Cor 2:11)? But if from you they hear about themselves, they cannot say: "The Lord is lying." For to hear about themselves from you is simply to know themselves. And who knowing himself can say "it is false" unless he himself is lying? But because "charity believes all things" (1 Cor 13:7) (that is, among those whom it binds together to make one), I confess to you so that men may hear me though I cannot prove to them that I am telling the truth; but they whose ears charity opens to me believe me.

Yet, I ask you, my inmost Physician, to clarify for me what benefit I gain in doing it. For the confessions of my past sins (which you have forgiven and covered so that you might make me happy in you, transforming my soul by faith and your sacrament), when read and heard, stir up the heart lest it fall asleep in despair saying: "I cannot," but that it may awaken in the love of your mercy and the sweetness of your grace by which when aware of his own weakness, every weak person becomes strong. And it delights good people to hear of the past evils of those who are now freed from them; they are delighted with the evils but only because they who were evil no longer are.

Then with what benefit, my Lord, to whom my conscience, more secure in your mercy than in its innocence, daily confesses, with what benefit, I ask you, do I confess before you and also before men through this book not what I once was but what I now am? As to my confession of the past, I have both seen and recounted that. But as to what I now am, at this very moment of writing my confessions, there are also many people who desire to know this, those who know me and those who do not know me who have heard of me or from me; but their ear is not against my heart where I am whatever I am. They wish, therefore, to hear me confessing what I am within myself—which is beyond the reach of their eyes, ears, or understanding. Although they wish to believe, will they understand? That charity by which they are good tells them that in my confessions I would not lie, and that charity in them believes in me.

4

But what benefit do they wish from this? Do they desire to congratulate me when they hear how close I have come to you by your Grace, and to pray for me when they hear how I am kept back by my own weight? To such people I shall reveal myself. For it is no small benefit, O Lord my God, that thanks should be given to you for me by so many and that many should pray to you for me. Let the brotherly mind love in me what you teach should be loved and lament in me what you teach should be lamented. Let the mind doing this be brotherly not alien, not of "strange children whose mouth speaks of vanity, and their right hand is a right hand of iniquity" (Ps 144:11), but that brotherly mind which, when it approves of me, rejoices over me, and when it disapproves, sorrows on my behalf, because whether it approves or disapproves, it loves me. To such I shall reveal myself: Let them breathe freely at my good deeds, sigh for my evil ones. My good deeds are your work and your gift; my evil ones are my faults and your judgments. Let them breathe freely at the one, sigh at the other, and let hymns and lamentations arise in your sight from fraternal hearts, your censers. When you, O Lord, are delighted with the incense of your Holy Temple, "have mercy upon me according to Your great mercy, for your own name's sake" (Ps 51:1), and in no way deserting what you have begun in me, perfect my imperfections.

The benefit of confessing, not what I have been, but what I am is this: I confess not only before you, in a secret "exaltation with trembling" (Ps 2:11) and in secret sorrow with hope, but also in the ears of the believing sons of men, companions of my joy and partners in my mortality, my fellow citizens and fellow pilgrims: both those who have gone before and those who follow after and my companions on the way. These are your servants, my brethren, whom you have willed to be your sons, my masters whom you have commanded me to serve, if I wish to live with you and from you. And this word of yours would be a minor matter if it only gave me a spoken command and did not precede me in action. I serve these men by deeds and words. This I do "under your wings" (Ps 35:8), and the danger would be too great if under your wings my soul were not protected by you and my weakness known to you. I am very little, but my Father lives forever, and my Protector is adequate for me. For He is the same who begot me and who watches over me, and you yourself are my total good, you, Almighty, who are with me even before I am with you. Therefore, to such people whom you have commanded me to serve, I shall reveal not what I was, but what I now am and continue to be. "But neither do I judge myself" (1 Cor 4:3). And so in this way let me be heard.

5

For "you, Lord, judge me," because, although "no man knoweth the things of a man, but the spirit of man which is in him" (1 Cor 2:11), yet there is still something of man which even the spirit of man that is in him does not know, but you, O Lord, who made him, know everything about him. As for me, though in your sight I despise myself and esteem myself but dust and ashes, yet I know something of you which I know not of myself. And certainly we see "now through a glass darkly, not yet face to face" (1 Cor 13:12), and therefore, as long as I wander away from you, I am more present to myself than to you; yet I know that you are in no way subject to violence, whereas in my case I do not know what temptations I can and cannot resist. Yet there is still hope, because "you are faithful, who will not suffer us to be tempted above that we are able: but will with the temptation also make a way to escape, that we may be able to bear it" (1 Cor 10:13). Therefore, I shall confess what I know of myself, I shall confess also what I do not know of myself, since what I know of myself I know by means of your light shining upon me, and what I do not know remains unknown to me until in your countenance "my darkness be made as the noonday" (Is 58:10).

6

It is not with doubtful but with assured awareness, O Lord, that I love you. You pierced my heart with your Word and I loved you. But also heaven and earth and all within them, behold, they bid me on every side to love you, nor do they cease telling this to all, "that they may be without excuse" (Rom 1:20). But more deeply "will you have mercy or whom you will have mercy, and will show compassion to whom you will show compassion" (Rom 9:15); otherwise, heaven and earth proclaim your praises to deaf ears. But what do I love when I love you? Not the beauty of body nor the gracefulness of temporal rhythm, not the brightness of light so friendly to the eyes, not the sweet and various melodies of songs, not the fragrance of flowers and ointments and spices, not manna and honey; not limbs receptive to fleshly embraces: I love not these when I love my God. And yet I do love a kind of light, melody, fragrance, food, embracement when I love my God; for He is the light, the melody, the fragrance, the food, the embracement of my inner self: Where that light shines into my soul which no place can contain, and where that voice sounds which time does not take away, and where that fragrance smells which no wind scatters, and where there is that flavor which eating does not diminish, and where there is that clinging that no satiety will separate. This is what I love when I love my God.

And what is this? I asked the earth and it said: "I am not He," and all things in it made the same confession. I asked the sea and the deeps and the creeping things and they answered: "We are not your god; seek above us." I asked the blowing breezes, and the entire air with its inhabitants said: "Anaximenes was deceived; I am not god." I questioned the sky, the sun, the moon, the stars: "Nor are we the god whom you seek," they said. And I said to all these which surround the doors of my flesh: "Tell me about my God, since you are not he, tell me something about Him." And they exclaimed in a loud voice: "He made us." My question was in my contemplation of them; and their answer was in their beauty. And I turned my attention upon myself and said: "Who are you?" and I answered: "A man." Now I find in myself a soul and body, one exterior, the other interior. Which of these should I have used in seeking for my God? I had already searched for Him by means of the body, searching from earth to sky, as far as I could direct the beams of my eyes as messengers. But the interior part of me is the better. To this part all my bodily messengers gave in their reports and this inner reality sat in judgment weighing the replies of heaven and earth and all things within them when they said: "We are not God," and when they said: "He made us." The inner man knew these things through the ministry of the outer man; I, the inner man, knew all this; I, the soul, through my bodily senses; I asked the whole mass of the world about my God, and it answered me: "I am not He, but He made me."

Is not the face of the earth clearly seen by all who have sound senses? Why then does it not speak the same things to all? Animals great and small see it well enough but they cannot ask questions of it. Reason does not preside over their senses to judge on what they report. Men can ask so that they may clearly understand "the invisible things of God, which are understood by the things which are made" (Rom 1:20), but by loving these things, they become subject to them, and subjects cannot judge. Nor will these creatures answer those questioning unless the questioners are capable of judging. Not that they alter their speech, that is, their beautiful appearance. If one man merely looks at them while another not only looks but questions, they do not appear one thing to one man, and a different thing to the other. They look identically the same to both, but to one man they say nothing and to the other they speak. It would be truer to say that they speak to all but are understood only by those who compare the voice which comes to them from outside with the truth within. For truth says to me: "Your God is not sky or earth, or any body." Their own nature declares this. They recognize that there is less bulk in a part than in a whole. Now, my soul, I tell you that you are my better part, since you animate the whole bulk of the body, giving life to it, which no body confers on a body. But God, however, is even for you the Life of your life.

7

What then do I love when I love my God? Who is He above the summit of my soul? Through this very soul of mine I shall ascend to Him. I shall go beyond my life-force by which I cling to the body and fill its frame with life. Not by that force do I find my God: If so, "the horses and mules which lack understanding" (Ps 32:9) could find him since their bodies also live by that same force. But there is another force, not only that by which I not only give life, but give sensation to my flesh which the Lord fashioned for me, commanding the eye not to hear, and the ear not to see, but giving me the eye to see by and the ear to hear by, assigning to each of the other senses its own particular duty and function. Through these senses, with all their different functions, I act as one soul. I shall also go beyond this force, for this also the horse and the mule have: They also sense through the body.

8

I shall therefore also go beyond this power of my nature, ascending by degrees to Him who made me. And I come to the fields and spacious palaces of memory where lie the treasures of innumerable images of all kinds of things brought into it by the senses. There is stored up whatever we think, if by thought we have enlarged or diminished or in any way altered those things which the sense has touched, and there also is everything else that has been brought in and deposited and has not yet been swallowed up and buried in forgetfulness. When I am in this treasure house, I ask for whatever I like to be brought forth to me; whereupon, some things are produced at once, some things take longer and have, so to speak, to be fetched from a more remote part of the store, and some things come pouring out all together and, when indeed we want and are searching for something quite different, they thrust themselves forward as though saying: "Perhaps you are looking for us?" These I drive away with the hand of my heart from the face of my remembrance until I discover at last what I desire, emerging from its hidden place into my sight. Some things are produced easily and in perfect order just as they are desired: What comes first gives place to what comes next, and, as it gives place, it is stored up ready to be brought forth when I need it again. This all takes place when I repeat anything by heart.

There all sensations are preserved distinctly and in categories according to how they enter, such as light and all colors and bodily shapes brought in by the eyes; all sorts of sounds through the ears, and all odors through the nostrils; all tastes through the mouth; and by the sensation of the whole body we derive our impression of what is hard or soft, of whatever is hot or cold, or whatever is smooth or rugged, heavy or light, whether from outside or inside the body itself. All these sensations are received into the great harbor of memory with its many secret and indefinable recesses, to be produced when need requires, each coming in by its own entry and there stored up. Yet the things themselves do not enter, but the images of things perceived are there ready at hand for thought to recall.

Who can say how these things are formed? Yet it is clear by which senses they entered and were stored up. For even while I remain in darkness and silence I can, if I wish, call forth colors in my memory and note the difference between black and white and any other colors I like, and when I reflect on the images drawn in by my eyes, sounds do not come running in to disturb them, though they also are in my memory, stored up, as it were, in a separate compartment. For I can summon forth sounds also, if I wish, and they are immediately present; with no movement of tongue or vocal chords I sing as much as I please, nor do those images of color, although present in the memory, intrude and interrupt when I summon something from that other storehouse containing impressions brought in by the ear. And so I call forth as I like all other things brought in and stored up by the other senses. I can discern the difference between the smell of lilies and violets though I am actually smelling nothing at the time, and I prefer honey to sweet wine, something smooth to something rough merely by memory, using neither the sense of taste nor that of touch.

This I do within, in that huge court of my memory. There I have available to me the sky, the earth, the sea, and all those things in them which I have been able to perceive—apart from what I have forgotten. There also I encounter myself; I recall myself, what, when, and where I have done something; and how I felt at the time. There are all things I remember to have experienced myself or to have heard from others. From the same storehouse also I can summon forth pictures of things which have either happened to me or are believed on the basis of experience. I can myself weave them into the context of the past; and from these I infer future actions and events and hopes, and on these again I contemplate as if they were present. "I shall do this and that," I say to myself in this deep recess of my mind, full of the images of so many and such great things, "and this or that follows." "Oh, if only this or that could happen!" or "May God prevent this or that!" So I say to myself, and while I am speaking, the images of all the things that I am saying are present to my mind, all from this same treasury of my memory: in fact, if the images were not there, I would not be able to speak of these things at all.

How great is the power of memory, how exceedingly great, O God; a vast and unlimited interior; who has plumbed its depths? Yet this is a power of my mind and belongs to my nature; I myself do not grasp all that I am. Is then the mind too narrow to hold itself so that the questions arise: Where is this which belongs to it, and it cannot grasp? Is it outside itself and not inside? How then does it not grasp itself? Faced with all this, great wonder arises in me, astonishment seizes me. And men go abroad marveling at the heights of mountains, at the huge waves of the sea, at the broad courses of the rivers, the vastness of the ocean, the circular motions of the stars, and yet do not notice themselves and see nothing marvelous in the fact that when I was mentioning all these things I was not observing them with my eyes. Yet I could not have spoken of them unless these mountains and waves and rivers and stars, which I have seen, and the ocean of which I have heard, had been visible to me inside, in my memory, and with precisely the same great intervals and proportions as if I were really seeing them outside myself. Yet by the act of seeing I did not draw them into myself; not they themselves but only their images are within me, and I know by what bodily sense each impression came to me.

9

But this immense capacity of my memory contains far more than this. Here also are all those things I have learned of the liberal sciences, and have not yet forgotten, removed, somehow, to an inner place which is not really a place. Nor do I have with me the images of these but the sciences themselves. For what literature is, what the art of disputation is, or how many kinds of questions there are, everything of this kind which I know is in my memory in a special way. In this case I do not retain the image and leave the thing outside me. It is not a matter of the sound of words which has ceased sounding, like a voice, having left a definite impression upon the ear through a vestigial image by which it can be recalled as though it were sounding, when in fact it is not sounding; nor like an odor which, while passing and vanishing into air affects the sense of smell and so brings into the memory an image of itself which can be recalled by an act of recollection; nor like food, which surely has no taste when already in the stomach but yet has a kind of taste when in our memory; nor like something perceived by the sense of bodily touch which can still be imagined in our memory when we are no longer in contact with it. Certainly these things are not brought into our memory but only their images are captured with marvelous swiftness and stored up in wonderful secret places and are marvelously brought forth by the act of remembering.

10

But when I hear that there are three kinds of questions—"Does the thing exist? What is it? What kind is it?"—I do indeed hold in mind the images of the sounds of which these words are composed, and I know that they have noisily passed through the air and have now ceased to be. But as to the things themselves signified by these sounds, I never attained them by any bodily sense nor discerned them anywhere else than in my mind; yet in my memory I have stored up not their images, but the things themselves. How they got into me, let them say if they can. For as I examine all the gateways of my body, I cannot find by which one they entered. The eyes say: "If these images were colored, we announced them." The ears say: "If they made a sound, we reported them." The nostrils say: "If they had an odor, they entered through us." And the sense of taste says: "Unless there is a taste to them, do not ask me." Touch says: "If the thing is not a body, I did not handle it, and if I did not handle it, I gave no information about it."

From where then and how did they enter into my memory? I do not know. For when I learned them, I was not accepting them because of trust in another; I was recognizing them in my own mind; I approved them as true and committed them to my own mind, so storing them that I might recall them when I wished. So they were in my mind even before I learned them but they were not in my memory. Then where were they? Or why was it that, when I heard them spoken, I recognized them and said: "That is right; that is true" unless indeed they were already in my memory, but so remote and so buried, as it were, in the deepest recesses that if they had not been drawn forth by the encouragement of someone else I should perhaps not have been able to conceive of them?

11

We find, consequently, that to learn those things which we do not draw into us as images through our senses, but which we discern inside ourselves as they actually are without the help of images, means merely this: By thinking we are, so to speak, collecting together things which the memory did contain, though in a disorganized and dispersed way, and by attending carefully to them we arrange for them to be, so to speak, stored up ready at hand in that same memory where previously they lay hidden, disregarded and dispersed; so that now they will readily come forward to the mind which becomes familiar with them. My memory included many things like this which have been discovered, and, as I said, placed ready at hand. These are the things which we are said to have learned and to know. Yet if I stop, even for a brief span of time, bringing them up into my mind, they are submerged again and slip back into some kind of distant hiding place, so that I have to think them out anew from that same place—for they have no other place—and once again collect them so that they may be known. They must be collected as from their scattered sites: so one speaks of "cogitating." For *cogo* [collect] and *cogito* [recollect] are related to each other as *ago* [do] is to *agito* [do constantly], as *facio* [make] is to *factito* [make frequently]. But the mind has appropriated to itself this word ("cogitation") so that we correctly use that word only of things "collected" in the mind, not of things gathered together elsewhere.

12

Likewise, the memory contains the innumerable principles and laws of numbers and dimensions which no bodily sense impressed on it because they have neither color, nor sound, nor taste, nor smell, nor feeling. I have heard the sounds of the words by which these principles are signified when we speak of them, but sounds differ from principles. The sounds will vary according to whether the words used are Greek or Latin but the principles are neither Greek nor Latin nor any other language. I have seen the lines drawn by architects, lines as small as the thread of a spider's web. But the principles involved are something different;

they are not images of those things reported to me by my bodily eye, and whoever knows these principles recognizes them within himself without any conception of any kind of body. I have also perceived with all my bodily senses the numbers we use in counting; but the numbers by which we count are not the same as these, nor are they images of these, and therefore they really exist. Anyone who does not see them may laugh at me for speaking thus of them, and while he laughs at me, I shall pity him.

13

All these things I hold in my memory and how I learned them I also hold in my memory. I have also heard and hold in memory false arguments against these things. Although they are false, it is not false to say that I remember them, and I also remember that I have distinguished between the truths and the false objections made to these truths. Therefore, I often remember that I have previously understood these things, and what I now discern and understand I record in my memory so that later I may remember what I have understood now. So I remember that I have understood these things, and if later I recall that I have now been able to remember these things, I shall recall this through the force of memory.

14

The same memory also contains the affections of my mind not in the way that my mind contains them when it experiences them but in another way appropriate to the nature of memory. For I remember that I was happy when I am not happy now, and I recall my past sadness when I am not sad now; when I am not frightened, I can remember that I was once frightened, and I remember a former desire when I am without that desire. Sometimes, on the contrary, when I am happy I remember my past sadness, and when I am sad I remember my past happiness. This is not to be wondered at with respect to the body, for the mind is one thing and the body is another, and so if I remember some past pain of the body, that is not so surprising. But since the mind is also the same as the memory—for when we tell someone to remember something we say: "See that you keep it in mind," and when we forget something we say: "It did not come to mind" or "It slipped my mind," calling the memory itself mind—since this is the case, how is it that when I, being happy, remember my past sadness—so that the mind contains happiness and the memory contains sadness—the mind is happy because of the happiness in it, but the memory is not sad because of the sadness in it? Does the memory have no connection with the mind? Who would say such a thing? Therefore, the memory must be, as it were, the stomach of the mind, and happiness and sadness like sweet and bitter food, and when they are committed to the memory, it is as if they passed into the stomach where they are stored away but where there is no taste. A ridiculous comparison, perhaps, and yet there is some similarity.

But notice that I bring them forth from my memory when I name the four emotions of the mind—desire, joy, fear, sadness—and however I discuss these by defining or classifying under genus and species, it is in my memory that I find what I say and it is from my memory that I bring it forth. Yet I am not disturbed by any emotion when I take note of them by remembering them. Yet, they were there in the memory before I recalled them and reviewed them. Only because they were there was I able to recollect them. Perhaps, therefore, just as food is brought up from the stomach by chewing the cud, so these things are brought forth from the memory by recollection. Why, then, is the actual sweetness of joy or bitterness of sorrow not tasted in the cogitational mouth of the one discussing, that is, remembering these things? Is the comparison unlike in this, that it is not alike in every way? For we would be unwilling to speak of such things if whenever we used the words "sorrow" or "fear" we had actually to feel sorrow or fear. And yet we could not speak about them at all unless we could find within our memory not only the sounds of the words (according to their images impressed on it by the bodily senses) but even the very notions of the things themselves, and we did not receive these notions through the entry of any bodily sense. It was the mind itself which by the experience of its own passions felt them and committed them to the memory; or else the memory retained them even if they were not committed to it.

15

But who will easily say whether this is done through images or not? I pronounce the word "stone" or "sun" when the things themselves are not present to my senses; yet before my memory images of them are present. I speak of some bodily pain; this pain is not present to me since I am not in pain; but unless the image of it was in my memory, I should not know how to speak of it and in any discussion, I should be unable to distinguish it from pleasure. I mention bodily health when I myself am in good health: The thing signified by the word is actually present in me, yet unless its image was also in my memory, I could in no way recall what the sound of the name signifies. Nor when the word "health" was mentioned would sick people recognize the meaning of what was said, unless, despite the fact that health itself was not present in their bodies, they still retained through the force of memory an image of health. I name the numbers used in counting; the numbers themselves and not their images are in my memory. I name the image of the sun, and this image is in my memory—not the image of its image, but the image itself; that is before me when I recall it. I mention memory and I recognize what I mean by it. But where do I recognize it except in memory itself? Can memory itself be present to itself through its image rather than through its reality?

16

Now when I say "forgetfulness" and recognize what I mean by the word, how do I recognize the thing itself except by remembering it? I am not speaking of the sound of the word, but of what the word signifies. For if I had forgotten the reality I certainly would not be able to recognize what the word meant. When I remember memory, memory itself is, through itself, present to itself; but when I remember forgetfulness, memory and forgetfulness are both present—memory by which I remember, forgetfulness which I remember. But what is forgetfulness except privation of memory? How then can that be present for me to remember which when present I am not able to remember? But if what we remember we retain in memory and if, unless we remembered forgetfulness, we could never recognize what was meant by the word when we heard it, then forgetfulness must be retained in the memory. It is therefore present so that we may not forget that which when it is present we do forget. Must we understand from this that forgetfulness, when we remember it, is not present to the memory in itself, but by its image, because if it were present in itself, it would cause us not to remember but to forget? Who can search such a thing out? Who shall understand how that should be?

Certainly, Lord, I labor over this and I labor over myself. I have become to myself a piece of difficult ground, not to be worked over without much labor. For we are not now investigating the region of the sky nor measuring the distance of the stars or the weight of the earth. I am the one who remembers—I, the mind. It is then no wonder that something other than myself is far away from me; but what is closer to me than my own self? Yet this power of my memory is incomprehensible to me, although without it I may not speak of myself. What shall I say when I so surely see that I remember forgetfulness? Shall I say that what I remember is not in my memory? Or that forgetfulness is in my memory so that I may not forget? Each of these statements is absurd. What is to be said of the third? Can I say that the image of forgetfulness, not forgetfulness itself, is retained in my memory when I remember it? How can I say this since when something's image is impressed in the memory, the thing itself from which the impression is derived must necessarily be present? So it is that I remember Carthage and all other places I have been; in this way I remember men's faces which I have seen, and the reports of the other senses; so also I remember the health or sickness of the body. When these things were present, my memory received their images from them and these images remained present for me to contemplate and consider anew when I recollected the absent objects themselves. If, therefore, forgetfulness is retained in the memory by means of its image and not in itself then clearly forgetfulness must have at some time been present so that its image might be received. But when it was present how did it impress its image upon the memory since forgetfulness by its pressure erases whatever it finds already recorded there? Nevertheless, howsoever it be, however incomprehensible and inexplicable, I am very certain that I well remember this very forgetfulness by which whatever we remember is concealed.

17

Great is the power of memory! It is something terrifying, my God, a profound and infinite multiplicity; and this is the mind, and I am this myself. What therefore, am I, my God? What is my nature? A life various, manifold, and utterly immeasurable.

CONFESSIONS

Behold the plains, caverns and abysses of my memory; they are filled beyond number with innumerable kinds of things, present either in their images as in the case of all bodies or by means of their own presence, as with the arts, or in the form of some kind of notions or impressions, as with the affections of the mind which, even when the mind is not experiencing them, the memory still retains, although whatever is in the memory is also in the mind! Through all this I range in all directions and flit here and there. I dive down as deeply as I can, yet there is no limit. So great is the power of memory, so great is the power of life in man who lives mortally.

What, then, shall I do, my true Life, my God? I shall pass even beyond this power of mine called memory, I shall pass beyond it that I may draw near to you, sweet Light. What are you saying to me? I am now ascending through my mind to you who dwells above me. I shall pass beyond this power of mine called memory in the desire to touch you at the point where you may be touched, to cleave to you where it is possible to be in contact with you. For even beasts and birds have memory; otherwise, they could never find their lairs and nests, or the many other things to which they become accustomed. In fact, without memory they could not become accustomed to anything. I shall pass beyond my memory, therefore, to attain Him who separated me from four-footed beasts and made me wiser than the birds of the air. I shall pass beyond memory to find you—oh, where, where shall I find you my truly good and serene delight? If I find you without memory, I shall not remember you. And how shall I find you if I do not remember you?

18

For the woman had lost her groat and sought it with a light (Lk 15:8) and unless she had remembered it, she would never have found it. For when it was found, how would she know that it was hers if she did not remember it? I remember many times when I have looked for and found something I had lost and from these occasions I know that when I was looking for the thing and people asked me, "Is this it?" or "Is that it?" I would continue to say: "No, it is not," until the thing I was really searching for was produced. But I would not have found it even if it were produced in front of me unless I had remembered it; otherwise, I would not

137

have recognized it. And this is always the case when we search for and find something lost. Yet if anything happens to disappear from our eyes, not from memory, such as any visible body, its image is retained within and searched for until it is restored to sight. When found, it is recognized through the interior image. We do not say that we have found what was lost unless we recognize it, and we cannot recognize it unless we remember it. It certainly disappeared from the eyes but it was retained in the memory.

19

What then? When memory itself loses something, as occurs when we forget something and seek to recall it, where finally do we seek it if not in memory itself? And there if something other than what we are searching for is presented to us, we reject it until what we are seeking is encountered. And when it is encountered we say: "That is it." We would not say this unless we recognized it, and we would not recognize it unless we remembered it. For certainly we had forgotten it. Or could it be that the whole of it had not slipped from our memory; from the part which was retained the other part was sought for because the memory sensed that it did not have its accustomed totality, and feeling the defect in a habit which was, as it were, defective in some part, it strove to recover what was missing. For example, if we see or think of some man known to us, but have forgotten his name and are trying to recall it, any name occurring to us other than his will be rejected because we are not accustomed to thinking of that name and that person together. Therefore we continue rejecting names until that name presents itself with which our knowledge can rest satisfied. And where does that name come to us except from the memory itself? Even if we recognize it when reminded of it by someone else, the recognition still comes from the memory. So we do not accept it as something new, but we agree to what is told us because it agrees with what we remember. If it were completely obliterated from our mind we should never remember it even when reminded of it. For if we can remember that we have forgotten something, then we have not completely forgotten it. Whatever has been completely forgotten cannot even be reflected upon as lost and cannot be sought.

20

How, then, Lord, do I seek you? For when I seek you, my God, I am seeking the happy life. "I shall seek you that my soul may live" (Is 4:3). For my body lives by my soul, and my soul lives by you. How then do I seek the happy life? Because it is not mine until I say: "Enough; there it is." Whereas I ought to say how I am seeking it, whether through recollection as though I had forgotten it, remembering that I had forgotten it, or through the desire of learning something unknown which either I never knew or I have so forgotten it that I do not remember that I have forgotten it. Is not the happy life desired by all men so that there is no one who does not desire it? Where did they know it so that they so much want it? Where did they see it so as to love it? Certainly we have it, in some way, but how we have it I do not know. There is a way by which one may have it and be happy in having it, and there are others who are happy in hope. The latter do not have it as fully as those who are already to some degree happy, but they are better off than those who are neither happy in fact nor in hope. Yet even the latter must have it in some sense or other or they would not wish to be happy: because it is most certain that they do wish it. Somehow they know it and therefore may be said to possess it in some form of knowledge. I am concerned as to whether this form of knowledge is in the memory, because if it is there then at some previous time we were happy; I am not now asking whether we experienced happiness individually or whether the experience was in that man who first sinned, in whom we all died and of whom we are all born in misery, but I do ask whether the happy life is in our memory. For unless we knew it, we would not love it. We have heard the name "happiness" and all of us would agree that we seek that which is signified by the name; for what pleases us is not merely the sound of the word. If a Greek hears this word in Latin, he derives no pleasure from it since he does not know what has been said; but we are pleased just as he would have been pleased if he had heard the word in Greek. For happiness itself is neither Greek nor Latin, but it is that which Greeks, Latins, and men of all other languages long to attain. It is then known to all of them, and if they could all be asked: "Do you wish to be happy?" they would without doubt answer with one voice: "We do." And

139

this would not be the case unless the reality itself, signified by the name, was retained in their memory.

21

How is this like my remembering Carthage, which I have seen? For the happy life is not seen with the eyes because it is not a body. Do I remember it as I remember numbers? No. Whoever has a knowledge of numbers does not go on trying to obtain them, but we who have knowledge of the happy life and therefore love it nevertheless wish to possess it so that we may be happy. Do we remember it, then, as we do eloquence? No. Although on hearing the word "eloquence" many who are not yet eloquent recall the reality signified by the word and desire to be eloquent, which indicates that the reality is in their knowledge. Yet by means of the bodily senses they have observed others who are eloquent, have been pleased by it, desiring to become eloquent themselves: though unless they possessed some interior knowledge, they would not be pleased, and, if they were not pleased, they would not want to possess eloquence. By no bodily sense, however, can we experience the happy life in others. Do we then remember it as we remember joy? Perhaps so. For I remember my joy even when I am sad as I remember the happy life when I am miserable. And never by any bodily sense did I see my joy or hear it or smell it or taste it or touch it. But when I was joyful I experienced it in my mind and the knowledge of it so clung to my memory that I am well able to remember it, sometimes with contempt, sometimes with desire according to the diversity of things which I remember enjoying. For even base things filled me with a kind of joy, which on recalling I detest and curse, and at other times I have enjoyed good and worthy things which I remember with desire, though they are no longer with me so that I am sad when I recall my past joy.

Where was it, then, and when was it that I experienced the happy life so that I now recall it and love it and desire it? And not I alone, or I and a few others, but all of us; we all want to be happy. And unless we knew it with certain knowledge, we could not will it with such a certain act of will. But what about this? Suppose two men are asked whether they want to join the army; it might happen that one would say yes and the other would say no. But if they are asked whether they want to be happy, both, without doubt, would immediately answer, "Yes." Nor did one want to join the army and the other not want it except because they both wanted to be happy. Is not this so because one man rejoices about this, another rejoices about that? So all then agree that they wish to be happy just as they would agree, if asked, that they wish to be joyful, and they call joy itself the happy life. Although one obtains joy in one way, another in a different way, the end at which they all aim is the same, that is, a state of joy. And joy is a reality that no one can say he has not experienced; therefore, he finds it in his memory and recognizes it when he hears the words "the happy life."

22

Far be it, O Lord, far be it from the heart of your servant who is confessing to you, far be it from me to think that just any joy I experience makes me happy. For there is a joy not granted to the ungodly but only to those who cherish you for your own sake, whose joy is yourself. And this is the happy life, to rejoice in you and for you and because of you. This is the happy life, and there is no other. Those who think there is another are pursuing a different joy, which is not the true joy. Nevertheless their will is not utterly turned away from some image of joy.

23

It is not certain, therefore, that all men want to be happy, since those who do not want to rejoice in you, which alone is the happy life, certainly do not want the happy life. Or do all want it, but "because the flesh lusts against the spirit and the spirit against the flesh, they do not do what they want" (Gal 5:17), they fall into whatever they are able to do and are content with it, because they do not will sufficiently earnestly what they are not able to do so as to become able to do it? I ask anyone whether he would rather rejoice in the truth or in falsehood? They would say that they would rather have their joy in truth, as spontaneously as they would say that they want to be happy. And certainly the happy life is joy in truth, which means joy in you, who are the Truth, O God, "my Light, health of my countenance, my God" (Jn 14:6). This is the happy life that all desire; this life which alone is happy all desire; all desire joy in truth. I have met many people who wanted to deceive, but no one who wanted to be deceived. Where, then, did they attain this knowledge of the happy life except where they also attained the knowledge of truth? For they love truth also because they do not wish to be deceived, and in loving the happy life (which merely means joy in truth) they certainly also love truth; and they could not love it unless there were some knowledge of it in their memory. Why then do they not find their joy in it? Why are they not happy? Because they are more strongly occupied with other things which have more power to make them unhappy than that, which they faintly remember, has to make them happy. "Yet a little while the light is" (Jn 12:35) in men; let them walk, walk lest darkness overtake them.

But why does truth give birth to hatred and why does your man speaking the truth become an enemy to them since the happy life is loved and is nothing but joy arising from truth? It is because truth is so loved that those who love something else would like to believe that what they love is the truth, and because they do not like to be deceived, they object to being shown that in fact they are deceived. And so—for the sake of whatever it is they love instead of truth, they hate truth. They love the truth when it enlightens, but hate it when it accuses them. Because they do not want to be deceived and do want to deceive, they love truth when it reveals itself and hate it when it reveals them. And their retribution is this: Those who are unwilling to be discovered by the truth, the truth will discover them and will not reveal itself to them. So it is, yes, so indeed it is: this human mind of ours, so blind and weak, so offensive and disgraceful, wants to be hidden itself but hates to have anything hidden from it. But quite the contrary happens: It cannot hide from truth, but truth can be hidden from it. But even so, while wretched, it prefers to find joy in truth rather than in falsehoods. Therefore, it will be happy, when, with no interfering disturbance, it will find its joy in that sole Truth through which all things are true.

24

See what a distance I have covered searching for you, O Lord, in my memory! And I have not found you outside it. Nor have I found anything about you which I did not retain in my memory from the time I first learned about you. For ever since I learned about you, I never forgot you. For wherever I found truth, there I found my God, Truth itself, and ever since I learned it, I never forgot it. And so ever since I learned of you, you have remained in my memory, and there I find you whenever I call you to mind and delight in you. These are my holy delights which you gave me in your mercy, having regard for my poverty.

25

But where do you dwell in my memory, O Lord, where do you dwell? What resting place have you fashioned for yourself? What sanctuary have you built for yourself? You have honored my memory by dwelling within it: but in what part of it do you dwell? This I am now considering. For I transcended those parts of it which the beasts also have when I was recalling you (because I did not find you there among the images of material things), and I came to those parts of it where I had stored up the affections of my mind, nor did I find you there. And I entered into the seat of my mind itself (which the mind has in my memory, since the mind remembers itself) and you were not there. For just as you are not a bodily image nor an affection of any living being, such as we feel when we rejoice, sorrow, desire, fear, remember, forget, or whatever else like this we do, no, you are not the mind itself, because you are the Lord God of the mind, and all these things change, but you remain changeless over all things, and you deigned to dwell in my memory ever since I first learned of you. And why do I enquire in what place of my memory you dwell, as though there were any places at all there? Certainly you dwell in my memory, because I remember you ever since I first learned of you, and I find you there when I recall you to mind.

26

Where then did I find you so that I might learn of you? For you were not already in my memory before I learned of you. Where, then, did I find you so that I might learn of you unless in yourself above me? There is no place; we go "backward and forward" (Jb 23:8) yet there is no place. Everywhere, O Truth, you preside over all asking counsel of you and you simultaneously respond to all the diverse requests for counsel. You respond clearly, but not all hear clearly. All ask what they wish, but they do not always hear what they wish. He is your best servant who is not so eager to hear from you what he himself wills as to will what he hears from you.

27

Late have I loved you, O Beauty, so ancient and so new, late have I loved you! And behold, you were within me and I was outside, and there I sought for you, and in my deformity I rushed headlong into the well-formed things that you have made. You were with me, and I was not with you. Those outer beauties held me far from you, yet if they had not been in you, they would not have existed at all. You called, and cried out to me and broke open my deafness; you shone forth upon me and you scattered my blindness: You breathed fragrance, and I drew in my breath and I now pant for you: I tasted and I hunger and thirst; you touched me, and I burned for Your peace.

28

When I with my whole self shall cleave to you, there will no longer be for me sorrow nor labor; wholly alive will my life be, being wholly filled with you. Those whom you fill you raise up and now, since I am not yet full of you, I am a burden to myself. Pleasures of this life in which I should find sorrow conflict with the sorrows of this life in which I should rejoice, and on which side stands the victory I do not know. Woe is me, O Lord, have pity on me: My evil sorrows conflict with my good joys, and on which side stands the victory I do not know: Woe is me, O Lord, have mercy on me! Woe is me! Look, I am not concealing my wounds: You are the physician and I am ill, you are merciful, I need mercy. "Is not human life on earth a trial" (Jb 7:1)? Who wishes to have troubles and difficulties? These you order us to tolerate, not to love. No one loves what he tolerates, even though he loves to tolerate. For however greatly he rejoices in his toleration, he would yet prefer to have nothing to tolerate. In adversity I desire prosperity, in prosperity I fear adversity. What middle place is there between these two where human life is not all trial? All the prosperities of this world are caused again and again—by the fear of adversity and by the corruption of joy. And the adversities of this world are cursed once, twice, and thrice—by the desire for prosperity, by the very bitterness of adversity itself, and by the fear that it may break down our toleration. Is not then human life on earth a trial without intermission?

29

All my hope is in your great mercy. Give what you command, and command what you will. You command continence for us. And "when I knew," as it is said, "that no man can be continent, unless God gave it, this also was a part of wisdom to know whose gift it was" (Wis 8:21). Certainly it is through continence that we are brought together and returned to the One from whom we have flowed out in the many. For he loves you too little who loves anything together with you which he does not love for your sake. O love, ever burning and never quenched! O Charity, my God, kindle me! You command continence: Give what you command and command what you will.

30

Certainly you command me to refrain from the "lust of the flesh, the lust of the eyes, and the ambition of this world" (1 Jn 2:16). You command me also to abstain from concubinage, and with reference to marriage you have advised something better. Since you gave it, it was done, even before I became a minister of your Sacrament. But there still live in my memory, of which I have spoken much, the images of such things which habit has fixed there. They rush into my thoughts and though when I am awake they lack strength, in sleep they not only cause pleasure but go so far as to obtain assent and something very like reality. The illusion of the image so prevails in my soul and my flesh that false visions in my sleep obtain from me what true things cannot when I am awake. Am I not myself at that time, O Lord my God? Yet there is a very great difference between myself at one moment and myself at another, between the moment when I go to sleep and that when I awaken from it!

Where then is my reason which, when I am awake, resists such suggestions and remains unshaken when the realities themselves are presented to it? Do reason's eyes close with the bodily eyes? Does reason sleep when the bodily senses sleep? If so, how explain that even in our sleep we often resist and, remembering our resolution and most chastely abiding by it, give no assent to such enticements? Yet there is so much difference that, when it happens otherwise, we return on waking to peace of conscience, and by the distance between our state now and then find that it was not we who did something, which was, regretfully, somehow or other done in us.

Almighty God, certainly your hand is powerful enough to cure all the sickness of my soul and with a more abundant grace to extinguish even the lustful impulses of my sleep. Lord, you will increase in me your gifts ever more and more, so that my soul, loosened from the birdlime of concupiscence, may follow me to you; so that it may not rebel against itself and may not, even in dreams, succumb to or even give the slightest assent to those degrading corruptions which by means of sensual images disturb and pollute the flesh. It is not difficult for you, the Almighty who is "able to do above all that we ask or think" (Eph 3:20), to prevent something like this, the very slight inclination, so small that a mere nod would check it, from affecting the chaste mind of a sleeper—even now in the prime of my life. But now I have explained to my good Lord what is still my state with regard to this kind of evil, "rejoicing with trembling" in your gifts and bemoaning my imperfection and hoping that you will perfect your mercies in me unto a fullness of peace which both my inner and my outer self will possess with you when "death shall be swallowed up in victory" (1 Cor 15:54).

31

There is another "evil of the day" (Mt 6:34) which I wish were "sufficient unto it." For by eating and drinking we repair the daily losses of the body until such time as you destroy "both belly and meat" (1 Cor 6:13) when you will kill all hunger with a wonderful plentitude and clothe this "corruptible body" with everlasting "incorruption" (1 Cor 15:54). But now this necessity is sweet to me, and I struggle against this sweetness in order not to be enslaved by it; by fasting I wage daily war, often "bringing my body into subjection," yet my pains are expelled by sensual pleasure. For hunger and thirst are pains of a sort; they burn and kill, like a fever, unless the medicine of nourishment relieve us. And this medicine is available through the comfort of your gifts in which earth and sea and sky serve our weakness; this very weakness is called delight.

CONFESSIONS

This you have taught me: that I should approach the taking of food as I approach medicine. But while I pass from the discomfort of hunger to the comfort of sufficiency, in that very passage there lies before me the share of concupiscence. For that passage is pleasurable, and there is no other way to pass except that way which necessity imposes. And while for the sake of health we eat and drink, a dangerous pleasure accompanies health and very frequently tries to give itself priority, so that what I say I am doing, and mean to do, for the sake of health is done for the sake of pleasure. Nor is there the same measure for both; what suffices for health does not suffice for pleasure, and frequently it is difficult to discern whether the needed care of my body is asking for sustenance or whether a deceitful voluptuousness of greed is trying to seduce me. By reason of uncertainty the unhappy soul rejoices and this provides it with the protection of an excuse, and it rejoices that it is not perfectly clear what is sufficient for the needs of health so that under the cloak of health it may hide the business of pleasure. Daily I try to resist these temptations; I call upon your right hand and refer my perplexities to you, because I have no clear guidance upon this matter.

I hear the voice of my God commanding: "Let not your hearts be overcharged with surfeiting and drunkenness" (Lk 21:34). I am not at all inclined to drunkenness, and in your mercy you will keep it from me. But overeating has sometimes overtaken your servant: You will have mercy so that it may be far from me. For no one can be continent unless you give it. You grant us many things when we pray, and everything good that we receive before we pray, we receive from you; and for this purpose we have received it: so that we might afterwards realize that we have received it from you. I have never been a drunkard but I have known drunkards who were made sober people by you. Therefore, it is your doing that some people have never been drunkards; it is your doing that others who have been drunkards should not always remain so, and it is also your doing that both kinds of men should acknowledge that it is your doing.

I heard another command of yours: "Go not after your lusts, and from your pleasure turn away" (Eccl 18:30). By your gift, I have heard another statement and have greatly loved it: "Neither if we eat, shall we abound; neither if we eat not, shall we lack" (1 Cor 8:8), which means that one will not make me wealthy and the other will not make me poor. And I also heard: "For I have learned in whatever condition I am, to be content with it; I know how to live in abundance and how to suffer need. I can do all things in Him who strengthens me" (Phil 4:13). Behold the soldier of the heavenly army and not dust such as we are. But "remember, Lord, that we are dust," and that "of dust you have made man" (Gen 3:19), and "he was lost and is found." Nor did Paul do it by his own power since he was the same dust—he, I mean, who said through the influence of your inspiration these words which I love: "I can do all things," he said, "in Him who strengthens me" (Phil 4:13). Strengthen me, so that I can. Give what you command, and command what you will. Paul confesses that he received it, and when he "glories, he glories in the Lord" (1 Cor 1:31). I have also heard another begging that he may receive: "Take from me," he says, "the greediness of the belly" (Eccl 23:5–6). From all this it is evident, O holy God, that it is your gift when what you command to be done is done.

Good Father, you have taught me that "to the pure all things are pure" (Ti 1:15) but that "a thing is evil for the man who eats through scandal" (1 Cor 8:8); and that "every creature of yours is good, and nothing is to be refused which is received with thanksgiving" (Col 2:16); and that "food commends us not to God"; and that "no man should judge us in respect to meat or drink"; and that "he who eats, let him not despise him who eats not, and let him who eats not, not judge him who eats" (Rom 14:13).

These things I have learned, thanks to you; praise to you, my God, my Teacher, knocking at my ears, enlightening my heart: Deliver me from every temptation. It is not the uncleanness of meat that I fear; it is only the uncleanness of gluttony. I know that Noah was allowed to eat any kind of meat that served as food; that Elias was fed with meat; that John the Baptist, remarkable in his abstinence, was not polluted by partaking of living things, that is, the locusts, given him for food. I know that Esau was deceived by his greediness for lentils, that David reproached himself for craving water, and that our King was tempted not by meat but by bread. Furthermore, the people in the desert deserved blame not for desiring meat but for murmuring against the Lord (Gn 9:3; 1 Kgs 17:6; Mt 3:4; Gn 25:34; 2 Sm 23:15; Nm 11:14; Mt 4:3) because of their desire for meat.

Situated among these temptations, therefore, I struggle daily against concupiscence in eating and drinking. This is not the kind of thing that I can decide to renounce once and for all, as I was able to do with fornication. And so I must keep a grip which is neither too loose nor too tight on the reins of my palate. And who, O Lord, is not sometimes carried beyond the bounds of necessity? If there is one who is not, he is a great man and should magnify your name. Yet I am not he because I am a sinful man. Yet I too magnify your name, and "He makes intercession to you" for my sins, He who has "overcome the world," numbering me among the "weak members" of His "body," because "your eyes have seen his imperfection, and in your book everything shall be written" (Ps 139:16).

32

As to the enticements of sweet scents I am not much concerned. When they are absent I do not need them; when they are present, I do not refuse them, but I am prepared to be without them forever. So it seems to me, though I may be deceiving myself. For here also is a lamentable darkness in which the capacities in me are hidden from myself, so that when my mind questions itself about its own powers it cannot be assured that its answers are to be believed. For what is in it is often hidden unless manifested by experience, and in this life, described as one continuous trial, no one ought to be oversure that, though he is capable of becoming better, instead of worse, he is not actually becoming worse instead of better. Our one hope, our one confidence, our one firm promise is your mercy.

33

The pleasures of the ear draw me and hold me more tenaciously, but you have set me free. Now when I hear sung in a sweet and well-trained voice those melodies into which your words breathe life, I do, I confess, feel a pleasurable relaxation, not so that I am captivated by it, for I am able to rise up and leave. Yet those words do request a place of some dignity in my heart so that they may be received into me along with the words that give them life, and to give them precisely a fitting place is not easy for me. Sometimes it seems to me that I am giving them more honor than is suitable when I feel that when these holy words themselves are well sung, our minds are stirred up more ardently and more religiously into a flame of devotion than if they are not so well sung. I realize that all feelings of our spirit, in the various dispositions, have their own modes in voice and song, which are stirred up because of some secret affinity with them. But this bodily pleasure, to which the mind should not succumb through enervation, often deceives me, when sense does not keep company with reason so as to follow it passively; but although it owes the fact of its admission to reason, it strives even to run ahead and lead it. So in these matters I sin without realizing it, but I later become aware of it.

Sometimes when I am overanxiously avoiding being deceived in this way, I fall into the error of being too severe—so much so that I would like banished from my own ears and those of the church as well all the sweet melody of the chants used with David's Psalter. The safer way then seems to be that of Athanasius, bishop of Alexandria, who as I have often been told caused the reader of the psalm to so modulate his voice that the result was more like speaking than singing.

Yet I recall the tears I shed on hearing the hymns of your church when I was beginning to recover my faith. And now when I am moved not by the singing but by the words which are sung, provided they are sung with a clear voice and suitable modulation, I again recognize the great usefulness of this practice. So I fluctuate between the peril of pleasure and my experience of the good coming from hymns. I tend to favor the custom of singing in church (though I do not consider this opinion irrevocable) so that through the delight of the ears weaker minds may be raised to a feeling of devotion. Yet whenever it happens that I am more moved by the singing than by what is sung, I admit that I have grievously sinned, and then I would prefer not to have heard the singing. See in what state I am. Weep with me and weep for me, all those of you who feel within yourselves that goodness from which good actions come. Those of you who have no such feeling will not be moved by what I am saying. And I pray that you, my Lord God, will hear me and look down upon me and observe me and heal me. In Your eyes I have become a question to myself, and that is my infirmity.

34

There remains the pleasure of the eyes of my flesh, of which I now make confession within the hearing of the ears of your temple—those brotherly and devout ears. This concludes the account of the temptations arising from "the lust of the flesh," temptations which still solicit me, "groaning earnestly, and desiring to be clothed with my house that is from heaven" (2 Cor 5:2).

The eyes love beautiful forms of various kinds, brilliant and pleasing colors. Let these not possess my soul; that is for God to do. Certainly God made these very good things, but He Himself, not these things, is my Good. These things affect me every day during my waking hours; I get no respite from them, as I get from the sound of music and sometimes, in a period of silence, from all voices. For light is the queen of colors, and she suffuses all things visible whenever I am abroad in daylight; she glides up to me in her varied forms, beguiling me when I am doing some other thing and not adverting to her. But she so forcibly insinuates herself that if the light is suddenly removed, I search for it with longing, and if it remains long absent, my mind grows sad.

O Light which Tobias (Tb 6:4) saw when, with blinded eyes, he showed his son the way of life and, with the feet of charity, preceded him, never losing the way. Light which Isaac (Gn 27:1) beheld when with his bodily eyes heavy and dim with age, it was granted him to bless his sons without being able to distinguish one from the other, and yet in the act of blessing he did recognize them. Light which Jacob (Gn 48:14) saw when he had become blind in his old age; yet his heart was illumined and he illuminated the tribes of the future, which were foreshadowed in the persons of his sons, and he laid his hands, mystically reversed, on his grandchildren, the sons of Joseph, not as their father, observing from without, directed, but according to his own inner discernment. This is the Light; it is one, and all who see it and love it are one. As to that corporeal light of which I spoke, it seasons the life of this world for its blind lovers with a perilous sweetness. Yet those who know how to praise you for it also take up its praise in your hymn, "Creator Thou of everything," and are not taken away by it into spiritual sleep: So I desire to be. I resist these allurements of the eyes so that my feet by which I progress on your way may not be ensnared, and to you I lift up my invisible eyes so that you may "pluck my feet out of the snare" (Ps 121:4). You pluck them out repeatedly, for they are easily caught. You do not cease to pluck them out while I so often entangle myself in the traps surrounding me on all sides; because "you who keep Israel shall neither slumber nor sleep."

How many allurements without number have men added to the things which entice the eyes through the various acts and by the work of craftsmen, in the form of vessels and other such artefacts, clothes, shoes, even in paintings and all kinds of statues—exceeding all necessary and moderate use and all faithful representation.

So men go outside themselves to pursue things of their own making, and inside themselves they are forsaking Him who made them and are destroying what He made in them. But I, my God and my Glory, also dedicate a hymn to you and offer praise in sacrifice to Him who sanctifies me; for all those beauties which pass through men's souls into their artistic hands come from that Beauty which is above souls and for which my soul is sighing day and night. From it artists and enthusiasts for external beauties derive the criterion by which to judge what is or is not beautiful, but they do not find the rule for making the right use of these forms of beauty. Yet this rule is there and they do not see it, a rule that they should not go too far and that they should keep their strength for you instead of wasting it upon delights that end in lassitude. Yet I who am saying this and discerning the truth of what I say still entangle my steps in these outer beauties. But you will pluck me out, Lord, you will pluck me out, "because your loving kindness is before my eyes." For I am miserably captured by them, but you will pity me and pluck me out, and at times, when I am only lightly caught in the trap, I scarcely realize what you are doing; at times, when I have become deeply involved, I feel pain.

35

I now come to another form of temptation, in many ways more dangerous. Over and above the concupiscence of the flesh which is found in the enjoyment of all sensations and pleasures, to which they who remove themselves far from you become slaves unto destruction, there is within the soul through these very bodily senses a kind of empty longing and curiosity cloaked under the name of knowledge and science—aiming not to take pleasure in the flesh but to gain personal experience through the flesh. Since this consists in the craving to know, and the eyes are the main agents for knowing among the senses, this is called in holy scripture "the lust of the eyes" (1 Jn 2:16). For "to see" is the proper function of the eyes; but we also use this word of the other senses when employing them to gain knowledge. We do not say: "Hear how it gleams," or "Smell how it glitters!" or "Taste how it shines," or "Feel how it glows." In all these instances "see" is the proper word. But not only do we say "See how it shines," something only perceptible to the eyes; we also say "see how it sounds; see how it smells; see how it tastes; see how hard it is."

Therefore, the general experience of the senses is, as was previously said, called the lust of the eyes, because seeing, belonging properly to the eyes, is used by analogy of other senses also when they are attempting to discover any kind of knowledge. From this it is easier to see what there is of pleasure and of curiosity in the functioning of the senses. Pleasure goes after what is beautiful, melodious, sweet-smelling, savory-tasting, soft things, whereas curiosity, for the sake of experience, may go after the exact opposite of these, not in order to suffer discomfort but merely because of the lust for experience and for knowledge.

What pleasure is to be had in looking at a mangled corpse which horrifies us? And yet if one lies nearby, people rush to see it in order to grow sad and pale at the sight. They also fear to see such a thing in their sleep as if anyone had forced them to see it while awake, or as if some report of its beauty had persuaded them to go.

So it is with the other senses, although this is too long to pursue. Because of this disease of curiosity monsters are exhibited in shows. Because of this craving men proceed to investigate the working of nature which is beyond our ken—things it does no good to know and which men want to know only out of curiosity. So also toward this same goal of perverted knowledge, people inquire by means of magic. Even in religion we find the same thing: God is put on trial when signs and portents are demanded and not desired for any salutary purpose but merely for the sake of experience.

In this vast forest full of pitfalls and dangers, see how many of them I have cut off and thrust out of my heart, as you, God of my salvation, have given me the power. Yet since so many things like this noisily intrude in all directions around our daily life, how can I dare to say, how can I ever dare to say that nothing like this can catch my attention and make me look upon it and be overcome by idle curiosity? True that I am no longer captivated by the theater; I no longer care to know the courses of the stars, nor has my soul ever sought answers from ghosts; I detest all sacrilegious rites. Yet, my Lord God, to whom I owe my humble and individual service, there are so many artifices of suggestion by which the enemy urges me to seek for some sign from you. But I beg you through our King and through our simple, chaste homeland that just as up to now it has been far from me to assent to such suggestions, so the possibility of doing so may become more and more remote. When I pray to you for the salvation of anyone, my intended end is quite different, for you do as you will, and you give me the grace and ever will give me the grace to accept and not to question.

Nevertheless there are many occasions, small and contemptible enough, in which our curiosity is daily tempted, and it is impossible to count the times we slip. Often people talk idly to us and at first we listen tolerantly so as not to offend the weak; but then we gradually begin to take a serious interest in their gossip. I no longer go to the games to see a dog chasing a hare; but if in going through a field I see this sport going on, it may distract me from some serious reflection—not, indeed, so as to make me turn my horse's body out of the way, but enough to alter my heart's inclination. And unless you showed me my infirmity and quickly admonished me either by some consideration related to the sight itself to arise toward you or to make no account of the thing at all and pass by, I would stand languidly gaping at it. What shall I say of those occasions when, sitting at home, my attention is attracted by a lizard catching flies or by a spider entangling them in his web? Although the animals are small, is it not the same thing? I do go on to praise you, wonderful Creator and Disposer of all things, but it was not this which first drew my attention. It is one thing to arise quickly and another not to fall down. My life is full of such things and my hope is in your great, great mercy. For when our heart is made the receptacle for things of this kind and overladen with the pressing throngs of vanity, the consequence is that even our prayers are interrupted and disturbed, and when, in your presence, we direct the voice of our hearts to your ears, this important matter is broken off by an invasion of idle, empty thoughts, coming from I know not where.

36

Shall we not consider this among things to be condemned, or shall anything return us to hope except your well-known mercy, since you have begun to change us? You know how much you have already changed me, you who first of all cured me of my lust for asserting myself against others, so that you may also be merciful to my remaining iniquities, and "heal all my infirmities, and redeem my life from corruption, and crown me with mercy and pity, and satisfy my desire with good things" (Ps 103:3–5); you who curbed my pride by fear of you and tamed my neck to your yoke. Now I bear that yoke and I find it light: because so you have promised and so you have done. And indeed it was always light and I knew it not when I was afraid to take it upon me.

But tell me, O Lord, you who alone are Lord without pride, because you alone are the true Lord who has no other Lord, has this third kind of temptation departed from me, or can it ever completely depart in this life: to wish to be feared and loved by men for no other reason but to attain joy which is not true joy? A miserable life this is and a disgraceful vanity. Hence it happens that men do not greatly love you or chastely fear you, and therefore "you resist the proud, and give grace to the humble" (1 Pt 5:5) and you thunder down upon the ambitions of this world, and "the foundations of the mountains tremble" (Jas 4:6). Therefore, because there are certain offices in human society where such officials must be loved and feared by men, the enemy of our true happiness keeps urging and spreading out his snares in the words "well done, well done," so that while we greedily entangle ourselves we shall be taken unaware so that we may cut off our joy from truth and place it in human deceits, and shall want to be loved and feared not because of you but instead of you. In this way the enemy will make us become like him, not in the concord of charity, but in the companionship of chastisement, he who decided to "set his throne in the north," so that there, in coldness and darkness, men might become his slaves as he attempts pervertedly and crookedly to imitate you.

But as to us, O Lord, see, we are your "little flock"; keep us in your possession. Stretch out your wings so that we may fly under them. You, be our glory: For the sake of you within us let us be loved and let your word be what is feared in us. Whoever wishes to be praised by men when you do not praise him will not be defended by men when you judge him, nor delivered by men when you condemn him. When, however, it is not a case of a "sinner being praised in the desires of his soul" (Ps 9:29) nor of a man "blessed who acts ungodly" (Ps 10:3), but it is a case of man being praised for some gift of yours and taking more pleasure in hearing himself praised than in having that gift for which he is praised, here this man is praised by men but not praised by you, and those who praise him are better than he who is praised. For what pleases them is God's gift in a man, but he takes more pleasure in man's gift than in God's.

37

Daily are we tempted by these temptations, O Lord; unceasingly we are tempted. The human tongue is our daily furnace in which we are tried. You also command us to be continent in this way: Give what you command and command what you will. You know with regard to this how my heart groans to you and my eyes stream tears. For I cannot easily learn how far I have become more purified of this disease and I greatly fear my secret sins visible to your eyes though not to mine. For in other kinds of temptation there is some way of self-examination, but in this there is almost no way. For as to the pleasures of the flesh and idle curiosity I can see how far I have progressed in controlling my mind when I lack these things either by choice or unavailability. For then I ask myself how more or less troublesome it is for me not to have them. So also with wealth, which is desired in order to satisfy one or two or all of those three concupiscences. If one cannot be certain in one's own mind whether or not one disdains them when one has them, they can be let go so as to test oneself. But how do we eliminate praise so that we can make the same experiment, or are we to live a wicked life, living so desperately and recklessly that everyone knowing us will detest us?

No madder proposal could be said or thought. But if praise both accompanies and ought to accompany a good life and good works, we should as little forgo it as the good life itself. Yet, unless something is absent, I cannot tell whether it is easy or difficult for me to be without it.

What, therefore, with respect to this kind of temptation shall I confess, O Lord? What except that I am delighted with praises? But more delighted with truth itself than with praises. For if I were given the choice of either playing the mad man and being wrong in all respects yet praised by everyone or being constant and certain in truth, yet blamed by everyone, I see what I should choose. Yet I wish it were not so that when someone praises me my joy in whatever good quality I may have is increased; but it does increase, I admit, and not only that, but disapproval diminishes it. And when I am troubled in this misery of mine, an excuse occurs to me, whether or not it is a good one, you know, O God; for it leaves me uncertain. For because you have commanded of us not only continence, that is, to restrain our love from certain things; but indeed also justice, that is, to direct our love to certain things, and it is your will not only that we should love you but also that we should love our neighbor, so it often seems to me that when I take delight in the praises of my neighbor I am delighting in his accomplishments and progress; and likewise when I hear him disapprove of something which he fails to understand or which is good, I regret this fault in him. At times I regret hearing myself praised, either when people praise things in me which I dislike in myself or when some trifling and unimportant good qualities in me are esteemed above their proper value. But again do I feel like this merely because I do not want someone who praises me to think differently from the way I think of myself not because I am moved by his advantage but because those good qualities of mine which I approve of in myself are all the more pleasing to me when someone else approves of them too? For in a sense I am not praised when my own judgment of myself is not praised, that is, when qualities of mine are praised of which I myself do not approve, or when a high value is placed on things in me which I consider unimportant. Am I not then uncertain of myself in this regard?

Behold, O Truth, in you I see that the pleasure I feel in being praised should not be for my own sake but for the sake of the good of my neighbor. But whether I do feel this way, I do not know. For in this matter I know less about myself than I know about you.

I beg you, my God, show me to myself, so that I may confess the faults within me to my brethren who will pray for me. Once again let me question myself more carefully. If when I am praised I am moved by the advantage of my neighbor, why am I less moved if another man is unjustly condemned than when I am? Why am I more wounded by a reproach made against me than by one which, with equal injustice, is made against another in my presence? Am I also unaware of this? Or does it finally amount to the fact that I deceive myself and neither in heart nor tongue think nor speak the truth before you? Remove this madness far from me, O Lord, that my own mouth may not be to me the "sinner's oil to make fat my head" (Ps 141:5).

38

"I am poor and needy," yet I am better when, with secret groans displeasing to myself, I seek your mercy until the time comes when what is defective in me will be repaired and perfected to the attaining of that peace which is unknown to the eye of the proud. Words proceeding from the mouth and actions known to men carry along with them a most dangerous temptation from the love of praise which for the advancing of our own personal glory goes about begging for compliments. Love of praise still tempts me even when I condemn it in myself; indeed it tempts me even in the very act of condemning it; frequently in our contempt of vainglory we are merely being all the more vainglorious, and so one cannot really say that one glories in the contempt of glory; for one does not feel contempt for something in which one glories.

39

Also within us is another evil belonging to the same kind of temptation. This is the vanity of those who are pleased with themselves, however much they may not please others, or may displease them, or may not care whether they displease them or not. But those who are pleased with themselves certainly do not please you. In this it is not so much a case of taking pleasure in things that are not good as though they were good. The mistake is to take pleasure in good things coming from you as though they came from oneself; or, even when they are acknowledged as coming from you, in assuming that one deserves to have them; or even when it is admitted that they come from your grace, in not rejoicing with their fellowmen, but grudging your grace to others. In all these and similar dangers and troubles you see the trembling of my heart, and truly I feel that my wounds will be healed by you over and over again rather than that they are not inflicted upon me any more.

40

Where have you not walked with me, O Truth, teaching me what to beware of and what to seek after, as I reported to you my views of lower things as far as possible and took counsel with you?

With my outer senses I observed, as best I could, the world, and I observed both my bodily life and my senses. From these I entered into the recesses of my memory, into those many spacious areas marvelously full of innumerable provisions, and I gazed and was amazed; not one of those things there could I discover without you, yet I found that none of them is you. Nor was I myself you, the discoverer of these things, though I surveyed them all and tried to distinguish each from each, evaluating them according to their proper worth, accepting some things on the report of my senses, and questioning them, noticing some that were mingled with myself, distinguishing and counting these messengers of my impressions, then in the vast treasury of memory scrutinizing some things, storing some away or taking something out. But it was not I myself who did all this—that is to say, the power by which I did it was not myself—nor were you that power, because you are the never-failing light which I consulted on all these things, asking whether they are, what they are, and what they are worth. And I heard you teaching and commanding me. And I often do this. It delights me, and whenever I can relax from my necessary duties I take refuge in this pleasure. And in all these things over which I range as I am consulting you I find no secure place for my soul except in you, and in you I pray that what is scattered in me may be brought together so that nothing of me may depart from you. And sometimes working within me you admit me to a state of feeling quite unlike any I am used to, a kind of sweet delight which if it were perfected in me would be something not of this world, not of this life. But by my sad weight I fall back again; I am swallowed up in ordinary affairs; I am held fast and heavily weep, but heavily am I held. So much are we weighed down by the burden of custom! Here I have the power but not the wish to stay; there I wish to be but cannot be; both ways, miserable.

41

And so I have considered the sickness of my sins in reference to that triple concupiscence, and I have called your right hand to my aid. For with a wounded heart I have looked upon your splendor and having been beaten back (1 Jn 2:16). I said: Who can reach there? "I am cast away from the sight of Your eyes" (Ps 31:22). You are Truth presiding over all reality. But I in my covetousness, while not wanting to lose you, wanted at the same time to possess a lie, just as no one wishes to speak so falsely that he himself becomes unaware of the truth. And therefore I lost you, because you will not deign to be possessed together with a lie.

42

Whom could I find to reconcile me to you? Was I to seek the favor of the angels? By what prayer? By what rites? Many trying to return to you and unable to do so through their own strength, as I hear, tried this way and have fallen into the desire for strange visions and have deserved to become the victims of delusions. For in seeking you they have drawn themselves up in the arrogance of their learning; they have thrust forth their breasts instead of beating them. Through likeness of heart they drew to themselves the "princes of the air" (Eph 2:2) as their fellow-conspirators in pride and were deceived by them in the power of magic even while they were seeking a mediator when there was none through whom to become clean. It was Satan distinguishing himself "as an angel of light" (2 Cor 11:14). For proud flesh it proved a strong attraction that he himself had not a body of flesh. They were mortal and sinners; you, O Lord, to whom they wished to be reconciled, were immortal and sinless. So a mediator between God and man should have something in common with God and something in common with men. If he were in both respects like men he would be far from God, and if he were in both respects like God he would be far from men, and so neither way could he be a mediator. That deceitful mediator by whom, according to your secret judgment, pride deserves to be mocked has in common with men one thing, namely, sin, and appears to have another thing in common with God, namely, that not being clothed in the mortality of the flesh, he can pretend to be immortal. But, since "the wages of sin is death" (Rom 6:20), he has in common with men the fact that he, like them, is condemned to death.

43

But the true Mediator, whom in your secret mercy you have manifested to men and have sent him so that they, by his example, might learn humility, that "Mediator between God and men, the Man Christ Jesus" (1 Tm 2:5) appeared between mortal sinners and the immortal Just One: mortal with men, just with God; so that, because the wages of justice is life and peace, He might by a justice conjoined with God make void the death of sinners justified by him; for He was willing to allow that death be common to Him and to them. He was revealed to the holy men of old so that they might be saved through faith in His coming passion as we are saved through faith in His passion which has come to pass. For insofar as He is man, He is mediator; but insofar as He is the Word, He is not midway between God and man; for He is equal to God, both God with God, and together one God.

How much you have loved us, Good Father, who "did not spare your only Son, but delivered Him up for us" (Rom 8:32), the ungodly! How you have loved us, for whom "He who thought it not robbery to be equal with you was made subject even to the death of the cross" (Phil 2:6, 8). He "alone free among the dead, having power to lay down His life, and power to take it up again" (Ps 88:5): For us He was to you both victor and victim (Jn 10:18) and victor because victim: For us He was to you both priest and sacrifice, and priest because sacrifice: and He made us sons to you instead of slaves by being born of you and becoming your slave. Deservedly, then, my hope in Him is strong, that "you will heal all my infirmities" (Ps 102:3) through Him who "sits at your right hand making intercession for us" (Rom 8:34), otherwise I should despair. For many and great are my infirmities, yes, many and great; but your medicine is still greater. We could have thought that your word was far removed from any union with man and thus despaired of ourselves, unless it had been "made flesh and dwelt amongst us" (Jn 1:14).

Terrified by my sins and the burden of my misery I pondered in my heart about a plan to fly to the wilderness. But you forbade me and strengthened me, saying: "Therefore Christ died for all, that they who live may now no longer live unto themselves, but unto Him who died for them" (2 Cor 5:15). See, Lord, "I cast my care upon you" (Ps 55:22) that I may live and "consider the wondrous things of Your law" (Ps 119:8). You know my unskillfulness and my weakness; teach me and heal me. He, your only Son, "in whom are hid all the treasures of wisdom and knowledge" (Col 2:3), has redeemed me with His blood. "Let not the proud speak evil of me" (Ps 119:22) for I meditate on the price of my redemption. I eat it and drink it and give it to others. And being poor myself, I desire to be satisfied by it among those who "eat and are satisfied, and they shall praise the Lord who seek Him" (Ps 31:16).

Augustine of Hippo

THE HAPPY LIFE

Introductory Note. This is the first dialogue begun by Augustine in the villa at Cassiciacum near Milan where he lived from the autumn of 386 while preparing for baptism to be received after Lent in 387. Here Monica, Adeodatus, his brother Navigius, two cousins (Lastidianus and Rusticus), two students (Licentius and Trygetius), and the friend Alypius prayed, studied, and held philosophical discussions, which were recorded by a stenographer.

This dialogue opens with a comparison of the search for Truth to a dangerous voyage with pride as the enormous boulder barring the way to the harbor and threatening ship-wreck. In Augustine's case, Manichaean rationalism had been the obstacle that was finally removed by his discovery of the spiritual and sacred nature of the soul through reading the Platonic books and listening to the sermons of Ambrose.

The discussants agree that happiness is more directly related with the soul's condition than with bodily well-being and wealth since the latter can be lost whereas the God loved by the virtuous is an abiding reality. In his Retractations *1.2 Augustine corrects the impression he gave in 2.14 of this dialogue that perfect happiness can be had in this life. The happiness condition of the soul is Wisdom. Although Augustine, his friends, and all people are merely seekers of Truth, they can be united within themselves to the Source of truth or happiness when they overcome the moral obstacles to the sincere desire for God. The reference to the soul's being in direct contact with God is a conviction derived from Neoplatonic teaching. Plotinus taught that the spiritual icon is always in immediate contact with its exemplar, the higher intelligible that is its source. In this earliest use of the soul as the image of God Augustine is holding that the intelligible source from which the soul comes and with which it remains in intellectual contact is the Eternal Truth or God Himself. This develops into his theory of illumination and his demon-*

stration of God's existence in the dialogue On Free Choice of the Will.

But it was in Ambrose's teaching of the soul as the image of God that Augustine had learned that although the natural quest for Truth is unending in this life, there is a happiness derived from being united through God's Spirit with the Source of Truth always in contact with the soul. Through Ambrose Augustine had found the "wind" that would waft his bark safely to port in the Blessed Fatherland (1.4).

Therefore, as early as his thirty-third year Augustine is already transfiguring his Neoplatonic sources in the light of Scripture mediated through Ambrose. He asserts that the spiritual sun illuminating our minds is the Divine Word or Wisdom of the Father. Only this Measure of our minds will give happiness by converting to the Father those souls strengthened by piety and made Godlike by Grace. The tri-une God is known intuitively only through the supernatural knowledge possessed by the soul whose faith and charity have transformed it into a likeness of the Trinity.

Most gracious and renowned Theodore, I am not certain that I would be speaking rashly in saying that if it were our own will and a course directed by reason which lead us to the port of philosophy, whence one proceeds to the land and Kingdom of the happy life, a much smaller number of men would have arrived there than actually have, although now also, as we see, only few arrive there and infrequently. For since God or nature or necessity or our own will or some assortment of these or all of them together have cast us into this world (for the matter is very obscure, but is proposed so that you can shed light on it) as into a stormy sea, accidently and indiscriminately, as it were, what man would know in what direction to struggle or where to return unless some tempest, to the foolish apparently bad luck, should push us unwilling, resisting, unwitting, and off our course, upon the land we most of all longed to reach?

2

Therefore, it seems to me that there are three classes of seafarers, whom philosophy can include. The first class consists of those who, on reaching the age of reason, with little effort and a lazy stroke of the oars, shove off a short distance and establish themselves in a state of tranquillity, in which they set up a striking sign of their work, such as it is, so that as many citizens as possible enticed by this sign, may try to join them.

Now the second class, quite different from the former, consists of those who, misled by the beguiling appearance of the sea, choose to proceed out into the middle of the deep, and venture to sail far away from their native land, which they often forget. If a wind from the stern, which they believe favorable, has sometimes mysteriously accompanied them they enter, elated and rejoicing, into the deep waters of misfortune because everywhere a most deceptive serenity of pleasure and honors continually entices them. What, indeed, should they desire more than some upset in those affairs by which they are pleasurably ensnared and, if that does not suffice, a completely devastating tempest and a gale blowing in the opposite direction to bring them despite their weeping and wailing to sound and genuine joys? Many of this class, however, if they have not yet sailed too far, are brought back by adversities that are not so serious. These are the men who, when the miserable tragedies of their fortunes or the anxious cares of their vain business affairs have driven them, as it were (as if they had nothing else to do), to the books of learned and wise men, somehow awaken in the harbor from which they cannot be lured by any promises of that deceitfully smiling sea.

There is a third class between these two who, either on the very threshold of youth or after being rocked long and far upon the sea, look back to certain beacons and recall their dearly beloved native land although they are now surrounded by waves. Either they set forth on a direct course for their homeland again, neither deceived nor delayed, or more often, wandering in the midst of a fog or intently watching the sinking stars, or held by some alluring charm, they neglect good opportunities for sailing and, off course too long, they are sometimes even in danger. They are also often driven by some adversity of shifting fortune like a tempest, as it were, opposing their efforts, back home and to a most welcome rest.

3

To the distress, moreover, of all who in any way are traveling to the land of the happy life, a large mountain bars the way to the port itself, causing the passage to be extremely narrow for incoming sailors. This mountain must be very seriously feared and carefully avoided. For it is so splendid and clothed in such deceptive light that it disguises itself as a dwelling place to those arriving and not yet landed, promising to quench their desire for the happy life itself. It often also attracts men from the harbor itself to come out, often captivating them by delight in its sheer height, whence they like to look down upon others. They often warn newcomers not to be deceived by hidden rocks nor to think that it is easy to climb them, and in a most helpful way, they show newcomers where, because of the nearness of the land, they may without danger enter. And so to newcomers envious of their vainglory they show a place of security.

Does reason teach those approaching and entering upon philosophy that they should fear any mountain more than the proud pursuit of empty glory? For within it there is nothing substantial or solid and, with a cracking of the ground-crust beneath, it collapses and swallows up those walking above, puffed up with themselves, and, as they tumble headlong into darkness, it withdraws from them the gleaming dwelling place just barely seen.

4

Since this is the case, please learn, my good Theodore—for to you alone I look for what I desire and at your great ability I always marvel—please learn which of the three classes of men has given me to you, in what place I myself seem to be, and what kind of help I confidently expect of you. At the age of nineteen, when in the school of rhetoric I came upon Cicero's book *Hortensius,* I was inflamed with such enthusiasm for philosophy that I thought of devoting myself to it immediately.

But there was no lack of mist to confuse my course and for some time, I confess, I followed stars falling into the ocean and so I was led astray. For a kind of childish superstition caused me to cringe before inquiry itself, and when having become self-reliant, I dispelled that mist and persuaded myself to submit to those who teach rather than to those who command, I met men by whom the light seen by the eyes was beheld as that which was an object of highest and even divine veneration. I did not agree, but I thought they were concealing within those veils some important secret which at some time they would divulge.

But when I shook off those men and escaped, especially after I had crossed this sea, for some time the Academics held the tiller of my ship as, surrounded by waves, it battled all winds. Then I came to this land. Here I have learned to know the North Star to which I entrusted myself.

Often I noticed in the sermons of our priest, and sometimes in yours, that when there was consideration of God or of the soul, which is nearest to God, there was to be no thought at all of anything corporeal. The enticements of a woman and of fame kept holding me back, I confess, from flying immediately into philosophy's embrace, so that not until I had satisfied my desire for these did I—and this has been granted only to the most fortunate few—under full sail and with all oars pulling make that harbor quickly and there find rest. But having read a few books of Plotinus, of whom I understand that you are a zealous student, and having compared them, as well as I could, with the authority of those who have handed down the divine mysteries, I was so inflamed that I would have cast off all those anchors holding me if my esteem for certain men had not restrained me. What then remained except that a storm which seemed ill luck should come to my rescue as I hesitated, occupied with unnecessary cares? And so such a violent chest ailment seized me that, unable to bear the burden of my profession, by which perhaps I was sailing to the Sirens, I threw everything overboard and brought my ship, battered and weary, to the desired resting place.

5

Therefore, you see the philosophy in which, as in a port, I am now sailing. But even the port itself lies wide open; although its great size presents less danger, yet it does not entirely exclude error. For I am not at all aware to what part of the land I should move—that part which alone is really happy—and how I should reach it. For what do I hold as firm, since up to now the question about the soul is still wavering and uncertain? Wherefore I entreat you through your virtue, through your kindness, through the spiritual bond and fellowship between us, that you extend your helping right hand, for this means that you love me and that you may believe that I in turn love you and hold you dear. If I obtain this request, I shall arrive very easily and with slight effort at that happy life in which I presume you already share.

But that you may know what I am doing and how I am gathering my dear ones at the port, and from this more completely understand my mind—for I cannot find any other signs by which to reveal myself to you—I thought that one of my discussions which seemed to me more religious in character and especially worthy of your fame should be addressed to you and dedicated to your name.

This is surely most appropriate for together we have inquired concerning the happy life, and I know nothing else which should rather be called a gift of God. I am not frightened by your eloquence, for whatever I love I cannot fear, although I may not attain it; much less am I frightened by the height of your good fortune. For, although it is great, it is truly secondary in your consideration because it puts in second place the very ones whom it dominates. But now please listen to what I say.

6

My birthday fell on the Ides of November. After a breakfast light enough not to in any way impede our thinking, I invited all who were living together, not only that day, but every day, to meet at the bathing quarters, a sequestered place appropriate for the season. The following were present—for I do not hesitate to present them to your kindness, though only by name: first of all, our mother, to whose merit I believe is due all that I am; Navigius, my brother; Trygetius and Licentius, fellow-citizens and students of mine; and I do not want to omit Lastidianus and Rusticus, my cousins. Although they had no grammatical training, I thought that their very common sense was necessary to the discussion which I was trying to lead. Also with us was Adeodatus, my son, the youngest of all, whose ability, if I am not blinded by love, promises something great. When I had gained their attention, I began thus.

7

"Does it seem clear to you that we are composed of soul and body?" Although all the others agreed, Navigius replied that he did not know.

"Do you know nothing at all," I said to him, "or is this to be counted as just one of the things of which you are ignorant?"

He replied, "I don't think I am ignorant about everything."

"Can you tell us some of the things which you know?"

"I can," he said.

"Unless it is difficult," I continued, "mention something."

Since he hesitated, I suggested, "You know at least that you are alive?"

"Yes," he declared.

"You know therefore that you have life, since no one can live except by life."

"This also," he said, "I know."

"You also know that you have a body?"

He assented.

"Then you already know that you consist of body and life."

"I know that much, but I am uncertain whether there are only these two."

"Therefore you are not in doubt," I said, "about these two, body and soul, but you are uncertain whether there is something else needed to make up and complete a human being."

"Yes," he replied.

"We shall later inquire into, if we can, what this something else is," I said. I now ask this question of all, since we all agree that man cannot exist without body or soul: On account of which of those do we seek food?

"On account of the body," said Licentius.

But the others hesitated now on this side, now on that, how food can seem necessary for the body when it is sought on account of life, and life pertains only to the soul. Then I asked, "Does it seem to you that food pertains to that part which we see grow and become stronger through food?" All agreed except Trygetius, who objected, "Why haven't I grown in proportion to my great appetite?"

"All bodies have a measure fixed by nature," I replied, "which they cannot exceed. Yet they would be smaller than this measure if they were deprived of food. We notice this very readily in regard to domestic cattle, and no one doubts that the bodies of all living things grow thin when denied food."

"Grow thin," replied Licentius, "not grow small."

"That is enough for my purpose," I said. "Indeed the question is whether food pertains to the body. But it does pertain to the body, since deprived of food, the body becomes emaciated." All agreed that this was the case.

8

"What, then, of the soul?" I continued. "Has it no nourishment of its own? Or does it seem to you that knowledge is its food?"

"Clearly," said Mother, "I believe that the soul has no other nourishment than knowledge and the understanding of things."

When Trygetius showed that he doubted this statement, she continued, "Today haven't you yourself taught us whence and where the soul is fed? For you said that only after breakfast had been going on for some time you noticed what bowl we were using, because you were thinking about something else, and yet your hand and mouth were not unused during the first part of the meal. Where, then, was your soul at the time you paid no attention to what you were eating? In this way, believe me, and by such repasts the soul is nourished, that is, on its thoughts and concerns, if through them it can learn something."

When they were murmuring their doubts on this point, I said, "Do you not concede that the souls of learned men are much fuller and in their own way much greater, as it were, than the souls of the uneducated?"

They said that this was obvious.

"Therefore we rightly say that the souls of those untrained in any studies and who have not become possessed of skills and arts, are, as it were, hungry and famished."

"I think their souls are also full," said Trygetius, "but full of vices and worthlessness."

"This very worthlessness," I said, "believe me, is a kind of barrenness and hunger of souls. For just as a body denied food is often afflicted with sickness and scabs, illnesses which point to hunger, so the souls of the uneducated are also filled with diseases which reveal their malnutrition. Indeed the ancients wanted it known that the very word *nequitia* [worthlessness], the mother of all vices, is derived from *nequicquam* [to no purpose], that is, from that which is nothing. The opposite virtue of this vice is called *frugalitas* [worth]. Therefore, as the latter word is from *frux* [fruit], which in turn is from *fructus* [productive of enjoyment], because of a kind of fruitfulness of souls, so the former word *nequitia* [worthlessness] takes its name from barrenness, that is, from that which is nothing. For *nihil* [nothing] is whatever is in a state of flux, and which disintegrates, dissolves, and, as it were, is always perishing (*perit*). For this reason we also say that such men are *perditi* [lost beyond recovery].

"But whatever endures, if it continues, if it is always the same, is something positive and real, as is virtue. A great and most beautiful part of virtue is called *temperentia* [moderation] and *frugalitas* [worth]. But if this is so obscure that you cannot now see it, you will certainly admit that if the souls of the uneducated are themselves also full, then there are two kinds of food for the soul just as there are two kinds of food for the body: one, wholesome and helpful, the other, unwholesome and harmful.

9

"Since this is the case, I think that on my birthday, insofar as we are agreed that there are two components of man, body and soul, I should serve a somewhat more festive meal not only for our bodies but also for our souls. And if you are hungry, I shall tell you what this meal will be. For if disdaining the food and against your will I try to feed you, in vain shall I exert myself and ought rather to pray that you will enjoy such feasts more than those for the body. This will be so if your souls are healthy; for sick souls, as we see in respect to physical illness, refuse their food and spit it out." All declared by their facial expressions as well as by their spoken agreement that they were ready to take and eagerly eat whatever I had prepared.

10

And so beginning again, I said: "*We want to be happy*, do we not?" As soon as I said this, they unanimously assented.

"Does a man who does not have what he wants," I said, "seem to you to be happy?" They said no. "Well, is everyone who has what he wants happy?"

Then Mother said: "If he wants and possesses good things, he is happy; but if he wants evil things, although he possesses them, he is unhappy."

Smiling at her, I exclaimed cheerfully: "You have truly gained the mastery of the very stronghold of philosophy, Mother. For without doubt only for lack of words you did not elaborate on this subject as did Tullius [Cicero], whose words will follow. For in the *Hortensius*, the book he wrote on the praise and defense of philosophy, he said: 'But see, surely not the philosophers but all given to argument say that those who live just as they wish are happy.' This is definitely false; for to want what is not appropriate is the worst of all miseries. It is not so miserable not to get what you want as to want to get what you ought not. Wickedness of will brings to everyone greater evil than good fortune brings good."

At these words, she so exclaimed that we, entirely oblivious of her sex, believed that some great man was with us. Meanwhile I understood, as well as possible, from what source those words came and how divine was the source.

Then Licentius said, "You must tell us what a person ought to wish for in order to be happy, and what kind of things he must desire."

"Invite me on your birthday," I answered, "if you will be so kind. I shall gladly receive whatever you serve. In this spirit I beg that you dine with me today and that you do not insist on having what has perhaps not been prepared."

When he regretted his excitement, although it was modest and proper, I asked, "Are we therefore in agreement on this point, that no one who does not have what he wants can be happy and not everyone who has what he wants is happy?"

They granted this.

11

"Well then," I continued, "do you grant that everyone who is not happy is miserable?"

They did not doubt that.

"Everyone, therefore," I went on, "who does not have what he wants is miserable."

This was accepted by all.

"How then, should a man provide for himself so that he may be happy?" I asked. "Perhaps this will also be supplied for our feast so that the eagerness of Licentius may not go unheeded for, in my opinion, he ought to obtain that which one possesses wherever one wants it."

They said that was evident.

"Then it must always be something enduring, not depending on chance, not subject to misfortunes, for we cannot have whatever is mortal and transient whenever we wish it, and as long as we wish to have it."

All except Trygetius assented. "There are many fortunate people who possess abundantly and lavishly these very same fragile possessions which are subject to misfortunes and yet give pleasure to this life, nor do they lack any of the things they want."

I responded: "Does it seem to you that he who fears is happy?"

"It does not seem so," he replied.

"Then if anyone can lose what he loves, is it possible for him not to fear?"

"It is not possible."

"But these things which depend on chance can be lost. Therefore, whoever loves and possesses such things can in no way be happy."

He did not continue arguing. But at this point Mother said, "Even if he is assured that he cannot lose all these things, yet with such things he will not be satisfied. Therefore, he is unhappy because he is always needy."

"Suppose," I said, "enriched and overflowing with all these things, he should limit his desire and contentedly, fittingly, pleasantly enjoy what he has, would he not seem happy to you?"

"Then he is not happy," she answered, "because of those things, but because of the moderation of his own mind."

"Very good," I cried. "No other answer should have been made to this question, and certainly no other by you. Hence, in no way do we doubt that if anyone has decided to be happy, he must secure for himself what is permanent, what no misfortune, however grave, can snatch away."

"To this," said Trygetius, "we already fully consent."

"Does God seem to be eternal and abiding forever?" I asked.

"This is so certain," said Licentius, "that there the question is superfluous." All the others with pious devotion assented.

"Therefore," I said, "whoever possesses God is happy."

12

While with joy they were most willingly accepting this statement, I added: "There is nothing, therefore, I think, which we must now inquire about other than what kind of man possesses God, for certainly he will be happy. On this I would like to know your opinion."

Whereupon Licentius said: "He who lives well possesses God."

Trygetius suggested: "He possesses God who does what God wills to be done."

Lastidianus concurred in this statement. But the boy, youngest of all, said: "He possesses God who does not have an unclean spirit."

Mother approved all the opinions but especially the last.

Navigius kept silence. When I asked him what he thought, he answered that the last statement pleased him.

Nor did it seem proper not to learn the opinion of Rusticus on such an important topic. It seems to me that he was tongue-tied by shyness rather than deliberately silent. He agreed with Trygetius.

13

Then I said: "I now have all your views on this obviously important topic beyond which it is not necessary to inquire nor can any conclusion be reached even if we continue to investigate it very calmly and earnestly, as we began to do. Since the investigation today would be tiring, and since even souls suffer from overabundance in their feasts, if they indulge in them greedily and to excess (for they get a kind of indigestion which should be guarded against for the sake of health no less than against that very hunger we have discussed), we shall better resume this question tomorrow when hungry, if that is satisfactory to you. Meanwhile, I should like to have you munch freely on a tidbit which has suddenly come into your host's mind as something that must be served, and which unless I am wrong, is—like those dishes usually served last—concocted and seasoned, as it were, with scholastic honey."

Having heard this, all reached forward, as it were, toward a dish being offered, and they insisted that I immediately tell them just what it was.

"Well," I said, "do you think that the whole business of discussion which we have undertaken with the Academics has been completed?"

Having heard that name, the three to whom this matter was familiar eagerly arose and, with outstretched hands, as it were, in the usual manner, helped the host to serve, showing with whatever words they could that there was nothing they could be more pleased to hear.

14

Then I proposed the matter this way: "If it is obvious that a man who does not have what he wants is not happy—which reason demonstrated a short time ago—but no one seeks what he does not want to find, and the Academics are always seeking truth, hence want to find truth, therefore wanting the power to find truth—but they do not find it—it follows that they do not have what they want, and from that it also follows that they are not happy. But no one is wise unless he is happy: Therefore there is no wise Academic."

Whereupon they suddenly exclaimed as if hastily grasping the whole thing. But Licentius, listening more carefully and cautiously, feared assent and added: "I joined you in that snack since the conclusion moved me to exclamation. But I shall swallow no more of this and shall save my share for Alypius; for either he will relish it together with me or he will advise me why it should not be touched."

"Navigius with his troublesome spleen ought to be more careful with sweets," I said.

He laughingly replied, "Such things will certainly cure me, for the dish you set before us, somehow concocted and spiced, is, as Cicero says of Hymettic honey, bitterly sweet and does not bloat my stomach. Hence, after a taste of it, I gladly swallow it all to the extent of my capacity. For I do not see how that conclusion can be refuted."

"In no way can it be refuted," said Trygetius, "and so I rejoice that long ago I began to oppose them. For impelled by natural impulse or, to speak more truly, by the grace of God, although I knew not how they were to be refuted, nevertheless I greatly opposed them."

15

Here Licentius interrupted. "As for me, I do not yet abandon them."

"Then," asked Trygetius, "you disagree with us?"

"Does anyone of you," he replied, "disagree with Alypius?"

"I have no doubt," I said, "that if Alypius were here he would assent to this conclusion. For he could not hold such an absurd opinion: either that a man who lacks such a great good for the soul and a good ardently desired seems happy; or that those men do not wish to find the truth; or that he who is not happy is wise. For the dish you fear to taste is concocted of these ingredients, as it were, honey, meal, and nuts."

"Would he yield to this miserable bait for children," he

replied, "forsaking the wonderfully rich argumentation of the Academics which by its abundance will either overwhelm this short and insignificant discussion of ours or extend it?"

"As if, indeed, we were seeking something long, especially against Alypius, for he himself would in no small way prove from his own body that those small ingredients provide vigor and utility. But you, who have chosen to depend on the authority of someone absent, which of these statements do you not approve? Is it the statement that he who does not have what he wants is not happy? Or do you deny that those men wish to find and possess the truth they eagerly seek? Or does it seem to you a wise man is not happy?"

"Certainly he who does not have what he wants is happy," he said, laughing almost peevishly.

When I requested that this statement be written down, he exclaimed, "I didn't say that."

When again I motioned that it be written down, he admitted, "I did say it."

And I ordered once and for all that every word should be committed to writing. Thus I kept the youth on their toes between modesty and constancy.

16

But while with these words I was jokingly urging him to eat his morsel, so to speak, I noticed that the others who had not heard this part of the discussion and were eager to know what was going on so pleasantly just between the two of us were looking at us without smiling. And to me they seemed especially like those who—as often happens—when they dine with very greedy and hungry guests, refrain from taking food quickly either through consideration or modesty.

And since it was I who had done the inviting—and you have shown how to play the role of a great man (that of a real man, to explain it fully) and how to remain the host even at feasts of this kind—the inequality and discrepancy at our table disturbed me. I smiled at Mother. Bidding them draw from her supply, as it were, what they needed, she said: "Now tell us who these Academics are and what purpose they have in mind."

When I had explained to her briefly and so clearly that none of the group might leave ignorant, she asserted: "Those men are epileptics"—(this term is used colloquially among us to designate those suffering from "falling sickness"). At the same time she stood up and left.

And at this point, having ended our discussion, we all departed, happy and laughing.

17

The next day when again we all assembled after breakfast in the same place but somewhat later than the previous day, I said, "You have come late to the feast. I don't think this has occurred from indigestion yesterday, but because, aware of the small number of courses, you thought it best not to come so early since you would finish eating quickly. For you believed that there could not be many leftovers when on the very day of the birthday celebration only a small amount of food was served. Perhaps you believed correctly. But I am with you in not knowing what has been prepared for you.

"For there is another who never ceases to supply not only all meals to all men but also especially such feasts as these, but we frequently cease eating either because of weakness, or satiety, or business. He is the one who, dwelling in men, makes them happy as, unless I am mistaken, we piously and firmly agreed yesterday. For since reason proved that he who possesses God is happy, and none of you opposed this conclusion, the question was asked: Who, in your opinion, possessed God. On this question, if I remember well, three opinions were expressed. Some held that whoever does what God wants possesses God; but others said that whoever lives well possesses God; but to the rest it seemed that God is in those in whom there is not present what is called an unclean spirit.

18

"But perhaps you all have one and the same feeling, though expressed in different words. For if we consider the first two statements, namely, everyone who lives well does what God wills, and everyone who does what God wills lives well, living well is nothing other than doing whatever pleases God, unless it seems otherwise to you."

They agreed.

"Truly that third opinion should be considered a little more carefully because, according to the rites of the most pure Mysteries, the term 'unclean spirit,' as far as I know, is usually interpreted in two ways: either a spirit which invades a soul from outside and confuses the senses and causes a sort of frenzy in people, and those qualified to dismiss such a spirit are said to lay hands upon or exorcise it—that is, to drive it out by adjuring it in the name of God—or else, every impure soul, that is, one defiled through vices and sins, is called an unclean spirit.

"Therefore, I ask you, my boy, you who expressed that opinion perhaps from a somewhat calmer and purer spirit, who do you think does not have an unclean spirit, that one who does not have a demon whereby men are usually made mad, or that one who has cleansed his soul from all vices and sins?"

"It seems to me," he said, "that he who lives purely does not have an unclean spirit."

"But," I continued, "whom do you call pure, he who does not sin at all, or only the one who refrains from illicit intercourse?"

"How can he be pure," he said, "who refrains only from illicit intercourse and does not cease to defile himself with other sins? That man who attends to God and devotes himself solely to Him is truly pure."

When I had ordered that the boy's words be written down just as he had uttered them, I then said: "Such a man necessarily lives well and whoever lives well has to be such a man, unless you think otherwise."

Along with the others he agreed.

"Therefore the opinion expressed here is unanimous," I said.

19

"But I shall question you a little on this point: whether God wishes man to seek Him."

They conceded this.

"I likewise ask whether we can say that a man who seeks God lives wickedly."

"In no way," they answered.

"Also tell me your answer to this third question: Can an unclean spirit seek God?"

They denied this possibility, although Navigius, at first hesitating, later yielded to the opinion of the others.

"If, then, a man who seeks God does what God wills, he lives well and has no unclean spirit. But he who seeks God does not yet possess Him. Therefore, not everyone who lives well or who does what God wills or who has no unclean spirit should be said forthwith to possess God."

At this point when all the others, deceived by their own concessions, were laughing at themselves, Mother, who had been dumbfounded for a time, requested me to unravel and clarify the logical knot I had been compelled to present. When I did this, she objected, "But no one who has not sought God can reach God."

"Very good point," I said, "but he who still seeks has not yet reached God, yet he is already living well. Therefore, not everyone who lives well possesses God."

"It seems to me," she replied, "that there is no one who does not have God, but those who live well have God favorably inclined, while those who live wickedly have Him inclined unfavorably."

"Yesterday then we were wrong," I said, "when we agreed that he who possesses God is happy if it is the case that everyone possesses God and yet not everyone is happy."

"Add, then, the phrase 'favorably inclined,' " she replied.

20

"At least," I went on, "are we agreed on this: that a man who has God favorably inclined toward him is happy?"

"I should like to agree," objected Navigius, "but I fear the case of the man still seeking, especially lest you conclude that the Academic is happy who in yesterday's discussion was designated by the term 'epileptic' (*caducarius* [faller] in vulgar and bad Latin, but most aptly, so it seemed to me).

"For I cannot say that God is unfavorable to a man who seeks Him. But if it is wrong to say that, He will be favorably inclined, and whoever has God favorably inclined is happy, therefore he who seeks will be happy. But anyone seeking does not yet possess what he wants; hence that man who has not what he wants will be happy, a conclusion which yesterday seemed absurd to all of us, whereupon we believed that we had dissipated the confusions of the Academics. Hence Licentius will now exult over us and like a wise physician he will warn that those sweets I rashly accepted against my health are exacting this punishment from me."

21

At this point, when even Mother had smiled, Trygetius said, "I do not absolutely agree that God is opposed to anyone toward whom He is not favorably inclined, but I think there is some middle position."

I questioned him: "Do you agree that a man in a middle position, that is, a man toward whom God is neither favorably nor unfavorably inclined, in some way possesses God?"

When he hesitated at this, Mother said, "It is one thing to possess God; it is another, not to be without God."

"Which then," I asked, "is better: to possess God, or not to be without Him?"

"As far as I can understand," she replied, "this is my opinion: Whoever lives well possesses God, but as favorably inclined; whoever lives wickedly possesses God, but as unfavorably inclined; but whoever is still seeking Him and has not yet found Him has God as neither favorably nor unfavorably inclined, but is not without God."

"Is this also the opinion of all of you?" I asked. They said that it was.

"Please tell me," I said, "doesn't it seem to you that God is favorably inclined to a man whom he favors?"

They admitted this.

"Then," I asked, "does not God favor a man who seeks Him?"

They replied that He does favor him.

"Therefore," I said, "whoever seeks God has God favorably inclined toward him, and everyone who has God favorably inclined toward him is happy; hence, he who is seeking is happy; but he who seeks does not yet possess what he wants; consequently, he who does not have what he wants will be happy."

"Surely," objected Mother, "a man who does not have what he wants does not seem happy to me."

"Therefore," I said, "not everyone who has God favorably inclined toward him is happy."

"If reasoning requires this," she replied, "I cannot deny it."

"Therefore, this will be the distinction," I said, "everyone who has already found God has God favorably inclined and is happy; but anyone seeking God has God favorably inclined but is not yet happy; however, whoever by vices and sins alienates himself from God not only is not happy but does not even live with God favorably inclined toward him."

22

When this pleased all, I said, "Very well, but I still fear that what we previously conceded may disturb you: namely, whoever is not happy is miserable. It will follow that a man is miserable who has God favorable to him since—as he said—he still seeks God and therefore is not yet happy. Or, to quote Tullius, 'shall we call the owners of large estates throughout the world "rich" and call the possessors of all virtues "poor"?' But consider this: whether, just as it is true that every needy person is miserable it is likewise true that every miserable one is needy. For thus it will be true that there is no other misery than neediness, an opinion which as soon as it is expressed, you notice that I commend. But it would be tedious to inquire into it today. So I ask you, lest you be satiated, to assemble please at this table again tomorrow."

When all had said that they would gladly do so, we arose.

23

On the third day of our discussion the morning mist which was keeping us in the bathing quarters lifted and a very bright afternoon returned. Hence it seemed good to descend to the small meadow nearby. When all were seated wherever they wanted, the rest of the discussion proceeded thus: "Almost everything," I said, "which I wanted you to concede when I questioned you, I have and retain. Therefore, today so that we can at last interrupt our feast by a space of days, there will be nothing or not much, in my opinion, to which you must reply. Mother stated that unhappiness is nothing but neediness, and we agreed that persons who are needy are unhappy. But whether all who are unhappy are also needy is an important question which yesterday we could not answer. But if reason demonstrates that this is the case, it will be most adequately discovered who is happy, for it will be the person who is not in need. For everyone who is not unhappy is happy.

Therefore whoever is without needs is happy, if what we call 'need' (*egestatem*) constitutes 'unhappiness' (*miseriam*)."

24

"Well then," said Trygetius, "because it is clear that everyone in need is unhappy, cannot the conclusion now be drawn that anyone not in need is happy? For I remember we agreed that there was no middle position between happiness and unhappiness."

"Does there seem to you to be any middle position between life and death, or is not every man either living or dead?" I asked.

"I admit," he said, "that there is no middle position in that; but why this question?"

"Because," I said, "I believe that you will also admit this: Whoever has been buried for a year is dead."

He did not deny this.

"Well, is everyone who has not been buried for a year alive?"

"It does not follow," he answered.

"Then," said I, "neither docs it follow that if everyone who is in need is unhappy, everyone not in need is happy, although there is no middle position between happy and unhappy, just as between life and death."

25

Since some of them only very slowly understood this argument, explaining and presenting as well as I could with words suitable for comprehension, I said: "Therefore no one doubts that everyone in need is unhappy, nor are we alarmed that even wise men need certain things for their bodies. The soul in which the happy life is placed does not need these things. For the soul itself is complete and no soul, being complete, needs anything; and while it takes whatever seems necessary for the body if it is there, if it is not there, the lack of such things will not crush it. Every wise man is strong, and the strong man entertains no fear. For every wise man fears neither bodily death nor sufferings. For the banishment, prevention, or delay of such pains he would need all those things of which he is capable of being in want. Yet he does not fail to use them well if they are there. For very true is that aphorism, 'It is foolish to suffer what you can avoid.' Therefore, he will avoid death and pain as far as it is possible and fitting so that, if he does not avoid them, he will not be unhappy when they occur but because he refused to avoid them when it was possible, behavior which is a clear sign of folly. And so whoever does not avoid these things will be unhappy not from enduring them but from folly.

"But if he cannot avoid them, although his behavior has been careful and proper, they will not make him unhappy. Indeed, this aphorism of the comic poet is no less true: 'Since what you wish for is impossible, better wish for what is possible.' How will he be unhappy to whom nothing happens against his will, since he cannot want anything which he sees he cannot get? For he has his will directed toward very definite things so that, whatever he does, he does only according to some precept of virtue or divine law of wisdom, and in no way can these be taken from him.

26

"Now then, consider whether everyone who is unhappy is also in need. To admit that is rather difficult in view of the fact that for many living amidst great abundance of fortuitous wealth and who have at their disposal all things so that at their nod they can have whatever their whims dictate, that life is indeed pleasant and easy.

"But let us imagine such a person as Tullius says that Orata was. For who would readily say that Orata suffered from need, he who was the richest, the most charming, the most pampered of men, who lacked nothing with respect to pleasure, popularity, and good sound health? For he had an abundance of lucrative land and genial friends, as many as he wanted, and all these he used very advantageously for his physical welfare and, briefly, a prosperous outcome followed his every plan and desire. Some of you, perhaps, will suggest that he wanted to have more than he had. Does he seem to you to have been in need?"

"Even if I agreed," objected Licentius, "that he wanted nothing more, which I would scarcely admit in the case of an unwise man, he must have feared (for he was, it is said, a man of no small intelligence) that he would lose all with one adverse stroke of fortune. For it was not very difficult to realize that all such things, however great they may be, were subject to chance."

Then I, smiling, said to him, "Licentius, you see how this

most fortunate man was kept by the keenness of his intellect from the happy life. For the keener he was, the more he realized that he could lose all those things. He was crushed by this fear and fully confirmed that commonplace: 'The faithless man is wise in his own folly.' "

27

When he and the others had laughed at this, I continued, "Let us, however, examine this question more carefully because, although he was afraid, he was not in need, and this raises a question. For to be in need consists in not having, not in fear of losing what you have. But this man was unhappy because he was afraid, although he was not in need. Not everyone, therefore, who is unhappy is in need."

Even Mother, whose position I was defending, along with the others approved this. Still a little in doubt, she said: "I still do not know nor do I yet clearly understand how unhappiness can be separated from need and need from unhappiness. For even this man who was rich in money and land and, as you say, desired nothing more, nevertheless because he feared to lose his wealth, he lacked wisdom. Therefore would we not say that he was in need if he lacked silver and money? Shall we not say that he was in need when he lacked wisdom?"

When all cried out in admiration and I myself was very excited and pleased because it was she in particular who had stated what I had learned with great trouble from the books of the philosophers and had planned to bring forth last, "Do you all see," I asked, "that a great difference exists between many and varied doctrines and a soul wholly attentive to God? For whence come those words which we admire unless from Him?"

Here Licentius joyfully exclaimed: "Surely nothing truer, nothing more divine could be said. For no need is greater and more unhappy than lack of wisdom, and whoever does not lack wisdom cannot lack anything at all."

28

"A needy mind, then," I said, "is nothing else but folly. For folly is the opposite of wisdom, and opposite in the way that death is the opposite of life and that the happy life is the opposite of the unhappy life, that is, with no middle position. Just as every man not happy is unhappy, and every man not dead is alive, so it is obvious that every man not foolish is wise."

"From this we also may see that Sergius Orata was unhappy, not so much because he feared losing those gifts of fortune, but because he was foolish. So it is that he would have been more unhappy if he had not at all feared for those things, unstable and perishable as they were, which he considered good. For he would have felt more secure through mental laziness than through the protection gained by courage, and by his greater folly he would have been steeped more deeply in unhappiness. Now if everyone who is foolish suffers great need and everyone possessing wisdom lacks nothing, it follows that folly is a need. And as everyone who is foolish is unhappy, so everyone unhappy is foolish. Therefore, just as all need is to be considered unhappiness, so all unhappiness is to be considered need."

29

When Trygetius said that he did not very well understand this conclusion, I said, "What did our reasoning convince us of?"

"That a man who lacks wisdom is in need," he answered.

"What, then, is being in need?" I asked.

"Not to have wisdom," he replied.

"What is not to have wisdom?" I went on.

When on this point he was silent, I asked, "Is not this to have folly?"

"It is," he assented.

"To have need, then, is nothing but to have folly," I said. From this it necessarily follows that 'need' (*egestas*) is merely designated by another name when it is called 'folly' (*stultia*), although I am unable to explain how we shall say, 'He has need' or 'He has folly.' For this is like saying that some place lacking light has darkness—which is nothing but lacking light. Now darkness does not come and go, as it were, but lack of light is itself identical with darkness just as lack of clothing is identical with being naked. When clothing is put on, nakedness does not depart as if it were a mobile thing. So we say that someone has need in the sense in which we say he has nakedness, for 'need' is an expression for not having. Accordingly, to explain my meaning as well as possible, when we say 'He has need,' this is identical with saying 'He has not-having.' And so if it has been shown that folly is a genuine, definite lack, let us see whether the question we just raised has now been answered. For among us there was some doubt whether we meant anything other than need when we used the word 'unhappiness.' But we have now given a reason why folly is correctly called need. Just as every man, therefore, who is foolish is unhappy, and every man who is unhappy is foolish, so we must concede not only that everyone who is in need is unhappy but also that everyone who is unhappy is in need. But if we conclude from the fact that everyone foolish is unhappy and everyone unhappy is foolish that folly is unhappiness, why do we not conclude from the fact that whoever is in need is unhappy and whoever is unhappy is in need that unhappiness is nothing but need?"

30

When they all admitted that this was so, I said: "This now follows, that we should see who is not in need, for he will be wise and happy. 'Folly' (*stultia*) is need and a synonym for 'need' and this word usually signifies a kind of sterility and lack. Notice therefore how either all the words of the ancients or, at least, what is apparent here, certain words were created to designate what is very necessary to know. For you already concede that everyone who is foolish is in need and everyone in need is foolish. I believe you will also agree that a soul without wisdom is vicious and that all the imperfections of the soul are included in the one term 'folly.' Moreover, on the first day of our discussion, we said that *nequitia* [worthlessness] was so called because it is *nequicquam* [not anything] and is the opposite of *frugalitas* [worth], which was derived from *frux* [fruit]. Therefore in these two opposites, namely, fruitfulness and unfruitfulness, these two qualities seem to stand out: 'to be' (*esse*) and 'not to be' (*non esse*). But what do we think to be the opposite of need, which is the question at hand?"

When they somewhat hesitated here, Trygetius said, "If I should speak about riches, I see that poverty is their opposite."

"That is certainly clear," I said, "for poverty and need are usually taken as one and the same thing. But another word must be discovered so that at least one positive synonym may not be lacking, for although there are adequate negative terms like 'poverty' (*paupertas*) and 'need', the term 'riches' (*divitiae*) is the only positive term opposed to them. Nothing is more absurd than the lack of a term as counterpart of 'need.' "

" 'Fullness,' " suggested Licentius, "if I may say so, seems to me the correct opposite of 'need.' "

31

"Later we shall inquire perhaps more carefully about the word," I said, "for this is not the main concern in our search for truth. For although Sallust, that most learned weigher of words, uses 'opulence' (*opulentia*) as the opposite of 'need,' nevertheless I accept your 'fullness' (*plenitudo*). For here, at least, we shall be freed from fear of grammarians or from fear of being chastised for the careless use of words by those who gave us the use of their property."

When they had laughed at this, I said, "Therefore since I did not plan while you were intent on God to disregard your minds as I would oracles, so to speak, let us see what this word signifies, for I think that no word is more suited to the truth. Fullness and need, then, are opposites. But likewise here also, as in unfruitfulness and fruitfulness, these two qualities appear, namely, 'to be' and 'not to be,' and if need is identical with folly, fullness will be wisdom. Justly have many said that worth is indeed the matter of all the virtues. And agreeing with them, Tullius also says in one of his orations before the people, 'Let everyone decide as he wishes, but I consider worth, that is, moderation and restraint, the greatest virtue.' Surely a very scholarly and fitting statement, for he considered *frux*, that is, what we are calling *esse* the opposite of *non esse*. But because of ordinary language in which *frugalitas* is commonly identified with *parsimonia* (thrift), he clarifies what he means by two following words, that is, adding *modestia* (moderation) and *temperantia* (restraint). Let us examine more closely these two words.

32

"*Modestia* is said to come from *modus* [measure] and *temperantia* from *temperies* [a proper blend]. Now where there is measure and proper blend, there is nothing too much or too little. Therefore, that word 'fullness' which we proposed as the opposite of 'need' is a much better choice than 'abundance' [*abundantia*]. For by abundance is understood affluence and a kind of overflow of something present in superabundance. If this happens in excess, measure is lacking, and the thing which is in excess lacks measure. Therefore, need is not alien to superabundance itself, but too much and too little are alien to measure. If you also analyze the word *opulentia* itself you will discover that it contains only measure, for the word is clearly derived from *ops* [wealth]. But how does that which is too much help, since too much is often more inconvenient than too little? Therefore, whatever is either too little or too much, because it lacks measure, is subject to need. Therefore the measure of the mind is wisdom. For it is not to be denied that wisdom is the opposite of folly, and folly is need. But fullness is the opposite of need. Therefore, wisdom is fullness, and in fullness there is measure; therefore, the measure for the mind is in wisdom. Hence that excellent and rightly famous aphorism: 'This is the most useful principle in life: nothing too much.' "

33

"At the outset of yesterday's discussion, however, we said that if we found that unhappiness was nothing but need, we would concede that a man who is not in need is happy. Now this has been discovered to be true. Hence to be happy is nothing but not to be in need, that is, to be wise. But if you seek what wisdom is, reason has already explained and declared this as far as presently possible. For wisdom is nothing but the measure of the soul, that is, that by which the mind is liberated so that it neither runs over into too much nor falls short of fullness. For there is a running over into luxuries, tyrannies, acts of pride, and other such things whereby the souls of unrestrained and unhappy men think they get for themselves pleasure and power. But there is a falling short of fullness through baseness, fear, sorrow, passion, and other things, of whatever kind, whereby unhappy men even admit that they are unhappy. But when one contemplates the wisdom that has been discovered, and to use this boy's words, devotes himself to it and, unmoved by any vanity, does not turn to the deceptions of idols, whose authority, when embraced, is wont to lead one away from God and plunge one into destruction, one fears no lack of restraint and therefore no need, and accordingly, no unhappiness. Whoever therefore has his own measure, that is, wisdom, is happy."

34

"But what should be called wisdom except the wisdom of God? Moreover, we have received on divine authority that the Son of God is none other than the wisdom of God, and the Son of God is truly God. Therefore, whoever possesses God is happy, which we all agreed upon at the outset of this symposium. But what do you think wisdom is except truth? For this was also said: 'I am the truth.' Now truth exists through some supreme measure from which it proceeds and unto which it is converted when perfected. Moreover, no other measure is imposed on the supreme measure, for if the supreme measure is a measure through the highest measure, it is the very measure through itself. But it is necessary that the highest measure also be a true measure. Therefore, just as truth is begotten of measure, so measure is known by truth. Therefore truth has never been without measure, and measure has never been without truth. Who is the Son of God? 'Truth,' it has been said. Who is it who has no father? Who other than the Supreme Measure? Whoever, then, has arrived at the Supreme Measure through truth is happy. For souls this is to possess God, that is, to enjoy God. For although other things are possessed by God, they do not possess God.

35

"Moreover a certain admonition which incites us to remember God, to seek Him, and having banished pride, to thirst after Him, comes forth to us from the source of truth. That secret sun pours that beaming light into our inward eyes. To this source belongs all the truth which we speak even when we still fear, on account of our weak or recently opened eyes, to turn boldly toward it and to gaze upon it in its entirety. And this light appears to be nothing other than God who is perfect and without any fault. For there we find every perfection in its entirety, and at the same time He is the most omnipotent God. But as long as we seek and are not yet satisfied by the source itself—and to use that word, by fullness (*plenitudo*)—let us confess that we have not yet attained our measure and therefore, although we already have God's help, nevertheless we are not yet wise and happy. This, therefore, is the complete satisfaction of souls, that is, the happy life: to know precisely and perfectly Him through whom you are led into the truth, the nature of the truth you enjoy, and the bond that connects you with the Supreme Measure! These three show to those who understand the one God, the one Substance, excluding the variety of all vain and superstitious images."

Whereupon Mother, having recalled words which dwelt firmly in her memory, as if awakening to her faith, uttered this verse of our priest: " 'Assist, O Trinity, those who pray,' " and added, "This is unmistakably the happy life, a life which is perfect, toward which it must be presumed that, hastening, we can be led by a well-founded faith, joyful hope, and ardent love."

36

"Therefore," I said, "since measure itself advises us to spread our colloquium over a certain number of days, to the best of my ability, I give thanks to the supreme and true God, the Father, the Master, the Liberator of souls, then to you who although cordially invited have generously heaped gifts upon me. You have contributed so much to our conversation that I cannot deny that I have been sumptuously fed by my own guests."

While all were rejoicing and praising God, Trygetius declared, "How I deeply wish that you would feed us with this same measure every day."

"This measure," I answered, "must be observed everywhere and must be loved everywhere, if you have at heart our return to God."

With these words we ended our discussion and departed.

Augustine of Hippo

HOMILIES ON THE PSALMS

Introductory Note. Augustine was commenting on these "Gradual" Psalms during the period he was giving the first homilies on the Gospel of St. John. He sees these "songs of steps" as encouraging the newly baptized Christian, the New Man, to yearn with his whole mind and heart for the heavenly Fatherland, to become part of the People of God ascending toward Jerusalem while singing together the Songs of Ascent. Here is the simple prescription for the happiness of true peace: Walking in faith and according to the measure of this faith working through love, the Christian constantly grows in spiritual understanding, participating ever more in Wisdom, until at last one comes face-to-face with God in the Beatific Vision. Only the Lord as the Interior Master can give this spiritual understanding of the Gospel, but preachers have to diminish the intellectual and cultural deafness to God's Word. For Christ would not have come in the form of a servant to preach the Gospel if He did not will us to understand it. The fruit of Faith is understanding, which is a foretaste of Vision.

It is especially in these commentaries that we recognize the centrality of the heart in Augustinian spirituality. The heart and its desires help us to understand the reality of heaven, from which Christ has descended to help us ascend. We ascend from this valley of tears, which He has sanctified by His own sufferings, His own humiliations. We cannot ascend to His divinity without beginning from His humility. The Christian will be tempted to avoid suffering, and often his neighbors by "deceitful tongues" will not support his desire for spiritual progress. The Word of God telling of His love for mankind is to be shared by preachers with Christians so that the assurance of God's love for them will strengthen them to overcome the temptations and taunts of the unchristian neighbor and rise above mediocrity. Open the heart to the love of God and one will advance spiritually. Not even sin is an obstacle to spiritual progress, only lack of love. The heart that enshrines love within it is the temple of eternal happiness. The spiritual happiness of growth in the love of God is the main prayer of the Church. In encouraging the spiritual man who is persecuted by the carnal man, Augustine is also encouraging today's Christians who strive for holiness in a secular society that gives priority to temporal values. Only at the world's end will the wheat be separated from the cockle.

Love, therefore, is the human longing toward God made effective by the Gift of the Holy Spirit, who impels us upward, metaphorically speaking, toward the peace of the Mystical Jerusalem. Love does not remove us from the valley of tears but lightens the burden and elevates the soul. The Spirit is the source of our love of neighbor and by loving the neighbor one's eye is purified so as to love God and eventually see Him. The Spirit unifies us with one another and with Father and Son as their common bond, their communion. True love of self exists only when one loves God more than self; only thus do we understand what it means to love one's neighbor as oneself in perfect freedom.

Love is indeed the central value in Augustine's numerous teachings on the spiritual life. It is love that gives vitality to Christianity and vitality to prayer. Only in the Old Testament was earthly prosperity promised to the faithful; the hope proper to the New Israel is the Resurrection. If Christ means more to the Christian than do any material goods, then the prosperity of the impious should not prove too problematic. Christians sigh for the return of Christ but they believe that they are on their way to the Fatherland and since the Way is Christ, by following Him they will arrive. To console and assist one another in the ascent they sing with joy the canticles of those who climbed in pilgrimage toward the Old Jerusalem, which foreshadows the eternal City of God they are approaching. By taking joy in God and acting out of love for neighbors, Christians will show forth the love of Christ, the Image of God.

Psalm 119: The Ascents of the Christian

The Psalm which we have just heard sung and to which we have responded in song is short and very helpful. You will not labor long in listening to it, nor will the labor you devote to practicing it be without fruit. As its title indicates, it is a "song of steps." Steps are either of ascent or descent, but as used in these Psalms, steps signify an ascent. Let us understand them, therefore, as ascending steps, and let us not seek to ascend with our feet and in a carnal manner but as suggested in another Psalm: "He has prepared ascents in his heart, in this valley of tears, in the place which He has fixed" (Ps 83:6–7).

Where then are these ascents? In the heart. From what should we ascend? From the valley of tears. In designating the place, the human tongue somehow fails us; one knows not how to speak of it nor even to think of it. You have previously heard this passage of St. Paul, that "eye has not seen, nor ear heard, and that it has not entered into the heart of man" (1 Cor 2:9). If it has not entered into the heart of man, then the heart of man ascends to it. Therefore, if "eye has not seen, if ear has not heard, if it has not entered into the heart of man," how are we to say where we should ascend? So in his powerlessness to say where, the Prophet says to us: "To the place fixed."

What more shall I say to you than this man in whom speaks the Holy Spirit has said to us? Is it to this place or to another? Whatever I say, you imagine some earthly place, crawling on the ground, weighed down by the flesh, the soul burdened by the corruptible body, this earthly dwelling place beating down the mind capable of the highest thoughts (Wis 9:15). To whom shall I say it? Who will hear? Who will understand where we shall be in the afterlife if we ascend in heart? Since no one can understand it, let us hope for an ineffable realm of bliss which He who has set

199

steps of ascent in your heart has prepared for you. But where? In the valley of tears. A valley is a symbol of humility as the mountain is the symbol of loftiness. The mountain which we must ascend is a kind of spiritual loftiness. And what is this mountain which we must ascend if not Our Lord Jesus Christ? It is He who, by His sufferings, has made for us a valley of tears, as He has made by His abiding a mountain of ascent. What is a valley of tears? "The Word was made flesh and dwelt among us" (Jn 1:14). What is a valley of tears? He has turned His cheek to those who would strike Him and was covered with opprobrium (Lam 3:30). What is a valley of tears? He was scourged, covered with spittle, crowned with thorns, nailed to the cross. From this valley of tears you must ascend. But ascend where? "In the beginning was the Word, and the Word was with God, and the Word was God" (Jn 1:1). For He Himself, the "Word was made flesh and dwelt among us." Abiding in Himself, He descended to you. He descended to you so as to become for you a valley of tears; He abode in Himself so as to be for you a mountain of ascent. And "In the days to come," said Isaiah, "the mountain of the Lord shall tower above the hills" (Is 2:2).

It is there we must ascend. But because one speaks of mountains, do not entertain any earthly image, any visible height; and when there is mention of stone or rock, do not imagine some hard body, nor think of ferocity when one mentions lion, nor of brute animal when there is a question of the lamb. Christ in Himself is nothing of all that, and He became all these for your sake. From here below we must ascend; it is there that we must ascend: from His example to His divinity. He has become your model by humbling Himself. Those unwilling to ascend from the valley of tears were rebuked by Him. They wished to ascend too quickly, they dreamed of great honors and considered not the way of humility.

Beloved Brothers, understand me. Two disciples of the Savior asked to sit next to the Lord, one on His right, one on His left. The Lord saw that they were too quickly and out of due order ambitious for honors whereas it was necessary that they learn to be humiliated before being elevated, and He said to them: "Can you drink the cup that I myself shall drink?" (Mt 20:21–22). For in this valley of tears He was to drink the cup of His passion; but they, paying no attention to Christ's humiliation, wished to attain only His loftiness. He called them back to the road as men gone astray, not to refuse what they desired but to show them how they must attain it.

2

Let us sing, then, my Brothers, this "Song of Steps," resolved to ascend in heart; for Christ descended to us so that we might ascend. Jacob saw a ladder, and on this ladder he saw some ascending, others descending (Gn 28:12); he saw both. In those who ascended we can recognize those who progressed in piety; and in those who descended those who lagged behind. This is in fact what we find among the People of God. Some progress, others remain behind. Such is perhaps the meaning of the ladder, and yet it is possible to see only the good on this ladder, those ascending and those descending. For it is not without reason that it is not said that they fall but that they descend. To fall and to descend are surely different. Adam fell (Gn 3:5) and that is why Christ descended. The first then has fallen but the second has descended. One fell by pride; the other descended by mercy.

But it was not only Jesus Christ who descended from heaven; many other saints descended to us in His footsteps. The Apostle was exalted in heart when he said: "If we seemed out of our senses, it was for God" (2 Cor 5:13). Thus his ecstasies of mind were ecstasies in God. Ascending above all human weakness, above all temporal interests, above all that comes into the world only to vanish by death, above all that passes, he dwelt in heart in a kind of ineffable contemplation as long as he could; of this he said that "he heard unspeakable words not lawful for man to utter" (2 Cor 12:5). Notwithstanding the lack of words, he yet in some way saw what he could not describe to us. Yet if he had wished to remain in what he saw and could not describe, he could not raise you and make you see what he himself saw. What then did he do? He descended. For in the same place he said: "When we have ecstasies it is to God; when we are sober, it is for you."

But what does it mean to say that we are sober? That we speak in such a way as to be understood by you. For Christ was made in His birth and in His passion so that men could speak of Him since a man easily speaks of another man. But how can a man speak of God as God is? A man easily speaks then of a man; and so that those who are great might descend to the humble and yet might reveal nought but great things, the One who is great became humble so that the great might speak of Him to the humble. You just heard in the reading from St. Paul what I have just said; for the Apostle said, if you noticed: "I have not been able to speak to you as to spiritual men, but only as to carnal men" (1 Cor 3:1). It is therefore in lofty terms that he speaks to spiritual men, and he descends to speak to the carnal. And to show you that when he descends, he speaks of the One who descended, this is how St. John speaks of Christ abiding in Himself: "In the beginning was the Word, and the Word was with God, and the Word was God. This is what was with God in the beginning. All things have been made by Him, and nothing was made without Him" (Jn 1:1–2). Grasp it if you can, accept it eagerly, it is food. But, you will say, I admit that it is food and yet I am only a child who has need of milk to become capable of taking more solid nourishment. Therefore, because you need food, and the Word is solid nourishment, through the flesh this nourishment has been brought to your mouth. Just as by means of the flesh the nourishment of a mother becomes milk that she transmits to her child, likewise the Lord who is the food of angels, the Word was made flesh and became milk.

And the Apostle said: "What I fed you with was milk, not solid food, for you were not ready for it; and indeed you are still not ready" (1 Cor 3:2). But to give this milk to children, the Apostle descended to their level; thus descending, he gave to them the One who descended. For he said: "During my stay with you, the only knowledge I claimed to have was about Jesus, and only about him as the crucified Christ" (1 Cor 2:2). If he had simply said Jesus Christ, this Jesus Christ is also in His divinity the Word who was with God, Jesus Christ the Son of God, but in this aspect children could not receive Him. How then do those with the capacity only for milk receive Him? Jesus Christ, said the Apostle, and Him crucified. Suck what He became for you, and you will grow into that which He is.

On that ladder, therefore, some ascend, others descend. Who are they who ascend? They who progress toward spiritual understanding. And who are they who descend? They who have the taste and understanding for spiritual things, as far as human beings may, and who nevertheless descend to the level of little ones, keeping to a language suitable to their weakness, nourishing them with milk so that they may become strong enough to take spiritual food. Isaiah, my Brothers, was himself among those descending to our level; one easily sees through what steps he descended. In speaking of the Holy Spirit: "Upon him," said he, "will rest the Spirit of Wisdom and of Understanding, the Spirit of Counsel and of Fortitude, and Spirit of Knowledge and of Piety, the Spirit of the Fear of the Lord" (Is 11:2–3); he begins with Wisdom and descends to Fear.

Just as the one who teaches descended from Wisdom to Fear, you whom he teaches, if you progress, ascend from Fear to Wisdom. For it is written that the beginning of Wisdom is the Fear of the Lord. Now listen to the Psalm. Let us represent to ourselves a man who will ascend. Where will he ascend? In his heart. From whence will he ascend? From humility or from the valley of tears. Where will he ascend? To that ineffable place which, failing all description, is called "the place that He has fixed."

3

As soon as a man has prepared his ascent, or, more specifically, as soon as a Christian seriously considers advancing in virtue, he is the object of his adversaries' tongues. Whoever has not yet endured these attacks has not yet advanced, and whoever does not endure them does not even try to advance. Does he wish to understand what we mean? Let him experience without delay what we have heard. Let him begin to advance, let him conceive the desire to ascend, the desire to despise all that is earthly, fragile, temporal, of holding worldly happiness for nothing, of thinking of God alone, not pleased by gain nor displeased by loss, desiring to sell all to give to the poor and to follow Christ. Let us see how he suffers the tongues of detractors and of constant enemies, and what is more serious, of counselors turning him away from salvation under pretext of giving him advice. When a man gives advice, let him do so for the good, for salvation; but these false advisers turn one away from salvation. Since then under the mantle of benevolence they hide a deadly malice, they are called in Scripture deceitful tongues. Therefore, before ascending, the Prophet implores God's help against these treacherous tongues, and exclaims: "Lord, in my troubles I called on You and You answered me" (Ps 119:1). Why did He answer him? In order to set him upon the steps of ascent.

4

And since now that he has been answered, he goes to ascend, what does he ask? "Lord, deliver my soul from unjust lips and from treacherous tongues." What is a treacherous tongue? A deceitful tongue which has the appearance of counseling us and the treachery of destroying us. Such are those who say to us: And you also, will you do what no one else will do, will you be the only Christian? What if we prove to them that many others before us have acted this way; if we read to them in the Gospel the precept that the Lord gives us, or the Acts of the Apostles, how will their deceitful tongues answer us, their treacherous lips? The enterprise is indeed difficult, and you will not be able to complete it. Some deter by their dissuasion, others with their praises discourage. As this Christian life is expanded into the entire world, the authority of Christ is so great there that the pagans do not dare to raise their voices against Him. They read this word of the One whom they know not how to contradict: "Go, sell all that you have, distribute to the poor and follow Me" (Mt 19:21). They cannot contradict Christ, nor contradict the Gospel, nor blame Christ; therefore the deceitful tongue raises up an obstacle by its praises. O tongue, if you have praises, at least exhort: Why do you discourage by praises? Blame would be preferable to false praise. What could you say in your invectives? Far from us such a life; it is shameful, it is criminal.

But, as you know, in speaking this way the authority of the Gospel would silence you; you turn to another kind of dissuasion that by false praise you may turn me away from true praise; nay, that by praising Christ you may keep me away from Christ. What is this Christian life, you say to me? Some succeed in it, but you will not. While trying to ascend you will fall. It seems to warn you: It is the serpent, a treacherous tongue, full of poison. Defend yourself from it by prayer, and if you wish to ascend, say to your God: "Deliver my soul, O my God, from unjust lips and from treacherous tongues."

5

And the Lord answers you: "What shall I give you, what shall I put before you against the 'treacherous tongue,' that is, what are your weapons against the treacherous tongue, what can you oppose to it, how defend yourself from it? What shall I give you, what shall I put before you?" He questions us to try us, for He will answer His own question; and He does so by saying: "The arrows of the powerful are sharp, 'like desolating coals'" (Ps 119:4). They who desolate or who lay waste (for one finds one or the other expression in different copies) are the same, because by laying waste, as you may note, they easily lead to desolation.

What are these coals? First, my Beloved, understand what arrows are. "The sharp arrows of the powerful" are the words of God. When one shoots them, they penetrate hearts. But these arrows in entering hearts enkindle there a lively love instead of bringing death. The Lord knows how to shoot arrows of love, and no one shoots an arrow of love better than the One who sends forth the arrow of the Word. He pierces the heart of him who loves so as to help him to love the more; he pierces it so as to make him loving. When with words we plead, these are arrows. But what are those coals that lay waste? Why they are called coals, my Beloved, briefly hear. Notice first of all how we should deal with examples. The deceitful tongue, the more deceitful it is, knows nothing better to say than this: Take care that such a life is not beyond your strength, for is it not too much to undertake? But you know the Gospel precept; this is your arrow and you have not as yet the coals. It is to be feared that the arrow alone is too feeble against the deceitful tongue; there are also coals. For instance, suppose God begins to say to you: You cannot undertake it? Why then can that one do it? And this one? Are you weaker than this senator? Feebler in health than this man or that one? Are you weaker than women? Women have been able to do it, are not men able? Delicate wealthy men have been able, are poor men not able? It is true, you will say, but as for me, I am a great sinner, I have sinned much. You are reminded of great sinners who have loved more, the more they have been pardoned; it is the word of the Gospel: "The one who is forgiven less, loves less" (Lk 7:47).

After this account and after men have been named who have succeeded, he, pierced to the heart by an arrow, with the hot coals which lay waste, has his earthly thoughts laid waste. What is meant by "laid waste"? Is brought to desolation. A baneful vegetation had grown in his soul, vegetation of earthly thoughts, of worldly affections; this is what these destroying coals are burning, so that the field may be cleared and purified, and that God can construct his temple there. For the devil there has come to ruin, Christ is now built there. For as long as the devil abides there, Christ cannot be built. These desolating coals come then to destroy what had been built for evil, and when this place is cleared, there rises the temple of eternal happiness.

Notice: Why this name of coals? Because to convert to the Lord is to pass from death to life. When coals are set on fire, before they were lighted, they were extinguished. But an extinguished coal is called a dead coal; on the contrary, it is alive when it is burning. The word "coals" then is used to denote the examples of many sinners converted to the Lord. You sometimes hear men say with surprise: I knew that man, what a drunkard, what a villain! What a lover of the circus, or of the amphitheatre! What a cheat! And now how fervently he serves God, how innocent his life! Why so surprised? He is a live coal. You wept for him as dead, and with joy you see him alive. But in praising this live coal, if you can wisely do it, place it near an extinguished coal, that is, whoever is slow to follow God, apply to him the coal which was extinguished, and have the arrow of God's word, and the coal that lays waste so that you may meet the deceitful tongue and lying lips.

6

What then happens? This man has received flaming arrows, let him also receive destroying coals. He now represses the treacherous tongue, the unjust lips; he now ascends a step, he begins to improve, but he is still in the midst of the wicked, unjust men. The floor has not yet been winnowed; the wheat may be formed but is it in the barn? It must be crowded with much chaff, and the more he advances, the more he sees offences in the people. For the less advanced he is, the less he notices iniquities; the less he is a true Christian, the less he notices what is only appearance. The Lord, in fact, teaches us this by the parable of the wheat and the cockle. "After the seed had been planted and produced its fruit, the cockle was also discovered" (Mt 13:26). That is to say, no man discovers the wicked unless he himself has become good, since the cockle appeared only when the seed was planted and produced its fruit.

Our questioner advances therefore; he notices the wicked and many more evils not previously discovered, and he exclaims to the

Lord: "Alas, that my sojourning is become far off" (Mt 13:5). I am very far from you, O my God: My sojourn here below is indeed prolonged! I am not yet in that country where I shall see no wicked one; I am not yet in that society of angels where I shall no longer fear offenses. Why am I not yet there? Because "my sojourning is become so far off." Sojourning is exile. The exiled is one who dwells in a land other than his own. "My exile," said the Psalmist, "has become far off." Why far off? Sometimes, my Brothers, a man in a foreign country meets better men than those of his own country; but that is not the case when we are outside that heavenly Jerusalem. The man who changes country sometimes finds himself better off in the sojourn; he finds more faithful friends. Enemies have banished him from his country, and in the foreign land he finds what he had not found in his fatherland. It is not thus with our Fatherland, which is Jerusalem. There one meets only the just; whoever travels away from there is among the wicked from whom he cannot be separated, except by entering into the society of angels so as to return to where he left. There are all the just ones and the holy ones who rejoice in the word of God without reading, without letters. For whatever is written to us on pages, they discover through the Face of God. What a country! What a great country, and how unfortunate to be estranged from it!

7

But this cry of the Psalmist: "Too long is my exile here below" is above all the cry of the Church that toils on this earth. It is her voice which cries out from the ends of the earth in another Psalm, saying: "From the ends of the earth I have cried out to you" (Ps 60:3). Who among us cries from the ends of the earth? Neither I, nor you, nor he, but the entire Church. It is the entire inheritance of Christ that cries toward God from the ends of the earth, for the Church is His heritage, and it is said of the Church: "Ask me and I shall give you the nations for your heritage, and the ends of the earth for your possession" (Ps 2:8).

If therefore Christ's possession extends to the ends of the earth, the saints are the possession of Christ, and all the saints form only one man in Christ, since holy unity is in Christ. And this one man exclaims: "From the ends of the earth I have cried out to you, when my heart was in anguish." The exile of this man, then, among the wicked became ever more distant. And if one should ask him: "With whom do you dwell that you groan in this way?" "My sojourn is become distant," he answers. But, you will say, suppose it were with the good? If it were with the good, he would not say, "Alas!" This word "alas" signifies affliction, misery; but yet in hope since he has already learned even to groan. Many are unhappy and groan not, wander afar and yet are reluctant to return. This one now wishing to return learns the misfortune of his exile, and because he has experienced this, he returns.

He begins to ascend because he begins to sing the Song of Steps. Where is he groaning, where is he dwelling? He dwells in the tents of Kedar. But perhaps you do not understand this Hebrew expression? What is meant by: "I have dwelt among the tents of Kedar?" The word Kedar, as far as I remember Hebraic etymologies, signifies "darkness." One translates Kedar into Latin by *tenebrae* (darkness). But you know the two sons of Abraham about whom St. Paul tells us, telling us that they are the types of the two covenants; one was born of a bondwoman, the other of a free woman. Of the bondwoman was born Ishmael (Gn 6:5), of Sara or the free woman was born Isaac, conceived through Faith contrary to all hope. Both issued from Abraham without both being heirs. One is born of Abraham, yet he does not receive the heritage; the other is also the heir, not the son only but the heir. In Ishmael are all those who have for God only a carnal worship, and they belong to the old covenant, according to this word of St. Paul: "You who wish to be under the Law, do you not understand the Law? It is written indeed that Abraham had two sons, one by a bondmaid and the other by a free woman; there is there an allegory, for these are the two covenants."

What are these two covenants? The old and the new. The old covenant comes from God, and the new covenant is from God just as from Abraham there came forth Ishmael and Isaac. But Ishmael belonged to the earthly kingdom, Isaac to the heavenly kingdom. Therefore the old covenant has earthly promises, an earthly Jerusalem, an earthly Palestine, an earthly kingdom, an earthly salvation, victory over enemies, numerous sons, abundant fruits; all these are earthly promises. They are to be understood spiritually as figurative just as the earthly Jerusalem typified the heavenly Jerusalem, and the earthly kingdom typified the heavenly kingdom. Ishmael was in the shadow, Isaac in the light. If Ishmael was in the shadow, it was not astonishing that there was darkness there, since darkness is only deepened shadow. Ishmael was therefore in darkness, Isaac in light. All those in the Church today who only know how to ask God for temporal happiness belong to Ishmael. These are the ones in conflict with spiritual men who advance in virtue, who vilify them, who have unrighteous lips, deceitful tongues.

Against these the Psalmist, when ascending, prayed and was given hot coals which lay waste and the sharp arrows of the Mighty One for his defense. He still lives in the midst of them until the whole floor be winnowed, and therefore said: "I have dwelt under the tents of Kedar." For the tents of Ishmael are called those of Kedar. Thus one reads in Genesis that Kedar belongs to Ishmael (Gn 25:13). Isaac is therefore with Ishmael, that is, those who belong to Isaac live amidst those who belong to Ishmael. These wish to ascend, those wish to topple them; these wish to fly to God, those try to pluck their wings. Indeed we read in St. Paul: "And just as the one who was born according to the flesh" persecuted the one who was born according to the Spirit, it is still the same today: The spiritual man suffers persecution from the carnal man.

But what does Scripture say? "Send away the slave and her son, for the son of the slave will not be heir with the son of the free woman, with my son Isaac" (Gn 16:15; 21:2–3, 10). But this word "cast out," when will it be fulfilled? When the floor shall begin to be winnowed. But now, before he is cast out, "alas to me, because my sojourning has become far off. Among the tents of Kedar I have dwelt." And he explains to us who belong to the tents of Kedar.

8

"My soul has wandered far." Lest you should imagine bodily wandering, he said that the soul wandered. The body wanders in places, the soul by affections. If you love the earth, you wander far from God; to love God is to ascend toward Him. Let us exercise ourselves in the love of God and of neighbor so as to return to love. To fall upon the earth is to go into decay, to corruption. But One descended to this one who had fallen in order that he might arise. In considering the time of his wandering he said that he wandered among the tents of Kedar. Why? Because "my soul has wandered far." He wanders there where he ascends. He wanders not in the body, he ascends not in the body. But where does he ascend? "In the heart," said the Psalmist, "are the steps." If then one ascends in heart only the wandering soul ascends through the ascent of the heart. But until he arrives, "my soul has wandered far." Where? Among the "tents of Kedar."

9

"With those who hate peace, I was peaceful." To tell the truth, my well beloved Brothers, you can understand the truth of what you sing only if you practice it. However I say this, in whatever way I may express it, with whatever choice of words, this word does not enter into a heart which does not practice it. Therefore begin to act, and you will understand what we are saying. Then each word of the Psalm will make the tears flow, then the Psalm is sung and the heart does what is sung in the Psalm. Alas! How many there are who chant with the voice and are remote in heart! Also, how many have silent lips when the heart utters cries of love! But at the heart of man is the ear of God. Just as man's ear hears the bodily voice, so God's ear hears the heart's voice. God hears many of those whose mouths are closed, many others with their loud cries are not heard. Therefore with our feelings we should pray and say: "My soul has wandered far; with those who hate peace I was peaceful." What else shall we say to these heretics except learn peace, love peace. You call yourselves righteous. If you were, you would groan as wheat among chaff. Since there are ears of wheat in the Catholic Church and they are true ears, they endure the chaff until the floor be threshed and because they cry among the chaff: "I have dwelt among the tents of Kedar; alas that my sojourning has been far off." I have dwelt, he says, with chaff. But just as dust goes out of the chaff, so darkness goes forth from Kedar. "I have dwelt with the tents of Kedar: my soul has wandered far." These are the words of the ears of wheat, groaning in the midst of chaff.

Thus we say to those who hate peace: "I was peaceful with those who hate peace." Who therefore hates peace? The one who breaks unity. They dwell in unity if they do not hate peace. But because they were righteous they made a schism for the sake of not being mingled with the unrighteous. Either we speak here through the mouth of the Psalmist or else they do. Choose. The Catholic Church declares that unity must not be lost, the Church of God must not be divided. Later God will judge the good and the evil ones. If today it is impossible to separate the good from the wicked, it is necessary to tolerate this for a time. The wicked may indeed be mingled with us on the floor, but not in the heavenly granaries. If some appear evil today, tomorrow perhaps they will be good. Those who today take pride in their own goodness may tomorrow be wicked. Whoever humbly bears with the wicked for a time will come to eternal rest. So speaks the Catholic Church.

What now do our adversaries say, who know neither what they say nor what they affirm (1 Tm 1:7): "Touch nothing impure"; and again "Whoever will touch something impure will himself be impure." Let us separate ourselves; no mingling with the wicked. Love peace, we say in our turn, love unity. Are you unaware of from how many good persons you are separated while you slanderously call them wicked? They rage and storm when we say this; for they wish even to slay us. Often we have witnessed their attempts, discovered their snares. While therefore we live in the midst of their snares and while they to whom we say "Love peace" are our foes, are not these our words: "With those who hate peace I was peaceful, and when I spoke to them, they attacked me without cause." What does this mean, Brothers, "they attacked me"? And shortly after, the Psalmist adds, "without cause." To them we say: Love peace, love Christ. Is this then to say to them: Love us and honor us? No, but honor Christ; no honor for us, but all honor to Jesus Christ.

Who indeed are we compared to the Apostle St. Paul? And yet what did he say to those little ones that the wicked, that the treacherous advisers wished to separate from unity and cast out into schism, what did he say to them? "Was it Paul who was crucified for you, or indeed was it in the name of Paul that you were baptized?" (1 Cor 1:13). This is also what we say to them: Love peace, love Christ. For to love peace is to love Christ; and to say to them: Love peace is to say to them: Love Christ. Why? Because the Apostle has said of Christ that He is our peace, he who of two peoples has made only one (Eph 2:14). If then Christ is the peace because He has reunited two peoples into one, why from one people do you make two? How would you be peacemakers, you who from one sole people make two peoples, when Jesus Christ, from two peoples, has made only one? But to say this to those who hate peace is to be peaceful, and yet when we speak to them in this way, these enemies of peace attack us without cause.

Psalm 120: Our Confidence in the Lord

Here is the second of the Psalms entitled "A Song of Steps." There are several of them, indeed, as you have understood in the first of them, which signify the ascent through which our heart rises to God from the depth of this valley of tears, that is, from the abasement of our miseries. We cannot in fact profitably ascend unless we are first humiliated, so as to remind ourselves that we must ascend from the valley (for an earthly valley is a low place; and these low places are called valleys just as the lofty places are called mountains and hills), for fear that in seeking to ascend hurriedly and before the proper time to be exalted we should find ourselves falling instead of ascending. The Lord indeed showed us that we should ascend from this valley of tears when He deigned to abase Himself even to suffer for us the death of the Cross. Let us not abandon His example; the martyrs understood this valley of tears. And whence have they understood it? Whence? It was from this valley of tears that they ascended to be crowned.

2

This Psalm, this song of steps, suits perfectly our solemnity; for of these martyrs it was elsewhere said: "They walk and weep in sowing their seeds" (Ps 125:6). This is surely a valley of tears where one sows while weeping. What are these seeds? The good works one does amidst the tribulations of this life. Whoever works well in the valley of tears is like a man who sows seed during the winter. Does the cold prevent him from working? Thus the tribulations of the world ought not to turn us from good works. See indeed what follows: "They walk while weeping," said the Psalmist, and "they scatter their seeds." Miserable if they weep always; miserable if no one wipes away their tears. But we next read:

"When they will come, on the contrary, they will come in joy carrying their sheaves" (Ps 125:6).

3

These songs, my Brothers, teach us then not only to ascend but to ascend in heart, in holy desires, in faith, hope, and charity, in the desire of eternity or of life without end. Thus we ascend. It is our duty to explain how we are to ascend. What terrible threats do you not discover in the reading of the Gospel! You see there that the day of the Lord will come like a thief in the night. "If the master of the house," he said, "knew at what moment the thief would come, I declare to you, he would not allow him to enter the house" (Mt 24:43). Do you now say: How can one know at what hour it will come since it will come like a thief? In your ignorance of the hour, watch constantly, so that despite your ignorance, this moment finds you constantly ready. And perhaps so that you might be always ready, this moment is unknown. This hour will surprise the master of the house who is here the type of a proud man. Be not then a master of the house, and this hour will not surprise you. What shall I be? you say to me. Such as you have heard in the Psalm: "As for me, I am poor and afflicted" (Ps 68:30).

If you are poor and afflicted, you will not be a master of the house that this hour will surprise and suddenly overwhelm. They are masters of houses who pride themselves on giving free rein to their lusts and who swell with the abundance of this world's delights. They exalt themselves against the humble and trample on the saints who understand the narrow way leading to life. These men will be surprised by the final hour, for such were those who lived in the days of Noah of whom the Gospel spoke earlier, as you have heard (Mt 24:37–41). "They ate, they drank, the men married their daughters, they espoused women, planted, built until Noah entered the ark and the deluge came and destroyed them all" (Lk 17:26–27). What then! Are they condemned to perish—those who married their daughters, who espoused women, who planted, who built? No, but those who glorified themselves in all this, who preferred all these things to God, who for the sake of them are always ready to offend God.

As for those who do not resort to these things, or who use them only as not using them, they trust more in the One who has given these things than in the goods which are given. They recognize in these gifts the mercy which consoles them. Without passion for these gifts they do not fall away from God. Such persons will not be surprised when the hour will come like a thief. To them the Apostle said: "As for you, you are not in darkness to be surprised by that day as by a thief; you are all children of light and children of day" (1 Thes 5:4). Also the Lord in telling us of the fear of this hour, has He not said that it will become night, and the Apostle expressed it this way: "The day of the Lord will become as a thief in the night" (1 Thes 5:2). Do you wish not to be surprised? Do not be in the night. And what does this mean: Do not be in the night? "You are children of the light, children of day; we are not children of the night, nor of darkness." But who are these children of darkness and of the night? The unjust, the ungodly, the unbelieving.

4

But in their turn, before the hour comes, let them listen also to what the Apostle says to them: "You were once darkness, and now you are light in the Lord" (Eph 5:8). Let them awaken according to the admonition of our Psalm. Already the mountains are lightened, why then sleep? "Let them lift their eyes toward the mountains whence help will come to them" (Ps 120:1). What does it mean to say that the mountains are already lightened? Already there has arisen the Sun of Justice, already the Apostles have preached the Gospel, preached the Holy Scriptures, all the Mysteries have been laid open, the veil has been rent, the secret of the temple has been revealed; let them finally lift their eyes toward the mountain whence help will come to them.

This is what this Psalm entreats, the second among the song of steps. But let no one trust in the mountains, for these mountains, far from being lightened by themselves, receive the light of the One of whom it is said: "And that One was the true light who enlightens every man coming into this world" (Mt 27:51). By mountains we mean of outstanding piety, great men. And who was greater than John the Baptist? What greater mountain than this man of whom the Savior said: "Among those born of women no one is greater than John the Baptist" (Mt 11:11). Assuredly you see this mountain shining; hear him now confessing. Confessing what? "And of his fullness we have all received" (Jn 1:9). From the One who has given to the mountains of His fullness will come help for you also and not from the mountains" (Mt 11:11). And yet if you do not lift your eyes upon these mountains by means of the Scriptures you cannot approach so as to be enlightened by the One who enlightens them.

5

Chant then what follows: If you wish to know how you may securely set your feet on the steps so as to ascend without fatigue and without falling (Jn 1:16), repeat what follows: "Do not permit that my foot be moved." By what are our feet moved? Who moved the feet of Adam when he was in Paradise? But first of all, see how the feet of the one who was among the angels was moved, and who fell by this jolt and from being an angel became a devil: He fell because his feet were moved. Seek the cause of his fall. He fell by pride. It is only pride that moves our feet; only pride makes us totter and fall. Charity, on the contrary, moves us to improve and to ascend; pride, to make us fall. Also what is said in our Psalm? "The children of men will trust in the shadow of your wings" (Ps 35:8). If they are in the shadow, they are always humble, always trusting in God, always without self-presumption. "Under the shadow of your wings they shall put their trust." For not in satisfying themselves do they taste happiness.

But what does the Psalmist say next? "They will be inebriated with the abundance of your house and you will water them in the torrents of your delights" (Ps 35:9). Behold them thirsty, behold them satisfied; behold they thirst, behold, they drink; but they do not drink of themselves, for they are not wells. Where then do they drink? "Under the shadow of your wings they put their trust" (Ps 35:8). If they are in the shadow of your wings, they are humble. Why? "Because with you," said the Psalmist, "is the well of life" (Ps 35:10). These mountains then do not water themselves nor do they illumine themselves. See in fact what follows. "In your light we see the light" (Ps 35:10). If then in His light we shall see light, who falls from that light except the one to whom He is not a light? Whoever wishes to be his own light deprives himself of the light whereby he is lighted. Thus, knowing that no one falls save he who wishes to enlighten himself, since by himself he is darkness, the Psalmist adds: "Let the foot of the proud not come against me and the hand of the sinner not move me," that is, in imitating sinners I should not be moved and separated from you.

But why have you feared and said: "Let the foot of the proud not come against me?" The Psalmist answers: "There those who commit iniquity have fallen" (Ps 35:12–13). All those who now commit iniquity under your eyes are already condemned; but to arrive there they have fallen when the foot of pride came into them. The Psalmist, then, who listens so as to ascend and not to fall, prays to God that he may profit from this valley of tears without failing in the swelling of pride, in these words: "Do not permit that my foot be moved." And to him God replies: "Let your guardian not fall asleep." Listen well, my Brothers. It is as if one thought were expressed in two sentences: the man while ascending and chanting this song of steps says: "Do not permit that my foot be moved." And God seems to reply to him: "You say to me: Do not permit that my foot be moved, add then: Let Him Who guards you not sleep" and your foot will not be moved.

6

But suppose he replied: Is it in my power that my guardian may not fall asleep? I wish him not to fall asleep or slumber. Choose then to guard you the one who does not fall asleep, who does not slumber, and your foot will not be moved. But God never sleeps. Therefore choose God for your guardian, if you wish one who never sleeps. "Do not permit that my foot be moved," you say; that is good, very good. But God answers you: "Let not him who guards you slumber." You were about to search among men for a guardian, saying: Whom shall I find who will not sleep? What man is there who will not slumber? Who can be found? Where can one go? The Psalmist tells you: "He who guards Israel shall neither slumber nor sleep." Do you wish as guardian one who neither slumbers nor sleeps? Behold, "He who guards Israel neither slumbers nor sleeps" (Ps 120:4). Christ guards Israel. Be Israel, therefore, you yourself be Israel.

What does Israel mean? Israel signifies seeing God. And how does one see God? First of all, by faith, and then by sight. If you cannot see His face since that is seeing Him by sight, then at least see His back parts. This is what the Lord said to Moses: "You cannot see my face, but when I pass by, you will see me from behind" (Ex 33:20, 23). Perhaps you await His passing: He has already passed by; see His back parts; where has He passed? Listen to St. John: "When the hour was come," he tells us, "that He should pass from this world to the Father" (Jn 13:1). Already Our Lord Jesus Christ has accomplished the Passover, for the meaning of the word *pascha* is "passing over." For it is a Hebrew word, and not, as many have believed, a Greek word signifying passion; but this is not so. Others, more exact and more learned, discovered that *pascha* is a Hebrew word meaning "passing over" and not "suffering."

By His passion, Our Lord passed from death to life, thus making for us the way, for us who believe in His Resurrection, so that we may also pass from death to life. It is little enough to believe that Christ died; the pagans, the Jews, the wicked believe this. All believe that He died; Christian faith consists in believing in His Resurrection. To believe that He arose from the dead is the important thing for us. He has therefore willed to be seen when He was passing, or in His Resurrection. He has willed that all should believe in Him when He passed by, because "He was delivered for our sins and has arisen for our justification" (Rom 4:25).

Such is faith in the Resurrection of Christ which the Apostle strongly recommended: "You will be saved," he said, "if you believe with all your heart that God has risen from the dead" (Rom 10:9). He did not say: If you believe that Christ died, which the pagans believe, the Jews and all His enemies; but indeed: If you believe with all your heart that God has raised Him from the dead, you will be saved. To believe this is to be Israel, it is to see God. And although you see Him only from behind, when you believe in His back parts you will come to the sight of His Face. What does this mean? When you have believed in what Jesus Christ became afterwards for you, when you have believed in what Christ took upon Himself later.

For at the outset what is His state? "In the beginning was the Word, and the Word was with God, and the Word was God." What are His back parts? "And the Word was made flesh and dwelt among us" (Jn 1:14). When, therefore, you believe in this, that the Word was made flesh for your sake and that the Word rose again in the flesh that you might not despair of your flesh, you become Israel. But as soon as you are Israel, your Guardian will not sleep, will not slumber. For you are now Israel and you have heard the Psalmist: "This is the guardian of Israel who will not sleep, who will not slumber." Christ himself slept, but He has arisen. What does He Himself say in a Psalm? "I have slept, I have taken my sleep." Did He remain asleep? "I have arisen," he said, "because the Lord will take me up" (Ps 3:16).

If then He has already arisen, He has already passed by; if He has passed by, look at His back parts. What does this mean? Believe in His Resurrection. And since the Apostle said: "Although He was crucified according to the weakness of the flesh, He is nevertheless living by the power of God"; and again: "Christ, arisen from the dead, dies no more; death no longer has victory over him" (Rom 6:9); he rightly sings to you: "This is the one who will not fall asleep, who will not slumber, the Guardian of Israel." You still search perhaps in a carnal sense for one who does not fall asleep, who does not slumber? You vainly seek him among men; you will not find him. Do not put your confidence in any man since every man falls asleep, every man slumbers. When does he sleep? When he bears here below a weak flesh. When will he sleep? When he will be dead. Do not therefore put your confidence in a man. A mortal may slumber, he sleeps in death. Do not seek a guardian among men.

7

And who then, you ask, shall keep watch without slumbering or sleeping? Hear what follows: "The Lord will guard you." It is not a man who sleeps and slumbers but the Lord who guards you. How does He guard you? "The Lord is your defense upon the hand of your right hand." Courage, my Brothers, understand with God's help what this word signifies: "The Lord is your defense, upon your right hand." There is, I believe, some mysterious reason which prevented the Psalmist from saying purely and simply: "The Lord will protect you," but made him add "on your right hand." Does God shield only our right hand and neglect our left? Has He not made us entirely? And the One who made our right hand, has He not also made our left hand? If it pleased Him to speak only of the right hand, why this expression: "on the hand of your right hand" and not at once "upon your right hand"? Why this language if there were not some mysterious reason that he conceals from us so that we may knock at the door? For He could say, without adding anything, either: The Lord will guard you; or, if He wished to add the right hand: The Lord will protect you on your right, or indeed, if He wished to add the hand, He might say:

The Lord will shield your right hand, and not the "hand of the right." I shall tell you what the Lord will deign to suggest to me; He who dwells in your souls will doubtless cause you to approve of that which I say as true. For you know not what I am about to say, but when we shall have said it, it is not I who shall show you the truth of my words, but you yourselves will recognize the truth.

How will you recognize the truth if not in the light of the One who dwells within you because you are among the number of those who say: "Do not let my foot be moved," and to whom He Himself replies: "Let your guardian not fall asleep, let him not slumber." Let Jesus Christ not sleep within you, and then you will understand the truth of my words. How so, you say? Because if your faith is asleep, Jesus Christ is asleep within you. For Christ is in your heart when you believe in Christ. The Apostle says: "That Christ may dwell by faith in your hearts" (Eph 3:17). Let our faith not slumber, and Christ watches within us. And if your faith should slumber and you therefore wavered when you asked that question, like that vessel that encountered the tempest when Christ slept (Mt 8:24–26), awaken Christ, and the tempest will be stilled.

8

I appeal therefore to your faith, my Brothers, you who are the sons of the Church, and have progressed in the Church, and who will progress if you have not done so, and you who will progress more and more, I ask you how you understand this word that you hear in the Gospel: "Let your left hand not know what your right hand does?" To understand this word is to understand what is your left hand and what is your right; you will also understand that God made both, the right and the left, and yet the left ought not to know what the right does. The left signifies all temporal possessions, and the right, the eternal and immutable good that God has promised us. But the same God who will give us eternal life and who consoles us during this life by temporal goods has assuredly made the right and the left hand. David said in a Psalm about some people that "their mouth has uttered vanities, and their right hand is the right hand of iniquity." Therefore he discovers and blames those who take their true right hand for the left, and their left hand for their right, and he shows us who these people are.

Whoever sees happiness for man only in temporal goods and pleasures, in worldly abundance and riches, such a one is foolish and perverse, taking his left hand for his right. These are they of whom the Psalm speaks, not that they had not received from God the temporal goods that they possessed but that they made the happy life consist only of these joys, seeking nothing else. Hear, indeed, what he next says on this topic: "Their mouth has spoken vanities and their right hand is the right hand of iniquity." And next: "Their children are like young trees, their daughters are adorned as the idol of a temple, their cellars are full and overflow on all sides, their sheep are prolific and crowd their tables, their oxen are fatted, neither break nor ruin is seen in their fences, and no one cries out in public places" (Ps 143:11–15). Such is the great happiness of some. At times this happiness could befall a just man as it befell Job. But Job regarded it as his left hand and not his right hand, for he counted as his right hand only the continual and endless happiness which was promised him in God. That is why God permitted that he be struck on the left hand, and his right hand sufficed for him. How was the left hand struck? By the devil's temptations. The devil suddenly withdrew his goods from him, the devil whom God allowed to act to try the just and to chastise the impious withdrew everything from Job. But Job knew that the left hand was the left hand and that only the right hand is the right hand. How did he hold onto his right hand? He rejoiced in the Lord, he was consoled for his losses because he did not let go of his interior wealth: His heart was full of God.

"The Lord has given," he said, "the Lord has taken away; thus he cried to the Lord, it has been done that the name of the Lord may be blessed" (Jb 1:21). Such was his right hand, the Lord Himself, eternal life itself, the possession of ineffable light, the source of light, the light in the light. "They will be inebriated with the abundance of your house" (Ps 33:9). This was his right hand. As for his left hand, it was only an aid to consolation and not the foundation of happiness. For God was his true and genuine happiness. But those of whom David says that "their mouth uttered vanities, that their right hand is the right hand of injustice" (Ps 143:8), he does not blame them for possessing all these goods but for talking vanity. In fact, what happens next? After having enumerated all their riches, he exclaims: "They have called happy the people who possess these goods" (Ps 143:5).

Such is the vanity their mouth uttered: to have proclaimed happy the people who have such goods. But what will you say, O Psalmist, you who know how to discern what is your left hand and what is your right? He continues by saying: "Blessed are the people who have the Lord for their God" (Ps 143:5).

9

Listen then, my Beloved. We have seen what is the left hand and also what is the right. Hear this confirmed in the Song of Songs: "His left hand is under my head," the spouse tells us in speaking of her husband, the Church, in speaking of Christ in the embrace of piety and love. What does she say? "His left hand is under my head, and He embraces me with His right" (Cant 2:6). But how? Because His right hand was above, His left hand below, and thus the husband embraced the spouse, supporting her with the consolation of his left hand and laying upon her his right hand to protect her. "His left hand is under my head," she tells us. This left hand comes from God, therefore it is His left hand because He gives all temporal goods. How very vain, how impious are those who beg for these goods from idols, from demons! How many there are who ask for them from demons without obtaining them; how many others there are who obtain them without asking demons; for demons do not give them.

Likewise many ask God for temporal goods and do not obtain them. God who calls us to the right hand knows also how to dispense with the left hand. If therefore it is the left hand, let it be the left hand, but let it be under your head, and let the head be raised above it, or let your faith be above it, your faith wherein Christ dwells. Prefer not to your faith anything temporal, and the left hand will not be above your head. Subject to your faith everything temporal, and place your faith above every temporal thing; then the left hand will be under your head, and His right hand will rightly embrace you.

10

Hear the Proverbs also tell you what is the right hand and what is the left. It is said with reference to Wisdom. "The length of days, the years of life are in His right hand; and in His left, glory and riches" (Prv 3:16). The "length of days" is eternity, for Scripture gives the name of length only to that which is eternal; indeed, everything which has an end is brief. "With long life I shall satisfy him" (Ps 90:16), it is said elsewhere. Otherwise, would it have been said as something great: "Honor your father and your mother so that you may live long in the land" (Ex 20:12)? What land but that of which it is said: "You are my hope, my inheritance in the land of the living" (Ps 141:6)? What is living a long time there if not to live eternally? Here below what, in fact, is living a long time if not arriving at old age? However long that age may appear to us now, as soon as one arrives there, it appears short because it has an end. Many grow old here on earth after having cursed their parents; many others after having honored them go soon to the Lord.

Is the promise of living long fulfilled in this world? No, this long life is understood of eternity. The long life is in His right hand, but in His left is found riches, glory, that which is needed here below and which men call wealth. But someone arises against you and wishes to strike you on the right, that is, to destroy your faith: You have received a blow on the right, offer the left (Mt 5:39), that is, let go of the temporal not of the eternal possessions. Hear how the Apostle St. Paul practiced this. Men persecuted him for being a Christian; they struck his right face, he offered them his left. "I am a Roman citizen," he said (Acts 22:25). They scorned his right hand, and he frightened them with his left. They could not fear his right hand since they did not yet believe in Christ.

If then the right hand embraces, the left is under your head, what does this word signify: "Let your left hand not know what your right hand does"? That means, when you do a good work, do it in view of eternal life. Because if on earth you do good only to possess an abundance of earthly goods, the left hand knows what the right is doing; you have mingled your right hand with your left. Never act except for eternal life. Yes, act in that way and you will act without fear; such is God's command. If you act only for earthly goods and in view of the present life, only your left hand is acting. But if you work in view of eternal life, and let some desire for temporal life slip in so as to work also in view of this and by desire of earthly reward, that is to mingle the left hand with the works of the right hand, and that is what God forbids.

11

Let us come now to this verse of the Psalm: "It is the Lord who shields the hand of your right hand." The hand signifies power; how do we prove this? The hand of God stands for the power of God. For the devil who tempted Job said to God: "Extend your hand, touch his possessions, and see if he curses you to your face" (Jb 1:11). What does it mean to say: "Extend your hand," if not use your power? But listen more closely still, Brothers, so as to cut short carnal thoughts lest you imagine a God who has members; see more clearly in what sense the hand of God is called power.

It is said somewhere in Scripture: "Death and life are in the hands of the tongue" (Prv 18:21). We know the morsel of flesh called tongue moving back and forth in the mouth, striking the palate and the teeth to articulate sounds which form the word. Show me the hands of the tongue. The tongue then has no hands, and yet it has a hand. What is the hand of the tongue? The power of the tongue. What is meant by: "Death and life are in the hands of the tongue. Your mouth will justify you and your mouth will condemn you" (Mt 12:37)? If then the hand is power, what is the hand of the right hand? I see no more consistent sense than to understand by the hand of the right hand the power that God has given you to take your place at His right hand with the help of His grace, if you wish it. For all the impious will be at His left, and at His right will be the sons of God, faithful to His will, to whom He will say: "Come, blessed of my Father, receive the Kingdom which has been prepared for you from the beginning of the world" (Mt 25:34).

You have therefore received the power to be at the right hand, the power to become a child of God. What power? The one St. John speaks of: "He has given them power to become children of God" (Jn 1:12). Whence have you received this power? "It is given to those who believe in His name." If then you have faith, you also have the power to be among the children of God. But to be among the children of God is to be at His right hand. Therefore your faith is the hand of your right hand, that is, the hand of the right hand is the power given to be among the children of God. But what would have become of this received power if God had not protected man? There is the one who believes, who walks in the faith; he is feeble, agitated in the midst of temptations, afflictions, carnal attractions, pricks of covetousness, guiles and snares of the enemy.

What assists him to believe in Christ and to have the power to be among the children of God? Unhappy that man if God does not come to the aid of his faith, that is, if He does not prevent you from being tempted beyond your strength, as the Apostle said: "God is faithful and will not allow you to be tempted beyond what you can endure" (1 Cor 10:13). The One then who does not allow us to be tempted beyond our strength, although we possess the hand of our right hand, is God who shields us on the hand of our right hand. It does not suffice that we have the hand of our right hand if He Himself does not shield with His protection this hand of our right hand.

12

So much for temptations: hear what follows: "Let the Lord shield you on the hand of your right hand." I have explained it to you, and as far as I can judge, I have awakened your recognition. If you had not already known it and known it through Holy Scripture, your voices would not have made known that you understood it. Therefore, my Brothers, since you have understood it, see what follows, why God protects you, and on the right hand, that is, in that very faith in which we have received the power of being children of God and of being at His right hand.

Why is it necessary for God to protect us? Because of scandals. Whence come scandals? They have to be feared from two sources, because there are two precepts which comprise the whole Law and the Prophets, the love of God and the love of neighbor (Mt 22:37–40). One loves the Church because of the neighbor and one loves God for Himself: but the sun is a symbol of God as the moon is the symbol of the Church. Whoever is in error by believing about God what should not be believed or by not believing that the Father, the Son, and the Holy Spirit are one same substance has been deceived by the cunning of the heretics, principally the Arians. If he has believed that the Son or the Holy Spirit is something less than the Father, he has fallen into scandal in respect to God and is scorched by the sun. Whoever also believes that the Church is in one part of the world and does not recognize that it has expanded into the entire world, who believes in those who say to him: "Here is the Christ, there is the Christ" (Mt 24:23), as you previously heard in the Gospel reading that Christ has redeemed the entire world for which He has given such a ransom: This one is scandalized, so to speak, in his neighbor and is burned by the moon.

Thus whoever is in error with regard to the very substance of truth is burned by the sun, burned during the day because he errs on the subject of Wisdom of which it is said: "Day speaks to day." Whence this word of the Apostle: "We communicate spiritual things to those who are spiritual." Day announces the word to day by communicating the things of the Spirit to spiritual men. "Day announces the word to day; but we announce Wisdom to the perfect" (1 Cor 2:13). And "night announces knowledge to night" (Ps 18:3)—what does this signify? To the little ones are preached the humility of Christ, the Incarnation of Christ, the Cross of Christ. This is the milk which suffices for infants. Therefore, infants are not forsaken during the night since the moon shines in the night; that is, only by the flesh of Christ does the Church preach because the Head of the Church is Christ in His flesh. Whoever is not scandalized in the Church, the flesh of Christ Itself, that one is not burned by the moon. Whoever is not scandalized with regard to the immutable and unchangeable Truth is not burned by the sun. Not that he is spared by that sun which flies and beasts see, but I speak of that Sun which will say to the impious on the last day: "What will come to us from our pride and what has availed the display of our riches? All that has passed like a shadow." And after saying that: "We have therefore strayed far from the path of truth, and the light of justice has not shone for us, the sun never rose on us" (Wis 5:6–9).

But does not the sun shine daily upon the impious by order of the One who "makes His sun shine on the good and the wicked" (Mt 5:45)? God has indeed made one sun which shines on the good and the wicked and which both can see; but there is another Sun, not made but begotten, through whom all has been made, in whom is the total understanding of immutable Truth. Of Him the impious say: "And the Sun has not shone upon us." The one who does not err about Wisdom itself is not burned by the sun; and the one who does not err in respect to the Church and the Lord's flesh and in those things which were done for us in time is not burned by the moon.

But although a man believes in Jesus, he will fall into error on all sides if this word is not accomplished on his behalf: "The Lord shields you on the hand of your right hand." Also after having said: "The Lord shields you on the hand of your right hand," as if there were inquiry, he replied: This is how I have the hand of my right hand: I have already chosen faith in Christ, I have received power to be among the children of God, why do I still need God to protect me, that is, to shield the hand of my right hand? This is how the Psalmist continues: "The sun will not burn you during the day, nor the moon during the night" (Ps 120:6). Thus therefore the Lord shields the hand of your right hand so that you be not burned by the sun in the day nor by the moon at night.

Understand by that, my Brothers, that this language is figurative; for if we think only of the visible sun, truly it burns during the day, but does the moon burn at night? But what is a burn? A scandal. Hear this word of the Apostle: "Who is weak that I am not weak with him? Who is scandalized" (2 Cor 11:29) without my burning?

13

Therefore "the sun will not burn you by day, nor the moon by night." Why? Because the "Lord will preseve you from every evil"—from scandals with regard to the sun, from scandals with regard to the moon. From every evil shall He preserve, He who shields the hand of your right hand, He Who does not fall asleep, He who does not slumber. Why this promise? Because we are in the midst of temptations: "And the Lord will guard you from every evil; let the Lord guard your soul." Yes, even your very soul. "Let Him watch over your coming and your going, both today and unto the end of time." Not your body, for with the martyrs the body was made to die, but the "Lord will guard your soul," for the martyrs yielded not up their souls. The persecutors raged against Crispina whose birthday we celebrate today. They treated cruelly a rich and delicate woman. But she was strong because the Lord who guarded her shielded the hand of her right hand. Is there anyone in all Africa, my Brothers, who does not know Crispina? She was illustrious, noble in birth, abundantly rich. But all that was in the left hand; it was under her head. The enemy came to strike her head, and the left hand which was under her head was presented to him. But her head was above, and the right hand of God embraced her from on high. What could all the persecutor's malice do against this delicate woman? Doubtless she had both the weakness of her sex and that feebleness which riches and long-established indolence produce. But what is all that when compared with God's great defense? What is all that to that Husband who puts His left hand under the head and embraces her with His right hand? What enemy could strike one thus defended? Yet he struck, but he struck the body. But what did the Psalm say: "Let God guard your soul." The soul did not yield, the body was struck; still it was struck only for a time since it was to rise at the world's end.

The One who deigned to become Head of the Church gave up His body to be struck for a time, but He quickened His flesh on the third day and He will quicken ours at the world's end. The Head was raised that the body might heed Its Resurrection and thus might not faint. "Let the Lord guard your soul." Let it not yield, let it not be broken down by scandals nor by giving way in persecutions and in tribulations, even as the Lord says: "Do not fear those who kill the body without being able to kill the soul, but fear the one who can cast both body and soul into hell" (Mt 10:28). Let the Lord henceforth keep your soul lest you be seduced by the enemy, a victim of false promises, a victim of threats against temporal goods, and "the Lord shall guard your soul."

14

Next, "Let the Lord watch over your coming and going, both today and to the end of time" (Ps 120:8). Reflect a moment on your coming. "Let the Lord watch over your coming and going, from this day to the end of time." Let Him also watch over your going. What is this coming? What is this going? For us the coming is temptation; the victory over temptation is the going. See this coming and going in Scripture: "The kiln tests the work of the potter, and sorrowful tribulation tests just men" (Eccl 27:6). If just men are like the potter's vessels, these vessels must be put in the kiln. And it is not when they enter that the potter is sure of them but when they go out. As for the Lord, He does not fear, for He knows those who belong to Him (2 Tm 2:19). He knows those who will not crack in the kiln. Those who are without pride will not crack.

Therefore in every temptation it is humility which guards us; for we ascend from the valley of tears while singing the Song of Steps, and the Lord watches over the entrance so that we may enter in all security. Let us in temptation keep a pure faith and the Lord "will watch our going out now and to the end of time." When we shall have gone out from every trial, no temptation will come to frighten us in eternity, no lust will even solicit us. Listen to the Apostle who recalls to us what we have just now heard: "God is faithful and will not permit that we be tempted beyond our strength."

In this way God watches over your coming: When He removes from you the trial you cannot overcome, He watches over your coming. See whether He does not also watch over your going. "But," pursues the Apostle, "He will give you a way out of temptation so that you can support it" (1 Cor 10:13). Can we, my Brothers, explain this in any other way than the Apostle does? Therefore, protect yourselves not by yourselves because God protects you and guards you, He who does not sleep, who does not slumber. Once upon a time He did sleep for you; He is risen and will nevermore sleep. Let no one count on himself.

From the valley of tears we ascend; do not tarry on the way. We have yet some steps to ascend; we ought not to tarry by laziness nor fall by pride. Let us say to God: "Let our foot be not moved": He who guards us will not sleep. This is in our power, if, with God's help, we choose for guardian the one who does not sleep, who does not slumber, who watches over Israel. What is Israel except the one who sees God? Thus help will come to you from the Lord, thus He will protect you on the hand of your right hand, thus will be guarded both your coming and going, from now until the end of time. If you trust in yourself, your foot has been moved, and if your foot is moved, even though you believe to some degree, you will fall because of your pride. For he who is humble in this valley of tears says to God: "Do not permit that my foot be moved."

15

The Psalm was short, and yet this was a long explanation, a long discourse. Imagine, my Brothers, that on the occasion of the feast of St. Crispina, I had invited you to a banquet and that I had not there guarded temperance: I kept you at table too long. Could that not happen to you if a military officer invited you and forced you to drink too much? Let us be allowed to do this in regard to the divine Word so that it may inebriate you and satisfy you to the full even as the Lord has deigned to water the earth with His temporal rain that we may go forth with greater joy to the abode of the martyrs as we promised yesterday. For those martyrs now without suffering are here with us.

Psalm 121: The Ecstasy of Love

Just as impure love inflames the soul and brings it to desire those earthly and perishable goods which make it also perish, plunging it into the abyss, so holy love raises us to heavenly things, inflames it with the desire of eternal good, urges it toward those goods which will neither pass away nor perish, and from the abyss of hell raises it to heaven. All love has its own power nor can love in the soul of the lover be idle; it necessarily urges on. Do you wish to know the quality of love? See where it leads. I do not exhort you not to love, only not to love the world so as to love more freely the One who has made the world. A soul tied by an earthly love has, as it were, birdlime on its wings and cannot fly. Once purified of the coarse affections of this world, extending, as it were, its pair of wings and freeing them from every weight, it flies with them, that is, with the two commandments of the love of God and the love of neighbor (Mt 22:40). But where, however, does it direct its flight if not toward God, since it rises by loving? But before arriving there, if it already has the desire to fly, it groans on the earth; it exclaims: "Who will give me wings like the dove, and I shall fly and take my rest" (Ps 54:7)? Whence will it take flight if not from the midst of the scandals where also groaned that Psalmist from whom I have borrowed these words? It is therefore from the midst of scandals, from the medley of evil men, from the chaff mingled with wheat it longs to fly, to go where it may not endure the society of any wicked one but may live in the holy company of the angels, citizens of the eternal Jerusalem.

2

This Psalm that we attempt to explain to you today, or rather the one who speaks and who ascends in this Psalm, aspires to the heavenly Jerusalem. It is indeed a song of steps. And as I have often said to you, these steps are not made to descend but to ascend. The questioner wishes then to ascend; and where does he wish to ascend if not to heaven? What does this mean—to ascend to heaven? Does he wish to ascend so as to be in the heavens with the sun, the moon, and the stars? Far from that! But there is in heaven an eternal Jerusalem where the angels, our co-citizens, are. From these co-citizens we on earth are estranged. In this exile we sigh; in the city we shall have joy. But in this exile we shall sometimes meet companions who have seen the holy city and who urge us to hasten there. With them he also rejoices who exclaims: "I rejoiced with this word which was spoken to me: We shall go into the house of the Lord" (Ps 121:1). My Beloved, recall to mind that when one speaks on a feast of martyrs or of a holy shrine, a crowd assembles to celebrate the anniversary. These crowds mutually encourage one another, exhorting one another, saying: Let us go, let us go! And where shall we go, some say. To such a place, answer the others, to the consecrated shrine. They stimulate one another, are enkindled until little by little they form only one flame, and this unique flame, enkindled by each one's ardent words, carries them to the designated holy place while holy thought sanctifies them.

If then holy love thus urges them to a temporal place, what must be the love which hurries people with one heart and soul toward heaven, saying to one another: "Let us go into the house of the Lord"? Let us run, then, to go into the house of the Lord. Let us run, and not grow weary; for we shall arrive there where there is no more weariness. Let us run into the house of the Lord, let our soul be rejoiced in those who say these words to us. For those who speak thus have seen before us that country, crying from a distant age to their posterity: "We shall go into the house of the Lord": walk, run. The Apostles have seen it and have said to us: Walk, run, follow us, "we shall go into the house of the Lord." And what does each of us answer? "I have rejoiced with the words that have been said to me, we shall go into the house of the Lord." I have rejoiced with the Prophets, I have rejoiced with the Apostles. For you have all said to us: "We shall go into the house of the Lord."

3

"Our feet were standing in the courts of Jerusalem" (Ps 121:2). Behold, you have the Lord's house if you seek it. In this house of the Lord He who built the house is praised. He is the delight of those who dwell in this house, He is their only hope here and their reality there. They who run there, what should they be thinking of? They should think of already being there, already standing there. For it is a great experience to stand among the angels and not to fail. The one who fell from there stood not in the truth. All those who have not fallen are standing in the truth; he stands who enjoys God. But whoever wishes to enjoy himself, falls. Who wishes to enjoy himself? He who is proud. He, therefore, who wished always to stand in the courts of Jerusalem says: "In your light we shall see the light" (Ps 34:10), not in any light. And again: "In you, not in myself, is the source of life." What did he add? "Do not let arrogant feet crush me or wicked hands expel me. Thus all those who committed iniquity have fallen; they are banished, they were unable to stand" (Ps 35:12).

If then they were unable to stand because of their pride, ascend humbly so as to say: "Our feet stood in the courts of Jerusalem." Reflect on what you will be there, and although you are still on pilgrimage, imagine that you have arrived, associate yourself with the unchanging joy of the angels as if that which is written were realized in you: "Blessed are those who dwell in Your house and can praise You all day long" (Ps 83:5).

Our feet stood in the courts of Jerusalem. Of what Jerusalem? For this name is that of an earthly city which is but the shadow of the heavenly Jerusalem. What would be the advantage of standing in that Jerusalem which itself was unable to stand, which has fallen into ruin? Is it of such an advantage that the Holy Spirit would sing, his heart inflamed with love, exclaiming: "Our feet stood in the courts of Jerusalem?" Is it not of that earthly Jerusalem that the Lord said: "Jerusalem, who kills the prophets and stones those sent to you"(Mt 23:37)? What great thing would the Psalmist have desired if he had willed to stand among those who killed the Prophets and stoned those sent to them? God forbid that he should think of that Jerusalem, he whose heart was so ardent, so burning with love, so impatient to arrive at that Jerusalem which is our mother and of which the Apostle said that she is "eternal in the Heavens" (Gal 4:26).

4

Hear for yourself, then, instead of believing me, hear what follows, and to what Jerusalem he summons our thoughts. After saying: "Our feet stood in the courts of Jerusalem," as if we had asked him: Of what Jerusalem are you speaking, the Psalmist adds immediately: "That Jerusalem that is being built as a city." My Brothers, when David thus spoke, Jerusalem was constructed, it was not being built. He speaks of a city that is now being built, to which living stones run in faith, of whom Peter says: "You also be living stones to form a building according to the Spirit" (2 Cor 5:1), that is, the holy temple of God. What does it mean to say: "You are built as living stones?" You are living if you are believing. And if you have faith, you become the temple of God, for St. Paul says: "You are the temple of God, yes, you are that temple" (1 Cor 3:17).

This city then is now being built. The hand of those who preach the truth cut stones from the hills; they are squared that they may enter into an everlasting building. The Builder has in His hands yet many stones; let them not fall from His hand so that they may be perfectly built into the structure of the temple. Such is "the Jerusalem that is being built as a city," of which the foundation is Christ. The Apostle Paul says: "For the foundation, no one can lay any other than the one which has already been laid, that is, Jesus Christ" (1 Cor 3:11). When a foundation is laid on earth, the walls are built above, and the weight of the walls tends toward the lowest parts because the foundation is placed below. But if our foundation is in heaven, let us be built toward heaven. Some material forces have built the edifice of this basilica, and you see its ample size; since material forces built it, they placed the foundations below. But since we are spiritually built, our foundation is placed at the highest point.

It is there that we must run, where we may be built; indeed of this Jerusalem it is said: "Our feet stand in the courts of Jerusalem." Of what Jerusalem? Of Jerusalem that is being built as a city. It is not enough to designate this Jerusalem by saying that it is built as a city, for this can be said of the earthly Jerusalem. But finally, how answer the one who would say: It is true that in

David's time when he sang thus the city was completely built; but David saw in spirit that it would fall into ruin and that it would be built anew. Jerusalem, in fact, was taken by assault and its people led captive to Babylon, which Scripture calls the Babylonian captivity. But the prophet Jeremiah had prophesied that this city after seventy years of captivity would be rebuilt, a city which had been destroyed by a conquering army (Jer 29:4–10). Perhaps, you say, that is what David saw in spirit: Jerusalem destroyed by its enemies and reconstructed seventy years later; hence this expression: "Jerusalem that is being built as a city"; be careful not to think then that the city of which there is question here is that city of which the saints would be as living stones. What did he then say to remove all doubt? "Our feet," he said, "stand in the courts of Jerusalem." But of what Jerusalem is there question here? Is it of that Jerusalem which we see standing, whose walls are material? No; but the Jerusalem "that is being built as a city." Why "as a city," and not "a city that is being built"? Why, if not because those walls so built in Jerusalem were a visible city, what in everyday language is called a city while this other is being built "as a city" for they who enter into it are like living stones since they are not literally stones? Just as they are called stones without being stones, likewise, what is being built "as a city" is not a city. For he says: is being built. For by the word "building" he intended to be understood the structure and the cohesion of stones and walls. For a city is understood strictly of the people who dwell there. But in saying "is being built" he showed us that he meant a town. And since a spiritual building resembles somewhat a material building, therefore it is being built as a city.

5

The Psalmist continues and shows us without any doubt that we should not understand of a material city these words: "Jerusalem is being built as a city, all the inhabitants of which are in unity." Here, my Brothers, I entreat whoever lifts up the gaze of the mind, whoever puts aside the obscurity of the flesh, whoever cleanses the eye of his heart, let him lift up his mind to contemplate the Selfsame. What is the Selfsame? How express it if not as the Selfsame? Understand the Selfsame, my Brothers, if you can. For in using any other word I do not express the Selfsame. Let us yet try by some expressions approaching it to lead our feeble

235

minds to think upon the Selfsame (*Idipsum*). What is the Selfsame? That which exists always in the same way, which is not now one thing, and again something else.

What then is the Selfsame save That Which Is? What is That Which Is? That which is eternal. For that which is now one way and now another does not exist, for it does not endure. It is not completely nonexistent, but in the highest sense it does not exist. And what is That Which Is if not the One who said to Moses in sending him: "I am Who am" (Ex 3:14)? And what is that if not the One who when His servant said, "Behold, you send me; if the people say to me, who sent you? what shall I reply?" would give no other name than, "I am Who am." He then added: "Say then to the children of Israel: 'He Who Is has sent me to you.'" But you cannot understand this, this is too high for you, it is much to take in. Remember what He whom you cannot comprehend has done for you. Remember the flesh of Christ toward which you were raised when sick and when left half-dead from the wounds of robbers, that you might be carried to the inn and there be cured.

Let us run then to the house of the Lord and reach the city where our feet may stand, the city "which is being built as a city: whose partaking is in the Selfsame." For what ought you to hold? That which Christ became for you; for he is Christ, and Christ Himself is rightly understood in the words "I am Who am," as He exists in the form of God where "He did not think it robbery to be equal to God" (Phil 2:6); there He is the Selfsame. But that you may partake of the Selfsame He first participated in your nature. And the Word was made flesh so that flesh might participate in the Word. But in that the Word was made flesh and dwelt among us (Jn 1:14), He came from the seed of Abraham. But it was promised to Abraham, to Isaac, and to Jacob that in their seed all nations should be blessed (Gn 22:18). And consequently the Church expanded through all the earth; God speaks to the weak. In saying: "I am Who am" He asks for firmness of heart, and He asks for a high contemplation when He says: "He Who Is sent me to you."

But if perhaps you have not yet this power of contemplation, faint not, do not despair. The "One Who Is" willed to be a human being like you, and therefore tells Moses His Name when Moses was, as it were, terrified. What Name? That is, "Is." And the Lord said to Moses: "I am the God of Abraham, the God of Isaac, the

God of Jacob" (Ex 3:13–15); this is my name forever. Do not be discouraged because He said "I am Who am"; and again: "He Who Is has sent me to you," because at present you waver and through the mutability of things and the variety of temporal things cannot know the meaning of the Selfsame. Since you cannot ascend, I descend. "I am the God of Abraham, the God of Isaac, the God of Jacob." In the seed of Abraham hope so that you may be strengthened to see the One who descended to you in the seed of Abraham.

6

This then is the Selfsame, of Whom it is said: "You will change them and they will be changed; but for you, you are eternally the same, and your years are without end (Ps 101:27–28). Behold the Selfsame whose years shall not fail. Alas, my Brothers, our years, do they not daily fail and abide not at all? For those which have come already are gone, and they that are to come do not yet exist; these have already gone, and others destined to go are yet to come. In this one day, my Brothers, notice that our speaking is at one moment of time. Past hours have already passed by, future hours do not yet exist, and when they arrive, they will pass, no longer to exist.

What are the years which will not pass save those that abide? If then the years stand there, the very years that stand are also one year, and that very year which stands is one day. For this one day has neither rising nor setting, nor did it arise from a yesterday nor will it be followed by a tomorrow, but that day abides forever. And you may call that day whatever you please: If you choose, they are years; if you choose, it is a day. However you say it, it nevertheless stands: That city "which partakes in the Selfsame" partakes in its stability. Rightly then, because he is partaker in its stability, does he who runs there say: "Our feet were standing in the courts of Jerusalem." For there where nothing passes away everything stands.

Do you wish to stand there without ever passing away? Hasten to come there. No one has the Selfsame from himself. Listen well, my Brothers: The body that he has is not the Selfsame, for it stands not in itself. It changes with the years, it changes with places and times, it changes with illnesses, weaknesses of the flesh: It has then no stability in itself. No more are the heavenly bodies stable in themselves. They have their secret changes; certainly they change their place, they ascend from east to west; therefore they do not stand, they are not the same. Even the human soul does not remain stable. To how many changes, to how many different imaginations is it not subject? By how many pleasures is it changed? By what powerful lusts is it afflicted and torn apart? Man's mind, called rational, is changeable, never the same. Sometimes it wishes, sometimes it does not wish; sometimes it knows; sometimes it does not know; sometimes it remembers and sometimes it forgets. No one has, therefore, Selfsameness from himself.

He who wished to have the Selfsame from himself so that he might in some way be the Selfsame unto himself fell: The angel fell and became a devil. The devil has plunged man into the cup of pride. By jealousy he made fall with himself one who was standing (Gn 3:1). Both have willed to be their own Selfsameness, to be princes and lords over themselves. They did not will to recognize the true Lord, who truly is the Selfsame, to whom it was said: "You will change them and they will be changed; but you, you are always the Selfsame (Ps 101:27–28). Therefore, after so much weariness, so many illnesses, difficulties, toils, let the humble soul return to itself and let it enter into that city "whose partaking is in the Selfsame."

7

"There the tribes ascended" (Ps 121:4). We were asking where he who has fallen ascends; for, we said, it is the voice of a man who is ascending, of the Church ascending. Can we know where it ascends? Where it is going? Where it is raised? "There," he says, "the tribes went up." Where have they ascended? "To a city whose partaking is the Selfsame." Therefore they ascend to Jerusalem. But the man who descended from Jerusalem to Jericho fell into the hands of robbers (Lk 10:30). He would not have fallen among robbers if he had not descended. But since in descending he fell into the power of robbers, let him by ascending come to the angels. Let him ascend, then, since the tribes have descended.

What tribes? Many know them, but many do not know them. But we who know them, let us descend toward those who do not know these tribes, so that they may ascend with us where the tribes have ascended. The tribes may be called *curies*, but improperly. Strictly speaking, no other name can replace the word tribe;

that of *curies* only approaches it. For if we use *curies* properly it will mean only the *curies* which exist in each particular city; whence the terms "*curiales*" and "*decuriones*," that is, the citizens of a *curia* or a *decuria*; and you know that each city has such *curies*. But there are or were at one time *curies* of the people in those cities, and one city has many of them; thus, in Rome the population is divided into thirty-five *curies*. That is what one calls tribes, and the people of Israel had twelve of these, according to the number of the sons of Jacob.

8

There were twelve tribes of the people of Israel but they contained the good and the wicked. What wickedness in those tribes who crucified our Lord! What goodness in those who acknowledged Him? The tribes who crucified the Lord were the tribes of the devil. When the Psalmist said: "For there the tribes go up," fearing lest we understand by that all the tribes, he adds: "The tribes of the Lord." What is meant by the tribes of the Lord? Those who acknowledged the Lord. Among these wicked tribes there were good people who came from those good tribes which had acknowledged the Builder of the city; they were in these very tribes like grains of wheat mingled with the chaff. For they went up, not with the chaff, but as wheat winnowed, chosen, as the tribes of the Lord. There the tribes go up, even the tribes of the Lord.

What are the tribes of the Lord? A testimony to Israel. Hear, my Brothers, what this signifies: "A testimony to Israel," that is, that whereby it may be known that it is truly Israel. What does Israel signify? I have already explained it to you, but it is well to repeat it; although we recently said it, it can have been forgotten. In repeating it, let us do so in such a way that they cannot forget it, those who do not know how to read or do not wish to; let us be their dictionary. Israel signifies "seeing God," and even more carefully interpreted, Israel will be found to mean "is seeing God": both meanings: "is" and "seeing God." Man of himself is not; he is changed and altered if he does not partake in Him who is the Selfsame. Then when he sees God, he is. He is when he sees Him Who Is, and in seeing Him Who Is, he is also himself, as far as his capacity allows, beginning to be. He is then Israel, and Israel is seeing God.

The proud man is therefore not Israel, since he does not partake of the Selfsame, since he chooses to be the Selfsame to himself. He who wishes to be the origin of himself is not Israel. No false one, therefore, is Israel, and every proud man is necessarily false. Yes, my Brothers, I repeat it, every proud man wishes to appear what he is not; otherwise, my Brothers, it cannot be. And I wish the proud man wanted to appear what he is not, so as to appear to be a flute player, for example, when not really one. He could then be tested. One would say: Play, let us see if you are a flute player. He would not be able and would be discovered to have wished falsely to appear what he was not. If he pretended to be eloquent, one would say to him: Speak, and prove yourself eloquent. If he should speak, he would be discovered not to be what he pretended to be. The proud man (and this is worse) wishes to appear righteous without being so, and as it is difficult to detect righteousness, it is difficult to discern the proud. The proud therefore wish to appear what they are not; hence they have no share in the Selfsame; they do not belong to Israel, which means "seeing God."

Who then belongs to Israel? He who partakes of the Selfsame. Who is he? He is one who acknowledges that he is not what God is, and that he holds from God all the capacity for good he has, that of himself he is only a sinner, and that his righteousness comes to him from God. Such is the one without guile. But, what did the Lord say in seeing Nathaniel? "Here is a true child of Israel, without guile" (Jn 1:47). If therefore he is a true Israelite in whom there is no guile, those tribes go up to Jerusalem in whom there is no guile. And these are "the testimony to Israel," that is, through them it is evident that there were grains mingled with the chaff, since when the floor was examined, all was thought to be chaff. Therefore, grains were there, but when they have ascended into that glory above, when the floor shall have been winnowed, then they will be "a testimony to Israel." All the wicked will then say: Truly there were here righteous people among the wicked, although all appeared wicked to us, and we judged them similar to ourselves. This is the testimony to Israel.

Where are these tribes ascending, and why? "To confess to your name, O Lord." Nothing greater could be said. As pride presumes, so does humility confess. Just as there is presumption in the one who wishes to appear what he is not, so is he a confessor who does not wish that to be seen which he himself is and loves that which He is. To this, therefore, do Israelites go up, in whom there is no guile because they are true Israelites, because in them is the testimony to Israel. To this they go up: "to confess to your name, O Lord."

9

There were seated seats for "judgment" (Ps 121:5). Strange enigma! Strange question, not easy to comprehend. Here what the Greeks called thrones are called seats, and the Greeks called chairs thrones as a term of honor. It is not astonishing that we should sit on seats, on chairs, but that these seats themselves should sit, how can we understand this? As if someone should say: Let stools or chairs sit here. We sit on chairs, we sit on seats, we sit on stools; the seats themselves do not sit. What then does this mean: "For there were seated seats for judgment?" You hear it said of God: "Heaven is my throne, the earth is my footstool" (Is 66:1), which is rendered in Latin by *Coelum mihi sedes est:* Heaven is my seat.

Who are these, save the righteous? Who are the heavens, save the righteous? They who are heaven are heavens themselves; for they which are the Church are themselves churches. They are many so as to be only one; so therefore are the righteous also. The righteous are heaven in such a way that they are heavens. It is on them that God is seated, and from them that He judges. And not without deep meaning is it said that "the heavens declare the glory of God" (Acts 7:43). For the Apostles have become a heaven. Why have they become heaven? Because they have been justified. As the sinner has become earth, for to him it is said: "You are dust, and you will return to dust" (Ps 18:2), so have the justified become heaven. They bore God, and from them He shone forth His wonders, thundered terrors, rained consolations.

They were, therefore, heaven, and they declared the glory of God. So that you may know that they were called heaven, the same Psalm adds: "The sound of their voice has gone out to all the earth, and their words to the ends of the world" (Ps 18:2–5). Seek to know whose voices these are, and you will discover that they are the voices of the heavens. If then heaven is the seat of God, and if the Apostles are heaven, they themselves are the seat of God, the throne of God. In another place it is said: "The soul of the righteous is the throne of wisdom." A great truth, a great truth is declared: The throne of wisdom is the soul of the righteous, that is, wisdom sits on the soul of the righteous as on her chair, as on her throne, and there judges whatever she judges.

There were, therefore, thrones of wisdom, and hence the Lord said to them: "You will be seated on twelve thrones to judge the twelve tribes of Israel" (Mt 19:28). Thus they will be seated upon twelve seats and they are themselves the seats of God; for of them it is said: "For there were seated seats." Who sat? Seats. And who are the seats? Those of whom it is said: The soul of the righteous is the seat of wisdom. Who are the seats? The heavens. Who are the heavens? Heaven. What is heaven? That of which the Lord says: "Heaven is my seat." The righteous, then, are themselves seats and have seats; and seats shall be seated in that Jerusalem. Why? For judgment. You shall sit upon twelve thrones, O you thrones, judging the twelve tribes of Israel. Judging whom? Those who are below on earth. Who will judge? Those who have become heaven.

But those who are to be judged will be divided into two parts, one on the right, the other on the left. The saints will judge with Christ. For "the Lord will come to judge with the ancients of His people" (Is 3:14), said Isaiah. Thus some will judge with Him; others will be judged by Him and by those who will judge with Him. These will then be divided into two parts: one on the right, and account will be rendered of the merciful deeds they have done; the others will be set on the left, and they will be reproached for their cruelty, their lack of mercy. And to those on the right it will be said: "Come, blessed of my Father, receive the kingdom which has been prepared for you since the beginning of the world." Why? "I was hungry," He will say, "and you gave me to eat." And these will say: "When have we seen you hungry?" And the Lord will say: "Whatever you have done to the least of my brothers, you have done it to me." And what then, my Brothers? They shall judge, those of whom it was said that men should "make friends with the mammon of iniquity," so that, he added, "they may receive you into eternal dwellings" (Lk 16:19). The saints will be seated with the Lord to mark those who have shown mercy and will bring them, set apart on the right, into the kingdom of heaven. Such is the peace of Jerusalem. What is this peace of Jerusalem? It consists in joining the corporal works of mercy with the spiritual works of preaching, that peace may result from giving and receiving. For the Apostle who said that this almsgiving is a balance of giving and receiving says: "If we have sown with you spiritual goods, is it then too much to receive temporal goods" (1 Cor 9:11)? And elsewhere on the same subject: "The one who has gathered much has not more than the others, and the one who has gathered little has not less" (2 Cor 8:15). Why had he who had gathered much nothing left over? Because he gave to the poor whatever "more" he had. In what sense does the one who gathered little not have less? Because he received from the one who possessed in abundance, so that there might be equality, as he says. Such is the peace of which it is said: "Let peace be established in your strength."

10

After having said: "There will be seated the seats for judgment, the seats above the house of David," that is, over the family of Christ, to whom they gave meat in season, he at once adds as to the seats themselves: "Inquire into the things that are for the peace of Jerusalem" (Ps 121:6). O you seats who are already seated to judge, who are the thrones of the sovereign Judge (since those who judge, inquire; those who are judged are interrogated), "inquire," he says, "into the things that are for the peace of Jerusalem."

In inquiring what will they find? That some have done deeds of charity and others have not. And they will call those found to have done deeds of charity to Jerusalem, for these deeds are "for the peace of Jerusalem." Love is powerful, my Brothers, yes, love is powerful. Do you wish to see how great is the power of love? Whoever through an insurmountable obstacle cannot accomplish what God commands him, let him love the one who accomplishes it, and thus he accomplishes it in that other. Listen, my Brothers, here is a man who has a wife whom he may not divorce since he must obey the Apostle's injunction: "Let the husband render to his wife due benevolence" and again: "Are you joined to a wife? do not seek to separate from her." But there comes to him the thought that it is more perfect to live as the same Apostle said: "I would wish that you were all as I am" (1 Cor 7:3, 27). He observes those who have acted like that; he loves them and accomplishes in them what he himself cannot do, so great is the power of love.

Love is your strength, for without charity, everything we

have amounts to nothing. "Though I speak with the tongues of men and of angels," says the Apostle, "if I have no charity, I am as sounding brass or tinkling cymbal." He adds this serious word: "When I shall have distributed all my riches to the poor, when I shall have delivered my body to be burned; if I have no charity, this amounts to nothing"(1 Cor 13:1–3). If one with charity is without means to distribute to the poor, let him love, let him give "one cup of cold water" (Mt 10:42); as much shall be charged to his account as to Zaccheus, who gave half his patrimony to the poor (Lk 19:8). Why? One gave so little, the other so much, and both will be equally treated? Yes, equally. The resources are unequal, the charity is equal.

11

They therefore ask: Reflect upon what you are. It has already been said to us: "We shall go into the house of the Lord." We took delight in those who said to us: "We shall go into the house of the Lord." Consider then whether we really go. For we go not with our feet but by our affections. See then if we are to go; let each one of you examine his conduct toward the saints who are poor, toward an indigent brother, toward a poor beggar; see whether one's heart is closed. For the seats which will sit to judge you are going to examine you; they must find things which are for the peace of Jerusalem. How will they question? As the seats of God, it is God who questions. If anything can escape God, it can also escape these seats who question. "Inquire into the things that are for the peace of Jerusalem."

But what things are for the peace of Jerusalem? "Let abundance," he adds, "be for those who love you." He speaks to Jerusalem herself and says that abundance is the share of those who love her. Abundance after poverty; here below, poverty, there above, abundance; here below, weakness, there above, strength; here below, indigence, there above, riches. How have they become rich? Because what they received here from God for a time they gave, and on high they have received for eternity what God gives. Here below, my Brothers, even rich men are poor: It is good for the rich man to acknowledge his poverty. If he thinks himself full, that is mere puffing, not abundance. Let him recognize that his hands are empty so that God can fill them. In fact, what has he? Gold. What has he not? Eternal life. Let him examine what he has and what he has not; and with what he has, let him give that he may receive what he has not, "Abundance to all those who love you."

12

"Peace be in your strength" (Ps 121:7). O Jerusalem, O City being built as a city, whose partaking is in the Selfsame: "peace be in your strength"; peace be in your love; for your strength is your love. Hear the Song of Songs: "Love is strong as death" (Cant 8:6). What a magnificent word, my Brothers! Love is strong as death! A great saying, that: "Love is strong as death." The strength of love cannot be expressed in grander terms than these: "Love is strong as death." Who indeed resists death, my Brothers? Consider well. Fire, waves, the sword are resisted; we resist principalities, we resist kings. Death comes alone and who can resist it? There is nothing stronger. Hence to this strength charity is compared, when it is said: "Love is strong as death."

And since this love destroys what we were so that we may become what we were not, love makes us undergo a certain death. This death he died who said: "The world is crucified to me, and I to the world" (Gal 6:14). This death they had died to whom he said, "You are dead, and your life is hid with Christ in God" (Col 3:3). Love is strong as death. If therefore it is strong, it is courageous and of great power and is strength itself. Through it the weak are ruled by the firm, earth by heaven, peoples by the "seats." Therefore, "Peace be in your strength" means peace be in your love. And by that strength, by that love, by that peace, "let there be abundance in your towers," that is, in your exalted ones. For few will sit in judgment but many set at the right hand will compose the people of that city. Many will belong to each of those eminent saints who will receive them into eternal habitations: and abundance will be in their towers. But the fullness of delights, the sufficiency of riches, is God Himself, He always the Selfsame, He in Whom the partaking of the city is in the Selfsame; such will be our abundance also. But how will it come to us? Through love, that is, through strength.

Where is this love, my Brothers? In the one who does not in this life seek his own interests (Phil 2:4, 21). Hear the Apostle consumed with this love: "Seek to please everyone in all things," he said, "as I try to please you in all things" (1 Cor 10:33). But what happens, O blessed Apostle, to what you said elsewhere: "If I wish also to please men, I shall not be a servant of Christ" (Gal 1:10)? And now you are pleasing them, you tell us, now you engage us to please them. But the end he proposes is not to please others for our own sake, it is to please for the sake of charity. Whoever seeks his own glory does not seek the salvation of others. St. Paul in fact says: "Just as I pleased all in everything, not seeking my own advantage, but that which was advantageous to many so that they might be saved" (1 Cor 10:32–33).

13

Thus as he was speaking here of charity, he adds: "Because of my brothers and my neighbors, O Jerusalem, I spoke of your peace" (Ps 121:8). O Jerusalem, City whose partaking is in the Selfsame, I in this life and on this earth, I poor, he says, I a stranger and groaning, not as yet enjoying your peace fully, and preaching your peace, I preach it not for my own sake as the heretics who, seeking their own glory, say: Peace be with you, and who have not the peace that they preach to the people.

If they had peace, they would not destroy unity. "As for me," he says, "I spoke of your peace." But why? For the sake of my brothers and my neighbors, not for my own honor, not for my own money, not for my life, for "to me, to live is Christ, and to die is gain." But "I spoke peace of you because of my brothers and my neighbors." For the Apostle desired to depart and to be with Christ, but since he must preach these things to his neighbors and his brothers, "That I abide in the flesh," he adds, "is more needful for you" (1 Phil 1:21–24). "For the sake of my brothers and my neighbors I spoke peace of you."

14

"Because of the house of the Lord, my God, I have sought good things for you" (Ps 121:9). Not for myself have I sought good things, for then I would be seeking myself and not you, and so I should not have them because I should not seek them for you. But "because of the house of the Lord, my God," because of the Church, because of the saints, because of the pilgrims, because of the poor, so that they may go up, because we say to them: "We shall go into the house of the Lord: because of the house of the Lord my God itself I have sought good things for you."

Gather up these long and necessary words, my Brothers, eat them, drink them, and grow strong, run, and seize!

Psalm 122: God Is True Wealth

I have been engaged in treating in sequence with you, holy Brothers, the songs of one who ascends: of one ascending and loving, and ascending because he loves. All love either ascends or descends. A good desire lifts us up to God, and by an evil desire we are cast down to the depths. But because through evil desire we have already fallen, it behooves us, if we know who did not fall but descended to us, to ascend by clinging to Him; for by our own strength we cannot ascend. Our Lord Jesus Christ Himself said, "No man ascends up to heaven except He who came down from heaven, even the Son of Man who is in heaven" (Jn 3:13). He apparently was speaking only of Himself. Did the rest remain below because He who alone came down, alone ascended? What should the rest do? Be united with His Body, so that Christ Who came down and ascended may be One. The Head descended and with the Body ascended, clothed with His Church which He presented to Himself "without spot or wrinkle" (Eph 5:7). Therefore He alone ascended. But when with Him we are His members in Him, and with us He is alone and therefore One, and always One, unity binding us into One. Only those who have not chosen to be one with Him do not ascend with Him.

Now He who was in heaven and immortal since He had raised up the flesh because of which He was mortal for a time, and in heaven suffering no persecution, no malice or reproaches as when He condescended to endure on earth all things for our sake, yet sympathizing with His Body suffering on earth, said: "Saul, Saul, why do you persecute me" (Acts 9:4)? Although He Himself was not being touched, He nevertheless cried from heaven that He was suffering persecution. We should not then lose hope but confidently trust that if through love He is Himself with us on earth, we also are with Him in heaven through the same love.

But we have said how He is Himself with us on earth; we said that it was His voice which sounded from heaven, "Saul, Saul, why do you persecute me?" when Saul had not touched Him nor seen Him. But how is it evident that we also are with Him in heaven? By the words of the same Paul, "If you be risen with Christ, seek the things which are above, where Christ sits on the right hand of God. Set your heart on things above, not on earthly things. For you are dead, and your life is hid with Christ in God" (Col 3:13). He is still here, therefore, and we are now there: Through the compassion of love He is here, through the hope of love we are there. "For we are saved by hope" (Rom 8:24). Because our hope is certain. Although it refers to what is to come, we are described as though hope had already reached fruition.

2

Therefore let this singer ascend, and let him sing from each one's heart, and let each of you be this singer, for when each one says this, because you are all one in Christ, one person says this. He does not say, "To you, O Lord, we lift up our eyes"; but "To you, O Lord, I lift up my eyes." Certainly you should imagine that each one of you is speaking but that One in a special sense speaks who is also spread abroad over the entire world. That One speaks who elsewhere says, "From the ends of the earth I cried to You, when my heart was heavy" (Ps 61:2). Who is crying from the ends of the earth? Each one can cry out from where he is but from the ends of the earth can he cry out? But Christ's inheritance of which it is said, "I shall give you the heathen for your inheritance, and the uttermost parts of the earth for your possession," itself cries out. "From the ends of the earth I cried to You, when my heart was heavy." If our heart is heavy, let us cry out. Why should our heart be heavy? Not because of what the wicked suffer here, that is, when they suffer a loss; for if that is why the heart is heavy, it is ashes. Perhaps by God's will you have lost a relative: If your heart is heavy for that reason, what great thing is this? For such a reason the hearts of unbelievers are heavy. They who do not yet believe in Christ also suffer such things.

What makes a Christian's heart heavy? He is a pilgrim and yearns for his country. If for this reason your heart is heavy, although you enjoy worldly prosperity, you yet groan. And if all things work together to make you fortunate, and the world in every way smiles on you, you nevertheless groan because you see that you are set on a pilgrimage. You feel that in the eyes of the foolish you certainly possess happiness but not as yet according to Christ's promises. You seek this with groans, you seek it by longing. By longing you ascend, and while you ascend you sing the Song of Steps, saying, "To you I lift up my eyes, O You who dwell in heaven."

3

 While ascending where was he to raise his eyes except toward that heaven to which he was linked and to which he longed to ascend? For from earth to heaven he ascends. Behold, here is the earth which we tread with our feet; behold, there is the heaven which we see with our eyes. And as we ascend, we sing, "To you I lift up my eyes, O You who dwell in heaven."

 Where then are the ladders? For we see so great a distance between earth and heaven, there is such a great separation, such a great space between them: We want to climb there, we see no ladder. Do we deceive ourselves because we sing the Song of Steps, that is, the Song of Ascent?

 We ascend to heaven if we think of God who has put ascending steps in the heart. What is this: to ascend in heart? To advance toward God. Just as everyone who fails falls rather than descends, so everyone who succeeds ascends if in succeeding he avoids pride, if he so ascends as not to fall. But if in succeeding he becomes proud, in ascending he again falls. But what should he do to avoid pride? Let him lift up his eyes to Him who dwells in heaven, let him not heed himself. For every proud man heeds himself, and he who pleases himself seems great to himself. But he who pleases himself pleases a fool, for he himself is a fool when he is pleasing to himself. Only he who is pleasing to God is pleasing without danger. And who is pleasing to God? He whom God has pleased. God cannot displease Himself; may He please you also that you may be pleasing to Him. But unless you displease yourself, He cannot please you. But if you displease yourself, lift your eyes from yourself. Why do you have self-regard? For if you sincerely regard yourself, you find in yourself that which will displease you. And you say to God, "My sin is ever before me" (Ps 51:3).

 Let your sin be before you that it may not be before God.

And refuse to be before yourself that you may be before God. For just as we want God not to turn away His face from us, so we want Him to turn His face from our sins; for both these prayers are present in the Psalms. "Oh, hide not your face from me" (Ps 27:9) are the words of the Psalm and ours also. And see what he who says, "Oh, hide not your face from me," says elsewhere: "Turn your face from my sins" (Ps 51:9). If you want Him to turn His face from your sins, then turn your face away from yourself and do not turn your face away from your sins. You are yourself indignant over your sins if you do not turn your face away from them. But if you do not turn your face away from your sins, you acknowledge them and He forgets them.

4

But lift your eyes from yourself to Him and say, "To you I lift up my eyes, O You who dwell in heaven." If, my Brothers, by heaven we understand the firmament visible to bodily eyes, we shall certainly so err as to imagine that we cannot ascend there without ladders or some scaling machines. But if we ascend spiritually we should understand heaven spiritually. If the ascent is by affection, heaven is righteousness. What then is God's heaven? All holy souls, all righteous ones. The Apostles also, although in the flesh and on earth, were heaven. For the Lord, enthroned in them, traversed the entire world. He then dwells in heaven. How? In what sense does he say in another Psalm, "But You dwell in holiness, O praise of Israel" (Ps 22:3)? He who dwells in heaven dwells in holiness. What is holiness but His temple? For "the temple of God is holy, which temple you are" (1 Cor 3:17). But all who are still weak and "walking according to faith" (2 Cor 5:7) are the temple of God according to faith. How long according to faith are they the temple of God? As long as through faith Christ dwells in them, as the Apostle says: "That Christ may dwell in your hearts through faith." But they in whom God already visibly dwells are already heaven, those who see Him face to face: all the holy Apostles, all the holy Virtues, Powers, Thrones, Lordships, that heavenly Jerusalem from which we are groaning wanderers and for which we pray with longing; and there God dwells. To that the Psalmist lifted up his faith, to that one rises by affection, with longing hope. And this very longing causes the soul to purify the filth of sins and to be cleansed from all stains in order itself to become heaven: because it has lifted up its eyes to Him who dwells in heaven.

For if we have decided that the heaven visible to bodily eyes is God's dwelling, then God's dwelling will pass away; for "heaven and earth will pass away" (Mt 24:35). Then, before God created heaven and earth, where did He dwell? But someone says: and before God made the saints where did He dwell? God dwelt in Himself, He dwelt with Himself, and God is with Himself. And when He consents to dwell in the saints, the saints are not God's house in such a way that God would fall if it were removed. For our way of dwelling in a house is not God's way of dwelling in the saints. You dwell in a house; if it is removed you fall. But God so dwells in the saints that if He Himself should depart, they fall.

Whoever then so bears God as to be God's temple, let him not think that God is so present in him that if he removes himself he may make God tremble. Woe to him if God removes Himself, for then he falls because God abides in Himself forever. The houses in which we live hold us; those in which God dwells are upheld by Him. Now consider the great difference between our dwelling and that of God and let the soul say, "To you I lift up my eyes, O You who dwell in heaven," that it may know that God does not even need heaven to dwell in, but heaven needs Him, to be upheld by Him.

5

What follows, therefore, because he has said, "To you I lift up my eyes, O You who dwell in heaven?" How have you lifted up your eyes? "Behold, even as the eyes of servants look to the hand of their masters, and as the eyes of a maiden to the hand of her mistress: even so our eyes wait upon the Lord our God until He have mercy upon us." We are both servants and handmaiden; He is both our Master and our Mistress. What do these words signify? What do these couplets mean? Listen for a time, beloved Brothers. It is not remarkable that we are servants and that He is Our Master, but it is remarkable if we are a maiden and He our Mistress. But not even our being a maiden is remarkable; for we are the Church. Nor is it remarkable that He is our Mistress, for He is the Power and Wisdom of God.

Hear the Apostle speaking: "We preach Christ crucified, to

the Jews a stumbling block, and to the Greeks foolishness; but to them that are called, both Jews and Greeks, Christ the Power of God, and the Wisdom of God" (1 Cor 1:23–24). So that how both the people may be a servant and the Church a handmaid you have heard: Christ the Power of God and the Wisdom of God. When, therefore, you hear Christ, then lift up your eyes to the hands of your Master. When you hear the Power of God and the Wisdom of God, lift up your eyes to the hands of your Mistress. For you are both servant and handmaiden; servant, for you are a people; handmaiden, for you are the Church.

But this maiden has found a great dignity with God; she has been made a wife. But until she comes to those spiritual embraces where without fear she may enjoy Him whom she has loved and for whom she has sighed in this wearisome pilgrimage, she is betrothed and has received a mighty pledge, the blood of the Spouse for whom she sighed without fear. Nor is it said to her: Do not love, as is sometimes said to any betrothed virgin not as yet married, and rightly said, do not love; when you have become a wife, then love. It is rightly said because it is a rash and irrational and an unchaste desire to love one whom she is not sure of marrying. For one man may be betrothed to her, and another man may marry her. But since there is no one preferable to Christ, let her love without fear. And before being joined to Him, let her love and sigh from a distance and from her far pilgrimage. He alone will marry her, for He alone has given such a pledge. For who can so marry as to die for her whom he wishes to marry? If he choose to die for her, he will no longer be there to marry her. But He who when He arose as to marry His betrothed, died for her without fear.

Nevertheless, Brothers, let us meanwhile be as servants and handmaidens. It is said in fact, "I call you not servants but friends" (Jn 15:15), but perhaps Our Lord said this only to his disciples? Hear the Apostle Paul, saying: "You are no longer a servant but a Son; and if a Son, then an heir through God" (Gal 4:7). He was speaking to the people, he was speaking to the faithful. Now then being redeemed in the name of the Lord by His own blood, washed in His laver, we are sons, we are a Son; because, although many, we are one in Him. Why then do we still speak as servants? Although we have been made sons instead of servants, can we deserve in the Church as much as the Apostle

Paul? And yet, what does he say in his epistle? "Paul, a servant of Jesus Christ" (Rom 1:1). If he calls himself a servant and through him the Gospel has been preached to us, how much more ought we to acknowledge our condition so that His grace in us may be greater? For those He redeemed He first made servants. For His blood was a price for servants, a pledge for His spouse.

Although now sons through grace, acknowledging our condition as servants by creation (for the entire creation serves God), let us say: "As the eyes of servants look to the hand of their masters, and as the eyes of a maiden to the hands of her mistress, even so our eyes wait upon the Lord our God, until He have mercy upon us."

6

He has also told the reason why "our eyes" should "wait upon the Lord our God," even as the eyes of a servant look to the hands of his master, and as the eyes of a maiden to the hands of her mistress. As though you would be asking why, he says, "Until He have mercy upon us." What kind of servants did he wish to be understood by those whose eyes look to the hands of their masters; and what kind of maidens are those whose eyes look to the hand of their mistress until their mistress have mercy upon them? Who are these servants and handmaidens whose eyes thus look to the hands of their masters except those destined to be beaten? "Our eyes look to the Lord our God, until He have mercy upon us." How? "As the eyes of servants look to the hand of their masters and as the eyes of a maiden unto the hands of her mistress." Therefore, both servants and maidens look thus, until their master or mistress have mercy upon them. Suppose then that a master has commanded his servant to be beaten. The servant is beaten; he feels the pain of the strokes; he looks upon the hands of his master until he says: Enough.

For by the hand is meant the master's power. What then shall we say, Brothers? Our Lord has commanded us to be beaten, and our Mistress, the Wisdom of God, has ordered us to be beaten. And in this life we are beaten, and the whole of this mortal life is a punishment. Hear the words of the Psalm: "You have chastened man for sin, and you have made my soul to consume away as if it were a spider" (Ps 39:11). Remember, Brothers, how fragile is a spider, and with how slight a touch it is shattered and dies. And so that we might not think that only our flesh is easily consumed from the weakness of our mortal nature, he did not say, "You have made me to consume away," lest we should understand this of the flesh, but "You have made my soul to consume away as if it were a spider." For there is nothing more fragile than our soul situated in the midst of worldly temptations, in the midst of groans and the torments of sorrows. There is nothing more fragile than it until it clings to the firmness of heaven and is in the temple of God, from where it may no longer fall. At first it was made as fragile as a spider and coming into this weak and perishable nature it was expelled from Paradise.

Then the servant was ordered to be beaten. Consider, my Brothers, from what point in time we have been beaten. In all who were born from the origin of the human race, in all who now exist and will exist, Adam is being beaten. Adam is being beaten, that is, the human race. And many have grown so hardened that they do not feel their own bruises. But they who have been made sons have regained the sense of pain. They feel that they are being beaten and they know who commanded them to be beaten. They have lifted up their eyes to Him who dwells in heaven so that their eyes are on the hands of their Lord until He have mercy upon them, even as the eyes of servants are on the hands of their masters, and as the eyes of the maiden are on the hands of her mistress. You see some prosperous people in this world all smiles, boasting that they are not being beaten; nay, they are worse beaten; in having lost feeling, they are worse beaten. Let them awake and be beaten. Let them feel that they are being beaten, let them know that they are being beaten, and let them sorrow that they are beaten. For "he who increases knowledge, increases sorrow" (Eccl 1:18), as Scripture says. So also the Lord in the Gospel: "Blessed are they who mourn, for they shall be comforted."

7

Let us listen to the words of the man who is beaten, and let these be the words of each of us, even when it is well with us. For who cannot know that he is being beaten when he is ill, when he is imprisoned, when perhaps he is enslaved or endures robbery? When disasters are inflicted upon him by wicked men, he feels that he is being beaten. But it is a better sensitivity to perceive that one is being beaten when all is going well. For Scripture does not say in Job, "Human life is full of temptations," but it says, "What is the life of man upon earth, except a temptation" (Jb 7:1)? He called the whole of life a temptation. Your whole life on earth is therefore a beating. Mourn as long as you live upon earth: whether you live happily or whether you are in trouble, cry: "Unto You I lift up my eyes, O You who dwells in heaven." Look to the hands of the Lord who ordered you to be beaten, to whom in another Psalm you say: "You have chastened man for sin and have made my soul to consume away like a spider"; cry to the hands of Him who beats you, and say, "Have mercy upon us, O Lord, have mercy upon us." Are not these the words of one who is being beaten, "Have mercy upon us, O Lord, have mercy upon us"?

8

"For we have been greatly filled with contempt, our soul has been filled to the utmost, a reproach to the wealthy, and a contempt to the proud" (2 Tm 3:12). All who piously live according to Christ must necessarily suffer reprimand and be despised by those who do not choose to live piously, those whose happiness is earthly. Those who speak of that happiness that is invisible to eyes are derided, and to them it is said: What do you believe, mad man? Do you see what you believe? Has anyone returned from the other world and described what is going on there? Behold I see and enjoy what I love here. You are disdained because you hope for what you do not see; and he who apparently possesses what he sees, disdains you. Reflect carefully on whether he really possesses it. Be not disquieted; discover whether he possesses it of himself, and let him not disdain you, lest thinking him to be happy in the present you may lose happiness in the future. Be not, I say, disquieted; reflect upon whether he really possesses it. What he possesses slips from his hands or he slips away from what he possesses: Either he has to pass through his property or it through him. Through whom do his possessions pass? Through him who is ruined while alive, who goes through his property? He who dies in his wealth. For when he dies, he does not take it with him to the other world. He boasted: "I own my house." You ask: What is his own house? The one my father left me. And where did he get it? From my grandfather. Go back even to his great-grandfather, then to his great-grandfather's father, and he cannot remember their names. Does not this frighten you, that you see how many have passed through this house and yet none of them took it with him to his everlasting home? Your father left it; he passed through it and so will you pass through it. Therefore if you have merely a passing stay in your house, it is an inn for transient guests, not a dwelling for a permanent stay. Nevertheless because we hope for that which is to come and sigh for future happiness, and because it has not yet appeared what we shall be, although already we are "sons of God" for "our life is hid with Christ in God," "we are utterly despised" (1 Jn 3:2; Col 3:3) by those who seek or enjoy happiness in this world.

9

"Our soul is filled exceedingly; a reproach to the wealthy, and a contempt to the proud." We were asking who were the "wealthy": He explained them as "the proud." "Reproach and contempt" are the same, and "wealthy" is the same as "proud." It repeats the sentence, "a reproach to the wealthy, and a contempt to the proud." Why are the proud wealthy? Because they wish to be happy here. Why, since they themselves are miserable are they called wealthy? Perhaps when they are miserable they do not disdain us? Listen, my Beloved. Perhaps they disdain when they are happy, when they extol themselves in the pomp of their wealth! When they extol themselves in the inflated state of false honors, then they disdain us and seem to say, see how well it goes with me: I enjoy good things here and now; let those who promise what they cannot show leave me alone. What I see, I possess, what I see, I enjoy; I want good fortune in this life.

You are more secure; for Christ has risen and has taught you what He will give in the next life: be sure that He will give it. But that man because he possesses what he does disdains you. Endure his disdain and you will laugh at his groans. For there will come a later time when these persons will say, "This was he whom we held sometimes in derision" (Wis 5:3). Such are the words of the Book of Wisdom; Scripture has told us what they who disdain us shall say, they who mock us, they by whom we are filled with reproach and contempt: What words will they then utter, when they shall be despised by the Truth. They shall see those among them whom they disdained shine on the right hand when that which the Apostle described has been fulfilled in them: "When Christ, who is our Life, shall appear, then shall you also appear with Him in glory" (Col 3:14), and they shall say, "This was he whom we held sometimes in derision, and a byword of reproach. We fools account his life madness and his end to be without honor. How is he numbered among the children of God, and his lot is among the Saints" (Wis 5:3–8)! And they continue: "Therefore we erred from the way of truth, and the light of righteousness did not shine on us nor the sun shine on us. What has pride gained for us? And what have riches with our boasting brought us?" There you do not disdain them for they disdain themselves. Until this happens, Brothers, let us lift up our eyes to Him who dwells in heaven: and let us not remove our eyes from Him "until He have mercy upon us," and free us from all temptation and reproach and contempt.

10

We must also add that at times those who suffer the scourge of worldly unhappiness disdain us. You see someone punished for his wickedness, whether by God's secret judgment or by a public condemnation sent to prison dragging a chain: and even he disdains you. And when asked, why did you not live rightly, see to what you have come by living wickedly, he answers: Why then do they who live rightly suffer these things? But they suffer so that they may be proven, that they may be tried by temptation, that they may profit by scourging: "for God scourges every son whom He receives" (Heb 12:6). And if He scourged His only Son without sin and "delivered Him up for us all," how much more should we be scourged who have done things which deserve scourging.

When we so answer, they still show pride even in their misery; afflicted though not humbled, they reply: These are the words of idle Christians who believe what they do not see. If even these people disdain us, why should we not imagine, Brothers, that they are referred to in this Psalm, in the words: "A reproach to the wealthy and a contempt to the proud"; because even those who are not wealthy disdain Christians and even in poverty and misery do not cease disdaining?

Surely then "we are a reproach to the wealthy," or is there no one to mock us even when afflicted with some disaster? Did not the thief who was crucified with our crucified Lord mock Him?

So if they who are not wealthy mock us, why does the Psalm say, "a reproach to the wealthy"? If we analyze carefully, even these, the unfortunate, are wealthy. How so? If they were not wealthy, they would not be proud. For one man is wealthy in money, and for that reason proud; another is wealthy in honors, and for that reason proud; another thinks himself wealthy in righteousness and hence his worse pride. They who seem not to be wealthy in money seem to themselves to be wealthy in righteousness toward God. And when misfortune comes, they justify themselves, accuse God, and say, why am I guilty, what wrong have I done? You reply: Reflect, recall your sins, see if you have done nothing wrong. His conscience is awakened and on reflection he thinks of his evil actions. Not even then does he choose to confess that he deserves his suffering but says, Behold, I have certainly done many wrong things but I notice that many have done worse and suffer no evil. He is righteous against God. He also, therefore, is wealthy. His breast is puffed out with righteousness because God seems to him to do wrong and he seems to suffer unjustly. And if you gave him a ship to pilot, he would be shipwrecked with it, yet he wants to deny to God the government of this world and take for himself the helm of creation, distributing pains and pleasures, punishments and rewards to all. Unhappy soul! Yet why wonder? He is wealthy, but wealthy in wickedness, wealthy in malice. He is more wealthy in wickedness in porportion as he seems to himself to be wealthy in righteousness.

11

A Christian should not be wealthy but acknowledge his poverty. And if he possesses wealth he should realize that it is not true wealth so that he may desire the other kind. For he who desires false riches does not seek true riches, while he who seeks true riches is as yet poor, and rightly says, "I am poor and in heaviness" (Ps 69:29). Again, how is it that whoever is poor and full of wickedness is called wealthy? Because he is displeased with being poor and in his own heart he seems wealthy in righteousness against the righteousness of God.

And what is the wealth of our righteousness? However great our righteousness, it is like dew compared to that fountain; compared to that abundance it is only a few drops which may soften our life and relax our hard iniquity. Let us only desire to be filled from the full fountain of righteousness, let us long to be filled with that abundant wealth of which the Psalm says: "They shall be satisfied with the abundance of your house: and You shall give them drink out of the torrent of Your pleasure" (Ps 36:8).

But while here let us realize that we are destitute and poor not only in regard to riches, which are not true riches, but in regard to salvation itself. And when we are healthy, let us realize that we are weak. For as long as this body hungers and thirsts, as long as this body is weary with watching, weary with standing, weary with walking, weary with sitting, weary with eating, wherever it turns for relief from weariness, there it finds another source of fatigue. There is therefore no perfect soundness, not even in the body itself.

Those [so-called] riches are then not riches but penury; for the more they abound the greater one's destitution and avarice. This is not soundness of body but weakness. Every day we are refreshed with cordials from God when we eat and drink; the things set before us are medicines. If you want to know, Brothers, what kind of disease we have: Whoever fasts for seven days dies of hunger. That hunger is here but you do not feel it because you daily give it medicine. Not even health then is perfect in us.

12

Realize, my Brothers, in what sense we are poor so that we may rejoice in Him and may lift up our eyes to Him who dwells in heaven. They are not true riches which increase ever more greatly the covetousness of those who possess them. This is not true health of body when we sustain a weakness that fails in every way; wherever it turns, it fails. There is no permanence even in relief: He is tired standing, he wants to sit: Will he remain sitting? He finds a flaw in whatever he takes as a remedy for fatigue. He is weary watching, he is about to sleep; does he never again grow weary because he slept? He is tired of fasting and is about to eat; if he takes too much he becomes weak. Our weakness then eliminates perseverance in anything.

What is our righteousness? How much is there in the midst of such great temptations? We can refrain from homicide, from adultery, from thefts, from perjuries, from frauds; but can we refrain from unrighteous thoughts? Can we refrain from the suggestion of evil desires? What then is our righteousness?

Let then our whole hunger, our whole thirst, be for true wealth, for true health, for true righteousness. What is true wealth? That heavenly dwelling in Jerusalem. Who is called wealthy on earth? When a wealthy man is praised, what is meant? He is very wealthy, he wants for nothing. That certainly is the praise of one who praises another, but it is not so when it is said that he wants nothing. Consider if he really wants nothing. If he desires nothing, he wants nothing? But if he still desires more than what he has, his riches have so increased that his wants have also increased.

But in that city there will be true wealth since there will be nothing wanting to us there. We shall not be in need of anything; there we shall have true health. What is true health? When "death shall have been swallowed up in victory," and when "this corruptible body shall have put on incorruption, and this mortal body shall have put on immortality" (1 Cor 15:53–54). Then there will be true health, then there will be true and perfect righteousness, so that we shall not only be incapable of doing but even of thinking any evil.

Now destitute, poor, in want, in heaviness we sigh, we groan, we pray, we lift up our eyes to God because they who are happy in this world disdain us, for they are wealthy. And they who are unhappy in this world despise us, for they are also wealthy: There is a righteousness in their hearts but a false kind. Because they are filled with false righteousness they do not come to true righteousness. But so that you may come to true righteousness, be poor and be a beggar as to righteousness itself, and hear the Gospel: "Blessed are they who hunger and thirst after righteousness, for they shall be filled" (Mt 5:6).

Augustine of Hippo

HOMILIES ON THE GOSPEL OF ST. JOHN

Introductory Note. In these homilies Augustine is speaking directly to the People of God in order to teach them, to persuade them, and to allow them to be touched by the Word of God. Stenographers actually recorded the sermons as given. Sitting in his cathedral, he is sharing with those standing around him the fruits of his own meditation on the Gospel made the previous evening. Whatever has nourished his own mind and heart he offers to them while making great efforts to reconcile apparent contradictions in Divine Revelation, usually introducing his sermon with a question. This was the method of catechesis in the Patristic era when religious instruction was the direct responsibility of the bishops. The episcopal office linked the priest more closely to the people. Out of love for his people Augustine wanted to preach effectively. That is why he meditated long and deeply the previous evening, structured his sermons to accomplish some progress in understanding the Gospel, and gave numerous examples from daily life to clarify the meaning of the Divine Word. He considered his preaching responsibility to extend not merely to giving the sermon but to changing minds and hearts, attitudes and lives. "What is it I want," he said to the people one day; "what do I desire? Why do I give sermons? Why am I seated here in my cathedral? What is the purpose of my life? My only purpose is that we should live together with Christ. This is my desire, my honor, my riches, this is my joy and my glory. But if you do not listen to me, since I have not kept silence, I shall save my soul. However, I do not wish to be saved without you" (Sermon 17:2). With his flock he listens to the Interior Master in a common search for truth that will work through love, always asking for light from the Lord.

In the First Homily Augustine preached of the Word of God, asking that we hear it in our hearts—this Word through whom we were made and through whom we shall be remade. And Augustine speaks of all things being in God as divine ideas before being created through the Word. Christians are to come to this Divine Word through the Incarnate Word, that Life which is the Light of men. Those too insensitive to receive the Light, which is always with us, need their eyes cleansed by ridding themselves of sins. Wisdom is always present but one must purify the heart to see it.

Whereas in the First Homily Augustine discusses being made through the Word, in the Twelfth Homily he speaks of being remade through the Spirit, which requires humility. "Two births of Christ are understood: one divine, the other human, one to create us, the other to re-create us, both admirable: in one, there is no mother, in the other, no father. ... He descended because of us; we ascend because of him." In the unity of Christ we shall ascend to heaven; how important then is unity! This is the Christ who entered into death to free us from death. But we shall not be freed from death until we are cured from sin by looking at the crucified Christ in faith. In the Light of Christ, sin is seen for what it is: separation from God and others.

In the two homilies presented here we see references to Manichaeism, Arianism, and Donatism. The many allusions to the Donatists in the early Johannine homilies can be explained by Augustine's position that the African schism was an injury done to Christ. Although the majority of African Christians were Donatists, the Catholic Party defended the primary role of Christ in the Sacraments. The Donatists grounded the validity of the Sacraments and the communication of Grace on the holiness of the human minister of the Sacraments. Hence they rebaptized Christians joining them from the Catholic Party. Augustine looked on this as the Donatist priests putting themselves in the place of Christ, the true and effective power of the sacraments. The Church puts all its hope in Christ; we are the receivers, Christ the giver. John the Baptizer and Paul knew that they baptized only in the name of Christ, who alone is to be glorified. Christ is the seed or descendant of Abraham and all those who belong to Christ belong to the Covenant of Faith.

The Mystery of the Incarnate Word is related to the Mystery of the Church and the Sacraments and to Christ's universal Lordship.

First Homily

On this passage of John: *"In the beginning was the Word, and the Word was with God, and the Word was God,"* and so forth, until *"and the darkness understood Him not."*

In considering what we have heard from Paul (1 Cor 2) that "the natural man does not understand that which is of the Spirit of God" (1 Cor 2:14) and realizing that in this present congregation of church members there are necessarily many natural men who continue to think according to the flesh and are not yet capable of rising to spiritual understanding, my hesitation is great: How, with God's help, can I declare and, what is more, explain properly what is read in the Gospel: "In the beginning was the Word, and the Word was with God, and the Word was God"; for the natural man does not understand this. What then, Brothers, shall we keep silence? Why then read it if only to keep silence about it? Or why hear it if it is not to be explained? But also, why explain it if it is not to be understood?

And so since I do not doubt that there are among you those who cannot only understand the explanation of this passage but the passage itself before it is explained, I shall not deprive those who are not capable of understanding even though I fear wasting the time of those who can understand. Finally perhaps the mercy of God will assist us so that all may be satisfied and each one receive what he can, since he who speaks also says what he can. For who can say what is actually the case? I daresay, my Brothers, that perhaps neither did John himself say what is actually the case, but he also has said what he could, doubtless a man inspired by God, but nevertheless a man.

2

For this John, my very dear Brothers, was one of those mountains of which it was written: "Let the mountains receive peace for your people, and the hills justice" (Ps 71:3). The mountains are great souls; the hills are ordinary souls. But the mountains receive peace so that the hills may receive justice. And what is the justice that the hills receive? Faith, because the just man lives by faith (Hb 2:4; Rom 1:17). For ordinary souls would not receive faith unless the great souls, called mountains, were enlightened by Wisdom itself, so that they might transmit to the little ones whatever the little ones can understand, and so the hills live by faith because the mountains receive peace. By these mountains it was said to the Church: Peace be with you. And in announcing peace to the Church, these mountains have not separated themselves against the one from whom they have received peace, so that they announce peace truly and not hypocritically (Ps 121:3; 124:5).

3

For there are other shipwrecking mountains which destroy any ship striking against them. For it is easy when the earth is sighted by those in peril to direct the ship toward the earth, but sometimes the earth is a mountain, and rocks are hidden at the foot of the mountain and whoever steers toward the mountain is hurled upon the rocks; one does not find a port there but disaster. There were certain mountains like this, and they appeared great among men, and they made heresies and schisms and divided the Church of God. But those who divided the Church of God were not those mountains of which it was said: "Let the mountains receive peace for your people" (Ps 71:3). For how have those who divided unity received peace?

4

But those who received peace to announce to the people have contemplated Wisdom itself insofar as it is possible for human hearts to attain "what eye has not seen, nor ear heard, what has not entered the heart of man" (1 Cor 2:9). But if Wisdom has not entered the heart of man, how did it enter the heart of John? Was not John a man? Or, perhaps, it did not enter the heart of John, but the heart of John ascended to it? For that which ascends into the heart of man is below man; but that to which the heart of man ascends is above man. Also, Brothers, it can be said that if Wisdom ascended into the heart of John it did so insofar as John was not a man. What does this mean: He was not a man? Insofar as he began to be an angel, because all the saints are angels insofar as they are messengers of God.

What in fact does the Apostle say to carnal and natural men who cannot understand the things of God? "When you say: I am Paul, I am Apollo, are you not men" (1 Cor 3:4)? What does he wish to make them, whom he blames for being men? Listen to the Psalm: "I have said: You are gods, and sons of the Most High, all of you" (Ps 81:6). To this, therefore, God calls us, that we no longer be men. But then we shall not be men in a better way if we do not first recognize ourselves as men, that is, if we do not rise to that heavenly state from humility, lest in thinking ourselves to be something we are nothing (Gal 6:3); not only we shall not receive what we are not, but we shall also lose what we are.

5

Therefore, Brothers, John was also among those mountains, he who said: "In the beginning was the Word, and the Word was with God, and the Word was God" (Jn 1:1). This mountain had received peace so that the divinity of the Word was contemplated. What was this mountain like, how high? It surpassed all earthly summits, it surpassed all the spaces of the air, it surpassed the highest stars, it surpassed all the choirs and all the legions of angels. If indeed it had not surpassed everything created it would not have come to the One through whom everything has been made (Jn 1:3). You cannot realize what He surpassed unless you see where He arrived. You question regarding heaven and earth? They have been made. You question regarding all that is in heaven and earth? It is evident with greater reason that they have been made. You question regarding spiritual creatures, Angels, Archangels, Thrones, Dominations, Virtues, Principalities? They themselves have been made. For, after enumerating all these the Psalm concluded thus: "He spoke and they were made; He commanded and they were created" (Ps 148:5). Since He said that they were made, it was through the mediation of the Word that they were made. But if they were made through the Word, the heart of John could not arrive at what he said: "In the beginning was the Word and the Word was with God and the Word was God" unless he transcended all those things which were made through the Word. What, therefore, was this mountain like, how holy, how high among those mountains which received peace for the People of God so that the hills could receive justice (Ps 71:3)?

6

See then, my Brothers, whether John was not among those mountains of which we have previously sung: "I have lifted my eyes to the mountains whence help comes to me" (Ps 120:1). Therefore, my Brothers, if you wish to understand, lift your eyes to this mountain, that is, hearken to the Evangelist, hearken to his meaning. But because these mountains receive peace and "he who places his hope in man" (Jer 17:5) cannot be in peace, do not lift your eyes toward the mountain so that you think that you are placing your hope in man. Say: "I have lifted my eyes toward the mountains whence help comes to me," but also add: "My help comes from the Lord who has made heaven and earth" (Ps 120:2). Let us lift then our eyes toward the mountains whence help will come to us, and yet we must not place our hope in the mountains themselves, for the mountains receive what they have to transmit to us; therefore we must place our hope in the One from whom the mountains themselves receive.

When we raise our eyes toward the Scriptures, because through men the Scriptures are transmitted to us, we raise our eyes to the mountains whence help will come to us, but because those who wrote the Scriptures were men, they were not enlightened by their own light; but he "was the true Light who enlightens every man coming into this world" (Jn 1:9). He was also a mountain, that John the Baptist who said: "I am not the Christ" (Jn 1:20); lest someone placing his hope in the mountain should abandon the One who illumines the mountains, he himself confessed: "Since from his fullness we have all received" (Jn 1:16). You then ought to say: "I have lifted my eyes toward the mountains whence help will come to me," but without attributing to the mountains the help which comes, and adding: "My help comes from the Lord, who has made heaven and earth."

7

Therefore, Brothers, for this I warn you so that when you have raised your heart to the Scriptures when the Gospel announces: "In the beginning was the Word and the Word was with God and the Word was God" and the rest which has been read, you will know that you have raised your eyes to the mountains. For unless the mountains made these things understood, you would not have the least awareness of them. Help has then come from the mountains so that you can first of all hear them; but you are not yet capable of understanding what you have heard. Implore help from the Lord who made heaven and earth, because if the mountains could speak, they could not enlighten by their own light since they themselves have been enlightened in hearing. Hence the one who said these words received them, that John, Brothers, who reclined on the Lord's bosom (Jn 13:23) and who drank from the Lord's bosom what he was to give us to drink. But he gave us words; you must seek understanding from that source whence he has himself imbibed it. You must raise your eyes to the mountains whence help will come to you so that you may receive the cup, that is, the effusion of the Word, and yet because your help comes from the Lord, who made heaven and earth, you must fill your heart at the source where John has filled his: That is why you have said: "My help comes from the Lord who made heaven and earth" (Ps 120:2). Whoever can fill his heart, do so. Brothers, I have said this: Let each one raise his heart as far as he can and let him understand what is said.

But perhaps you think that I am more present to you than God. Not so! He is much closer to you, for I appear to your eyes, but he presides over your consciences. To me your ears, to him your heart, so that each one will be filled. You raise your eyes and your bodily senses toward us and yet not even toward us, for we are not among the mountains, but toward the Gospel itself, toward the Evangelist himself. But as for your heart, toward the Lord you raise it so that he will fill it. Let each one raise his heart, considering well what he is raising and toward whom he raises it. What does this mean: what he raises and toward whom he raises it? Let him consider what heart he raises, because he raises it toward the Lord for fear that, weighed down by the burden of carnal pleasure, this heart may fall back again before having been lifted up. But it seems that each one bears a burden of flesh? Let him work through continence to purify what he will raise toward God. For "blessed are the clean of heart, because they will see God" (Mt 5:8).

8

But what comes from the announcement of these words: "In the beginning was the Word, and the Word was with God, and the Word was God" (Jn 1:1)? And we also in speaking have uttered words. Is it a word of this sort that was with God? These words that we have said, have they not sounded and disappeared? Has the Word of God then sounded and disappeared? How then has "everything been made by it and nothing has been made without it" (Jn 1:3)? How is whatever has been created by it governed by it if it has sounded and disappeared? What then is the Word which is uttered and does not disappear? My Beloved be attentive: This is a great reality. In speaking daily our words have lost their value for us; because they sound and disappear we count them worthless, we consider them only words. But there is also in man himself a word that remains within, for the sound does not proceed from the mouth. There is a word truly spoken spiritually; it is not itself a sound but what you understand from the sound. Thus, I utter a word when I say: God. A very short word, three letters, one syllable. Is it this totality that is God: three letters and one syllable? But as much as this is without value, so much more value is what is understood by them. What happened in your heart when you heard the word God? What happened in my heart when I said the word God? A certain great and highest substance is thought of, which transcends all changing creatures, bodily and animal. And if I say to you: Is God changing or unchangeable? you will immediately answer: Far from me to believe or feel that God is changeable: God is unchangeable. Your soul, although ordinary, although perhaps still carnal, has been able to give only one answer: God is unchangeable. Every creature, however, is changeable.

How then were you able to have this flash of light on what surpasses every creature, to answer me in all certitude that God is unchangeable? What is there then in the depths of your heart when you think of a living substance, eternal, all-powerful, infinite, omnipresent, wholly everywhere, enclosed nowhere? When you think this, this is the Word of God in your heart. But is this that sound which consists of three letters and one syllable? Therefore, those words which are said and which disappear are sounds, are letters, are syllables. This word which sounds disappears; but what the sound signifies and what is found in the thought of the one who spoke and in the understanding of the one who listened, that remains, even when the sounds disappear.

9

Be attentive to this word. If you can have in your heart a word, which is a deliberation born in your mind, such that your mind engenders that deliberation, and the deliberation remains there as the conception of your mind, like the son of your heart —for it is your heart which begins by engendering the deliberation to construct an edifice, to raise up on the earth a vast building—already this plan has been born and the work is not yet realized. You yourself see what you are going to do, but no one else admires it before you have constructed and completed its structure and brought the building to its final construction and perfect completion; men then look at this marvelous building and admire the plan of the builder. They are astonished at what they see and they like what they do not see: the plan, indeed, who can see it?

If, then, beginning from some vast building, we praise a plan of man, do you wish to know that plan of God who is the Lord Jesus Christ, the Word of God? Look at this edifice of the world: See what has been made by the Word, and you will know what the Word is. Look at these two parts of the universe, heaven and earth: Who can tell with words the beauty of heaven; who can tell with words the fruitfulness of the earth? Who will praise, as they merit it, both the cycle of seasons and the power of seeds? You see all that I pass over in silence, fearing by too long an enumeration to say perhaps less than what you can think of. Understand then, starting from this edifice, what is the Word through whom it has been realized; and this is not His only work. All that is indeed seen because it falls under the eye of the body but by this Word the Angels also have been made, and the Powers, the Thrones, the Dominations, the Principalities; by this Word, everything has been made. Judge by that what such a Word is!

10

Someone will perhaps answer me thus: And who is thinking of this Word? When you hear the Word, be unwilling to think of something unworthy and to explain the words you daily hear: Such a one has said such words, he has spoken such words, you relate such words to me: For by constantly using words, words lose their value. Thus when you hear: "In the beginning was the Word," so that you do not imagine something of little value, similar to what you are used to thinking when you hear human words spoken, hear what you must think: "The Word was God!"

11

Let some incredulous Arian now present himself saying: The Word of God was created. How can the Word of God have been created when through the Word of God everything has been made? If the Word of God itself has been made, through what other word has it been made? If you say that there exists a Word of the Word through which it has been made, it is that one that I call the only Son of God; but if you do not speak of a Word of the Word, agree that this Word through whom everything has been made has not itself been made, for the One through whom everything has been made could not have been made through itself.

Believe then in what the Evangelist says. He could indeed say: In the beginning God made the Word, as Moses said: "In the beginning God made heaven and earth" (Gn 1:1), and as he said in naming each one of the creatures: "God said: Let it be made," and it was made (Gn 1:3–27). If he said, who has said it? God, evidently. And what has been made? A creature. Between God who spoke and the creature that was made, what is that through whom was made that which was made, if not the Word? For "God said: Let that be done," and it was done. This Word is unchangeable; although changing things were made by the Word, it itself is unchangeable.

12

Therefore be unwilling to believe that He was made, the One through whom everything has been made, lest you be not remade through the Word through whom all things are remade. For you have already been made through the Word, but it is necessary that you be remade through the Word. But if your faith in the Word is touched by error, you cannot be remade through the Word. And if it has fallen to your lot to be made through the Word, so that through it you were made, through yourself you are defective. If you are defective through yourself, it is necessary that the One who has made you should remake you; if you have deteriorated through yourself, it is necessary that the One who has created you should re-create you.

But how can you be re-created through the Word if you think ill of the Word? The Evangelist says: "In the beginning was the Word"; and you say: In the beginning the Word was made. He says: "All things were made through him," and you say that the Word itself was also made. The Evangelist could have said: In the beginning the Word was made; but what did he say? "In the beginning was the Word." If it was, it was not made, so that all those things were made through it, and without it, nothing. If therefore "In the beginning was the Word, and the Word was with God, and the Word was God," if you cannot think what it is, be attentive and you will grow. He is solid food; take the milk so that you may be nourished and so grow strong enough to take solid food.

13

Certainly, Brothers, as to what follows: "All things were made through him, and without him there was made nothing" (Jn 1:3), see that you do not think that nothing is something. Many indeed who erroneously hear this word: "Without him nothing has been made" are accustomed to thinking that nothing is something. Sin, certainly, has not been made by Him, and it is evident that sin is nothing and that men fall away to nothingness when they sin. And the idol was not made through the Word: It doubtless has a human form, but it is man himself who was made through the Word, for the human form of the idol was not made through the Word, and it is written: "We know that the idol is nothing" (1 Cor 8:4). That has not then been made through the Word. But made through Him are all things which are naturally made, all that is in creatures, absolutely all that dwells in heaven and shines in the firmament, that which flies above in the sky, whatever moves in the universe, every creature without exception; I shall speak most clearly, I shall speak, my Brothers, so that you may understand, everything from the angel to the worm.

What is there among creatures more elevated than the angel, more miserable than the worm? The One who made the angel is also the one who made the worm; but He made the angel worthy of heaven and adapted the worm to the earth. He who created fixed the places of things. If he had placed the worm in heaven you would rebuke Him; if it pleased Him to make the angels be born of rotting flesh, you would rebuke Him for it, and yet it is almost what God did and He is not reprehensible. For all men who are born of flesh, what are they if not worms? And from these worms God made angels. If the Lord said of Himself: "I am a worm and not a man" (Ps 21:7), who would hesitate to say what is written in the book of Job: "How much more is man from decay, and the son of man a worm" (Jb 25:6)? He said first of all: "Man is from decay," and next: "The son of man is a worm" because the worm is born from decay, man is decay and the son of man is a worm. This is what He willed to become for you, the One who "in the beginning was the Word, and the Word was with God, and the Word was God." Why did He become that for you? In order to nourish you, you who could not eat. Therefore, Brothers, receive this absolutely: "All things have been made through Him, and without Him nothing has been made." For all creatures have been made through Him, the greatest, the smallest, the higher and the lower have been made through Him; the spiritual and the corporeal have been made through Him. No form, indeed, no structure, no harmony of parts, no substance of any nature whatsoever which can have weight, number, and measure exists except through this Word, that creative Word of which it was said: "You have disposed all things with measure, number, and weight" (Wis 11:21).

14

Let no one therefore deceive you when perhaps you are disgusted with flies. For some have been held up to ridicule by the devil and they have allowed themselves to be captured by flies. Bird hunters are accustomed, indeed, to place flies in their traps so as to catch hungry birds; these people the devil has likewise caught with flies. There was once someone who was disgusted with flies; a Manichaean found him in the midst of his disgust, and as the other told him that he could not stand flies, he asked him: "And who made them?" And because he was disgusted and hated them he did not dare to say: God made them; but he was a Catholic. Immediately the other exclaimed: "If God did not make them, who made them?" "To speak frankly," the Catholic said, "it seems to me that the devil made the flies." And he immediately said: "If the devil made the fly, as I see that you admit because you think prudently, who made the bee, which is worse than the fly?" The Catholic did not dare to say that God had made the bee and that he had not made the fly when there was so little difference between them! The Manichaean led him from the bee to the locust, from the locust to the lizard, from the lizard to the bird, from the bird to the fish, thence to the ox, thence to the elephant, afterward to man, and persuaded the man that man was not made by God. Thus this unfortunate man, disgusted by flies, became himself a fly by falling into the power of the devil. It is indeed said that Beelzebub signifies prince of flies, of those flies of which it is written: "The flies about to die give forth an oil of sweetness" (Eccl 10:1).

15

What then, Brothers! Why have I said this? Close the ears of your heart to the deceits of the enemy; understand that God has made everything and placed everything in its rank. Why then have we so many evils to suffer from a creature that God has made? Because we have offended God. Must the angels endure these evils? We also, perhaps, do not have to fear them in this life. Of your pain accuse your sin, and not your Judge. For because of pride God has made of this small and most abject creature the instrument of our punishment: Since man has made himself proud and risen up against God, since, mortal, he has terrified another mortal and, man, has refused to recognize in man his neighbor; since he has exalted himself, let him be submitted to insects.

What is it that inflates you with human pride? A man has spoken to you injuriously, and you grow proud and get angry; shove off the flies so that you may sleep, recognize who you are. So that you may know, Brothers, that on account of our pride this insect was created to torment us, God could have subdued the proud people of Pharaoh with bears, with lions, with serpents; he sent them flies and frogs (Ex 8:6, 24) that their pride might be subdued with the vilest things.

16

All things, therefore, absolutely "all things have been made through Him, and without Him nothing was made." But how are all things made through Him? What was made in Him is life (Jn 1:4). It can also be said: That which was made in Him is life: therefore, everything is life if we say it this way. For what is there that was not made in Him? For He Himself is the Wisdom of God, and it is said in the Psalm: "You have made everything in Wisdom" (Ps 103:24). If then Christ is the Wisdom of God and the Psalm says "You have made everything in Wisdom," everything has been made in Him just as everything has been made through Him.

If then everything has been made in Him, dearest Brothers, and that which was made in Him was life, the earth is also life and wood is life—we say, it is true, that the wood is life, but we then understand the wood of the Cross whence we have received life—therefore the stone is also life. This is an unfortunate interpretation which would furnish a new occasion to the abominable Manichaean sect to jump all over us and pretend that the stone has life, that the wall has a soul and rope has a soul, also wool and clothing. This is what they habitually say in their insanity and when opposed and refuted they proclaim it as coming from Scripture! Why then was it said: That which was made in Him is life? If, indeed, everything has been made in Him, everything is life. That they may not lead you astray, say it this way: "That-which-was-made" (stop here and next add): "in Him is life." What does this mean? The earth was made; yet the very earth that was made is not life; but there exists in Wisdom itself, on the spiritual level, an idea according to which the earth was made: This is life.

17

I shall explain it as best I can to you, my Beloved. A worker makes a chest. At first he has the chest in his skill-knowledge: For if he did not have it in his skill-knowledge, how could it be brought forth by making? But the chest as it is in his skill-knowledge is not the chest as it appears to our eyes. In skill-knowledge it exists invisibly, in the work it will exist visibly.

Behold it made in the work; now has it ceased to be in the skill-knowledge? For the former can decay but from the skill-knowledge another can be made. Distinguish then the chest in the skill-knowledge from the chest in the external work. The chest in the external work is not life; the chest in the skill-knowledge is life, because the soul of the worker is living: wherein are all those things before they are externalized. Likewise, very dear Brothers, because the Wisdom of God, through whom all things have been made, contains the knowledge of all things before making them, it follows that all that is realized by means of this knowledge is not of itself life, but that all that has been made is life in Him.

You see the earth, there is also the earth in knowledge; you see the heavens, the heavens are in knowledge; you see the sun and moon; these are also in knowledge; but externally they are bodies, in knowledge they are life. Understand as far as possible how this is so; for a great reality has been stated, and if I am not great, from whom and through whom this comes to you, it nevertheless comes from someone great. For it is not my littleness which has spoken to you of it, but He is not little, He in whose interest I have spoken to you.

Let each one take what he can, as much as he can, and let the one who cannot take nourish his heart so that he can. With what nourishment? Let him be nourished with milk so that later he may come to solid food. Let him not withdraw from Christ born through flesh until he arrive at Christ born from the one Father, the Word God with God, through whom all things have been made, because such is the life which in Him is the Light of men.

18

For this follows: "And the life was the Light of men," and from this life men are enlightened. Beasts are not enlightened because beasts have no rational minds which can see wisdom. But man made to the image of God has a rational mind through which he can perceive wisdom. Therefore that life through whom everything has been made, that life is itself the Light, not of all animals but of men.

Hence a little later the Evangelist says: "He was the true Light which enlightens every man coming into this world" (Jn 1:9). Through this Light John the Baptizer was enlightened, and through it also John the Evangelist. With this Light he was filled, he who said: "I am not the Christ, but it is He who comes after me and I am not worthy to touch the hem of His garment" (Jn 1:20, 27). Through this Light he was enlightened, he who said: "In the beginning was the Word, and the Word was with God, and the Word was God" (Jn 1:1). This life is therefore the Light of men.

19

But perhaps there are insensitive hearts, still incapable of receiving this Light because the weight of their sins prevents them from seeing it. Let them not imagine that the Light is absent because they do not see it, for on account of their sins they are in darkness. "And the Light shone in the darkness, and the darkness understood it not" (Jn 1:5). Therefore, Brothers, like the blind man exposed to the sun, the sun being present to him but he being absent from the sun, so the insensitive one, the sinner, the impious has a blind heart.

Wisdom is present but although present to the blind man, it is absent from his eyes; not that it itself is absent, but that he himself is absent from it. What must be done? Purify that through which God can be seen. Just as when something cannot be seen because one's eyes are soiled and wounded with dust, pus, or smoke, the physician would say: Cleanse your eye of the soils so that you can with your eyes see the light. Dust, pus, smoke, are sins and iniquities; cleanse all that away and you will see the Wisdom who is always present, for God is Wisdom itself, and it is written: "Blessed are the pure in heart because they will see God" (Mt 5:8).

Twelfth Homily

From that place of the Gospel: *"That which is born of flesh is flesh,"* and so forth, to *"But he who does the truth comes to the Light so that it may appear that his works are done in God."*

We realize that you came more quickly and in greater numbers because yesterday we held your attention. But if it is satisfactory we shall be faithful to the ordinary readings in this sermon; later, my Beloved, you will learn with respect to the peace of the Church what we have done and what we hope to do. Now then let the whole intention of your heart bear on the Gospel, let no one think of anything else. For if the one who is wholly attentive scarcely understands, how can the one distracted by various thoughts retain what he understands? My Beloved recall last Sunday when the Lord deigned to help us when we discussed spiritual rebirth (11th Homily). This is the very text that we have reread so that we can complete, in the name of Christ and with the help of your prayers, that which has not yet been explained.

2

There is one spiritual rebirth as there is one carnal birth. And what Nicodemus said to the Lord is true: Man when he is old cannot enter anew into his mother's womb and be reborn. He only said, it is true, that man cannot do it when he is old as though he could do it when he is only a child. For it absolutely cannot be done whether one is newly born or many years old, to enter anew into the maternal womb and be reborn. Just as carnal birth can bring the same man to birth only once, likewise when it is a question of spiritual birth, the womb of the Church can assure to each one only one baptism. That is so that no one may say: But that one was born in heresy, and the other was born in schism; all the difficulties have been eliminated, you may remember by the discussion of our three Fathers, by whom God willed to be called God not because they were themselves alone but because in them alone the future people has been perfectly represented in their totality.

We find a son of a disinherited servant and a son of an inheriting free woman, but we also find a son of a disinherited free woman and a son of an inheriting servant. The son of the disinherited servant: Ishmael; the son of the inheriting free woman: Isaac; the son of the disinherited free woman: Esau; the son of the sons of the inheriting servants: the sons of Jacob. Thus in these three Patriarchs there is presented to us the image of the future people, and God justly proclaims: "I am the God of Abraham, the God of Isaac and the God of Jacob: such is my name forever" (Ex 3:15). Let us recall what was promised to Abraham; for this was promised to Isaac and also to Jacob. What do we find? In your posterity all nations will be blessed (Gn 22:18). Then this one alone believed what he did not see; men see and they are blind. What was promised to one alone is realized in the nations, and those who refuse to see even this realization are separated from the communion of nations. But what use is it to refuse to see? They see, willing or unwilling; the truth is evident and strikes even closed eyes.

3

We have explained the Lord's answer to Nicodemus, who was among those who believed in Jesus, and Jesus Himself did not trust them. For He did not trust Himself to them although they already believed in Him. Thus it was written: "Many believed in his name, seeing the miracles he did. But Jesus did not entrust Himself to them. He had no need in fact that anyone should give testimony on the subject of man, for He Himself knew what was in man" (Jn 2:23–25). Thus already they believed in Jesus and Jesus Himself did not entrust Himself to them. Why? Because they were not yet reborn of water and of the Spirit.

We have therefore exhorted and we again exhort our catechumen brothers. For, if you question them, they have already given their faith to Jesus, but because they do not yet receive His flesh and blood, Jesus is not yet entrusted to them. What should they do so that Jesus may entrust Himself to them? Let them be reborn of water and of the Spirit; let the Church bring into the world those whom she bears. They are conceived; let them be born; let them have breasts to nourish them; let them not fear being suffocated at birth; let them not recede into the maternal womb.

4

No one can return to the womb of his mother and be born anew. But it happens that someone is born of a servant. Is it the case that those who have servants as mothers have returned to the womb of a free woman to be born anew? The seed of Abraham is found also in Ishmael, and that Abraham might be able to have a son of the servant, his wife was the cause of it. Ishmael was born of the seed of the husband, and if not of the seed, at least at the sole instigation of the spouse. Was he disinherited because he was born of a servant? But if he had been disinherited because he was born of a servant, no sons of servants would have been admitted to the inheritance. But the sons of Jacob have been admitted to the inheritance. As for Ishmael, he has been disinherited, not because he was born of a servant, but because he showed himself proud toward his mother, proud toward his mother's son. For his mother was Sara rather than Agar. The one contributed her womb, the other her will: Abraham would not have acted against Sara's will; Ishmael was then, first of all, her son. But because he was proud toward his brother, making sport of him, what did Sara say? "Dismiss the servant and her son, for the son of the servant will not be an heir with my son Isaac" (Gn 21:10).

It was not then his servile birth which brought dismissal but his enslaving pride. Even if he is of free birth, he is a slave, and what is worse, the slave of a bad master, his pride. And so, my Brothers, reply to men that no man can be born again; answer securely that no man can be born again. Whatever is done a second time is illusion; whatever is done a second time is a game. Ishmael plays, let him be dismissed. Sara indeed perceives the children playing, Scripture relates, and she asks Abraham: "Dismiss the servant and her son." This children's game displeases Sara; she perceives something strange about this children's game. Is it that the mothers do not wish their sons to play together? She saw and she disapproved. I do not know what she perceived in the game; she saw an illusion in this game, she noticed the pride of the slave; it displeased her and she dismissed him. The sons of servants are dismissed if they are bad, but Esau, born of a free woman, is likewise dismissed.

Let no one therefore presume on account of their good birth, let no one presume because they are baptized through saints. Let whoever is baptized through saints take care to be Jacob and not Esau. Therefore I shall say this, Brothers: It is better to be baptized by men seeking their own interests and who love the world, which the name of servant signifies, and spiritually seek the inheritance of Christ to be like a son of Jacob born of a servant than to be baptized by saints and be proud like Esau, who had to be dismissed although he was born of a free woman. Retain this teaching, my Brothers. We do not flatter you so that you may place no hope in us; we flatter no one, neither you nor ourselves: Each one has his own burden to carry. Ours is to speak so as not to be condemned: yours is to listen and to listen with your heart, lest an account be asked of what we give or indeed when an account is asked that a gain and not a loss be revealed.

5

The Lord says to Nicodemus and explains to him: "Amen I say unto you, unless someone is reborn of water and the Holy Spirit, he cannot enter into the kingdom of God" (Jn 3:5). You have in mind carnal generation when you object: "Is it possible for a man to enter again into his mother's womb?" (Jn 3:4). But it is of water and the Spirit that it is necessary to be born for the kingdom of God. If one is born to possess the temporal inheritance of a human father, it is necessary to be born of the womb of a carnal mother; but to possess the eternal inheritance of that Father who is God, it is necessary to be born of the womb of the Church. It is through his spouse that a father who will die generates the son who will succeed him. It is through the Church that God generates sons destined not to succeed Him but to dwell with Him. And the Lord continues: "That which is born of the flesh is flesh, and that which is born of the Spirit is spirit" (Jn 3:6).

We are born therefore spiritually, and we are born in the Spirit through the word and the Sacrament. The Spirit intervenes to bring us to birth; the Spirit of whom you are born is invisibly present, since this birth is itself also invisible. The Lord continues and says: "Do not be astonished because I said to you: You must be born again; the Spirit breathes where He wills, you hear His voice, but you know not whence it comes and whither it goes" (Jn 3:7–8). No one sees the Spirit; how do we hear the voice of the Spirit? A Psalm is sung, it is the voice of the Spirit; the Gospel is read, it is the voice of the Spirit; the Word of God is preached, it is the voice of the Spirit. You hear His voice, but you know not whence it comes or whither it goes. And you also, if you are born of the Spirit, you will become such that the one who is not yet born of the Spirit will not know whence you come or whither you go. This is what the Lord said next: "Such is everyone who is born of the Spirit."

6

Nicodemus answered and said to him: "How can this be done?" (Jn 3:9). And truly it cannot be understood in any carnal sense. What the Lord said was accomplished in Him: He heard the voice of the Spirit but he knew not whence it came nor whither it went. Jesus answered him: "You are a master in Israel and you are ignorant of these things?" (Jn 3:10). Oh Brothers, do you think that the Lord wished to insult this master of the Jews? The Lord knew what He was doing; He wished him to be born of the Spirit. No one is born of the Spirit unless he humbles himself, because it is humility which makes us to be born of the Spirit since the Lord is close to the contrite of heart. As a master this man was inflated and believed himself to be important because he was a Doctor of the Jews. The Lord deflates his pride so that he can be born of the Spirit, he mocks him as ignorant without wishing, however, to appear superior to him.

What comparison is there between God and man, truth and falsehood? It would already be ridiculous to say that Christ is greater than the angels, for He is incomparably greater than all creatures, the one through whom all creatures have been made. But He satirizes the pride of man: "You are master in Israel, and you are ignorant of these things?" As if to say: You know nothing, proud leader, you must be born of the Spirit, for if you are born of the Spirit you will keep to the ways of God so that you may follow the humility of Christ. For thus He is above all angels, because "although He was in the form of God, He did not consider it robbery to be equal to God, but He lowered Himself taking the form of servant and was made in the likeness of man and looked like a man so that He humbled Himself as a man and became obedient even unto death (and lest you think it the kind of death which would please you), even to the death of the Cross" (Phil 2:6–8).

He was crucified and they insulted Him. He could descend from the Cross but He preferred to rise from the tomb. The Lord has supported the proud servants and the doctor the sick ones. If He has done that, He who is the true Master in heaven not only of men but also of angels, what should those do for whom it is necessary to be born again of the Spirit? For if the angels have been taught, they were taught through the Word of God. If they have been taught through the Word of God, seek the source of this teaching and you will find: "In the beginning was the Word, and the Word was with God, and the Word was God" (Jn 1:1). The neck of man is brought up, but rough and hard so that it may be a soft neck to carry the yoke of Christ, of which it is said: "My yoke is sweet, and my burden is light" (Mt 11:30).

7

Jesus continues: "If I have spoken of these earthly things and you do not believe, how will you believe if I speak to you of heavenly things?" (Jn 3:12). What earthly things did He speak of, Brothers? "Unless one is born anew," is that an earthly thing? "The Spirit breathes where He wills, and you hear His voice, but you know not whence He comes nor whither He goes," is that an earthly thing? If He indeed spoke of our earthly wind as certain ones understood when asked what the Lord had said that was earthly when He said: "If I have spoken to you of earthly things and you do not believe, how will you believe if I speak to you of heavenly things?"—then as they were asked what the Lord had said concerning the earth, certain ones answered in their embarrassment that by this word: "The Spirit breathes where He wills, and you hear His voice, but you know not whence He comes nor whither He goes," He had spoken of our earthly wind.

What indeed did He call earthly? He spoke of spiritual generation and He added: "So is it with all those born of the Spirit." Next, Brothers, which of us does not see, for example, that the noon south wind blows toward the north, and the wind coming from the east blows toward the west? Therefore how do we not know whence it comes and whither it goes? Then what earthly thing did He say that men did not believe? Or was it when He spoke of the temple that would arise? Indeed He took His body from the earth, and He prepared to raise that very body taken from an earthly body. They did not believe that He would raise up the earth. "If I have spoken to you of earthly things," He says, "and you do not believe, how will you believe if I speak to you of heavenly things?" That is to say: If you do not believe that I can raise up the temple that you have destroyed, how will you believe that men can be reborn through the Spirit?

8

And He continues: "And no one ascends into heaven except the one who descended from heaven, the Son of man who is in heaven" (Jn 3:13). He was on earth and He was in heaven; He was on earth through flesh; He was in Heaven through divinity, or, rather, He was everywhere through divinity. He was born of a mother without leaving His father. Two births of Christ are understood: one divine, the other human; one to create us, the other to re-create us; both admirable: In one there is no mother, in the other, no father. But because He had received His body from Adam, since Mary descended from Adam, and it was precisely this body which was to arise, He had spoken of something earthly in saying: "Destroy this temple and in three days I will raise it up" (Jn 2:19). On the contrary, He spoke of something heavenly in declaring: "No one if not reborn of water and the Spirit will see the Kingdom of God" (Jn 3:5, 3:3).

Yes, Brothers, God willed to be son of man and willed that men become sons of God. He descended because of us; we ascend because of Him. Alone indeed He descended and ascended, He who said: "No one has ascended into heaven except the one who descended from heaven." Those whom He made sons of God, will they not ascend into heaven? Certainly they will ascend, for this promise is made to us: "They will be equal to the angels of God" (Mt 22:30). How is it then that no one has ascended except the one who has descended? Because one descended, one ascended. What of the others? What is to be understood except that they are His members, and one ascended? That is why He continues: "No one has ascended into heaven except the one who descended from heaven, the Son of man who is in heaven. You are astonished that He was simultaneously in heaven and here below? He has given the same privilege to His disciples. Hear Paul the Apostle saying: "But our conversation is in heaven" (Phil 3:20). If as man the Apostle Paul walked in the flesh on earth and conversed in heaven, could not the God of heaven and earth be both in heaven and also on earth?

9

If therefore no other than He descended and ascended, what hope for the others? This hope is for the others: Because He descended so that they may be one in Him and with Him, those who will ascend ascend through Him. The Apostle does not say: "And in your seeds, as if there were many, but as if there were one: And in your seed, which is Christ" (Gal 3:16). And he says to the faithful: "You are of Christ, and since you are of Christ, you are therefore the seed of Abraham" (Gal 3:29). He asserts that we are, altogether, this seed which he had declared unique. That is why in the Psalms sometimes many chant to show that many become one, and sometimes one chants to show that one becomes many. That is also why one sick man was cured at the pool, and all the others who descended there after him were not cured (Jn 5:2–9). Therefore this one manifests the unity of the Church.

How unfortunate those who hate unity and form parties among men! Let them listen to the one who wished to lead men to unity in One alone and for One alone, let them hear him say: You do not multiply! I have planted, Apollo has watered, but it is God who has given the increase; the one who plants is nothing, nor the one who waters, but God who gives the increase, is. They say: "I am Paul's; I am Apollo's; I am Cephas's." And he replies: "Is Christ divided?" (1 Cor 1:12–13). Be in One alone, be a unity, be only one. "No one has ascended into heaven except the one who descended from heaven." We wish to be yours, they say to Paul. And he says: Do not wish to be Paul's, be His to whom Paul belongs along with you.

10

Indeed Christ descended and died and by His death freed us from death; killed by death, He has killed death. And you know, Brothers, that this death entered into the world through the devil's envy. "God did not make death," says Scripture, "and He does not rejoice at the loss of the living, for He has created everything for existence" (Wis 1:13). And what does it say in the same book? "But it is by the devil's envy that death has entered into the universe" (Wis 2:24). Man could not have been forcibly brought to death by the devil: for the devil did not have the power of forcing but the wiliness of persuading. Without your consent the devil would have done no evil; your consent, O man, has led you to death. We are born mortal from mortal parents; from immortals we have been made mortal men. From Adam all men are mortal; as to Jesus, Son of God, Word of God through whom all has been created, only Son equal to the Father, He made Himself mortal, since "the Word was made flesh and dwelt amongst us" (Jn 1:14).

11

Therefore he has taken death and attached death to the Cross, and from death itself mortal men are freed. What was done in figure among the ancients the Lord here recalls: "And just as," He says, "Moses raised the serpent in the desert, so must the Son of man be raised so that all those who believe in Him may not perish, but that they may have life eternal" (Jn 3:14, 16). Profound mystery! Those who have read it know this. But let them listen, those who have not read it or who have perhaps forgotten it after having read or heard it. The people of Israel perished in the desert by the stings of serpents, and there was a great heap of corpses for it was a plague from God which punished and struck them to teach them. This is an admirable symbol of a future reality which was then shown. The Lord Himself witnesses to it in this passage so well that no one can give any other interpretation than the one indicated by the Truth in person. For the Lord ordered Moses to make a brazen serpent and raise it upon wood in the desert and to warn the people of Israel that if anyone were stung by a serpent he had only to look at the serpent raised on the wood. Thus was it done. They were stung, they looked, and they were cured (Nm 21:6–9).

What are the stinging serpents? Sins from the mortality of the flesh. Who is the uplifted serpent? The Lord's death on the Cross. As death came through the serpent it has been imaged by the serpent. The serpent's sting gives death, the Lord's death gives life. One looks at the serpent so that the serpent may no longer have power. What does that mean? So that death may no longer have power, one looks at death. But whose death? The death of Life, if one can speak of Life's death, and, one might say, the expression is marvelous. But must one not say what was done? Shall I hesitate to say what the Lord deigned to do for me? Is Christ not Life? And yet Christ was crucified. Is Christ not Life? And yet Christ died. But in the death of Christ death has died because Life struck by death killed death, the plenitude of Life has engulfed death, death has been destroyed in the body of Christ. So we shall say at the Resurrection when in triumph we shall sing: "Death where is your power? Death, where is your sting?" (1 Cor 15:55).

Until we are cured, Brothers, from sin, let us look at the crucified Christ for, He says, "just as Moses raised the serpent in the desert, so must the Son of man be raised so that those who believe in Him may not perish but may have eternal life" (Jn 3:14, 16). Just as those who already have looked at the serpent did not die from the stings of the serpents, so those who through faith look at the death of Christ are cured of the stings of sins. They were cured from death to enjoy a temporal life but Christ asserts here: so that they may have eternal life. Such is indeed the difference between the figure and the reality: The figure gives only a temporal life, the reality of which it was the figure gives eternal life.

12

"For God has not sent His Son into the World to judge the world but that the world may be saved through Him" (Jn 3:17). Therefore as a physician He comes to cure the sick. He who refuses to follow the prescriptions of the physician really kills himself. The Savior came into the world: Why is He called the Savior of the world except that He came to save the world and not to judge it? If you do not wish to be saved by Him, you will be judged by yourself. And what is meant by: You will be judged? Hear what He says: "He who believes in Him is not judged, but he who does not believe." What do you think He will say if not: He is judged? "Already," He said, "he has been judged." The judgment has not yet taken place and yet judgment has already been rendered. "The Lord knows indeed those who are His own"

(2 Tm 2:19). He knows those who endure for the crown and those who endure for the flame; He knows the wheat in His field, He knows the straw; He knows the wheat, He knows the cockle. Already he who does not believe has been judged: "Because he has not believed in the name of the only Son of God" (Jn 3:18).

13

But this is the judgment, because the Light came into the world and men loved darkness rather than light because their works were evil (Jn 3:19). My Brothers, whose works did the Lord find good? The works of none; He found the works of all evil. How therefore have certain ones done the truth and come to the Light? For He continues thus: "But he who does the truth comes to the light so that it may appear that his works are done in God" (Jn 3:21). How have certain ones done a good work to come to the Light, that is, to Christ? And how have certain ones loved darkness? If indeed He has found all sinners and has cured all from sin, and if that serpent which symbolized the death of Christ cured those who had been stung and if it is because of the sting of the serpent that the serpent was lifted up, that is, the death of the Lord, on account of mortal men whom He found unjust, how is this to be understood: "Such is the judgment: Light came into the world, and men have loved darkness rather than Light because their works were evil"? What is that trying to say? Who are those whose works were good? Did you not come to justify the impious?

But, He said, they have loved darkness rather than the Light. There is the main point: Many in fact have loved their sins, many have confessed their sins, because he who confesses his sins acts already with God. God accuses your sins; if you also accuse them, you join yourself to God. Man and the sinner are, so to speak, two realities; when you hear man spoken of, it is God who has made him; when you hear the sinner spoken of, it is man who has made him. You must hate in yourself your work and love in yourself God's work.

When you begin to detest what you have made, then your good works begin because you accuse yourself of your bad works. The beginning of good works is the confession of bad works. You do the truth and you come to the Light. What does this mean: You do the truth? You cease to praise yourself, to flatter yourself, to worship yourself, to say to yourself "I am just" when you are unjust; you begin then to do the truth. And you come to the Light to show that your works are done in God. That very thing which displeases you, your sin, would not displease you if God did not enlighten you and if His truth did not show it to your eyes. On the contrary, a man, even after having been warned, hates the Light and flies from it so that it may not reveal his evil deeds, which he loves.

Whoever loves the truth accuses his evils; he does not spare himself, he does not pardon himself so that God will pardon him, for he himself recognizes what he wishes, that God may pardon him, and he comes to the Light, to whom he gives thanks for having shown him what he should hate in himself. He says to God: "Turn your face from my sins" (Ps 50:11), and by what shame he says this is clear when he says: "Since I know my deeds, and my sin is always before me" (Ps 50:5). Keep in front of you what you do not wish to be in front of God. But if you put your sin behind you, God will restore it before your eyes when there will be no fruit of penance.

14

Run, lest darkness overcome you, my Brothers; be vigilant for your salvation, watch while there is time: Let no one keep you from coming to the temple of God, let no one keep you from doing the work of the Lord, let no one turn you from continual prayer, let no one deprive you of your customary devotion. Be vigilant then while it is still day; the day shines, Christ is the day. He is ready to pardon those who recognize their faults; He is ready to punish those who defend themselves, professing themselves just, thinking themselves to be something when they are nothing (Gal 6:3).

As for the one who walks in His love and His mercy, although freed from grave and mortal sins like crimes, homicides, thefts, adulteries, he still does the truth by confessing those faults which might appear light, committed in his conversations, his thoughts, or the immoderate use of permitted things, and he comes to the Light by good works. Indeed, little sins by multiplying eventually kill the soul if one neglects them. They are all small, drops of water which fill the rivers; grains on the threshing floor are small, but if many are placed on the threshing floor, it bends and breaks. So it happens with neglected leaks, which bring about a rushing overflow: Little by little, drops enter through the leak but upon entering and not being emptied, they sink the ship. What is meant by our emptying the leak if not watching through good works, fasts, pardoning injuries, so as not to be engulfed by sins?

Our present culture is difficult, it is filled with temptations; one must not exult in prosperity nor be broken by adversity. He who gave the felicity of this century gave it to console you, not to corrupt you; if, on the contrary, He chastises you in this century, He does it to correct you, not to lose you. Accept the lessons from the Father so that you do not have to undergo the punishment of the Judge. This is what we repeat to you every day, and it is necessary to repeat it often because it is good and salutary.

Augustine of Hippo

HOMILY ON
THE FIRST EPISTLE
OF ST. JOHN

Introductory Note. Augustine tells us that after preaching his Twelfth Homily on the Gospel according to John he interrupted these Gospel homilies to comment on the First Epistle of John during the Easter Octave and the Paschal Season. The African Schism, Donatism, influenced Augustine's choice of this Epistle on charity and unity.

The commentary begins with an act of faith in the Divine-human Christ through whom we know God and commune with Him. God reveals Himself as the Light of our Faith and as Love, source of our charity. Through Divine Light we can break with sin and obey the commandments, overcome the demon and resist Antichrists. In opening ourselves to Divine Love we become the children of God, who is Love, and gradually grow in likeness to God by fraternal love until we shall see Him as He is when this likeness becomes perfect. "Where charity exists, there is peace; and where humility exists, there is charity."

In the first part of the commentary Augustine speaks of the heretics who deny the divinity of Christ and yet people can be practical heretics by agreeing that Christ is the Son of God who died for us out of love and yet not following Him in that love. The commandments are all grounded in the love of God and neighbor. Christian perfection is the perfection of charity, which includes the love of enemies. The first responsibility of the Christian is faith, but this really means Faith in God's love for us. Only such faith gives rise to the love that casts out fear and leads to doing the truth with joy and delight in the spirit of the freedom of the children of God.

In fraternal love one not only knows God but knows, in the obscurity of faith, the Trinity. "You see the Trinity if you see charity" (De Trin. VIII.8.12). All love has a relative character, and therefore if God is believed to be Love, something like divine Trinitarian Life is understood. The Holy Spirit is properly Love, the Gift that enables us to participate in that charity which is the Divine Essence and which the Incarnation so splendidly manifests. What Revelation told the pagan world was the Good News that God was Love and therefore loved all persons with a love that was self-giving. By giving Himself as charity through the Spirit, God restores the image of God in man through the likeness of love. As Augustine grew older, he sought for religious experience more in fraternal charity than in contemplation. The experience of loving the neighbor was an experience of God.

Treatise Seven

This world is for all the faithful seeking the Fatherland what the desert was for the people of Israel. Doubtless they still wandered and looked for the Fatherland: but with God as leader they could not lose their way. The way for them was God's commandment. Where they wandered for forty years, the way included very few steps and it was known to all. They were delayed because they were being tried, not because they were being abandoned. What God therefore promised us is ineffable sweetness and the good, as Scripture says, and as you have often heard us reminding you: "that which eye has not seen nor ear heard, nor has it entered into the heart of man" (Is 64:4; 1 Cor 2:9). But the works of this temporal life exercise us and the temptations of this present life instruct us. But if you do not wish to die of thirst in the desert, drink charity. This is the fountain the Lord has willed to place here, lest we faint on the way, and we shall drink it more abundantly when we come to the Fatherland.

Now the Gospel has been read; I shall speak of those words which ended the reading—what else except charity? Indeed we have made a pact with our God in prayer that if we wish our sins to be forgiven us, we ourselves must forgive the sins committed against us (Mt 6:12). Only charity forgives them. Remove charity from the heart; hatred remains and knows not how to pardon. Where there is charity, it pardons with confidence, for it is not a closed heart. But see if this entire epistle, which we have undertaken to comment on for you, recommends anything other than charity. And we should not fear that by speaking of it we shall conceive a strong aversion to it. What indeed could one love if one conceived a strong aversion to charity? This charity which makes other things be loved well, how should it not be loved? Therefore this reality which ought never to be absent from the heart, let it not be absent from our lips.

2

"Now you are children of God, and you have overcome him": who, if not the Antichrist? "Whoever divides Jesus Christ and denies that he has come in the flesh is not of God" (1 Jn 4:3). We have explained to you, if you remember, that all those who violate charity deny that Jesus Christ has come in the flesh. There would have been no reason for Jesus to come except for charity. Indeed this charity which is recommended to us is that which He Himself recommends in the Gospel: "Greater love than this no one can have than to give one's life for one's friends" (Jn 15:13). How could the Son of God give His life for us except by taking on flesh so that He could die? Then whoever violates charity, whatever he says in words, denies by his very life that Christ has come in the flesh: and this is the Antichrist, wherever he is, wherever he goes.

But what did John say to those who are the citizens of this Fatherland toward which we sigh? "You have overcome him." And how have they overcome him? Because he who is in you is greater than he who is in this world. Fearing lest they attribute the victory to their own strength and are conquered by their arrogant pride—whomever the devil makes proud, he conquers—and wishing them to keep humility, what does John say? "You have overcome him." Every man who hears these words raises his head, holds himself upright, looks for praise. Do not praise yourself, see who overcomes in you. Why have you overcome? "Because He who is in you is greater than he who is in this world." Be humble, bear your Lord: go quietly under your rider. It is good for you that He directs and leads. For if you had not Him for rider, you might raise your neck, you could kick; but woe to you without a guide; because this liberty delivers you to the beasts to be devoured.

3

As for them, they are of the world. Who? The Antichrists. John has already told you who they are. And if you are not among them, you know them; but whoever is among them does not know them. As for them, they are of the world: that is why they speak the language of the world and the world listens to them. Who are those who speak the language of the world? Notice those who speak against charity.

You have heard the Lord say: "If you pardon men their sins, your heavenly Father will also pardon you: but if you do not pardon, neither will your heavenly Father pardon you your sins" (Mt 6:14–15). This is a statement of truth: or, if it does not state the truth, contradict it. If you are a Christian and believe Christ, it is He who said: "I am the Truth" (Jn 14:6). This statement is true, that is certain. Now hear the men speaking the language of the world. What! You are not going to avenge yourself, and that one will boast of what he has done to you! By all means let him feel that he is dealing with a man. Such things are said every day. Those who say these things speak the language of the world and the world listens to them. Only those who love the world say such things; only those who love the world listen to such things. And he who loves the world and neglects charity, you have heard that he denies that Jesus has come in the flesh. Has the Lord who came into the flesh acted in such a way? When He was slapped on the cheek, did He will to avenge himself? When He hung on the Cross, did He not say: "Father, forgive them, for they know not what they do" (Lk 23:34)? But if He who has power does not threaten, why should you threaten, why should you get angry, you who are under the power of another? He died because he willed it, and He did not threaten; you do not know when you will die, and you threaten?

4

As for us, we are of God. Let us see why: see if this is on account of anything other than charity. We, we are of God. Whoever knows God listens to us; whoever is not of God does not listen to us. From this we know the spirit of truth and of error. Because whoever hears us has the spirit of truth; whoever does not hear us has the spirit of error. Let us see what he advises, and let us hear by preference the one advising in the spirit of truth; not Antichrists, not the lovers of the world, and not the world. If we are born of God, "Most dearly beloved," continues John, see what he said: "As to us, we are of God. Whoever knows God listens to us; whoever is not of God does not listen to us. That is why we recognize the spirit of truth and the spirit of error." Already we are attentive: for whoever knows God hears Him; and whoever does not know God does not hear Him: and this discernment is of the spirit of truth and of error. Let us see what he will teach us, in which we should listen to him: "Dearly beloved, love one another." Why? Because a man advises this? Because love is of God. He has greatly commended love because He said: "It is of God": He will say more if we listen intently. He simply said: "Love is of God, and anyone who loves is born of God and knows God." Whoever does not love does not know God. Why? Because God is Love. What more can be said, my Brothers? If one did not find one word in praise of love through all the pages of this epistle, nor the least word throughout all the other pages of Scripture, and we heard only this one word from the voice of the Spirit of God: Because "God is Love," we should seek for nothing more.

5

You see now that to act against love is to act against God. No one should say: I sin against man when I do not love my brother. Pay attention: To sin against man is a light matter; only against God I should not sin. How will you not sin against God when you sin against love? "God is Love." Do we say this? If we should say, "God is Love," perhaps one of you would be scandalized and would say: What does he say, what does he wish to say when he pretends that God is love? God gave love, God has made the gift of love. "Love is from God: God is Love." Behold you have here, my Brothers, the Scriptures of God: This epistle is canonical; it is declared among all peoples; it has authority in the entire world; it has edified the entire world. Here you hear the Spirit of God saying: "God is Love." Now, if you dare, act against God and refuse to love your brother.

6

But how reconcile what was previously said: "Love is from God"; and what is presently said: "God is Love." For God is Father, Son, and Holy Spirit: the Son, God from God; the Holy Spirit, God from God; and the three are only one God, not three Gods. If the Son is God, if the Holy Spirit is God, and if He loves in whom dwells the Holy Spirit: Therefore God is Love; but God who comes from God. For you find in the epistle the two formulas: "love is from God," and "love is God." Only of the Father does Scripture not mean to say that He is from God. But when you hear "from God," either the Son is to be understood or the Holy Spirit.

But because the Apostle tells us: "The charity of God has been poured out in our hearts through the Holy Spirit who is given to us," we should understand that the Holy Spirit is in love. For it is the Holy Spirit who cannot receive the wicked; he is the fountain of whom Scripture speaks: "The Fountain of water belongs to you as your own, and let no stranger share it with you" (Prv 5:16–17). All those who do not love God are strangers, are Antichrists. And although they enter the churches, they cannot be numbered among the sons of God; the Fountain of life does not belong to them. The wicked can also have baptism, the wicked can also have the gift of prophecy. We notice that King Saul had the gift of prophecy; he persecuted innocent David, and he was filled with the gift of prophecy and began to prophesy (1 Sm 19). The wicked can also receive the Sacrament of the body and blood of the Lord, for of such men it was said: "He who eats and drinks unworthily eats and drink his condemnation" (1 Cor 11:29). The wicked can also bear the name of Christ; in other words, the wicked can be called Christian; of them it was said: "They dishonor the name of God" (Ex 36:20). Therefore the wicked can participate in all these mysteries; but to have charity and to be wicked, this cannot be. This is the more intimate gift; this is the singular Fountain. The Spirit of God invites you to drink there; the Spirit of God invites you to imbibe Him.

7

In this is manifested the love of God for us. Behold, we are urged to love God. Could we love Him unless He has first loved us? If we were slow to love Him, we should not be slow to return His love. He has first loved us and not because we were loving. He loved the sinners but effaced the sin; He loved the sinners, but He did not call us together so that we might commit sin. He loved the sick but He cured them. Therefore God is Love. In this the love of God is shown forth in us, because He sent His only-begotten Son into this world that we might live through Him. The Lord Himself said this: "Greater love than this no man has than to give one's life for one's friends." And there the love of Christ for us was proven, because he died for us.

And what proof have we of the Father's love? This: That for

us He sent His only Son to death: The Apostle Paul says this: "He who did not spare his own Son but delivered Him for us all, how would He not have given all with him?" (Rom 8:32). Behold, the Father delivered over Christ, Judas delivered Him over; is this not apparently the same act? Judas is a traitor; therefore the Father is also a traitor? Far be such a thought from me, you say. I do not say, but the Apostle says: "He who did not spare His own son but delivered Him for us all." The Father has delivered Him over, and He delivered Himself over. This same Apostle said: "He has loved me and delivered Himself for me" (Gal 2:20). If the Father has delivered the Son and if the Son has delivered Himself, what has Judas done? This treacherous delivery was done by the Father, this treacherous delivery was done by the Son, this treacherous delivery was done by Judas; one same thing was done. But what distinguishes the Father delivering the Son from the Son delivering Himself from the disciple Judas delivering over his master?

The Father and the Son do this in charity; but Judas does this as betrayal. You see that not only what man does must be considered but the spirit and the intent in doing it. In one and the same action we find God the Father doing what Judas does; we bless the Father; we detest Judas. Why do we bless the Father and detest Judas? We bless charity; we detest iniquity. For how greatly is not the human race indebted to the delivering over of Christ? But did Judas have this in mind in delivering Him? God had in mind our salvation in redeeming us; Judas had in mind money for selling his master. The Son Himself had in mind the price He gave for us; Judas had in mind the price he would receive for selling his master. A different intention makes a different act. Only one same act: but if we measure it according to the difference in intention, we find matter to love, matter to condemn, matter to glorify, matter to detest. So it is with charity. See that it alone discerns, see that it alone distinguishes the acts of man.

8

We have spoken here of similar acts. In different acts we find a man acting cruelly through charity and acting agreeably through wickedness. A father beats his child, and a slave-master is kind to his slave. If you were to choose between the two things, lashes and kindness, who would not choose kindness and flee from lashes? If you consider the persons, charity does the beating, wickedness is kind. See what we have praised, because the acts of man are not distinguished except by being rooted in charity. For many things can appear to be good and not proceed from the root of charity. Therefore once for all this short command is given to you: "Love and do what you will." If you keep silent, keep silent by love, if you speak, speak by love; if you correct, correct by love; if you pardon, pardon by love: let love be rooted in you, and from this root nothing but good can grow.

9

"In this is love. In this is shown forth the love of God for us, that God has sent His only Son into this world so that we might live through Him. In this is love, not because we have loved Him but because He has loved us." We have not first loved Him: for He has loved us to this end, that we might love Him. "And He sent His Son as propriation for our sins"; propriation sacrifice. He has sacrificed Himself for our sins. Where did He find the offering? Where did He find the pure victim He wished to offer? He found no other, He offered Himself. "Most dearly beloved, if God has so loved us, we also ought to love one another." "Peter," He said, "do you love me?" And Peter answered: "I do love you." "Feed my sheep" (Jn 21:15–17).

10

No one has ever seen God. God is an invisible reality; He is to be sought not with the eyes but with the heart. But just as in order to see our sun we purify our bodily eyes so that we can see the light, likewise, if we wish to see God, let us purify the eye which allows us to see Him. Where is this eye? Listen to the Gospel: "Blessed are the pure of heart for they shall see God" (Mt 5:8). For no one through earnest desire of the eyes knows God. For either he represents to himself an immense form, an infinite greatness extending through space as this light seen by our eyes which advances as far as possible through the land; or, indeed, he represents to himself an old man of venerable form. Think of nothing like this.

This is what you should think, if you wish to see God: "God is Love." What face has love? What form has it? What height? What feet? What hands? No one can say. Yet it has feet, for they lead to the Church; it has hands, for they care for the poor; it has eyes, for through them the needy one is known: "Blessed," He said, "is he who watches over the poor and the needy" (Ps 40:2). Love has ears, of whom the Lord spoke: "He who has ears to hear, let him hear" (Lk 8:8). These are not members spatially separated, but whoever has charity sees everything simultaneously through thought. Dwell in it and it will dwell in you; remain in it, and it will remain in you.

But, my Brothers, who loves what he does not see? But then why when charity is praised do you stand up, acclaim and praise it? What have I shown you? Have I shown you some colors? Have I presented before you gold or silver? Have I dug up precious gems from a treasure hoard? Have I shown any such thing to your eyes? Has my face changed while I was speaking to you? I keep this face of flesh; I am in the same form in which I came here, and you are in the very same form in which you came. Charity is praised and you acclaim it. Certainly you see nothing. But if it pleases you to praise it, let it also please you to retain it in your heart.

Attend to what I am going to say, my Brothers: I exhort you, insofar as God gives me the grace, to seek a great treasure. If one were to show you a small vase of wrought gold, perfectly made, capable of charming your eyes, of fulfilling your heart's desire, entranced as you are with the work of the artist, the weight and splendor of the metal, would not each one of you say: "Oh, if I possessed that vase"? And in vain would you say this because this vase would not be yours. Or, if someone wanted it, he would think of stealing it from another's house. Charity is praised before you; if it pleases you, take it, possess it; there is no need to steal it from another, there is no need to buy it. It costs nothing. Take it, embrace it: there is nothing sweeter. If it is such when it is commended, what must it be when possessed?

11

If ever you wish to preserve charity, my Brothers, above all do not think of it as something languishing and idling; nor that it is preserved by a kind of meekness—I do not mean meekness, but by a kind of laziness and negligence. It is not preserved in that way. Do not think that you love your son when you do not strike him, or that you love your son when you do not discipline him, or that you love your neighbor when you do not correct him: That is not charity but weakness. Let your charity be fervent to correct, to amend. If behavior is good, take delight in it; if wicked, let it be amended, corrected. Do not love the error in man but love the man. For man is the work of God; error is the work of man. Love the work of God, not the work of man. To love the latter is to destroy the former; to cherish the former is to purify the latter. But even if you are sometimes roused to anger, let it be by love of setting things right.

That is why charity is represented by a dove, which comes above the Lord (Mt 3:16). Under this form of the dove the Holy Spirit comes to pour out His charity into you. Why so? The dove has no bitterness; yet it struggles with its beak and its wings to defend its nest; it strikes without harshness. The father also does this; when he punishes his son, he punishes for the sake of discipline. As I have said, the deceiver, in order to betray, flatters with great vehemence: The father, in order to correct, punishes without bitterness. So you should be to all.

Consider, my Brothers, this great teaching, this great rule: Each of you has children or desires to have them; or, if you have decided not to have children according to the flesh, at least you desire to have them according to the spirit. But who is he who does not correct his son; who is he to whom the father does not give discipline (Heb 12:7)? And yet he seems cruel. Love is cruel, charity is cruel: It is somehow cruel without bitterness, in the way of the dove rather than the snake.

So it enters my mind to tell you, my Brothers, that the violators of charity make a schism: Just as they hate charity, they likewise hate the dove. But the dove has convinced them of their fault: It proceeds from heaven, the heavens are opened and it rests above the head of the Lord. Why? In order to say: "It is He who baptizes" (Jn 1:33). Retire, you thieves, retire, you invaders of the possessions of Christ. To your possessions which you pretend to rule, you have dared to attach property titles. He knows his own titles. He will assert His claim to His own possession; He does not destroy the titles but enters and takes possession. So when a man returns to the Catholic Church, his baptism is not destroyed, lest the title of his Ruler be destroyed. But what happens in the Catholic Church? The title is recognized; the owner enters into his own titles where the robber entered under titles belonging to another.

Augustine of Hippo

ON THE TRINITY

Introductory Note. This work was undertaken by Augustine without his being asked to write it by others. It is true that a strong heresy of the fourth century was that of Arius, who attempted to be utterly faithful to Christianity as monotheism by teaching the "natural" subordination of the Son to the Father. He spoke of the Son and the Spirit as creatures.

Yet Augustine's treatise on the Trinity is theological rather than polemical, an instance of faith seeking understanding. It is, moreover, a work that manifests the intimate connection between theology and spirituality. He begins in Book I with the teaching of the Trinity derived from Scripture and articulated in the Council of Nicaea as well as by the Cappadocian Fathers, Basil of Caesarea, Gregory of Nyssa, Gregory of Nazianzus:

> *Father, Son, and Holy Spirit constitute a divine unity of one and the same substance in an indivisible equality. Therefore they are not three gods but one God; although the Father has begotten the Son and, therefore, He who is Father is not the Son; and the Son was begotten by the Father and, therefore, He who is the Son is not the Father; and the Holy Spirit is neither the Father nor the Son, but only the Spirit of the Father and the Son, and He Himself is also co-equal with the Father and the Son and belongs to the unity of the Trinity.*

In the first few books Augustine explains that Scriptural statements regarding the Son as less than the Father refer to the Son in the "form of a servant" when made flesh. He then discusses the "Missions" of Son and Spirit in the world. The Son's great Mission was the Incarnation. He became flesh to manifest God's love in order to cure us from pride, heal us from the wounds of sin, and unify us as His Mystical Body. The Holy Spirit's main Mission was made evident at Pente-

cost, and the Spirit continues in the Church to vivify it with truth and charity.

After interpreting Scripture Augustine uses reason to show that the distinction between substantive and relative terms can safeguard the divine simplicity and the unity in nature of the three divine Persons. Person, according to Augustine, is not an adequate term to use of any one of the three-in-one-God because it usually denotes a substance. In the Trinitarian context it is used to say that as Son (person), that is, related to the Father, the Son is not the Father (person), that is, Begetter of the Son. It is therefore more accurate to say: God is Father, Son, and Spirit than to say God is three Persons.

In Book VIII, which is presented here, Augustine enters into himself to study the soul in order the better to understand the Trinity. As image of God, there must be in man a unity in trinity, and Augustine first finds this in love, which is impossible without a lover, a beloved, and a loving. God has been revealed as Love and this demands plurality. The way to a knowledge of God is to be achieved by love, not any kind of love, but charity, the Gift of God. Augustine was greatly impressed by the Johannine Gospel and epistles where we learn that God becomes present where there is love.

But we cannot remain at the level of the image. The Christian is called to ascend from the image to the contemplation of the Divine Reality. In Book XIV, presented here, we find the culmination of the spiritual life to be the soul's participation in Divine Wisdom wherein God Himself is the object of the mind's memory, understanding, and will. If God has made us toward Himself, then our hearts will be restless until they rest in Him. Therefore the spiritual life embraces both time and eternity. The one reality that is present here below and will forever continue is that of charity, which requires the presence of God and our awareness of God as Love. Through the gift of charity, or Grace, God unites people together and as a temple or sacred city they are a dwelling place of the Trinity-God in whose likeness they grow in the measure of their love.

Book Eight

We have already noted that the only terms strictly suitable to distinguish the several Persons of the Trinity are those denoting their mutual relations: Father, Son, and Holy Spirit, the Gift of both Father and Son. The Trinity is neither Father nor Son nor Gift. But the terms suitable to the Persons, taken in themselves, denote not three beings in the plural, but one, that is, the Trinity itself: Hence the Father is God, the Son is God, the Holy Spirit is God; the Father is good, the Son is good, the Holy Spirit is good; the Father is almighty, the Son is almighty, the Holy Spirit is almighty. Nevertheless, there are not three Gods, nor three goods, nor three almightys but one God, good, almighty —the Trinity itself. This is the same for every other term denoting not a mutual relation but the Persons taken in themselves. Such terms may be called "essential" insofar as the essence or being of God is the same as His being great, good, wise and whatever else is true either of each person or of the Trinity itself. We make use of the expression "three Persons" or three Substances not to point to any difference in essence, but to provide some one word whereby to answer the question: *what* are these "three"?

There is in this Trinity an absolute equality. The Father is not greater in divinity than the Son; nor together are the Father and the Son greater than the Holy Spirit; nor is any single Person of the three anything less than the Trinity itself. All this has been previously asserted, and repetition may strengthen the idea in our minds. But we must set a limit to our treatise. Let us now reverently and devoutly invoke God to open our understanding and take from us a contentious spirit so that our mind, freed from the notion of material mass or motion, may contemplate the essence of truth. We now propose, insofar as the Creator's own marvelous mercy may help us, to resume our previous theme by using a more inward method of approach. We shall keep to the same rule of holding fast by faith the truth not yet clear to our understanding.

Chapter One

2

We affirm that two or three Persons in this Trinity are not a greater reality than any one of them. Our material way of thinking goes against our grasping this for the simple reason that although it is aware according to its capacity of the truly existing realities which were created, it cannot perceive Truth itself which has created them. If it could perceive Truth, the fact previously affirmed would be as clear as daylight. Only Truth itself has true being: There is nothing greater in substance except that which more truly is. But there cannot be degrees of truth in the sphere of the spiritual and the changeless, for in that sphere everything is equally changeless and eternal. What is called "great" is great from no other source than from that by which it truly is. If, therefore, greatness itself is truth, to have more greatness should mean to have more truth: Whatever has not more truth does not also have more greatness. Whatever has more truth is the truer being just as whatever has more greatness is the greater. So, in this sphere the truer being is the greater.

But Father and Son together have no more true being than the Father alone or the Son alone. Both together, therefore, are no greater reality than either of them alone. And since the Holy Spirit exists no less truly, neither are Father and Son together a greater reality than the Spirit, because they are not a reality existing more truly. The Father and Son together, since they do not surpass the Son in truth—for their being is no truer—do not surpass Him in greatness. So the Son and Holy Spirit together are as great a reality as the Father alone, because they exist no less truly. And the Trinity itself has the same greatness as any one Person, for where Truth itself is greatness, the Person who is not truer is not greater. In the essential reality of truth, to be true is to be: To be is to be great. To be great, therefore, is to be true. In this sphere, then, that which is equally true must there be also equally great.

Chapter Two

3

Among material things one piece of gold may be as true as another and yet one may not be as great as another since in the material sphere greatness is not identical with truth; it is one thing to be gold, another to be great. It is the same with the soul, which we do not call true in respect to the same quality which allows us to call it great. A true soul belongs no less to the one who is not great-souled. For the essence of body and soul is not the essence of truth itself, as the Trinity is God, one sole, great, truly real, really true, Truth itself.

If, as far as He allows and grants, we would think of Him, we should think of no spatial contact or connection, no conjoined structure like that of the three-bodied Geryon in the legend. Any image like that, greater in its three parts than in any one of them, less in one than in two, would be spontaneously rejected just as we reject everything material in thinking of God. Nothing change-able, even in the order of spirit, should be taken for God. Before we can know what God is as we rise from the lower depths in which we live and long for the heights of heaven, our knowledge will not be insignificant if we can at least know what He is not. Surely He is neither earth nor sky, nor of the nature of earth and sky nor of anything visible in the sky or that may exist there invisibly. Imagine the sun's light magnified; make it greater or brighter as you wish, a thousand times or innumerable times: God will not be there. Think of the being of pure angelic spirits, animating celestial bodies, changing and turning them at will for the service of God. Not if all the thousand thousands were made into one will God be any such reality, not even if you could think of those very spirits as bodiless, difficult as that is for our material-ly influenced thinking.

Behold, if you can, you a soul weighed down by many and various earthly thoughts, behold and see, if you can that God is Truth. It is written, "God is Light" (1 Jn 1:5)—not the light seen by our eyes but that seen by the heart upon hearing the words: "He is Truth." Ask not: What is Truth? Immediately there will arise the mists of sensible images, thick clouds of phantasms darkening that clear empyrean which shone forth momentarily upon your sight at that word "Truth." At that moment, hold fast—if possible—that flash of vision that touches you with the word "Truth." But it is not possible: You fall back into that familiar world of earthly realities. And I ask: What is the weight pulling you down again if not the defilements acquired from the mire of passion and the delusions of your earthly pilgrimage?

Chapter Three

4

Try again and think of it this way. Only what is good attracts your love. The earth with its high mountains, gentle hills, level plains is good. The lovely and fertile land is good; the sturdy house with its proportions, its spaciousness and light is good. The bodies of living things are good; the mild and healthy air is good; pleasurable and health-giving food is good; health itself, a freedom from pain and exhaustion, is good. The human face with its symmetrical features, its glad countenance, its high coloring is good; the heart of a friend whose companionship is sweet and whose love is loyal is good; a righteous man is good; wealth for what it enables us to do is good; the sky with its sun, moon, and stars is good; the angels by their holy obedience are good; speech which teaches persuasively and counsels suitably is good; the poem of musical rhythm and profound meaning is good.

But enough! This is good and that is good; take away "this" and "that," and gaze if you can upon good itself: Then you will behold God, good not through the having of any other good thing, but He is the goodness of every good. For we could not affirm by a true judgment that any one of those good things I have cited (or others you may see or think of) is better than another if in our mind there were not imprinted the idea of good itself as the standard by which we either approve or prefer. So our love must rise to God as the Good itself, not in the way we love this or that good thing. The soul has to seek that Good over which it does not act as judge in some superior way but to which it will cleave in love. And what is that Good but God? —not the good soul, the good angel, the good heavens, but the good Good!

Perhaps the following will enable you to see more readily what I mean. When, for example, I hear the phrase "good soul," those two words recall two facts: that there is a soul, and that it is good. Not by its own act was it made a soul, for it was not already existing in order to bring itself into being. But I can see that an act of the will is necessary for it to be a good soul; not that its very existence as soul is not good, for in that case it could not be called and truly called better than body. But it cannot yet be called a good soul without the will's activity giving it excellence. Neglect of such action rightly makes it blameworthy and allows us properly to speak of it as not a good soul.

Such a soul differs from one that has made itself good by acts of will. Since the latter is worthy of praise, obviously the former's neglect of voluntary action should be blamed. But when a soul tries to do this and is becoming a good soul, it cannot do so unless directed toward another. Yet in order to become good to what may the soul turn but to *the* Good, which it loves, desires, and attains? If it turns away and loses its goodness by the very act of forsaking the good, there will be nothing to which it may return when it wants to amend unless that Good from which it is departing still remains within it.

5

If there were not a changeless good, there would be no changeable goods. The word "good" is spoken of this or that, things at another time often called "not good." See then if you can go beyond the things which are good through participating in Goodness and rise to the sight of that Good whose participated presence makes them good. Then if you are able to set aside these goods and attain the sight of Good in itself, you will have attained the sight of God, and in that moment if in love you cleave to Him you will receive beatitude. It would be a pity to remain attached to those things and not to love the Good itself which makes them good. Even when the soul has not the goodness of conversion to the changeless God, simply as a soul we may value it more highly than any corporeal light. Yet for us its value is grounded not in itself but in the creative art which made it; our seeing that it was worth creating leads us to praise it as made.

This is the Truth, the absolute Good, nothing but the Good itself, and hence the Highest Good; for only that good whose goodness is derived from another good can be lessened or increased. The soul's goodness, therefore, is derived from the very

Source which made it a soul. From the conforming of will to nature, the will in love converted toward that Good from which it derives existence which cannot be lost even should the will forsake its Source comes the soul's completion in goodness. In forsaking the Highest Good, the soul ceases to be a good soul, but not to be a soul, itself a higher good than body. The will loses what the will acquires, for the soul already existed with power to will its conversion toward its Source, but before it existed it was not there to will to be a soul. The good for us is to understand how it was or is right for that thing to be when we can understand the rightness; and when we cannot understand the rightness of anything, to recognize that it could not have been unless it was right for it to be. And this Good is not far from each one of us, for "in Him we live and move and have our being" (Acts 17:27).

Chapter Four

6

But we have to remain steadfast in that Good by love and cleave to it, so that we may enjoy the presence of Him from whom we have our being, and whose absence would make it impossible for us to be at all. "We walk by faith as yet, and not by sight" (2 Cor 5:7). We do not yet see God, as the same Apostle says, "face to face" (1 Cor 13:12). But unless we now love Him, we shall never see Him.

Yet how can one love what one does not know? A reality may be known and not loved; but whether that which is not known can be loved is questionable. If that is impossible, no one can love God before knowing Him. To know God is to apprehend Him steadfastly with our mind; He is not a body observable by the bodily eye. But God is seen and apprehended as far as He can be by the pure in heart; they, we read, are "happy, for they shall see God" (Mt 5:8). Before we are strengthened to see Him there can be no purifying of the heart to see Him unless He is loved in faith. Faith, hope, and charity, those three virtues which the whole structure of the Bible exists to build up, are only in the soul which believes what it does not yet see, and hopes for and loves what it believes.

Therefore if He is believed in, there is already love even of Him who is not yet known. Certainly we must guard against the soul which believes in what it does not see constructing an image of unreality and placing its hope and love in a lie. Then there will not be that "charity from a pure heart and a good conscience and a faith unfeigned, which is the end of the commandment" (cf. 1 Tm 1:5) as Paul says.

7

Whenever we get beliefs from reading or hearing of unseen material realities, the mind must form for itself some image in whatever outline or shape presents itself to thought. But it will not be a true image; or, if it is, as rarely happens, it does not help us to maintain our belief, although it may serve the purpose of suggesting something else to us. Most people who read or hear the epistles of Paul or his history will form some picture of his face, and of those faces of all the others associated with him. Of the many persons who know his epistles, one will picture the shapes and features of these people in one way, one in another, but who can say whose picture is the best resemblance? Our faith is not concerned with the outer appearance of the men but only with the fact that by God's grace their lives and deaths were what Scripture records. This is the faith which is both profitable and attainable, the faith we should desire.

An innumerable variety of mental images represents the bodily appearance of the Lord Himself, but there was no more than one actual reality. In our faith in the Lord Jesus Christ, the saving element is not in the mental image, which may be far removed from the facts, but in the idea of man; present in our consciousness is a definite standard of human nature by which, upon seeing that which conforms to it, we immediately recognize that this is a man or a human form.

Chapter Five

When we believe that God was made man to be for us an example of humility and to demonstrate God's love for us, our thought is formed by this knowledge. It is good for us to believe and to keep steadfastly unshaken in our hearts that the humility whereby God was born of a woman and shamefully brought by mortal men to death is the supreme medicine to heal the swelling of our pride and the exalted mystery that can loose the shackles of sin. Likewise it is because we have the idea of omnipotence that we believe the power of His miracles and of His Resurrection to have come from the omnipotent God. And we think of such realities in accord with our structured knowledge of general and specific notions, whether innate or acquired through experience, so that our faith may not be feigned. We are unaware of the countenance of the Virgin Mary of whom Christ was wondrously born so that both in conceiving and in giving birth her virginity was preserved. We are unaware of the features of Lazarus; we have not seen Bethany, the Sepulcher nor the stone which Christ had them remove when He raised Lazarus from the dead, nor of that new tomb hewn out the rock from which He Himself arose, nor of Mount Olivet whence He ascended into heaven.

And if we have not seen them we are completely unaware whether they are as we imagine them; in fact, we suppose it the more likely that they are not. For if a place or a person or any physical object presents to our eyes the same appearance it had in our imagination before we saw it, we are astonished, so rarely does it happen, if ever. Nevertheless we have a steadfast belief in the Gospel story because we conceive it according to our firm knowledge of general and specific ideas. We believe that the Lord Jesus Christ was born of a virgin named Mary, but what a virgin is, what it means to be born, what a proper name is, we do not believe but simply know. We neither know nor believe whether Mary had that countenance which came to our mind when we said or recalled the story. And so without injury to faith we may say: "Perhaps she was like this, perhaps she was not." But no one without injury to his Christian faith can say: "Perhaps Christ was born of a virgin."

8

Now we desire to attain as much understanding as permissible of the Trinity, its eternity, its equality, its unity. But before we can understand, we have to believe, and we should see to it that our faith is not feigned. For our happiness resides in our enjoyment of the Trinity, and if our belief about it is false, our hope will be vain, our love not pure. How then are we able to love, through believing, the Trinity we do not know? Will the love we are able to have for Paul be based upon some special or general knowledge? We may be completely ignorant of his countenance, which may have been entirely different from our imagination of it. Yet we know what a man is for we need not go beyond what we ourselves are. Clearly, Paul was also a man; his soul was joined to a body, and he lived a mortal life. We believe of him what we find in ourselves according to the genus or species in which every human nature is likewise composed. But knowledge of genus and species can tell us nothing of the transcendent Trinity. There do not exist a number of such trinities so that experience of some of them could enable us to form a generalized idea and believe that the divine Trinity is similar; and thus, by analogy with what we know, love that which without yet knowing we believe. No; we can love our Lord Jesus Christ's Resurrection from the dead, although we have never seen anyone so rise again; but we cannot in the same way love, through believing, the Trinity we do not see and the like of which we have never seen. We know what death and life are because we are alive and have seen and experienced the death and the dying of others. To rise again, then, is simply to return from death to life.

But when we say and believe that the Trinity exists, we certainly know what the word Trinity means, since we know the meaning of "three"; but that is not what we love. By holding up three fingers we can have "three" whenever we wish. Is that which we love then not *any* trinity but the Trinity which is God? Is it God in the Trinity whom we love? But we have neither seen nor do we know of any other God; for there is but one God whom not having seen we love through believing. The question is: What likeness or comparison in things we know can promote the belief by which we may love God before He is known?

Chapter Six

9

Let us return to consider why we love the Apostle. Certainly not because of that appearance of humanity familiar to us and which we believe he shared? If that were the case, our love would now have no object, for his soul and body are separated and no longer does he exist in human form. That which in him we love is not living; for we love the righteous soul. But this entails reference to a general or special law by which we know what a soul is, and what "righteous" means. Now we may appropriately assert that we know what a soul is because we ourselves have a soul. With our eyes we have never seen it nor from a number of perceived realities have we formed a general or special idea of it; it is because we have a soul that we know it. I know nothing more intimately than that which I am aware of being, that by which I am aware of everything else—the soul itself.

The bodily movements whereby we are aware of the life of others we recognize by their likeness to our own; life makes us move our bodies as we observe other bodies moving. When a living body moves, our eyes do not penetrate to a vision of the soul which is invisible to our eyes; but we are aware that in that bodily mass there is something like what we have within ourselves to move our own bodily mass, namely, life and soul. And this is not peculiar to human intelligence and reason: Animals are aware of life, not only within themselves but within one another and within us. They do not see our souls, but with a simple and instinctive immediacy they become aware of them from bodily movements. From our own soul, therefore, we derive the knowledge of soul in anyone else, and the belief of it when we do not know it. Not only are we conscious of the soul but by considering our own soul we can know what soul is; for we have a soul.

But how do we know what "righteous" means? We said that the only reason we love the Apostle is that he is a "righteous soul"; me must know then what righteous is as well as what is soul. What soul is we know from ourselves, as we have said; for in us there is soul. But how do we know what is righteous if we are not righteous? If none except he who is righteous knows what righteous is, none can know the righteous but the righteous. The mere belief that a man is righteous cannot make one love him if one does not know what righteous is. As previously noted, without seeing, one can only love what one believes by virtue of some law based on a general or special knowledge. Therefore, if none except the righteous can love the righteous, how can anyone not yet righteous desire to be so? For no one desires to be what he does not love. Yet without willing to be righteous it is impossible to become so; and to will it one must love the righteous man. It follows that a man who is himself not yet righteous can love the righteous, but only if he knows what righteous is.

We have to grant that a man not yet righteous may know the word's meaning, and we ask how this knowledge occurs. Certainly not by the visual sense: A body is not righteous in the way that it is white or black or square or round; and nothing but bodies are seen by the eyes. The righteous element in man is the soul, and it is by reason of his soul, not his body, that a man is called righteous. Righteousness is a beauty of soul able to exist in men whose bodies are deformed or ugly, and the soul's beauty is no more visible to the outer eye than the soul itself. How, therefore, can a man not yet righteous discover the word's meaning and himself become righteous through loving the righteous? Bodily movements might indicate righteousness in this or that man; but if one were completely unaware of the meaning of righteousness one would fail to recognize that these movements signified a righteous soul.

The problem remains. In some way or other we understand what righteous means before we ourselves are righteous. If that awareness is derived from the external world, it must be derived from some bodily source; but its object does not at all belong to the bodily world. Therefore, within ourselves we must discover the meaning of the word righteous. When I seek for the appropriate description of it, I can find the answer nowhere but in my own mind. If I ask another man, he must look within for his answer; and no one who has not found the answer in himself can answer truly.

When I try to describe Carthage, I search within myself to discover an image of Carthage in my own mind. But having been bodily present in the town I gained that through sense perception, having seen the town and remembered it so that the right word is ready whenever I wish to describe it. Its "word" is the actual image in my memory, not the sound of two syllables when I say "Carthage" nor the silent saying of the name in my mind: It is the object of my inward vision when I say or before I say the two syllables "Carthage." Likewise, if I wish to describe Alexandria, which I never saw, an image of it is available. I have been duly informed that it is a great city, and as far as possible I have formed a picture of it as described. And when I wish to speak of it that is its "word" in my mind before I say the five syllables of the famous name. But if I could show my mental picture to people who know Alexandria, they would certainly say "That is not it!" or if they said: "It is," I would be greatly surprised, and when I reflected on my mental picture I would still not know that it was Alexandria: I would only believe those who had seen it.

But this is not how I seek what a righteous man is nor is it how I find it or contemplate it when I describe it, nor is it how my description is accepted nor how I accept another's description. It is not as if I had seen anything like this or perceived it by any bodily sense, or heard it from others who had such knowledge. When I say, and knowingly say, that "the righteous soul is that which by the rational principle in life and conduct gives to each his own," I am not thinking of an absent object like Carthage, or imagining correctly or incorrectly an object like Alexandria. I apprehend something present, apprehend it within myself, although I myself am not what I apprehend. Many, on hearing me, may accept my description; but whoever does so in knowledge will himself be apprehending within himself the same reality, although he himself is not what he apprehends. When a righteous man says it, he is apprehending and describing what he himself is, but he also apprehends it "within himself."

That is natural enough: Where should he see himself except within himself? The wonder is that the mind or soul should see within itself what it has seen nowhere else, that it should see truly, and should see the truly righteous soul, being itself soul but not the righteous soul which it sees in itself. We can scarcely suppose the presence of another righteous soul in the soul which is not yet righteous. But then what is present to the soul when it sees and defines the righteous soul and sees it completely within itself although it itself is not righteous? We answer that what it sees is an inner truth present to the soul which has the power to contemplate it. Not everyone has the power. All of those having the power are not themselves what they contemplate; not all are themselves righteous souls, although they can see and define the righteous soul. They themselves can only become righteous by cleaving to that same form itself which they contemplate, to be conformed to it and to become righteous souls. Then they will not only apprehend and say that the righteous soul is "that which by the rational principle in life and conduct gives to each his own," but they will make righteous life and conduct their own, giving to each his own, "owing no man anything but to love one another" (Rom 13:8).

Only by love may one cleave to that form. If we love another man whom we think to be righteous, we must love the very form in which we see what the righteous soul is, so that we may also become righteous. In fact, if we did not love the form we would be unable to love the man inasmuch as we love him on the basis of the form; it is merely that our love of the form does not suffice to make us righteous as long as we are not righteous.

We conclude that love for the man who is considered righteous is based upon that form and truth which he who loves, sees, and understands within himself. But this form and truth cannot be loved from anywhere else. We are unable to discover anything outside of it which might make our belief in it and our love for it, while it is as yet unknown, to be based upon a previous knowledge of anything of its kind. It itself is the reality one sees wherever one beholds any reality of this kind; in fact, there is nothing else of this "kind," since it alone is what it is.

Consequently, our love for men must have their righteousness either as the cause or as the purpose of our love. Likewise, should a man love himself also, either because he is righteous or that he may be righteous, only thus can he safely love his neighbor as himself. His self-love is unrighteous if it has any other ground, for he will be loving himself in order to be unrighteous, and therefore to be evil, so that there will be no real self-love; for "he who loves iniquity hates his own soul" (Ps 11:5).

Chapter Seven

10

Consequently, in this question of the Trinity and our knowledge of God, the first thing we should learn is the nature of true love, or rather the nature of love, since only true love deserves the name of love. Any other kind is covetousness; language is misused when we say of those who covet that they love just as it is misused when we say of those who love that they covet. The purpose of true love is the life of righteousness in cleaving to the truth, and this means that nothing should interest us but love for others, and this means the will that they may live righteously. This is what gives the whole value to the readiness to die for the brethren, which by His example the Lord Jesus Christ taught us. There are two commandments on which depend all the Law and the Prophets: love of God and love of neighbor; but with good reason the Scripture often expresses one of them for both. At times this is the love of God. "We know that all things work together for good to them that love God" (Rom 8:28). "Whosoever loves God, he is known of God" (Rom 5:5). "The love of God is shed abroad in our hearts by the Holy Spirit which is given to us" (1 Cor 8:3).

Such statements imply that whoever loves God should do what God has commanded, that one's love depends upon one's doing, and thus one must also love one's neighbor because God has commanded this. At times Scripture discusses only the love of neighbor. "Bear you one another's burdens and so you shall fulfill the law of Christ" (Gal 6:2). "The whole Law is fulfilled in one saying, namely, you shall love your neighbor as yourself" (Gal 5:14). Or, as in the Gospel, "Whatsoever you would that men should do unto you, even so do unto them; for this is the Law and the Prophets" (Mt 7:12). In many other places in Holy Scripture the love of neighbor alone seems to be advocated for our perfection and nothing is mentioned about the love of God, although the Law and the Prophets depend upon both commandments. This is because one who loves his neighbor must necessarily first have the love for Love itself. But "God is Love, and he who abides in Love, abides in God" (1 Jn 4:16). Consequently, first one must love God above all things.

11

Those who search for God by means of the spiritual powers placed over the world or its parts fall far away from Him, separated not by space but by opposing affection. Although God is more interior than the innermost, they tend toward the external, and forsake what resides within them. They have heard of or fancied some holy celestial power, but it is the admiration that human weakness feels for the works of power which attracts them rather than the model of reverent surrender which attains the peace of God. They prefer the pride of angelic power to the devotion of angelic being. Rather than rejoicing in his own power, a holy person rejoices in the power of Him from whom is derived all the power that he can appropriately have. He knows that it is a greater thing to be united in voluntary worship to the omnipotent than to manifest in his own power and will a power that is feared by those who do not possess it.

So when the Lord Jesus Christ Himself performed miracles, He tried to give a fuller truth to the astonished spectators, to convert them from their immersion in temporal signs to interior and eternal realities. "Come unto me, all you that labor and are heavily burdened, and I will 'refresh you,' take my yoke upon you" (Mt 11:28). He does not say, "Learn of me, for I raise up them that have been dead four days"; but, "Learn of me, for I am meek and lowly of heart" (Mt 11:29). The firm ground of humility is stronger and safer than any wind-swept elevation, so He continues, "and you shall find rest for your souls." For "Love is not puffed up" (1 Cor 13:4); "God is love" (1 Jn 4:8); "The faithful in love shall rest in him" (Wis 3:9), summoned from the noise-filled external world to joyful silence.

"God is Love" (1 Jn 4:8). Why speed to the heavenly heights and the lowest parts of the earth searching for Him who is with us if we wish to be with Him?

Chapter Eight

12

Let no one say: "I do not know what I am to love." Let him love his brother, and he will love that same love; he knows the love whereby he loves better than he knows the brother whom he loves. God can be more known to him than his brother, really more known because more present; more known because more interior; more known because more certain. Embrace the love that is God; through love embrace God. He is the very love that joins together in holy bond all good angels and all God's servants, uniting them and us to one another in subjection to Himself. The more cleansed we are from the swelling of pride, the more we are filled with love; and is not whoever is filled with love filled with God?

But now you will answer: "Indeed I see love; I gaze upon it mentally as far as possible, I believe the word of Scripture that God is love, and "he who abides in love abides in God" (1 Jn 4:16). But my vision of love is not a vision of the Trinity. Then let me help you see that you do see the Trinity if you see love, hoping that charity itself be present to move us to a good end. The love that we love is a loving love, and we love it because it loves. What, therefore, is the object of love's love which makes love itself lovable? If it loves nothing, it is not love. If it loves itself, it cannot love itself as love unless as love it has an object. A transitive word, in addition to connoting its object, denotes itself but it does not denote itself as transitive word unless it denotes itself as connoting an object. Likewise, love may love itself but it will only be loving itself as love if it loves itself as loving something. The object of love's love has to be something that love loves; and if we begin with what is nearest, that is our brother. Remember the Apostle John's praise of brotherly love: "Whosoever loves his brother abides in the light, and there is no cause of stumbling in him" (1 Jn 2:10). He has evidently placed the perfection of righteousness in brotherly love; he in whom there is no scandal is clearly perfect. Apparently he says nothing of the love of God. This must mean that he intends God to be included in brotherly love itself. Sometime later in the epistle he explicitly asserts: "Beloved, let us love one another; for love is of God; and everyone who loves is born of God and knows God. He who loves not has not known God; for God is love" (1 Jn 4:7). The sequence of thought shows clearly enough that this very brotherly love, the love whereby we love one another, is being declared with apostolic authority to be not only "from God," but "God." Thus, when love brings us to love our brother, this love is from God; and the first object of our love must be that very love whereby we love our brother.

From this we deduce that these two commandments cannot be separated. "God is Love" (1 Jn 4:7). Whoever loves love certainly loves God; whoever loves his brother must of necessity love love. Hence we later read: "He who loves not his brother whom he sees cannot love God whom he does not see" (1 Jn 4:20). The fact that he does not love his brother is the reason that he does not see God. Whoever does not love his brother is not in love, and he who is not in love is not in God, because God is Love.

Moreover, whoever is not in God is not in the light; for "God is light, and there is no darkness in him" (1 Jn 1:5). Naturally, then, whoever is not in the light does not see the light and this means that he does not see God, for he is in darkness. He sees his brother with that external human vision to which God is invisible. But if with spiritual charity he loved the brother whom he sees externally, he would see God, who is charity itself, with the interior vision by which God can be seen. Hence he who does not love the brother whom he sees cannot love God whom he does not see simply because God is the love which he lacks. We should not be anxious about the question of how much love we should give to our brother and how much to God. The answer is: to God far more than to ourselves, and to our brother as much as to ourselves; the more we love God the more we love ourselves. We love God and our neighbor from one and the same love, but we love God for

God's sake, and we love ourselves and our neighbor for God's sake.

Chapter Nine

13

I want to question what it is that kindles the fire in our hearts when we hear or read such words as these: "Behold now is the acceptable time, behold, now is the day of salvation; giving no occasion of stumbling in anything, that our ministration be not blamed, but in all things commending ourselves as God's ministers; in much patience, in afflictions, in necessities, in distresses, in stripes, in imprisonments, in tumults, in labors, in watchings, in fastings; in purity, in knowledge, in long-suffering, in kindness, in the Holy Spirit, in charity unfeigned, in the word of truth, in the power of God, by the armor of righteousness, on the right hand and on the left, by glory and dishonor, by evil report and good report; as deceivers and yet true, as unknown and yet well known, as dying and behold we live; as chastened and not killed, as sorrowful yet always rejoicing, as poor yet making many rich, as having nothing, and yet possessing all things" (2 Cor 6:2ff.).

If in reading this a love for Paul the Apostle is kindled within us, this is certainly because we believe that his life was like that. But that God's ministers ought to live that way is not something we believe on hearsay; it is what we see within ourselves, or rather above ourselves, in Truth itself. Because of what we see we love Paul, whom we believe to have lived this way. And if we did not primarily love that form which we perceive to be always immovable and changeless, we would not love the Apostle whom we love because we believe that his earthly life corresponded to that form. But we discover that we are somehow more greatly aroused to a love of the form itself through the faith whereby we believe that a man has lived in harmony with it, and by the hope which prohibits us, since there have been men who so lived, to despair of our being able to live like them inasmuch as they are men like ourselves. Hence we desire it more eagerly and pray for it more confidently.

It is the love for that form according to which we believe that they lived which makes us love their life. And when we believe this, their life arouses within us a more burning love toward the same form. So that the more ardently our love burns for God, the surer and the more unclouded is our vision of Him. For we behold in God the changeless form of righteousness and thereby judge how a man should live.

Faith, therefore, is a powerful aid to the knowledge and the love of God, not as if he were previously unknown and unloved but so that he may be known more clearly and loved more fervently.

Chapter Ten

14

Now what is love or charity which is praised and preached so highly by divine Scripture except the love of the Good? Love is the activity of a lover and it has a definite object. There we have three things: the lover, that which is loved, and love. Love itself is only a kind of life which unites together or tries to unite two beings, the lover and the beloved. This is the case in the carnal loves of the external world; but let us leave the body and ascend to the soul where we may drink of a purer and clearer source. What does the soul love in a friend except the soul? Even here there are three: the lover, the beloved, and love.

There still remains for us a further ascent from here to seek those higher things as far as this is possible to man. But here we may pause, not asserting that we have discovered what we were seeking, but as having discovered, as seekers do, the place to look. We have discovered, not the reality itself, but where it is to be sought. And that will suffice to provide a point from which a fresh start may be made.

Book Fourteen

Chapter One

Now we shall treat the nature of wisdom; but not the wisdom of God, which is certainly God Himself, inasmuch as it is the name given to his only-begotten Son (1 Cor. 1:24). We shall tell of the wisdom of man, which nevertheless is a true wisdom insofar as it is in accordance with God and is the true and principal worship of Him. In Greek this is denoted by the one word *Theosébia*, which our Latin translators, wishing to have one corresponding word, have translated (as previously noted) as *pietas* or godly fear. However, the more ordinary Greek word for *pietas* was *eusébia*. *Theosébia* however, cannot be fully translated by one word; it is preferable to use two words and speak of the worship of God (*Dei cultus*). That this is the wisdom of man (as declared in Book XII of this work) is demonstrated by the authority of Holy Scripture, in the Book of Job the servant of God. We read therein that God's Wisdom said to man: "Behold, the fear of the Lord (*pietas*) is wisdom; and to refrain from evil is knowledge" (Jb 28:28). But some have translated the Greek *epistéme*, "discipline": which can be taken as knowledge as being itself derived from *discendo* or learning; for our reason for learning anything is to know it. "Discipline in fact has another meaning, as used for the punishment endured by a man for his sins for the sake of correction. So the Epistle to the Hebrews says: 'Who is the son whom his father does not discipline?' or again, more obviously; 'All discipline for the moment seems not to be joyous but grievous; but later it will yield the peaceful fruit of righteousness to those who have been exercised through it' " (Heb 12:7, 11).

God himself then is the Supreme Wisdom; and the worship of God is the wisdom of man, of which we are now speaking. For

331

"the wisdom of this world is foolishness with God" (1 Cor 3:19). Of this wisdom which is the worship of God Holy Scripture says: "The multitude of the wise is the welfare of the whole world" (Wis 6:26).

2

But if we need wise men to speak of wisdom, we are in trouble. So that our discourse may not be impudent shall we presume to profess wisdom? Or, rather, we should be admonished by Pythagoras, who dared not profess himself wise and replied to his questioners that he was merely a philosopher, that is, a lover of wisdom (Cicero, *Tusc. Quest.* V.3). This originated the name which later generations so approved that the greatest learning in respect to wisdom, whether classical or real, would entitle a man only to the name of philosopher. Did such men hesitate to profess wisdom because they supposed that the wise man must be wholly without fault? On the contrary, that is not the teaching of our Scriptures, which say: "Rebuke a wise man and he will love you" (Prv 9:8). If a man is found in need of rebuke he is surely found guilty of sin. Nevertheless, I do not venture to call myself wise: for me it suffices for the philosopher or lover of wisdom to discuss wisdom. And no one can deny this because those who have declared themselves to be lovers of wisdom rather than wise have never ceased discussing it.

3

In these discussions wisdom was defined as "the knowledge of human and divine things" (Cicero, *De Officiciis,* II.2). Therefore in a previous book (Book XIII.1) I expressed the opinion that familiarity with things both divine and human should be called wisdom as well as knowledge. Yet if we were to adopt the Apostle's distinction—"to one is given the word of wisdom, to another the word of knowledge" (1 Cor 12:8)—it is appropriate to divide this definition, giving the name of wisdom strictly speaking to the knowledge of divine things whereas, strictly speaking, we have knowledge of human things. I have discussed this in my thirteenth book, where I included in knowledge of the human only that by which the most wholesome faith leading to true happiness is begotten, nourished, defined, strengthened, and not any kind of knowledge of human affairs, most of which is needless vanity or harmful curiosity. Many of the faithful are weak in this knowledge although they are very strong in faith itself.

For merely to know what should be believed to attain that eternal life which alone is blessed is one thing; it is another to know how this faith may help the godly and be defended against the ungodly—which the Apostle apparently describes by the special name "knowledge." When I spoke of it I was mainly concerned to praise faith itself. First of all I briefly distinguished the eternal from the temporal and began discussing the temporal things. I postponed to this book the discussion of eternal realities, but I indicated that even of them there is a faith that is indeed temporal and dwells temporally in the hearts of believers and this is nevertheless needed to attain the eternal. I discussed how beneficial for this attainment was the faith about things which the Eternal did for us and suffered in time, in the man whose humanity He bore in time and exalted to eternity. And I held that the virtues in this temporal and mortal state which give prudence, courage, temperance, and justice to life are true virtues only if they are related to this same faith which, although temporal, leads us to eternal realities (XIII.20).

Chapter Two

4

It is written: "While we are in the body we are exiled from the Lord—for we walk by faith and not by sight" (2 Cor 5:6). Therefore, as long as the just man lives by faith (Rom 1:17), although his life is that of the inner man, he is only able to strive toward truth and wend his way toward the eternal by temporal faith: and there cannot yet be in the retention and contemplation and love of this temporal faith a trinity fit to be called the image of God. Otherwise, that which has to be secured in the eternal would seem to be secured in things temporal. When man's mind sees its own faith, believing what it does not see, it is not gazing upon what is everlasting.

For this will not always be thus, certainly not when at the end of the pilgrimage in which we are absent from the Lord and must walk by faith shall come the conversion to sight whereby we shall see face-to-face (1 Cor 13:12). We do not see now; but we shall be found worthy to see because we believe, and we shall rejoice that faith has led us home to sight. In the place of the faith by which the unseen is believed, there will be sight by which what was previously believed is seen. Perhaps we shall then remember this mortal life that has passed away and recall our former belief in what we did not see; but that faith will be found among the things past and gone, not present and eternally abiding. Therefore we shall find that the Trinity which now appears in our remembering, beholding, and loving of our present and abiding faith will later be past and gone, not permanent. We must conclude that even if that trinity is already an image of God, this very image must be considered to belong not to permanent reality, but to passing reality.

But if the soul is naturally immortal, so that after its original creation it can never cease to be, far be it from us to think that the soul's most precious possession should not endure along with its own immortality. But what is there in its created nature that can be more precious than its having been made to the image of its Creator? Therefore it is not in the retention, contemplation, and love of faith which will not last forever, but in what will exist forever, that the image of God worthy of that name is to be found.

Chapter Three

5

But let us examine the truth of this conclusion through a closer and more careful inquiry. It may be argued that this trinity does not cease to be even when faith itself has ceased. For just as we now retain faith in our memory, perceive it in thought, love it with will, so afterward when we shall retain it in our memory and recall that we once had it, our will uniting this memory and reflection, the same trinity will remain. For if faith were to perish, leaving no trace within us, there would then be nothing of it in our memory to which we could turn to remember it as past, joining by the effort of attention these two elements—what was present in the memory without our perceiving it and what is given form by thought. This argument neglects the difference between two trinities: one, when our present faith is retained, seen, and loved within us; and another which will be there when not faith itself but a kind of trace of it stored in the memory is contemplated in recollection, the will uniting the content of memory and the trace of it in the mind's sight.

In order to understand this, let us take an example from the material world which was sufficiently discussed in the eleventh book. In the ascent from lower to higher, or the entry from outer to inner, we find a first trinity in the material object of sight, the sight of the beholder to which it gives form in the moment of vision, and the exercise of will which unites the two. We may propose a trinity on similar lines when the faith now present in us, like the material body in space, is held in our memory and from it form is given to the thought which recollects it, just as the material object gives form to the perception of the perceiver. These two elements become a trinity by the addition of will, which links and joins together the faith present in the memory and its representation in the recollecting contemplation: just as, in the trinity of bodily sight, the form of the body seen and the conformity to it of the perceiver's perception are united by the exercise of will.

Now suppose that the material body, the object of sight, has disintegrated and perished, with nothing left in space to which the eye could be redirected. The fact that an image of the material object, now past and gone, stays in the memory giving form to the recollecting perception so that these two elements may be linked by the will does not permit us to call the resulting trinity the same as what had existed when the real body was perceived in space. It is completely different: It not only belongs to the internal sphere whereas the previous one belonged to the external, but it is produced by the image of a body no longer present rather then by an actually present body.

So in what we are investigating for which the parallel has been proposed, the faith now in our mind, like the body in space, is a kind of trinity in being retained, contemplated, and loved; yet the trinity will not be the same when this faith is no longer present in the mind as the body is no longer present in space. When we begin to recollect its being in us as past and no longer present, it will doubtless be a different trinity. The one we now possess originates by the presence of the reality itself and its connection with the believing mind; the one we shall then possess will be the result of the imagining of what is no longer present, remaining in the memory as object of recollection.

Chapter Four

6

We may assert, therefore, neither that we shall possess the image of God in that trinity which does not presently exist, nor that we possess it now in the trinity which then will no longer be present. We must discover, in man's rational or intellectual soul, an image of its Creator fixed immortally in its immortal nature. We are able to speak only of a qualified immortality of the soul, for when the soul is deprived of that bliss which constitutes its true life, there is a death of the soul. It is called immortal because even in great misery it never stops living a certain kind of life. Likewise, although at some time reason and understanding may be inactive in it and at other times seem diminished or great, the human soul is never anything but rational and intellectual; and consequently, if its being made in God's image witnesses its power to exercise reason and intellect in order to understand and contemplate God, we may be certain that being so great and marvelous a creature from the very beginning that image always remains, whether it be so faded that almost no image is left, whether it be obscured and defaced or bright and beautiful.

Here we may appeal to God's Scriptural text expressing His pity for the defacement of its dignity: "Although man walks in an image, yet he is vainly disquieted: he heaps up treasures, and knows not for whom he shall gather them" (Ps 39:6). Vanity would not be referred to the image of God if it were not seen as a defacement; and that no defacement can destroy its nature as image is sufficiently clear from the words "although man walks in an image." Therefore, the statement will be equally true if its clauses are inverted and we read: "Although man is vainly disquieted, yet he walks in an image." Human nature is great, but because it is not the highest reality it could be corrupted; although as not the highest reality it is open to corruption, nevertheless because it has a capacity for the highest reality and can partake in it, human nature remains great.

We have to search, then, in this image of God, for a trinity of its own kind—confiding in the help of Him who created us in His image. For in no other way can we investigate these things for our salvation and, according to the wisdom which is from Him, find something. But the reader will not need more words here concerning the methodology if what was asserted in earlier books (especially the tenth) concerning the human soul or mind be recalled and reconsidered, or reference to the pages of the discussion be made.

Chapter Five

7

In the tenth book, among other things it was said that the mind of man knows itself—for nothing can be better known to the mind than what is immediately present to it; and nothing is more immediately present to the mind than it is to itself. This fact was also satisfactorily defended with other arguments. What, therefore, should we say of the mind of a child, as yet so little and so deeply ignorant that its intellectual darkness is almost frightening to the more or less knowledgeable adult? Perhaps even the child's mind may be considered to know itself, but to be so taken up with experiences of sense pleasures, all the greater for their novelty, that it cannot reflect upon itself, although unable to be unaware of itself. The intensity of the child's interest in the external objects of sensation is visible in the one example of its eagerness for light. If, through carelessness or ignorance of the possible result, a nightlight is placed by a child's cot so that where the child lies it can turn its eyes toward the candle but cannot move its head, it will so fixedly stare at the light that in some cases a squint has resulted by the eyes holding the position whereby their delicate young structure was set by habit.

And we discover in the child's soul the same intense concentrated interest upon the other bodily senses as far as its age allows; so that strong aversion or desire will only be excited in it by whatever displeases or pleases the flesh. Its thoughts are not turned inward upon itself, and to look inward cannot be suggested to it, since it is still unresponsive to suggestion made mainly by words of which it is, as of so much else, as yet ignorant. But in the same book it was indicated that not reflecting upon oneself is different from not knowing oneself.

8

We may, however, pass over the time of infancy, which cannot be questioned about its experiences and which we ourselves have mostly forgotten. It will suffice for us to be sure that when a man becomes able to think about his own mind's nature and to find the truth, he will not find it any other place than within himself. And what he will find is not something he did not know but something he did not think about. What can we know, if we are unaware of what is in our own mind, since the mind is the necessary means of all our knowledge?

Chapter Six

Yet so great is the power of thought that only by thinking can the mind, as it were, place itself within its own sight. Only when something is thought about is it in the mind's sight. That implies that even the mind itself, the only agent of thought, can be in its own sight only by thinking about itself. The question of how it can be understood not to be in its own sight when not thinking of itself, although it can never be separated from itself, is one I am unable to answer. Apparently, its "sight" and "itself" are two different realities—which in regard to the bodily eye is a reasonable way to speak; for whereas the eye itself has its own settled place in the body, its sight is directed to external objects and can be directed even to the stars. Nor is the eye in its own sight at all, inasmuch as it is unable to see itself unless reflected in a mirror, as we previously noted (X.3); while nothing corresponds with that reflection when the mind by thinking of itself places itself within its own sight. When the mind is thinking of itself we can scarcely suppose that it is seeing one part of itself by another part as we see other parts of our body with one part of our body, the eye. What can be thought or said that is more absurd than this? If the mind is removed, it is removed from itself; if placed in its own sight, it is placed before itself. This means that it has changed its position from that taken when not in its own sight, as if it were removed from one place and put in another. But if it has moved in order to be seen, where does it remain in order to see? Is it doubled so that it can take two positions, one for seeing and another for being seen, in itself for seeing, before itself for being seen?

To our inquiry truth brings none of these answers; for, in

fact, this mode of thinking pertains to images drawn from material objects, and it is absolutely certain that the mind is not material—at least for those few "minds" which can tell us the truth in this regard. It remains therefore, that the "sight" of the mind is essential to its nature, to which it is recalled when it thinks of itself not by a spatial movement but by an incorporeal conversion. And when not thinking of itself, although it is not within its own sight and its seeing is not defined by its nature, it nevertheless knows itself as if it were a remembrance of itself to itself. Likewise, the knowledge possessed by the expert in many sciences is present in his memory, and no part of it is in the sight of his mind unless he thinks of it, the rest being hidden in a kind of secret knowledge which is called memory.

Thus we unfolded an account of the mental trinity whereby memory provided the source from which the thinker's sight receives its form, the conformation itself being a sort of image impressed by the memory, with will or love as the agency by which the two are linked. Hence when the mind sees itself in the act of thought, it understands and knows itself, we may say that it begets this self-understanding and self-knowledge. For an immaterial object is seen when understood, and is known when it is understood. But this begetting of self-knowledge by the mind, when it sees itself as understood in thought, does not mean that previously it did not know itself. It was known as realities present in memory are known, though not thought about: as we say that a man, even when not thinking of literature but of other things, knows literature. And to these two, the begetter and the begotten, we should add the love which links them together, and this is nothing else than the will, seeking or embracing an object of enjoyment. Accordingly, we thought that a trinity was also suggested by these three names: memory, understanding, will.

Chapter Seven

9

Near the end of the same tenth book we stated that the mind always remembers itself and always understands and loves itself, although it does not always think of itself as distinct from all that differs in nature from itself. We should then ask why understanding is given over to the act of thinking whereas the knowledge of an object in the mind when not being thought about is properly given over only to memory. If this is the case, the three functions of memory, understanding, and love of itself will not have been always present together in the mind. Only the memory of itself will it have had, and only when it began to think of itself will it have understanding and love of itself. To solve this difficulty, let us more closely examine the previous case to demonstrate the difference between not knowing something and not thinking about it, so that a man can know something of which he is not thinking when his thought is taken up with something else. An expert in two or more arts may in thinking of one of them know another or many others although not thinking about them. But are we able rightly to say, "This musician knows music, but at this moment he does not understand it since he is not thinking about it; but at this moment he understands geometry since he is thinking about geometry"? Such an assertion seems absurd, and not less absurd would be the assertion, "This musician knows music, but at this moment he does not love it since he is not thinking of it; but at this moment he loves geometry since he is thinking about geometry." What we may very rightly assert is: "This man whom you observe discussing geometry is also an accomplished musician because he remembers that art, understands it, and loves it; but while knowing and loving it, he is not thinking of it at this moment because he is thinking of the geometry he is discussing."

This indicates to us the presence "in the recesses of our minds" of certain stores of knowledge of certain things which emerge, as it were, into the center and take a clearer position in the mind's sight when they become the object of thought. Then the mind discovers that it remembers, understands, and loves what it was not thinking about while thinking of something else. If there is a topic of which we have not thought for some time, and of which we are unable to begin thinking unless it is suggested to us, then with reference to it we are in the strange position and a highly paradoxical one of not knowing that we know it. Indeed, it is appropriate for the one reminding to say to the one reminded: "You know this, but you do not know that you know it: I shall remind you of it, and you will discover yourself knowing what you had thought you did not know." There is a similar result when a reader is led by reason to discover the truth of some theme written in a book. He does not accept its truth on trust from the writer when he reads history: he himself discovers it to be true, whether this is his own discovery or that of Truth itself, which is the mind's light. The man whose blindness of heart is such that no suggestion can enable him to recognize such truths is too deeply immersed in the darkness of ignorance and needs the miracle of divine assistance in order to attain to true wisdom.

10

This was why I tried to illustrate the process of thinking by an example which would indicate how the remembering attention takes form from the content of memory and in the thinking person something is brought to birth like what was in him as the possessor of memory before thinking. To distinguish things that are not simultaneous is easier, and where the parent is prior in time to the "offspring." If we examine the mind's inner memory by which it remembers itself, its inner understanding by which it understands itself, and its inner will by which it loves itself, we are concerned with a state in which these three are always present together and were so from the beginning, whether or not they were objects of thought. And so it will appear that the image of the trinity belongs only to the sphere of memory. Yet without thought there can be no "word," for we think whatever we say, even with the inner word that belongs to no particular language. So the image is discoverable in the three functions of memory, understanding, and will. I refer to "understanding" as denoting the faculty by which we come to understand by actually thinking: that is, when our thinking takes form through the "begetting" of what was present to the memory but not thought of. And the word "will" signifies the love which unites the "offspring" and its "parent," and which is somehow common to both.

In order that the reader might group these distinctions more easily I used to illustrate them in the eleventh book the sphere of external sense perception; then proceeded to consider that faculty of the inner man which exercises the reasoning power upon temporal realities, whereas I postponed for future discussion the other sovereign principal power by which he contemplates eternal realities. This covered two books, the twelfth treating how one faculty was differentiated from the other, as the lower from the higher to which it should be subject; and the thirteenth dealing with the function of the lower, which includes the saving knowledge of human things which during this temporal life helps us so to act as to attain eternal life. I dealt with this as exactly as I could but briefly; for I had to include within one book a subject rich in detail, the theme of many great works and many great writers. I also drew attention to a trinity in this sphere, although not yet one to be called the image of God.

Chapter Eight

11

We have now arrived at that point in our discussion where we begin to consider that highest part of the human mind by which it knows or can know God, in order to discover therein an image of God. Although the human mind is not of God's own nature, yet the image of that nature which transcends in excellence every other nature is to be sought and discovered in the most excellent part of our own nature.

But primarily we have to consider the mind in itself, before it participates in God, and there discover His image. We have asserted that it still remains the image of God, although an image obscured and defaced by the loss of its participation in God. This is His image because it has a capacity for God and can participate in God: It has this high destiny only because it is His image.

Here, therefore, is the mind remembering itself, understanding itself, loving itself. Perceiving this, we perceive a trinity—a trinity far less than God, but now finally an image of God. In this trinity the memory has not brought in from outside what it is to retain, nor has the understanding found in the outer world the object for its contemplating, as with the bodily eye. In this case the will has not made an outer union of these two, as of the material form and its derivative in the eye of the beholder. An image of the observed external object, taken up, so to speak, and stored in the memory, has not been found by thought directed toward it, with form having been given to the recollecting attention, while the two are linked by the additional activity of will. This was the arrangement manifest in those trinities which we found present in material processes, or somehow passing into our inner experience from the external body through the bodily sense. We treated all this in the eleventh book.

Nor is our present trinity identical with the one discovered as existing or presenting itself to us in our treatment of knowledge (as distinct from wisdom), the sphere of which is the activity of the inner man. The objects of this knowledge were, so to speak, adventitious to the mind: They may enter by historical information, like deeds and statements transacted in time and transient, or things locally and geographically situated in the natural world; or they may arise from nonbeing within the man himself, either through instruction from others or through one's own reflections, like faith, which we discussed at length in the thirteenth book, or like virtues by which, if genuine, we then live well in our present mortal condition so that we may reach in the immortality promised by God the happy life.

These and like matters are placed in temporal succession, making it easier for us to find the trinity of memory, vision, and love. For some of them exist before the learner's knowledge of them: they are knowable before they are known, and in the learners beget the knowledge of themselves. They either still exist in their own places or they belong to the past: In the latter case, that which exists is not themselves but certain signs of their past existence, the sight or hearing of which provides knowledge that they once were and now are past. Such signs may be situated in places, as tombs of the dead and so forth. They may be stored in reliable books like any credible and authoritative history. Or they may exist in the minds of men who already know the facts: What is already known to them is knowable to others, to whose knowledge it is prior and who, through instruction from those to whom it is known, can come to know it. All this, in the activity of learning, presents a kind of trinity: the reality knowable before known, the applying to it of the learner's knowledge coming into existence with the learning, and, thirdly, the will linking the two. And when knowledge is attained, another more inward trinity appears with its recollection in the mind itself, made up of the images impressed upon the memory in the process of learning, and derived from the informing of the thought when the recollecting attention is directed to them, and from the will which links the two.

As to that which arises in the mind where it had not previously been, such as faith and the like, although they indeed seem to be extrinsic elements added through teaching, yet, like the objects of belief, they are not situated or accomplished in the outer world but originate completely within the mind itself. Faith is not that which is believed but that by which it is believed: The former is believed, the latter is seen. But because it originates in the mind, which before faith began to exist there was already mind, it seems like something adventitious and will be considered among things which have passed when sight takes its place and faith itself ceases to be: Now by its presence it forms one trinity when it is retained, contemplated, and loved, but then it will form another trinity by a trace of itself left behind when passing through the memory, as has been previously said.

Chapter Nine

12

It may, moreover, be questioned whether in the afterlife the virtues by which one lives well in our state of mortality must cease existing when they have led the soul home to the eternal world; for they also originate in the mind which previously existed without them when it was mind nonetheless. Some have supposed that they will cease and in respect to three of them, prudence, fortitude, and temperance, this view has a great deal in its favor. But justice (or righteousness) at least is immortal, and, rather than cease to be, will be perfected in us in the afterlife; yet that great and eloquent writer Cicero, in his dialogue *Hortensius,* argues this way concerning all four: "If, when we have left this life, we should be allowed, as the fables relate, to live immortally in the islands of the blest, what need with no courts to plead in should we have of eloquence, or even of virtues themselves? We could not need fortitude when no labor or danger confronted us, or justice, when no other men's possessions could be coveted, or temperance for the ruling of passions which will no longer exist, or even prudence, when there would be no choice to make between good and evil. Our blessedness would consist only in the awareness and knowledge of nature which alone makes admirable even the life of gods. From this we may infer that all the rest serve some need and only this [blessedness] is the free choice of the will."

Thus that great orator, when he begins to sing the praises of philosophy, recalling what he owes to the philosophers and expressing it with power and grace, declared that all four virtues are needed only in this life filled, as we know, with anxieties and delusions; but when we have left this life, no virtue is needed, if we are allowed to live where life is blessed. He believes that the good soul is blessed only through learning and knowledge, that is, contemplation, of that Nature which is supremely good and lovable—the Nature, that is, which has created and ordered all other natures. If it is proper to justice to be subject to that Nature's rule, then certainly justice is immortal, nor will it in that blessed state cease to exist but will be of a perfection and a grandeur beyond the possibility of increase.

Perhaps the other three virtues also—prudence with no remaining risk of error, fortitude without ills to be endured, temperance with no resisting passions—may nevertheless exist in that state of happiness. It may be the function of prudence to consider no good preferable or equal to God; of fortitude, to cleave to him steadfastly; of temperance, to take pleasure in no harmful defection. But the present work of justice in supporting the oppressed, of prudence in warding off snares, of fortitude in the endurance of difficulties, of temperance in the restraint of corrupting pleasures—there will be nothing of these in that life where there is to be no evil.

Therefore, these activities of the virtues, needed in our mortal life as is faith to which they should be referred, will be considered as things past: and they form one trinity now when we retain, contemplate, and love them as present; they will form another trinity then, when we find (by means of some traces of their passing left in the memory) that they no longer exist but have been. Even then there will be a trinity when that trace will be both retained in the memory and truly known and both will be linked together by the will as a third.

Chapter Ten

13

In the knowledge of all those temporal things which we have mentioned here certain knowable things precede knowledge by an interval of time; such are the sensible properties already in the outer objects before being perceived or all those things known through history. Some others arise simultaneously with being known: If, for example, an object of sight having no previous existence should arise before our eyes, it cannot precede our knowing of it; or if a sound is made in the presence of a hearer, the sound and the hearing of it begin and end simultaneously. But whether their origin is prior or simultaneous, the "knowables" beget the knowledge, and not vice versa.

But when knowledge is begotten and things known are placed in memory and are recalled to sight in the act of recollection, the retention in the memory is obviously prior temporally both to the recollecting vision and to the union of the two by the will. But this is not the case with the mind itself. The mind cannot come from outside to itself, as if to a self already in existence there should be added an identical self previously nonexistent, or as if, rather than coming from outside, there should be born in the existing self an identical self which did not previously exist just as faith arises from nonexistence in the existing mind. Nor does the mind when it knows itself see itself by recollection as constituted in its own memory, as if it had not been there before it became the object of its own knowledge. From the time of its origin the mind has certainly never stopped remembering itself, understanding itself, and loving itself, as already indicated. Consequently in its act of conversion upon itself in thought, a trinity is manifested in which we can recognize a "word"—formed from the act of thinking and united to its origin by will. This is where we may recognize more clearly than before the image we seek.

Chapter Eleven

14

The objection may be raised that the power by which the mind, always present to itself, is asserted to "remember" itself cannot strictly be called memory. For memory is of past realities, not present ones. Some who write about virtues, including Cicero, have analyzed prudence into the three elements of memory, understanding, and foresight (Cicero, *De Inv. Rhet. II.*53), referring memory to the past, understanding to the present, and foresight to the future—the last being reliable only in those having foreknowledge of future events, a power belonging only to men when given from above, as to the Prophets. Thus the Scriptural Book of Wisdom says that "the thoughts of men are fearful, and our foresight uncertain" (Wis 9:14). Memory of past things and understanding of present things are reliable—that is, when the realities present are incorporeal: for corporeal realities are present to the gaze of bodily eyes and not to understanding. To meet the objection that there is no memory of present realities we may note a quotation from secular literature where there was more concern for verbal exactitude than for factual truth. "Ulysses would not brook such outrage, nor in that testing hour forget himself" (Vergil, *Aen.* III.628f).

In saying that Ulysses did not forget himself, Vergil is saying that the hero remembered himself; and, since he was surely present to himself, that could only be the case if we can have memory of present realities. Therefore in regard to past realities memory is that power by which they may be reviewed and recollected; in regard to a present reality as the mind is to itself, the name memory not unreasonably may be given to the mind's self-possession so as to be understandable by its own thinking activity and both can be joined together by the love of itself.

Chapter Twelve

15

Now this trinity of the mind is the image of God, not because the mind remembers, understands, and loves itself, but because it also has the power to remember, understand, and love its Maker. And in doing this it attains wisdom. If it does not do this, the memory, understanding, and love of itself is no more than an act of folly. Therefore, let the mind remember its God, to whose image it was made, let it understand and love him.

In brief, let it worship the uncreated God who created it with the capacity for Himself, and in whom it can be made partaker. Hence it is written: "Behold, the worship of God is wisdom" (Jb 28:28). By participating in that supreme Light wisdom will belong to the mind not by its own light, and it will reign in bliss only where the eternal Light is. The wisdom is so called the wisdom of man as to be also that of God. If wisdom were only human it would be vain, for only God's wisdom is true wisdom. Yet when we call it God's wisdom, we do not mean the wisdom by which God is wise: He is not wise by partaking in Himself as the mind is wise by partaking in God. It is more like speaking of the justice of God not only to mean that God is just but to mean the justice He gives to man when He "justifies the ungodly": to which the Apostle alludes when speaking of those who "being ignorant of God's justice, and wanting to establish their own justice, were not subject to the justice of God" (Rom 4:5, 10:3). In this way we might speak of those who, ignorant of the wisdom of God and wanting to establish their own, were not subject to the wisdom of God.

16

There is an uncreated Being who has made all other beings great and small, certainly more excellent than everything He made, and thus also more excellent than the rational and intellectual being which we have been discussing, namely, the mind of man, made to the image of its Creator. And the Being more excellent than all others is God. Indeed, He is "not far from any one of us," as the Apostle says, adding, "for in him we live and move and have our being" (Acts 17:27f). Were this said in a material sense we could understand it of our material world: for in it also, in respect to our body, we live and move and are. The text should be taken, however, in a more excellent and also invisible and intelligible way, namely, with respect to the mind that has been made to His image.

In fact, what is there that is not in Him of whom Holy Scripture says: "For from Him and through Him and in Him are all things" (Rom 11:36)? If all things are in Him, in whom except in Him in whom they are can the living live or the moving move? Yet all men are not with Him in the sense in which He says "I am always with you" (Ps 73:23). Nor is He with all things in the sense in which we say, "The Lord be with you." The great misery of man, therefore, is not to be with Him without whom he cannot exist. Unquestionably, man is never without Him in whom man is; but if a man does not remember Him, does not understand Him or love Him, he is not with Him. But complete forgetfulness makes it impossible even to be reminded of what we have forgotten.

Chapter Thirteen

17

To clarify this let us take an example from the visible world. A man whom you fail to recognize says: "You know me"; and to remind you, he says, where, when, and how you met him. After he gives all the clues to revive the memory of him and you still do not recognize him, this means that you have forgotten him so completely that there is no trace of your former knowledge and you can only believe his assurance that you once knew him, or you do not believe him if he does not seen credible. Clearly, however, if you do remember, you are returning to your memory, discovering therein what was not completely forgotten and erased. Now let us return to what led us to draw a parallel with human encounters. In the ninth Psalm we read the words: "Let the sinners be turned to hell, all the nations which forget God" (Ps 9:18). Or again, in the twenty-second: "All the ends of the earth shall be reminded, and shall turn unto the Lord" (Ps 22:27). Therefore, these nations had not so forgotten God that they could not remember Him when reminded. By forgetting God, which was like forgetting their own life, they had been turned toward death, that is, toward hell. But, when reminded, they are turned to the Lord, revived through the remembrance of their proper life of which forgetfulness had deprived them. We may compare the text of the ninety-fourth Psalm: "Understand now, you unwise among the people: return finally, you fools, to wisdom. He who planted the ear, shall he not hear?" and so forth (Ps 94:8f.). The words are addressed to those who have spoken vainly concerning God by not understanding Him.

Chapter Fourteen

18

There are many more testimonies in Scripture to the love of God and in this the other two mental elements are logically implied since no one can love what he does not remember nor love that which he does not know. This is the best-known and the principal commandment: "You shall love the Lord your God" (Dt 6:5). The human mind is naturally constituted so as never to be without the memory, the understanding, and the love of itself. But inasmuch as the desire to harm accompanies hatred of a man, it is reasonable to say that a man's mind hates itself when it is harmful to itself. When the mind does not know that what it wants is harmful, its ill will to itself is unconscious, but in wanting what is harmful, it is willing evil to itself. So it is written: "He who loves iniquity hates his own soul" (Ps 11:5). Consequently, the man who knows how to love himself properly loves God; whereas the man who does not love God, even if he retains a natural self-love, may properly be said to hate himself when he acts against his own good, acting as an enemy to himself. That is certainly a frightful delusion whereby, with all men desiring their own profit, so many do what brings ruin to them. Vergil describes a similar distemper in dumb animals in these words:

> God guard his servants from such delusion,
> And send it on his enemies!—to tear
> With uncovered fangs their mangled limbs.
> (Vergil, *Georg.* III.513f.)

The poet is able to speak of a bodily disease as delusion insofar as every creature is its own friend and guardian, and the disease resulted in making beasts mutilate their own body whose welfare was their aim.

When the mind loves God and, therefore, remembers Him and understands Him, there rightly follows the command to love one's neighbor as oneself.

For the mind's self-love becomes right instead of evil when it loves God by partaking of whom the image we mention not only exists but is transformed from old to new, from deformity to beauty, from unhappiness to happiness. The power of self-love is so strong that if a man has to choose he will lose all worldly things rather than lose himself. Only with God above, to whom the Psalmist sings "My strength will I keep safe with thee," and again, "Draw near unto Him, and be lightened," can a man secure his strength and enjoy the divine Light as his own. But the mind forsaking the God above becomes so weakened and darkened that through uncontrollable loves and inescapable delusions it falls miserably away from itself into alien and inferior things. So the penitent, who had already experienced God's mercy, exclaims in the Psalm: "My strength has forsaken me, and the light of my eyes is not with me" (Ps 38:10).

19

Nevertheless, even in evil situations of weakness and delusion, the mind is not able to lose its natural memory, understanding, and love of itself, and thus is justified the above quotation: "Though man walks in an image, yet is he vainly disquieted: he heaps up treasures, and knows not for whom he shall gather them" (Book XIV.4.ii). Why does he heap up treasures except that his strength has forsaken him—the strength in which by possessing God he needed nothing else? And why does he not know for whom he shall gather them but because the light of his eyes is not with him? So he is unable to see what truth would tell him: "You fool, this night they require your soul of you; then whose shall those things be which you have provided?" (Lk 12:20).

Yet man, although fallen, still "walks in an image," and his mind retains a memory, an understanding, and love of himself; so that if it were made clear to him that he cannot have both, and a choice offered of one of the two with loss of the other—either his stored-up treasures or his mind—there is no one so mindless as to prefer treasures to mind. Treasures very often can conquer the mind; but the mind not conquered by treasures is able to live an easier and more unobstructed life without them. Who can possess treasures except through the mind? A child born to the greatest wealth, though owner of all that he legally possesses, as long as his mind is dormant possesses nothing. How, therefore, can anything be possessed by one who has lost his mind? It is in fact needless to suggest that any man, facing the choice, should prefer the loss of treasures to the loss of mind. No one could prefer treasures or even find them of comparable value to his bodily eyes, which give possession not as of gold to a few fortunate ones but of the wide heaven to every man. By using the bodily eyes every one possesses whatever he delights in seeing. Who then would not choose, if he could not keep both and must be deprived of one, to lose his treasures rather than his eyes? Likewise if asked whether he would rather lose eyes or mind, every "mind" must see that he would rather keep his mind and lose his eyes. For without the bodily eyes the mind is still human, but the bodily eyes without the mind are the eyes of a beast—who would not prefer to be a blind man than a seeing beast?

20

My purpose in this argument was to convince even those slower in comprehension among those reading or hearing what I have written of the strength of the mind's self-love even when it is weak and erring through the misguided love and pursuit of inferior things. Now it would not be able to love itself if it were entirely ignorant of itself—that is, if it did not remember itself—and did not understand itself. Such power it has by virtue of God's image within it that it is able to cleave to Him whose image it is. It has been placed in that order of reality, not a spatial order, where there is none above it but God.

And when its cleaving to Him has become absolute, it will be one spirit with Him: Witness the words of the Apostle, "He that is joined to the Lord is one spirit" (1 Cor 6:17), by drawing near, in order to participate in that being, truth, and bliss without this adding anything to His own being, truth, and bliss. Joined to that Being in perfect happiness, the mind will live within that Being a changeless life, enjoying the changeless vision of all it beholds. Then, as Holy Scripture promises, its desire will be satisfied "with good things" (Ps 103:5), with unchanging goods, with the very Trinity itself, its God whose image it is. And that nothing may ever injure it, it will abide "in the secret place of his countenance" (Ps 31:20), so full of His abundance that sin can never again delight it. But here and now when the mind sees itself, what it sees is not unchangeable.

Chapter Fifteen

21

Of this it can have no doubt since it is miserable and longs for happiness. Only because it is able to change is it able to hope that happiness is possible for it. For if it were unchangeable it could change neither from bliss to misery nor from misery to bliss. Under an omnipotent and good Lord nothing but its own sin and its Lord's justice could have made it miserable. Nothing but its own merit and its Lord's rewarding will make it blissful; and even its merit is a grace from Him whose reward will also be its bliss. For the justice it has lost and now lacks it cannot give itself. That justice was received at creation and was lost inevitably by its own sinning. Therefore it must receive justice in order to deserve to receive bliss. To a mind inclining toward pride in a good considered its own doing, the Apostle asserts this truth: "What hast thou that thou hast not received? And if thou hast received, why does thou boast as if thou hast not received it?"

But when rightly remembering its Lord, it receives His spirit, becoming fully aware of the truth learned from the inner Teacher, that it can ascend only by the affection He freely gives, just as it could have fallen only by its own voluntary failure. In fact it has no memory of its own happiness, for that was once and is no longer, and the mind has entirely forgotten it, so that no reminder can bring it back. But it believes in the Scriptures of its God that are worthy of faith and written by His Prophet, when they tell of a paradisal happiness and relate the account of man's original good and evil yet remembers the Lord its God. For He always is—neither has He been and is not, nor is He and has not been, but just as He never will not be, so never was He not. And He is everywhere in His totality; so that in Him the mind lives and moves and has its being, and consequently can remember him. Not that it recollects that it had known Him in Adam, or anywhere else before this bodily life, or at its first making and settling in this body. Of none of these things has it any memory at all; all of them are buried in forgetfulness. But it is reminded that it should turn to the Lord as to that light by which it was somehow touched even when it was turned away from Him. Hence arises the ability even in the godless to think of eternity and to assign praise and blame rightly in the sphere of human morality.

By what norms do they make such judgments if not by those in which they recognize how every man should live, although their own lives are not an example of this? Where do they see such norms? Not in their own nature: for the mind unquestionably sees them, whereas their minds are admittedly changeable; but the changelessness of these norms is evident to all who have the power to see them. Nor does it see them in any state of their own mind; for the norms are norms of justice, and their minds are admittedly unjust.

Where are the norms written, whereby what is just is recognized by the unjust man, and in which he sees that he ought to have what he does not have? Where are they written except in the book of that light called Truth, out of which every just law is copied and passes into the heart of man who does justice—passes not by transference but by impression, just as the seal of a ring passes into the wax without leaving the ring? But as for him who does not do justice, seeing nevertheless what is to be done, he is turned away from the light by which he nevertheless is still touched. The man who does not even see how he ought to live sins with more excuse since he does not transgress a law he knows: yet even he at times may feel the touch of truth's omnipresent splendor when he admits the justice of a rebuke.

Chapter Sixteen

22

Those moved by the reminder to convert again to the Lord from that state of deformity wherein worldly desires conformed them to this world have to receive from the Lord their re-formation, as the Apostle says, "Be not conformed to this world, but be reformed in newness of your mind" (Rom 12:2), the beginning of the image's reforming must come from him who first formed it. It cannot of itself re-form the self which it could de-form. The Apostle says in another place: "Be renewed in the spirit of your mind, and put on the new man, which has been created according to God in justice and holiness of truth" (Eph 4:23). The words "according to God" agree with what we read elsewhere: "to the image of God" (Gn 1:27). Justice and holiness of truth were lost through sin; hence this image became deformed and discolored. When the image is re-formed and renewed the mind receives what it once had.

When he said, "in the spirit of your mind," this did not signify two separate realities, one the mind and the other the mind's spirit. It signifies that while every mind is spirit, not every spirit is mind. God also is a spirit, and He cannot be renewed since He cannot grow old. The word "spirit" is also used to denote something in a man which is not mind and to which belong imaginings in the likeness of bodily objects: We see this in the text of the letter to the Corinthians, "If I pray in a tongue, my spirit prays, but my mind is unfruitful" (1 Cor 14:14). That tells what happens when what is spoken is not understood. It could not be spoken unless the images of the material sounds were present in the thought of the spirit before their vocal articulation.

Again, the human soul may be called "spirit" as in the words of the Gospel: "And bowing His head, He gave up His spirit," signifying the death of the body when the soul leaves it. "Spirit" may even be spoken of a beast; this is evident in the book of Solomon, Ecclesiastes, where we read: "Who knows if the spirit of the children of men ascend upward and if the spirit of the beast descend downward to the earth?" (Eccl 3:21). It is also written in Genesis, where it says that all flesh died in the flood, "that had in it the spirit of life" (Gen 7:22). "Spirit" is also used of wind, something clearly material, as in the Psalms: "Fire and hail, snow and ice, the spirit of the storm" (Ps 148:8). Since "spirit" has many different meanings, Paul wished to signify by "the spirit of the mind" that spirit which is called mind. Likewise the same Apostle writes: "In the putting off of the body of flesh" (Col 2:11). Here two different realities are not signified: one flesh and the other body of flesh: but because there are fleshless bodies like the celestial bodies and earthly ones without flesh, Paul uses "body of flesh" for that body which is flesh. And in like manner he uses "spirit of the mind" for the spirit which is mind.

In other texts the image is named more explicitly as when the same advice is given in other words: "Putting off the old man with his deeds, put on the new man who is renewed in the knowledge of God according to the image of his Creator" (Col 3:9). Therefore, what we read in that other place: "Put on the new man that has been created according to God" means exactly what is said in this place, "Put on the new man, that is being renewed according to the image of him who created him." Where the former text reads "according to God," the latter reads "according to the image of his Creator," and where the former reads "in justice and holiness of truth," in the latter we read "in the knowledge of God." So the renewal and re-forming of the mind takes place "according to God" or "according to God's image": It is said to be according to God to exclude the supposition that it is according to another creature; and according to God's image, to clarify that the renewal is accomplished there where God's image is, in the mind. Likewise we say of the righteous and the faithful departed that he is dead according to the body but not according to the soul. Dead according to the body means dead with or in the body, and not dead with or in the soul. To call a man beautiful according to the body, or strong according to the body, not according to the mind, is to say that his beauty and strength are not mental but bodily. This manner of speaking is quite common. We are not, therefore, to understand "according to the image of his Creator" as if the image, according to which the mind is renewed, is different from the mind, and as if it is not the mind itself that is renewed.

Chapter Seventeen

23

Certainly the renewal we are discussing is not accomplished in one moment of conversion like the renewal occurring in the moment of baptism by the forgiveness of all sins, none remaining unforgiven. But it is one thing to recover from a fever, and another to regain one's health after weakness resulting from fever. It is one thing to remove a spear from the body, and another to heal the inflicted wound with treatment that follows. So to begin the cure is to remove the cause of sickness: and this occurs through the forgiveness of sins. There is in addition the healing of the sickness itself accomplished gradually by progressive renewal of the image. Both are manifest in one text of the Psalm where we read: "Who shows mercy upon all your iniquities," which occurs in baptism; and then: "Who heals all your sicknesses" (Ps 103:3), which refers to daily advances whereby the image is renewed. The Apostle spoke of this in clear words: "If our outer man decays, yet is our inner man renewed from day to day" (2 Cor 4:16)—but he is "renewed" as he said in the previously quoted texts, "in the knowledge of God," that is, "in justice and holiness of truth." He who is thus renewed by daily progressing in the knowledge of God, in justice and holiness of truth, is converting the direction of his love from the temporal to the eternal, from visible to intelligible things, from carnal to spiritual things, trying assiduously to control and reduce all desire for the former and to bind himself by love to the latter. All his success in this depends on divine assistance, for it is God's word that "without me you can do nothing" (Jn 15:5).

When the final day of life reveals a man, in the midst of this progress and growth, holding steadfast to the faith of the Mediator, the holy angels will await him to bring him home to the God whom he has served and by whom he must be perfected; and at the end of the world he will receive an incorruptible body, not for punishment but for glory. For the likeness of God will be perfect in this image only in the perfect vision of God: of which vision the Apostle Paul says: "Now we see through a glass darkly, but then face-to-face" (1 Cor 13:12). And again: "But we with unveiled face beholding the glory of the Lord are transformed into the same image from glory to glory, as from the spirit of the Lord" (2 Cor

3:18). This describes the daily process in those progressing as they should.

Chapter Eighteen

24

This statement is from the Apostle John: "Beloved, we are now the children of God, and it has not yet appeared what we shall be: but we know that when He appears we shall be like Him, for we shall see Him as he is" (Jn 3:2). This indicates that the full likeness of God is attained in His image only when it has attained the full vision of Him. John's words may indeed be considered as referring to the body's immortality; for also in that we shall be like God, but only like the Son, since He alone in the Trinity took a body in which He died, rose again, and which He bore with Him into heaven. We may also speak here of an image of the Son of God in which we, like Him, shall have an immortal body, conformed in that respect to the image of the Son only, not of the Father nor of the Holy Spirit. For of Him alone do we read and receive with very sound faith that "the Word was made flesh" (Jn 1:14). So the Apostle says: "Whom He foreknew, them He also predestined to be conformed to the image of His Son, that He might be firstborn among many brethren" (Rom 8:29). "First-born," in fact, "of the dead," in the words of the same Apostle (Col 1:18)—that death whereby His flesh was sown in dishonor and rose again in glory (1 Cor 15:43). According to this image of the Son, to which we are conformed through immortality in the body, we likewise do that which the same Paul says elsewhere: "As we have borne the image of the earthly, let us also bear the image of Him who is from heaven" (1 Cor 15:49). This means: Let us who were mortal according to Adam believe with true faith and sure and steadfast hope that we shall be immortal according to Christ. For thus we can bear the same image now, not yet in vision but through faith, not yet in reality but in hope. Indeed in this context the Apostle was speaking of the resurrection of the body.

Chapter Nineteen

25

But if we consider that image of which it is written: "Let us make man in our image and likeness" (Gn 1:26), not "in my image" or "in your image," we must believe that man was made in the image of the Trinity; and we have devoted our best efforts to discover and understand this. Therefore in respect to this image we may better interpret John's words: "We shall be like Him, for we shall see Him as He is!" Here the Apostle is speaking of Him of whom he has said: "We are the children of God!"

The immortality of the flesh, moreover, will be made perfect in the moment of resurrection which, as Paul says, will be "in the twinkling of an eye, at the last trumpet: and the dead shall be raised uncorrupted, and we shall be changed" (1 Cor 15:52). For in the twinkling of an eye there shall rise again before the judgment that spiritual body in strength, incorruption, and glory which now as a natural body is being sown in weakness, corruption, and dishonor. But the image that is being renewed day by day in the spirit of the mind, and in the knowledge of God, not outwardly but inwardly, will be perfected by that vision which shall exist after the judgment as face-to-face—the vision which now is only developing, through a glass darkly (1 Cor 13:12).

We ought to understand the perfecting of the image by these words: "We shall be like Him, for we shall see Him as He is." This is the gift to be given us then when we hear the call: "Come you blessed of my Father, possess the kingdom prepared for you" (Mt 25:34). Then the godless one shall be removed so that he does not see the glory of the Lord, when those on the left hand go into eternal punishment, and those on the right hand into eternal life. But as the Truth has told us, "This is eternal life, that they may know you the one true God, and Jesus Christ whom you have sent" (Jn 17:3).

This wisdom of contemplation is, I believe, in its strict sense, distinguished in Holy Scripture from knowledge, and called wisdom—a human wisdom, yet coming to man only from God: participating in whom, the reasonable and intellectual mind is able to become wise in truth. At the end of his dialogue *Hortensius*, we see Cicero praising this contemplative wisdom. "If," he says, "we meditate day and night, if we sharpen our understanding which is the mind's eye and take care that it not grow dull, if, that is, we live the life of philosophy, then we may have good hope that although our power of feeling and thinking is mortal and transient, it will be pleasant for us to pass away when life's duties are done. Nor will our death be offensive to us but a repose from living; and if, however, as the greatest and most famous of the ancient philosophers have believed, our souls are eternal and divine, then we may rightly suppose that the more constant a soul has been in following its own course, that is, in the use of reason and zeal in inquiry, and the less it has mingled and involved itself in the vices and delusions of man, so much the easier will be its ascent and return to its heavenly country." Afterward, he adds this final statement to summarize and conclude his discussion: "Therefore, to end this long discourse, after these pursuits have filled our life, if it is our will to pass quietly into nothingness or to go immediately from our present home to another far better one, we should dedicate all our energy and attention to these studies."

I cannot but wonder that so powerful a mind should offer to men who live the life of philosophy, the life-giving happiness in the contemplation of truth, a "pleasant passing away" when human life's duties are done, if our power of thinking and feeling is mortal and transient; as though this would be the death and destruction of that which we so little loved or so fiercely hated that its passing away would be pleasant to us. He did not learn that from the philosophers to whom he gives such great praise; his opinion smacked rather of the New Academy, which had led him to skepticism even about the most evident truths. But, as he admits, the tradition that came to him from those philosophers who were the greatest and most famous was that souls are eternal. Indeed, the advice is appropriate for eternal souls so that they may be found at the end of their life "following their own course, that is, in the use of reason and the zeal in inquiry," not "mingling and involving themselves in the vices and delusions of men," so that they may more easily return to God. But for unhappy men, as all men must be whose mortality is supported by reason alone without faith in the Mediator, this course which consists in the love of God and in the search for truth is not enough. I have done my best to demonstrate this in previous books of this treatise, especially the fourth and thirteenth.

Augustine of Hippo

ON SEEING GOD
ON THE PRESENCE OF GOD

Introductory Note. In the preface to the first letter written to Pauline, Augustine distinguishes between believing and seeing. He cites the Resurrection of Christ as an example of something that is believed on the authority of Scripture but not seen, and he places Scripture above all human authority.

He then proposes these texts: "Blessed are the clean of heart, for they shall see God" (Mt 5:8) and "No man hath seen God at any time" (Mt 5:8) and "I have seen God face-to-face, and my soul hath been saved" (Gn 32:30). He asserts that seeing God is correctly placed in the future tense, whereas in the past neither Moses nor the Apostles saw the "fullness of divinity." This is promised only to the saints in the afterlife.

The entire letter is a statement in various ways of the unknowability of God and can be used as an instance of Augustine's negative theology and great reliance on faith. It is faith, working through love and hope, that cleanses the heart so that it will see God.

Following Ambrose, Augustine admits that "although we have no power of seeing, there is a grace of meriting that we may be able to see." The indispensable condition is the desire to see God. Only those with this desire will cleanse their hearts by faith working through love. It is God who gives the desire and God who fulfills it by his gifts of faith and charity.

The final judgment as to whether we will see God is to be a judgment concerning love. God is not sought by eyes but by desire, nor is He found except through love.

In the second letter presented here Augustine takes up the question of Dardanus as to whether those who are united with God are also in paradise or heaven, since God is there. He responds that the "word paradise is a general term signifying a state of living in happiness." But since God is everywhere, those who are happily united to Him may be said to be in paradise. But just as when Christ was on earth He was not

363

in heaven as man, so we are not yet in heaven as human beings although the God of heaven is present to us here on earth.

Augustine then explains the various modes of God's presence: in the universe by His divinity, in God's People (His temple) by Grace. He is always wholly present in Himself, although He is not always received wholly, but according to each one's capacity. Paradise is knowledge of God's presence in the universe and in ourselves. God's presence by Grace occurs at baptism, and children have to grow up before they can, as spiritual persons, recognize the Holy Spirit's indwelling.

With Christ as the Cornerstone, the baptized are built throughout time into a temple of God, His Church. In this letter, therefore, Augustine is teaching the necessity of baptism in order for one to become a living stone of God's temple. "For we are the temple of the living God, as God said: I will dwell in them and I will be their God and they shall be my people" (2 Cor 6:16; Lv 26:12)—Christ, the Head, and the faithful, His Mystical Body, are this living temple, the City of God, the communion of saints.

Letter 147: Augustine to the Noble Lady, Pauline, greeting (413)

Chapter One

Aware of the debt that I have acquired through your request and my promise, devoted servant of God, Pauline, I should not have delayed in paying it. For, when you requested that I write you a long and detailed treatise about the invisible God, and whether He can be seen by bodily eyes, I was not able to refuse lest I affront your holy zeal, but I postponed fulfilling my promise, either on account of other business or because I needed much more time to reflect on what you requested. But since it is so profound a subject that it becomes more difficult the more one reflects on it—not so much in what is to be thought and said of it, but in the method of persuasion to be used with those who think otherwise—I decided it was high time to end my delay, in the hope that writing rather than postponing it would bring me divine help. Hence, in the first place, I think that the manner of life is more effective for this kind of research than the manner of speech. Those who have learned from Our Lord Jesus Christ to be meek and humble of heart make greater progress by meditation and prayer than by reading and hearing. I am not saying that speech will cease to play its part, but when he who plants and he who waters have fulfilled the requirements of their task, he leaves the rest to Him who gives the increase (1 Cor 3:7), since He made the one who plants and the one who waters.

Chapter Two

According to the inward man, then, receive the words of understanding renewed day by day, even when "the outward man is corrupted" (2 Cor 4:16), either by the chastisement of abstinence, or by a case of ill health, or by some accident, or even by the very onset of age, a necessary consequence even for those who long enjoy good health. Therefore, lift up the spirit of your mind which is renewed unto knowledge, unto the image of Him that created him (Col 3:10), where Christ dwells in you by faith (Eph 3:17), where there is no Jew or Greek, bond, free, male or female (Gal 3:28; 1 Cor 12:13; Col 3:11), where you will not die when you begin to be liberated from your body, because there you did not waste away although weighed down by years. Attentive to your interior life, take note and see what I say. I do not want you to depend on my authority by thinking that you must believe something because I have said it. If you do not see that something is true, in order that you may see clearly you should base your belief either on the Canonical Scriptures or on the truth manifested to you interiorly.

Chapter Three

As an example I shall say something to prepare you for greater certitude, and, preferably, I shall draw it from the source from which the task of expressing the argument in this subject originates. We believe that in the present life God is seen, but do we believe that we see Him with our bodily eyes, as we see the sun, or with the eye of the mind, as everyone sees himself inwardly, when he sees himself living, wishing, seeking, knowing or not knowing? You yourself, after having read this letter, remember that you have seen the sun with your bodily eyes; you can also immediately see it from the direction needed to see the sun if you are in a place where the sky is in your view and if it is the right time. But to see those things which I said are beheld by the mind, namely, that you are living, that you wish to see God, that you seek this, that you know that you are living and wishing and seeking, but you do not know in what way God is seen; to see all those things, I repeat, you do not use your bodily eyes, nor do you perceive or search for any spot through which your gaze may travel in order to reach the sight of these things. This is how you see your life, will, power of search, knowledge, ignorance—for it is no despicable part of this kind of sight to see that you do not know—this, I repeat, is how you see all these things; you see them in yourself, you possess them within yourself, and the more simply and inwardly you behold them, the more clearly and surely you see them, with no outline of forms nor brightness of colors.

Since, then, in this life we do not see God with bodily eyes, as we see heavenly or earthly bodies, or with mental vision, as we see some of those things I have noted, and which you most surely behold within yourself, why do we believe that He is seen, except that we base our faith upon Scripture, where we read: "Blessed are the clean of heart for they shall see God" (Mt 5:8) and upon any other writings like this with the same divine authority? We believe that it is forbidden to doubt this, and we do not doubt that it is an act of piety to believe.

Chapter Four

Therefore, remember this difference, if I suggest throughout my argument that you see something with bodily eyes or perceive it with any other sense, or recall that you have perceived it, as colors, noises, odors, tastes, warmth, are perceived, or if we experience anything at all in the body seeing, hearing, smelling, tasting, or touching, or that you see it by mental vision, as you see your life, will, thought, memory, understanding, knowledge, faith, or whatever else you see mentally, and you have no doubt about it, not by belief but by clear vision, you may conclude that I have proven my point. But what I shall not thus prove so that it is accepted as seen and perceived either by bodily or mental powers must be believed or not believed, if I shall say something which is necessarily true or false but is not seen to be either one. But if it is backed by Scriptures, namely, of those which in the Church are called Canonical, it must be unreservedly believed. With regard to other witnesses or evidence offered as guarantees of belief, you may or not believe, insofar as you esteem that they either have or have not the weight necessary to elicit belief.

Chapter Five

If we believed none at all of those things which we have not seen, that is, have not experienced as being actually present either mentally or corporally, or have not learned from Holy Scripture, either by reading or hearing them, how could we know of the origin of cities where we have never been, such as that Rome was founded by Romulus, or, to take more recent events, that Constantinople was founded by Constantine? Finally, how could we know

what parents begot us, or from what fathers, grandfathers, ances-
tors we have come? Since we obviously know many such things,
like the soul and its mental power of the will, which we have not
learned either as present to any of our faculties, or on the authority of the Canonical writings, as that Adam was the first man, or
that Christ was born in the flesh, suffered and rose again, we
know these things on the word of others, and we have concluded
that their testimony, at least in this area of knowledge, is completely trustworthy. If we are sometimes led astray in such matters, either by believing that something is the case when it is not
the case, or that it is not the case when it is, we conclude that there
is no danger as long as the matter does not contradict that faith on
which our devotion is based.

This preface of mine raises a question not yet articulated, but
it forewarns you and others who will read these words of what
judgment you should make either concerning my writings or
those of another, lest you think that you know what you do not
know or believe rashly what you have neither perceived by your
bodily sense or your mental vision on the evidence of the subject
to be known, nor learned on the authority of the Canonical
Scriptures, as something worthy of belief although not present to
bodily or mental powers.

Chapter Six

Shall we now come to the topic? Or do you need more
instruction before reading? Some people think that when the
mind considers something its only act is the very one we call
belief. If so, there is something wrong with my preface where I
made the distinction that it is one thing to perceive something
through the body, like the sun in the sky, or a mountain, a tree, or
some physical thing on earth; another, to perceive by mental
vision a fact no less evident, such as when we are inwardly aware
of our own will when we will something, or of our thought when
we think, or of our memory when we remember, or of any mental
experience without bodily intervention; and, finally, that it is
quite different to believe what is not present to bodily or mental
powers, nor remembered as having been present, as that without
parents Adam was created, and that Christ was born of a virgin,
suffered and rose again. These events were accomplished in the
body and surely could have been seen in the body, if we had been

present, but now they are not present to us as the light seen by our eyes is present, or as we are now mentally aware of the will by which we now are willing something. Because this distinction is not a false one, there is no doubt that my previous distinction between believing and being mentally aware of something was not unclearly worded.

Chapter Seven

What, therefore, shall we affirm? Is it sufficient to say that the difference between seeing and believing is that we see what is present and believe what is absent? Perhaps it really is sufficient if by the word "present" here we mean whatever is an object of our bodily or mental powers. Thus, I see a light by a bodily sense; thus, I am fully aware of my will, because these are presented to my mental powers, and are present within me. However, if anyone whose face and voice are present to me should show me his will, it would not be an object of my bodily or mental powers; therefore, I do not see it; I believe or, if I think he is lying, I do not believe, even if it should be as he says.

Hence, whatever is not present to our powers is believed if the authority on which they are offered for belief seems trustworthy; things which are present to us are seen, therefore said to be present to our mental or bodily powers. Although there are five bodily senses—seeing, hearing, smelling, tasting, touching—of these, sight is especially attributed to the eyes, but we also use this word of the others. Not only do we say, "See, how bright it is," but also "See, what a noise"; "See, what a smell"; "See, what a taste"; "See, how hot it is." My saying that things not present to the senses are believed is not to be taken as meaning that among them we include what we previously saw and now remember and have a certainty of having seen; for those are included not among the objects of our belief, but as things we have seen and, therefore, known, not because we base our belief on other evidence, but because we remember and know without any doubt that we have seen them.

Chapter Eight

Our knowledge, then, consists of things seen and things believed. Of the things which we have seen or now see, we are our own witnesses, but in those which we believe, we are led to assert by the testimony of others, since, of the things which we do not recall having seen, or do not now see, we are informed by spoken or written words, or by certain documents, and, when these have been seen, the unseen things are believed. There is every reason to say that we know not only what we have seen or see, but also what we believe, when, influenced by appropriate evidence or witnesses, we give assent to some fact. Moreover, if it is not inappropriate to say that we also know what we firmly believe, this comes from the fact that we are correctly said to see mentally what we believe, although this is not present to our senses. It is true that knowledge is attributed to the mind, whether the object of its perception and recognition came to it through the bodily senses or through the mind itself; and faith itself is surely seen by the mind, although what is believed by faith is not seen. Thus the Apostle Peter says: "In whom also now, though you see Him not, you believe" (1 Pt 1:8); and the Lord Himself said: "Blessed are they that have not seen and have believed" (Jn 20:29).

Chapter Nine

When, then, a man is told: "Believe that Christ rose from the dead," if he believes, notice what he sees, notice what he believes, and distinguish between them. He sees the man whose voice he hears, and the voice itself is included among the objects of the bodily senses, as we previously said. The witness and testimony are two different things, of which one pertains to his eyes, the other to his ears. But perhaps the importance of the witness is increased by the authority of other testimonies, namely, that of the Divine Scriptures, or by any others which induce him to believe. Hence, the Scriptures are included among the objects of bodily senses: of the eyes, if he reads them, or of the ears if he hears them read. He sees them in his mind and he understands whatever is signified by the shapes or sounds of the letters: He sees his own faith by which he responds instantly that he believes; he sees the thought by which he thinks what advantage can accrue to him by believing; he sees the will by which he approaches to embrace religion; he even sees a certain image of the Resurrection itself, as formed in his mind, and without this it is impossible to understand anything described as having happened corporeally, whether believed or not. But I think you do differentiate between the way he sees his own faith by which he believes and the way he sees that image of the Resurrection formed in his mind: something which upon hearing these words even the unbelieving one sees.

Chapter Ten

Hence, he sees all these things partly through the body and partly through the mind. But he does not see the will of the one from whom he hears the command to believe, nor the actual Resurrection of Christ, but he does believe; yet, he is spoken of as seeing it by a kind of mental vision, according to his faith in the testimonies rather than in things believed to be present. For the things he sees are present to the senses either of mind or body, although the will of the one from whom he hears the command to believe has not become something past, but remains in the speaker. The very one who speaks sees within himself this will; the hearer does not see it, he believes it. But the Resurrection of Christ is in past time, and the men who lived at that time did not see it; those who saw the living Christ had seen Him dying, but they did not see the actual Resurrection. They believed it very firmly by seeing and touching the living Christ whom they had known as dead. We completely believe that He rose again, that He was then seen and touched by men, that He lives now in heaven, and that "He dies now no more, death shall no more have dominion over Him" (1 Cor 2:11). But the actual fact is not present to our bodily senses, as are present this sky and earth, nor to our mental vision, as is present the very faith by which we believe.

Chapter Eleven

But I think you have understood through my preface what it is to see either mentally or corporeally, and the differences between that and believing. This certainly occurs in the mind and is seen by the mind, since our faith is apparent to our mind. However, what is believed by that faith is not apparent to our bodily senses, just as the very body in which Christ rose is not apparent, and it is not apparent to another's mind, as your faith is not perceived by my mind; although I believe it is in you, I do not see it corporeally—and neither can you; nor mentally, as you can; as I see mine, but you cannot. "For no man knows what is done in man but the spirit of a man that is in him" (Rom 6:9), "until the

Lord comes who both will bring to light the hidden things of darkness, and will make manifest the thoughts of hearts" (1 Cor 4:5), so that every one will see not only his own but those of others. In this sense the Apostle said that "no man knows what is done in man but the spirit of man that is in him" according to what we see in ourselves; for according to what we believe but do not see, we know that there are many faithful, and we are known to many.

Chapter Twelve

If those differences are now clear, let us come to the main point. We know that God can be seen, since it is written: "Blessed are the clean of heart, for they shall see God" (Mt 5:8). Perhaps I should not have said, "we know," but "we believe," since we have at no time seen God, either corporeally, as we see this light, or mentally, as we see within us the very faith by which we believe; but I say this only because it is so written in Scriptures. As believers in it, have we the least doubt that it is true? Yet when the Apostle John said something similar, his words were: "We know that when He shall appear, we shall be like to Him, because we shall see Him as he is." See! He said he knew something which had not happened, and which he knew by believing, though not by seeing. Therefore, we were right in saying, "We know that God can be seen," although we have not seen Him, but we have placed our faith in the divine authority contained in the holy books.

Chapter Thirteen

But what is the meaning of that word of the same authority: "No man has seen God at any time" (Mt 5:8)? Would the answer be that those words refer to seeing God, not to having seen Him? For it says, "They shall see God," not "they have seen"; and "we shall see Him as He is," not "we have seen." Hence, the words "No man has seen God at any time" do not contradict these persons' statements. The clean of heart, who wish to see God, shall see Him whom they have not seen. But what about this: "I have seen God face-to-face, and my soul has been saved" (Gn 32:30)? Does it not contradict that other passage: "No man has seen God at any time," and this, written about Moses, that he spoke to God face-to-face, as a man is wont to speak to his friend (Ex 33:11), and this: "I saw the Lord of hosts sitting upon a throne" (Is 6:1), and other like testimonies usually taken from the same authority—how can it be that they do not contradict the words "No man has seen God at any time"? Yet, the Gospel itself can be considered self-contradictory. For how can it be true to say, as it does say: "He that sees me sees the Father also" (Jn 14:9) if no man has seen God at any time? Or how is it true that "their angels always see the face of my Father," if no one has seen God at any time?

Chapter Fourteen

By what rule of interpretation shall we prove that these apparently contrary and contradictory statements are neither contrary nor contradictory? For it is not even remotely possible that the authority of the Scriptures should be erroneous at any point. When we say of the passage "No one has seen God at any time," we understand this of human beings alone; as it says elsewhere: "No one knows what is done in man, but the Spirit of a man who is in him" (1 Cor 2:11). This means: No human being knows, for this cannot be said of God, since of Christ it is written that "He needed not that any should give testimony of man, for He knew what was in man" (Jn 2:25). The Apostle, explaining this more fully, says: "Whom no man has seen, nor can see"; hence, if he says "No one has seen God at anytime," it is as if he said "No human being," and thus this problem will seem to be solved, at least to this extent, that it is not contrary to what the Lord says: "Their angels always see the face of my Father," since we certainly believe that the angels see God, "whom no one has seen at any time," that is, no human being. How, then, was God seen by Abraham (Gn 18:1), Isaac (Gn 26:2), Jacob (Gn 32:30), Job (Jb 38:1, 42:9), Moses (Ex 33:11), Micheas (3 Kgs 22:19), Isaiah (Is 6:1), of whom the absolutely truthful Scripture bears witness that they saw God, if no human being "has ever seen God, nor can see Him"?

Chapter Fifteen

Some even want to prove that the wicked will see God, and they think that God has been seen by the devil also, reading in that sense what is written in the Book of Job, that the devil came with the angels into the presence of God (Jb 1:6, 2:1), so they even question how this can be said: "Blessed are the clean of heart, for they shall see God" (Mt 5:8) and this, "Follow peace with all men, and holiness, without which no man shall see God" (Heb 12:14). I wonder very much whether those who think that the wicked will see God, and that God has been seen by the devil, go so far as to claim that they are also clean of heart and that they follow peace and holiness with all men.

Chapter Sixteen

The statement which the Lord makes: "He that sees me sees the Father also" (Jn 14:19) can on a more careful examination be shown as not contrary to the words, "No man has seen God at any time." He did not say: "Because you have seen me, you have seen the Father also," but by saying "He that sees me, sees the Father also," He wanted to show the unity of substance between the Father and the Son, that they might not be thought to differ from each other in any way. So, since it is true to say: "He that sees me, sees the Father also," and since it is clear that no one of men has seen God at any time, no one can be imagined to have seen either the Father or the Son, insofar as the Son is God and is one God with the Father; but, insofar as He is Man, surely "afterward He was seen upon earth, and conversed with men" (Bar 3:38; Jn 1:14).

Chapter Seventeen

But it is seriously problematic how there is no contradiction involved in so many men of old seeing God, if "no one has seen God at any time," whom "no man has seen, nor can see." Notice what a difficult question you have raised for me, about which you want me to speak at length and thoroughly within the limits of a brief letter, and which it seemed to you should be explained carefully and completely. Are you willing to attend to the answers I have found in the writings of other excellent Scripture commentators on what they think about seeing God—which may perhaps satisfy your desire, although you may already be acquainted with them? Pay attention, then, to these few points, please. When Blessed Ambrose, Bishop of Milan, in his commentary on the Gospel, had come to the place (*Expositio Evangelii Secundam Lucam* 1, 24–27 [CSEL 32.4.25]) where the angel appeared in the temple to the priest, Zachary (Lk 1:11), here are the great and noble things he on that occasion said about the vision of God.

Chapter Eighteen

"Not without reason," he says, "is the angel seen in the temple, because the coming of the true priest was then being proclaimed, and the heavenly sacrifice was being prepared, in which angels were to minister. "And well is He said to have appeared to one who beheld him suddenly. The Divine Scripture is wont to use this particular term, either of the angels or of God, so that what cannot be seen in advance is said to appear. Thus you have, "God appeared to Abraham at the oak of Mambre" (Gn 18:1), for he who is not perceived beforehand, but is suddenly presented to sight, is said to appear. But the objects of the senses are not seen in that way, and He on whose will it depends to be seen and whose nature it is not to be seen is seen because of His Will. For, if He does not wish it, He is not seen, but if He wishes, He is seen. Thus because He willed it, God appeared to Abraham; to others He did not appear because He did not will it. When Stephen was being stoned by the people, he saw the heavens opened and Jesus standing at the right hand of God (Acts 7:55), but this was not seen by the people. Isaiah saw the Lord of Hosts (Is 6:1), but no one else could see Him, because He appeared to whom He pleased. And why do we speak of men when of the heavenly powers and virtues themselves we read that "no one has seen God at any time"? To this the Apostle added: "The only-begotten Son, who is in the bosom of the Father, he hath declared Him" (Jn 1:18).

Hence, if no one has seen God the Father at any time, we must either necessarily assent to the Son having been seen in the Old Testament, and the heretics must stop attributing a beginning to Him who was seen before He was born of a virgin, or surely it is impossible to refute the argument that the Father or the Son or, at least, the Holy Spirit—if, however, the Holy Spirit can be seen—are seen under the appearance chosen by their will but not arising from their nature, since we learn that the Spirit also was seen under the form of a dove (Mt 3:16). Therefore, "no one has seen God at any time," because no one has beheld that plenitude of divinity which dwells in God (Col 2:9), no one has experienced it with mind or eyes, for the word "seen" pertains to both. Finally, when he adds, "The only Begotten Son, who is in the bosom of the Father, He hath declared Him" (Jn 1:18), it is the sight of minds rather than of eyes which is described. For beauty is seen, but virtue is declared; the former is grasped by the eyes, the latter by the mind.

But why should I speak of the Trinity? A seraphim appeared when he willed it, and Isaiah alone heard His voice (Is 6:67); an angel appeared and is now present but is not seen. It is not in our power to see, but in His to appear. However, although we have no power of seeing, there is a grace of meriting that we may be able to see. Thus, he who had the grace merited the occasion. We do not merit the occasion because we have not the grace of seeing God. Is it to be marveled at that the Lord is not seen in the present world except when He wills? Even in the Resurrection itself it is not easy to see God, except for the clean of heart; hence, "Blessed are the clean of heart, for they shall see God" (Mt 5:8). How many kinds of blessed He had enumerated, yet to none of them had He promised the ability to see God!

If, then, those who are clean of heart will see God, doubtless others will not see Him; the unworthy will not see Him, nor will he who does not wish to see God be able to see Him. God is not seen in any place but in the clean of heart; He is not sought by bodily eyes, nor limited by our sight, nor held by touch, nor heard through His speaking, nor perceived in His approach. When He is considered absent, He is seen; when He is present, He is not seen.

Finally, not all the Apostles saw Christ. Therefore, He says: "So long a time have I been with you, and you have not known me?" (Jn 14:9). But he who knew "what is the breadth and length and height and depth, and the charity of Christ which surpasseth all knowledge" (Eph 3:18–19) saw both Christ and the Father (Jn 14:9). For we do not know Christ according to the flesh (2 Cor 5:16) but according to the Spirit. For "our breath, Christ the Lord, is taken from before our face" (cf. Lam 4:20), and may He deign in His mercy to fill us unto all the fullness of God (Eph 3:19), that He may be able to be seen by us.

Chapter Nineteen

If you understand these words, what else do you want from me, since that problem, which seemed so difficult, is now solved?

But a distinction had been made between the meaning of "No one has seen God at any time" and the way in which those saints of old saw God, if those words were said because God is invisible; they saw—those of them who did see God—because He appeared to whomever He wished, and as He wished, in that form which His will chose, although His nature remained hidden. For if, when the Patriarchs saw God, His very nature appeared to them —although if He had not willed, doubtless it would not have appeared—how is it that no one has seen God at any time, when at His will, His very nature was beheld by so many Patriarchs, so that these words might be understood as spoken of God the Father, that no one has seen Him at any time?

Ambrose certainly did not lose his chance to refute certain heretics from this ground, namely, the Photinians, who declare that the Son of God originated from the womb of the Virgin, and who refused to believe that He preexisted. But because he saw others, namely, the Arians, promoting more dangerous views, whose error is doubtless included within that other, he asserted that if the Father is by nature invisible but the Son is believed to be visible, both have one equally invisible nature, and the Holy Spirit also. He transmitted this idea briefly but admirably when he later said: "Or certainly it is not possible to refute the argument that the Father or the Son, or at least the Holy Spirit (if the Holy Spirit can be seen), is seen under the appearance which their will has chosen but which their nature has not formed." He could have said "their nature has not manifested," but he chose to say "formed," lest the aspect under which God chose to appear should be thought to have the form of His nature, and from that an argument be drawn to prove that His substance is changeable and mutable. May the merciful and good God Himself keep this error far from the faith of His devoted children.

Chapter Twenty

Therefore, God is by nature invisible, and not only the Father, but also the Trinity itself, one God, and, because He is not only invisible but also unchangeable, He appears to whomever He wills and under the aspect that He wills, so that His invisible and unchangeable nature may remain completely within Himself. But the yearning of truly devoted souls, whereby they long to see God and burn with ardent love for Him, is not enkindled, in my opinion, by longing to see that aspect under which He appears as He wills, but which is not Himself; they long for the substance by which He is what He is. The holy Moses, His faithful servant, manifested the flame of this longing of his when he said to God, with whom he spoke as to a friend, face-to-face: "If I have found favor before Thee, show me yourself" (Ex 33:11–13). What, then? Was it not Himself? If it were not "Himself," he would not have said "show me yourself," but "show me God"; yet, if he actually beheld His nature and substance, he would have been far from saying "show me yourself." It was Himself, then, under that aspect in which He willed to appear, but He did not appear in His own nature which Moses longed to see because that is promised to the saints in another life.

Therefore, the answer given to Moses is true, that no one can see the face of God and live (Ex 33:20), that is, no one living in this life can see Him as He is. Many have seen, but what His will chose to show they saw, not what formed His nature, and this is what John said, if he is correctly understood: "Dearly beloved, we are the sons of God, and it hath not yet appeared what we shall be. We know that when He shall appear, we shall be like to Him, because we shall see Him as He is" (1 Jn 3:2), not as men saw Him when He willed to show Himself under the appearance that He willed; not as He is in His nature under which He lies hidden within Himself even when seen. This is what was asked of Him by the one who spoke to Him face-to-face, when he said to Him: "Show me yourself": but no one can at any time experience the plenitude of God through bodily eyes nor by the mind itself.

Chapter Twenty-One

It is one thing to see: it is quite another to take in the totality of something by seeing, since, in truth, a thing is seen when it is perceived as present in any way at all, but the totality is taken in when it is seen so that no part of it escapes notice, or when its outline can be included in the sight of it, as at present nothing of your will escapes your notice, or as you can take in at a glance the span of your ring. I have noted these two examples, the one referring to mental vision, the other to bodily eyes, for sight, as he [Ambrose] says, is to be referred to both, that is, to the eyes and the mind.

ON SEEING GOD

Chapter Twenty-Two

Moreover, if the reason why no one has at any time seen God, as Ambrose, whose words we are considering, says, is that "no one has beheld the fullness of His divinity, no one has experienced it with mind or eyes, for the phrase 'has seen' is to be referred to both," it remains for us to discover how the angels see God, because of that passage I quoted from the Gospel: "Their angels always see the face of my Father" (Mt 18:10). If He appears to them not as He is, but under whatever aspect He wills, whereas His nature remains hidden, we have greater and greater need to inquire how we shall see Him as He is, as Moses wanted to see Him when he asked God, then visible to him, to show him Himself. As our supreme reward it is promised to us that at the Resurrection we shall be like the angels of God (Lk 20:36; Mt 22:30; Mk 12:25) and if they do not see Him as He is, how, when we shall have become like to them at the Resurrection, shall we see Him? But notice what our Ambrose then says. "Finally," he says, "when this is added, the only-begotten Son Himself, He has declared Him, it is the vision of minds rather than of eyes which is described." For beauty is seen, but virtue is declared; the former is perceived by the eyes, the latter by the mind.

Just previously he had said that vision is to be referred to both; now he attributes it not to the mind, but to the eyes; yet I do not think this is done out of careless inattention to his own words, but because in speaking we more usually attribute vision to the eyes, as beauty is attributed to the body. Our way of speaking more often applies beauty to things limited by space and distinguished by color. But if there were no beauty to be seen by the mind, He would not be described as "beautiful in form, above the sons of men" (Ps 44:3). For this was not merely said according to the flesh, but also according to spiritual beauty. Hence, beauty is also used as applying to mental vision, but since it is more commonly used of corporeal things or in comparisons with them, he said: "Beauty is seen, but virtue is declared; the former is perceived by the eyes, the latter by the mind." Thus, when the only-begotten Son, who is in the bosom of the Father, declares Him with an indescribable utterance, the rational being, pure and holy, is filled with the indescribable vision of God which we shall attain when we have become like the angels. For it is true that no one

379

has seen God at any time, in the sense in which visible bodily things, known by the senses, are seen; because, if at any time He has been seen in that way, He is not seen according to His own nature but under that aspect in which he wills to appear, although that nature remains hidden and unchangeable within Him. He is seen now in the way by which He is seen as He is perhaps by some of the angels; when we have become like them, He will be seen in that way by us.

Chapter Twenty-Three

Later, when he had added that the heavenly powers, such as the Seraphim, are also not seen except when they will and how they will, he did this to indicate the depth of the Trinity's invisibility. "However," he says, "although we have no power of seeing, there is a grace of meriting that we may be able to see. Therefore, he who had the grace merited the occasion. We do not merit the occasion, because we have not the grace of seeing God." Obviously, by these words whereby he is not teaching his own doctrine, but explaining the Gospel, he does not mean that some of them will see God, but some will not see Him. "To them that believe He gave the power to be made the sons of God" (Jn 1:12), inasmuch as the following words apply to all: "We shall see Him as He is" (1 Jn 3:2); but by saying: "We do not merit the occasion because we have not the grace of seeing God," he indicates that He is speaking of this world. Although God has deigned to appear here under the aspect He willed, as to Abraham (Gen 18:1), to Isaiah (Is 6:1), and others like him, yet He shows Himself under no such appearance to innumerable others, although they belong to His people and His eternal inheritance. But in the world to come, those who are to receive the kingdom prepared from the beginning for them (Mt 25:34), all the clean of heart, shall see Him, and in that kingdom there will be no others.

Chapter Twenty-Four

Note, then, what he continues saying about that world, commencing with: "Is it any wonder that the Lord is not seen in the present world except when He wills? Even in the Resurrection itself it is not easy to see God, except for the clean of heart; therefore: 'Blessed are the clean of heart, for they shall see God.'

If, therefore, those who are clean of heart will see God, no doubt others will not see Him; the unworthy will not see Him, nor will he who does not want to see God be able to see Him." You see how carefully he speaks at present of those who will see God in the world to come: It will not be everyone; only those who are worthy. For the worthy and the unworthy will rise again, in that kingdom where God will be seen, since, "all that are in graves shall hear his voice . . . and come forth," but with a great difference, "for they that have done good things shall come forth unto the resurrection of life; but they that have done evil, unto the resurrection of judgment" (Jn 5:28–29). Thus judgment means eternal punishment, according to this other statement: "He that does not believe is already judged" (Jn 3:18).

Chapter Twenty-Five

When St. Ambrose said, "nor will he who does not want to see God be able to see Him," what else does he wish us to infer but that he who is unwilling to devote to his heart's cleansing an effort worthy of so great an aim does not want to see God? Note, then, that he adds: "God is not seen in any place, but in the clean heart." Nothing could be more explicitly, more strongly expressed. Hence, with no shadow of doubt, the devil and his angels and with them all the wicked are deprived of this vision because they are not clean of heart. Therefore, from what is written in the Book of Job (Jb 1:6, 2:1), of the angels entering the presence of God and the devil coming with them, we are not to believe that the devil saw God. It said that they came into God's presence, not God into their presence. The things we see come into our presence, but not those by which we are seen. They came, then, as it says in many versions of Scripture, "to stand before the Lord," not that God was before them. There is no need to emphasize this point, to attempt to show, as far as we can, how this happens also in time, since all things are in the sight of God always.

Chapter Twenty-Six

We ask now how God is seen, not under that aspect by which He willed to appear to certain people in that age when He spoke not only to Abraham and other just men, but even to Cain, the murderer (Gn 18:1–4), but we ask how He is seen in that kingdom where His sons will see Him as He is. Then, in truth, "He will satisfy their desire with good things" (Ps 102:5), that desire with which Moses burned, which left him unsatisfied with speaking to God face-to-face (Ex 33:11), and made him say: "Show me yourself openly, that I may see you" (Ex 33:13), as if he were saying what is said about that desire in the Psalm: "I shall be satisfied when your glory shall appear" (Ps 16:15).

With that desire, also, Philip burned and longed to be satisfied, when he said: "Show us the Father and it is enough for us" (Jn 14:8). Speaking of that vision, Ambrose, lover of God and man of desires said: "God is not seen in any place," as at the oak of Mambre, or on Mount Sinai, "but in the clean heart," and he continues, knowing what he longs and yearns and hopes for: "God is not sought by bodily eyes, through which He showed Himself to Abraham, Isaac, Jacob, and others in this world, nor is He limited by our sight because of this statement, 'Thou shalt see my back parts' (Ex 33:23). Nor is he held by touch, as when He wrestled with Jacob (Gn 32:24–30); nor heard by His utterance, as He was heard not only by so many saints but even by the devil (Gn 3:14); nor seen in His approach, as formerly when He walked in paradise in the afternoon air (Gn 3:8)."

Chapter Twenty-Seven

You notice how the holy man attempts to draw our minds away from all bodily senses in order to make them apt to see God. Nevertheless, what does such a one achieve outwardly, when he plants and waters, if God, "who gives the increase" (1 Cor 3:7), does not work inwardly? Without the help of the Spirit of God, who could think that there is something that is greater than all the things experienced through the body, and that it is not seen in any place, is not an object of search by the eyes, is not heard by any speaking, nor held by touch, nor seen in its approach, yet is seen by the clean heart? When he said this, he spoke not of this life, because he used the clearest kind of distinction, in distinguishing the life of the world to come from that of the present world where God does not appear as He is, but under that aspect which He wills. He said: "Is it any wonder that the Lord is not seen in this present world, except when He wills? In the Resurrection itself it is not easy to see God, except for those who are clean of heart; therefore: 'Blessed are the clean of heart, for they shall see God.' "

From here on he begins to speak of that world where all who rise again will not see God, but only those who rise to eternal life. The unworthy will not see Him, for of them it is said: "Let the wicked be taken away lest he behold the brightness of the Lord" (Is 26:10); but the worthy will see Him, and of those the Lord spoke when He, although present, was not seen, saying: "He that loves me keeps my commandments, and he that loves me shall be loved of my Father, and I will love him and will manifest myself to him" (Jn 14:21). Those to whom it will be said: "Depart . . . into everlasting fire which was prepared for the devil and his angels" (Mt 25:41) shall not see Him; but those who will hear the words: "Come, ye blessed of my Father, possess ye the kingdom prepared for you from the foundation of the world" (Mt. 25:34) shall see Him. The former, in truth, "shall go into everlasting burning, but the just into life everlasting" (Mt 25:46).

And what is everlasting life except that life he described elsewhere: "Now this is eternal life, that they may know you, the only true God, and Jesus Christ whom you have sent" (Jn 17:3), the life in which He promises to show Himself as one God with His Father to those who love Him, not as He was seen in the flesh in this world by both good and bad people?

Chapter Twenty-Eight

At the future judgment, when He will so come as He was seen going into heaven (Acts 1:11), that is, in the very form of Son of man, they will see that form and to them He will say: "I was hungry and you gave me not to eat" (Mt 25:42), because the Jews also shall "look upon one whom they have pierced" (Zec 12:10) but shall not see that form of God in which "He thought it not robbery to be equal with God" (Phil 2:6). Those who will see Him as He is will then see Him in that form of God; but they will not so see Him because in this life they were poor in spirit or because they were meek, or because they mourned or hungered and thirsted after justice, or were merciful or peacemakers, but because they are clean of heart. It is to be emphasized among those beatitudes that, although those with a clean heart may do everything else, the conclusion "They shall see God" is not given except to the words

"Blessed are the clean of heart" (Mt 5:3–10). Hence, He who is not seen in any place, is not sought by bodily eyes, nor limited by our sight, nor held by touch, nor heard by His speaking, nor seen in His approach, will be seen by the clean of heart. For "no man has seen God at any time," either in this life as He is, or even in the angelic life, as those visible things seen by bodily sight, because "the only-begotten Son who is in the bosom of the Father, He has declared Him" (Jn 1:18). Hence, what He declares is said to pertain to mental vision, not to bodily vision.

Chapter Twenty-Nine

But, again, lest our desire should be transferred from one bodily sense to another, that is, from eyes to ears, when he had said: "God is not sought by bodily eyes, nor limited by our sight, nor held by touch," he also added: "nor heard by His speaking," so that, if we are able, we are to realize that the only-begotten Son who is in the bosom of the Father declares Him insofar as He is the Word; not as a sound resounding in our ears, but as an image giving knowledge to our minds, that it may there shine with an ineffable light. This is what was said to Philip in the words "He that sees me, sees the Father also" (Jn 14:19), when he saw and did not see. Then Ambrose, whose yearning for that vision was so extraordinary, continues and says: "When He is considered absent, He is seen, and when He is present, He is not seen." He did not say "when He is absent," but "when He is considered absent," for He who fills heaven and earth (Jer 23:24) without being limited by finite space or extended through vast space is nowhere absent; He is completely present everywhere, but contained in no place. Whoever is carried beyond the bounds of his mind (2 Cor 5:13) to understand this sees God even when He is considered absent; whoever cannot do this should beg and endeavor to deserve to be able to do it. But let him not knock at the door of man, the disputant, to ask that he may read what he does not read, but at the door of God, the Savior, that he may be strengthened to do what he is not strong enough to do now. Later he makes clear to us why he said: "And when he is present, he is not seen," by adding: "Finally, not all the Apostles saw Christ." Therefore He says: "So long a time have I been with you, and you have not known me?" This is how God was present but was not seen.

ON SEEING GOD

Chapter Thirty

Why did he not dare to say "Finally, the Apostles did not see Christ," instead of "not all the Apostles," as if some of them by real vision saw how He and the Father are one (Jn 10:30)? Or was he, perhaps, referring to that time when Peter said: "Thou art Christ, the Son of the living God," and received the answer: "Blessed are you, Simon Bar-Jona, because flesh and blood have not revealed it to you, but my Father who is in heaven (Mt 16:16–17)? And yet it is not clear to me whether through his faith in so great a truth or by the sight of something seen that Revelation was given to his mind, inasmuch as Peter was to manifest himself as still so weak in faith as to fear the loss by death of the Son of the living God (Mt 16:21–22) whom so shortly before he had confessed.

Chapter Thirty-One

Another troubling aspect is how it was possible for God's very substance to be seen by some while still in this life, in view of what was said to Moses: "No man can see my face and live" (Ex 33:20), unless it can happen that the human mind is divinely caught up from this life to the angelic life before it is by our common death freed from the body. He who heard "secret words which it is not granted to man to utter" (2 Cor 12:2–4) was so enraptured that a certain withdrawal of his consciousness from the senses of this life occurred, and he said that he did not know "whether it was in the body or out of the body," that is, as usually occurs in advanced ecstasy, when the mind is withdrawn from this life unto that life without loosing the tie of the body, or whether there is a complete separation as occurs in real death.

So it is that this statement, "No man can see my face and live," is true, because the mind must necessarily be withdrawn from this life when it is caught up in the ineffable reality of that vision, and it is also not unbelievable that the perfection of that revelation was accorded to some saints who were not yet close enough to death that their bodies were ready for burial. This, in my opinion, was in the writer's mind when he would not say "the Apostles did not see Christ," but said "not all the Apostles saw Christ," believing that the sight of the Godhead itself, of which he spoke, could have been accorded to some of them even then; especially, blessed Paul, who, although he was, so to speak, the last of the Apostles, did not fail to mention his own ineffable revelation.

Chapter Thirty-Two

Moreover, in ancient days, in the case of Moses, God's faithful servant, destined to labor on this earth and to rule the chosen people, it would not be surprising that what he asked for was given: that he might see the glory of the Lord, to whom he said: "If I have found favor before you, show me yourself openly" (Ex 33:13). He received an answer appropriate to present conditions, that he could not see the face of God, because no man could see Him and live; thus God was explicit that the vision pertains to another and better life. Moreover, the mystery of the future Church of Christ was foretold by the words of God. Without a doubt, Moses in himself represented the type of the Jewish people who would believe in Christ after His passion, and that is why it says: "When I shall pass, you shall see my back parts" (Ex 33:21–23), and whatever else is said there, by a wonderful mystery which foretells the Church to come. But to discuss this now would take too long. As I had begun to say, however, it is later revealed in the Book of Numbers that even what he asked for was given for there the Lord reprimanded Moses' sister for her obstinacy, saying that He appeared to the other Prophets in a vision and in a dream, but to Moses plainly and not by riddles, and He added the words: "And he saw the glory of the Lord" (Nm 12:6–8). Why, therefore, did God grant him an exception unless, perhaps, that He thought him such a ruler of His people, so faithful a minister of His whole house, that even then he was worthy of that contemplation, so that, as he had wanted, he saw God as He is; a contemplation promised at the end of life (1 Jn 3:2) to all His sons?

Chapter Thirty-Three

I believe that holy man whose words we are considering was thinking of such things when he said: "not all the Apostles saw Christ," since probably some of them saw Him in the way I said. But, to prove that not all of them saw Him, as he said, he quickly adds: "Therefore He said: 'So long a time have I been with you and you have not known me?'" Then, explaining by what kind of man God is seen as He is in that contemplation, he says: "He who knows 'what is the breadth and length and height and depth, and the charity of Christ which surpasses all knowledge,' saw both Christ and the Father."

Chapter Thirty-Four

I usually understand these words of the Apostle Paul in this way: by "breadth," all good works of charity; by "length," perseverance to the end; by "height," hope of heavenly rewards; by "depth," the unsearchable judgments of God, from whom that grace has come to men. I also adapt this interpretation to the mystery of the Cross: for breadth I take the transverse beam on which the hands are stretched, because it signifies works; for length, that part of the upright which extends from the transverse beam down into the earth, where the entire crucified body was seen erect, which signifies to persevere, that is, to be steadfast and long-suffering; by height, that part which extends upward from the transverse beam, where the head is conspicuously seen, because of the expectation of heavenly things. This is to keep us from believing that good works should be done and continued for the sake of God's earthly and temporal forms, rather than for that heavenly and eternal good which "faith that works by charity" hopes for. By depth I understand that part of the Cross which is plunged into the earth's hidden part and is not seen, but from which rises the entire top part which is visible, just as man is called by God's secret will to a share in such great grace, "one after this manner, and another after that" (1 Cor 7:7); but that charity of Christ which surpasses all knowledge is doubtless found where "that peace is, which surpasses all understanding" (Phil 4:7). But, whether that champion of the Gospel sees this in these words of the Apostle, or whether he perhaps understands something more appropriate, you, in any case, see, if I am right, that it is not inconsistent with the role of faith.

Chapter Thirty-Five

Therefore, we now understand it as spiritual insight when he said: "He who knew 'what is the breadth and length and height and depth, and the charity of Christ which surpasses all knowledge,' saw both Christ and the Father"; and, lest to some dull-witted person it might seem that he was speaking of bodily sight, he said: "For we do not know Christ according to the flesh, but according to the spirit." For "our breath, Christ the Lord is taken before our face." When here he says "we know," he is speaking of our present knowledge by faith, not of our future knowledge by contemplation, since whatever we know by "unfeigned faith" (1 Tim 1:5), although by sight we do not yet see it, we now hold by unshaken belief. Finally, after he had said that he does not "now know Christ according to the flesh," as the Apostle says, and had added the Prophet's testimony: "Our breath Christ the Lord is taken before our face," he immediately continued: "May He deign in His mercy to fill us unto all the fullness of God, that He may be able to be seen by us." Surely it is evident that in saying "we know" he gained that knowledge from faith by which the just man now lives (Heb 2:4; Rom 1:17; Gal 3:11; Heb 10:38) and not from contemplation, by which we shall see God as He is (1 Jn 3:2). This gift He wants for Himself, and, therefore, for us, and he shows that it will be ours when He says: "May He deign, in His mercy, to fill us unto all the fullness of God, that He may be able to be seen by us."

Chapter Thirty-Six

In thinking that we shall become wholly what God is, some of the Apostles in their speech showed their understanding of this fullness of God. You remember that the Apostle expressed these words in this way when he said: "To know also the charity of Christ which surpasses all knowledge; that you may be filled unto all the fullness of God" (Eph 3:19). Hence, they say, if we have anything less than God has, and are less than He is in anyway, how shall we be filled unto all the fullness of God? But, when we are filled, surely we shall be equal to Him. You are shocked and turn aside with loathing from that error of that human mind, I am sure, and you are correct. Later, if God wills and according to the strength He gives, we shall discuss how that fullness is to be understood by which it is said that we are to be filled unto all the fullness of God.

Chapter Thirty-Seven

Now, take careful note and remember what has been said, to see whether I have explained what you requested and what seemed not easy to explain. If you ask whether God can be seen, I answer: He can. If you ask how I know, I answer that in Scripture, the source of truth, we read: "Blessed are the clean of heart, for they shall see God" (Mt 5:8), and other such passages. If you ask how He is said to be invisible if He can be seen, I answer that by nature He is invisible, but He is seen when He wills and as He wills. By mercy He has been seen, not as He is, but under whatever aspect he wanted to appear. If it is true that the clean of heart are blessed by seeing God and if you ask how even the evil Cain saw Him (Gn 4:6–15) when questioned by Him about his crime or how even the devil himself saw Him when with angels he came to stand before Him (Jb 1:6, 2:1), I answer that those who at times hear His words do not necessarily see Him. Those who have heard Him saying to His Son: "I have both glorified it and will glorify it again" (Jn 12:28), did not see Him, but we should not be surprised that some who are not clean of heart see God under the appearance made possible by His will, whereas His invisible nature, remaining unchanged, is still hidden.

If you ask whether He can also be seen at any time as He is, I answer that this was promised to His sons, of whom it is said: "We know that when He shall appear, we shall be like Him, because we shall see Him as He is" (1 Jn 3:2). If you ask how we shall see Him, I answer: as the angels see those things called visible; but no man has ever seen God nor can see Him, because "He inhabits light inaccessible" (1 Tm 6:16), and His nature is invisible as it is immortal. The Apostle declares this in a similar passage when he says: "Now to the King of ages, invisible and immortal" (1 Tm 1:17) since, as He is now immortal and will never be mortal, so He is invisible not only now but always. For He is not seen in any place, but in the "clean of heart"; He is not sought by bodily eyes, nor confined by our sight, nor held by touch, nor heard by His speaking, nor perceived in His approach. But the only-begotten Son who is in the bosom of the Father (Jn 1:18) soundlessly declares the nature and substance of the Godhead, and hence to eyes worthy and apt for such appearance He shows it invisibly. Those are the eyes of which the Apostle says: "The eyes of your heart enlightened" (Eph 1:18) and of which it is said: "Enlighten my eyes that I never sleep in death" (Ps 12:4). For the Lord is a spirit (2 Cor 3:17; Jn 4:24); hence, "he who is united to the Lord is one spirit" (1 Cor 6:17). Therefore, whoever can see God invisibly can be united to God spiritually.

Chapter Thirty-Eight

I think there is no further inquiry into your question. But consider in this whole discussion what you have seen, what you have believed, what you do not yet know, either because I have not spoken of it, or you have not understood, or you have not judged it worthy of faith. Among the facts you have seen as true, distinguish further how you saw them, whether by remembering that you had seen them through the body, like heavenly or earthly bodies, or whether you never saw them by bodily eyes but only by mental vision observed that they are true and certain, like your own will, concerning which I believe you when you speak, for truly I myself cannot see it as it is seen by you.

And in distinguishing between these two, take note also how you make your distinction. Although we see some things through the body, others through the mind, the distinction between these two kinds of sight is seen by the mind, not the body. Things seen by the mind need no bodily senses to let us know that they are true, but those seen through the body cannot become our knowledge without a mind to which these incoming messages can be referred. And it is the case that these incoming messages which the mind in some way is said to receive are left outside, but it forms images of them, that is, incorporeal likenesses of physical things, which it commits incorporeally to memory, so that when it has the will or power, it may pass judgment on them, after bringing them out of custody and displaying them before its mental vision. And when it has its full power, it also makes a distinction between these two: what remains outside in its corporeal aspect, what it sees within as a likeness. It discerns that the former is not there, yet the latter is there. In like manner while I am absent you think of my corporeal face; the image is present to you, yet the face whose image it is, is absent; the one is body, the other an incorporeal likeness of body.

Chapter Thirty-Nine

After carefully and diligently examining and distinguishing what you see, take care in making your distinction to assess the actual weight of evidence for what you believe in my entire speech which I began in this letter, and note how far you believe in what you do not see. You do not put the same faith in me as you do in Ambrose, from whose books I have taken this weighty testimony; or if you think we are of equal weight, you will not, of course, compare us in any way with the Gospel, or put our writings on the same footing with the Canonical Scriptures. Obviously, if you are wise enough to discern correctly, you recognize that we fall far short of that authority, and that I fall even further; however much credibility you give to us both, in vain do you compare us to that high standard. Hence, that saying, "No man has seen God at any time" (1 Jn 4:12), and: "He inhabits light inaccessible, whom no man has seen or can see" (1 Tm 6:16), and: "Blessed are the clean of heart, for they shall see God" (Mt 5:8), and other passages from the sacred books which I have cited: All these you believe more firmly than what Ambrose said: "God is not seen in any place, He is not sought by bodily eyes, nor confined by our sight, nor held by touch, nor heard by His speaking, nor perceived in His approach." No doubt he understood or believed that God who is seen by the clean of heart is like that, and I confess this is also my opinion.

Chapter Forty

Hence, in one way you have faith in these words, but in a very different way in the divine words. Perhaps some small doubt has entered your mind about us, that in respect to some of the divine words we may be somewhat less than clear, and that they are interpreted by us not literally but imaginatively. Maybe you say to yourself: Suppose God is seen by the clean of heart, and is also visible in some place? Or: Suppose the clean of heart will see God even with bodily eyes, when this corruptible flesh shall put on incorruption (1 Cor 15:33), when we shall be like the angels of God (Lk 20:36). Perhaps you do not know how far you should or should not believe us, and you are vigilant not to be misled by believing us either more or less than you should.

In regard to the Divine Scriptures, however, even when not clearly understood, you have no doubt that they are to be believed. But you certainly notice this wavering between belief or nonbelief, and the difficulties of knowing, and the storms of doubt, and the devout faith due to the divine words; all these in your mind you see as they are, and you do not in the least doubt that they are in your mind in this way, either as I described them or, rather, as you yourself knew them. Hence, you see your faith, you see your doubt, you see your desire and will to learn, and when you are induced by divine authority to believe what you do not see, you see at once that you believe these things; you analyze and discern all this.

Chapter Forty-One

Of course, you will not make any kind of comparison between your bodily eyes and these eyes of your heart, by which you perceive that all this is true and certain, by which you notice and discern what is invisibly present to you; especially when, from these same visible things which are, so to speak, reflected by the sight of the bodily eyes, and from these same bodily eyes and their power of sight, of whatever kind and degree it may be, you calculate what a difference exists between them and invisible things. I do not mean the higher ones in which you should believe even though unseen, but those, as I have said, which are mentally perceived as present—not the ones which by their absence demand belief—and which are seen with interior eyes rather than the eyes of flesh. Since, therefore, the interior eyes are judges of the exterior ones, and the latter are subject to the former, as it were, in their duty and ministry of gathering information; and since the former see many things which the latter do not see, whereas the latter see only what is subjected to the judgment of the former, acting as president of the tribunal, could anyone fail to prefer the former to the latter as incomparably superior?

Chapter Forty-Two

Therefore I ask whether you consider you are acting in darkness or in light when the great action occurs in you whereby you distinguish interior things from exterior and, without clamor of words, prefer the former to the latter, when you learn the exterior ones outside and dwell within, among the interior ones, estimating them by discerning their incorporeal limits? My opinion is that such great, such high, such true, manifest, and certain things cannot be seen without light. Behold that light, then, in which you behold all other things, and see whether any gaze of bodily eyes can approach it. Obviously, it cannot. Take note, also, and say whether in it you see any dimensions or limits of space.

You will find nothing like that there, I believe, if you carefully exclude from your inner vision whatever material images the senses of the outer man bring in.

But this is difficult, perhaps, since as happens in our carnal life, a host of fantasies in the likeness of material things invades those interior eyes, also; and when I made an attempt, at least, to resist them, I exclaimed in anguish in that short letter of mine (Letter 92), relying on divine authority, and I said: "Let flesh, drunk with carnal thoughts, hear this: God is a spirit" (Jn 4:24). I was restraining my own mind from that kind of vanity by that reproach rather than another. Indeed, we are more easily drawn to what is customary, and our soul, in its weakness, likes to bring in and permit worldly business to enter, not to rouse itself to health, but out of indulgence, and to give itself some kind of rest in its weariness.

Chapter Forty-Three

Therefore, if you cannot entirely clear your mind's eye from this apparent cloud of material images, examine them carefully within yourself. In your thought gaze upon heaven and earth, as you have been accustomed to gaze upon them with your bodily eyes, and note that these images of heaven and earth, set before your mental vision, are the likenesses of things, not the things themselves. Pass judgment, then, against yourself, on your own behalf, if you cannot drive from your mental vision those many fanciful images of material qualities, and from your own defeat win the victory. For no one, in my opinion, is so deceived by such imaginings as to believe that he actually has in his memory or in his mental vision the sun, moon, stars, rivers, seas, mountains, hills, cities, in a word, the walls of his house or even of his sleeping room, and whatever else he knows or experiences through his bodily eyes, in their dimensions or spatial limit, whether at rest or in movement.

Moreover, if those mental images resembling bodies or spaces are nevertheless unconfined by spatial relations or limits and are not stored in our memory with spaces between them, how much less likely that those things bearing the resemblance to physical objects: "charity, joy, peace, longanimity, benignity, goodness, faith, mildness, contingency" (Gal 5:22), should take up room, be spatially separated, or that the heart's eyes should seek out any such spaces in order to send forth their rays and so see these things! Are not all these things effortlessly together, and are they not known by their own limits, without any surrounding space? Tell me in what place you see charity, known to you only insofar as you can mentally perceive it. You do not know it as great in the sense of a huge mass that you survey; when it speaks within you, bidding you live by it, it does not shout with any sound of voice; you do not raise your bodily eyes to see it; you do not strain your bodily muscles to grasp it firmly; and when it enters your mind, you do not perceive its approach.

Chapter Forty-Four

This, therefore, is charity, however small it appears to us when it resides in our will: "It is not seen in any place, nor sought by bodily eyes, nor limited by our sight, nor held by touch, nor heard by speaking, nor perceived in its approach." How much more true this is of God, of whom charity within us is the pledge! If our inward man is an image of Him—indeed, insignificant—not begotten but created by Him, yet day by day renewed (2 Cor 4:16), it now dwells in such light that no corporeal sight comes near to it and if those things we perceive by that light are distinguished and not spatially separated, how much more is this true of God, who dwells in light inaccessible (1 Tm 6:16) to the bodily senses, whom only the pure of heart can approach! Since then we have chosen that light in preference to any corporeal light, not only by rational judgment, but also by the longing of our love, we shall increase that love the stronger it becomes, until all our soul's weaknesses will be healed by Him (Ps 102:3) who becomes merciful toward our iniquities. Having become in this life more fully alive, we shall be able to judge all things, but ourselves be judged by no man (1 Cor 2:15): "But the sensual man perceives not these things that are of the spiritual God, for it is foolishness to him, and he cannot understand, because it is spiritually examined" (1 Cor 2:14).

Chapter Forty-Five

But if we cannot yet prefer the light which judges to the light which is judged, or prefer the life of the mind to the life of sense-experience only, or prefer the nature which does not vary from place to place but has all it possesses in unity—like our intellect—to that nature composed of parts so that half is less than the whole—like our body—then it is useless for us to discuss such great and high topics.

But, if we can now do this, let us believe that God is something greater than our intellect, so that His peace, "which surpasses all understanding, may keep our hearts and minds in Christ Jesus" (Phil 4:7). For surely that peace which surpasses all understanding is not inferior to our mind, so that it should be thought visible to our bodily eyes, although the mind itself is invisible. Or is it true that the peace of God differs from the "brightness of His glory" (Heb 1:3), which is the same as the only-begotten Son; and that charity surpassing knowledge is His, also, whereby "we shall be filled unto all the fullness of God" (Eph 3:19), and that it is inferior to the light of our mind, bestowed by His illuminating act? But if this light is inaccessible to bodily eyes, how incomparably superior is that light! Therefore, since something of us is visible, like the body, and something invisible, like the interior man, and since the best part of us, that is, mind and intelligence, is invisible to bodily eyes, how shall that which is better than the higher part of us be visible to our lower part?

Chapter Forty-Six

After weighing all these arguments, you now agree, I think, that it is right to say that "God is not seen in any place, except in the pure heart; He is not sought by bodily eyes, nor limited by our sight, nor held by touch, nor heard by His speaking, nor perceived in His approach." If there is anything here we do not understand, or concerning which we are "otherwise minded, this also God will reveal to us if, whereunto we are come we continue in the same" (Phil 3:15). For we have come to believe that God is not body but spirit (Jn 4:24); we have come also to believe that "no man has seen God at any time" (Jn 1:18); and that "with Him there is no change nor shadow of alteration" (Jas 1:17); and that "He inhabits light inaccessible, whom no man has seen nor can see" (1 Tm 6:16); and that the Father and the Son and the Holy Spirit are one God (1 Jn 5:7), without any difference or separation of nature, and the clean of heart will see Him (Mt 5:8); and that "we shall be like to Him, because we shall see Him as He is" (1 Jn 3:2); and that "God is charity and he that abides in charity, abides in God and God in him" (1 Jn 4:16); and that we ought to "follow peace and holiness, without which no man shall see God" (Heb 12:14); and that this corruptible and mortal body of ours shall be changed at the Resurrection, and shall put on incorruption and immortality (1 Cor 15:53); and that "it is sown a natural body, it shall rise a spiritual body" (1 Cor 15:44) when the Lord will "reform the body of our lowness" and make it "like to the body of His glory" (Phil 3:21); and that God "made man to His image and likeness" (Gn 1:26); and that we are renewed in the spirit of our mind unto the knowledge of God "according to the image of Him that created us" (Col 3:10).

Those who walk by faith (2 Cor 5:7) in accordance with these and similar authoritative prescriptions of the Holy Scriptures, who have made spiritual progress by a divinely given or strengthened understanding, and who have been able to assess the value of spiritual realities have recognized that mental vision is superior to bodily vision, and that objects of this mental vision are not spatially limited; they are not spatially separated and their parts are not less than the whole.

Chapter Forty-Seven

This is why he so confidently said that "God is not seen in any place, but in the clean heart, that He is not sought by bodily eyes, nor limited by our sight, nor held by our touch, nor heard by His speaking, nor perceived in His approach." Hence, although His invisible substance is praised in Holy Scripture, it is nevertheless revealed in the same authorities that He has been seen by many in the body, and in corporeal places, or else in the spirit, through which corporeal images are perceived, in some incorporeal likeness of the body, however, as occurs in sleep or ecstasy. That saintly man Ambrose distinguished this kind of vision from the nature of God, and said that they represented the forms chosen by His will, not presented by His Nature. For God causes those visions in which he appears, as He wills, to whom He wills and when He wills, while His substance remains hidden and in itself unchangeable. If our will, remaining in itself and in itself unchangeable, speaks words through which it expresses itself, as it were, how much more readily can the omnipotent God, keeping His nature hidden and unchangeable, appear under any form He wills, and to whom He wills, since out of nothing He made all things (2 Mc 7:28) and remaining in Himself, "reneweth all things" (Wis 7:27)?

ON SEEING GOD

Chapter Forty-Eight

In order to attain that vision by which we see God as He is, He has warned us that our hearts must be cleansed. Since we ordinarily speak of material things as visible, God is called invisible (Col 1:15; 1 Tm 1:17) lest He be considered a material body. Nevertheless, He will not deprive pure hearts of the contemplation of His substance, since this great and sublime reward is promised, on the Lord's own word, to those who worship and love God. When he appeared visibly to bodily eyes, He promised that His invisible being also would be seen by the clean of heart: "He that loves Me shall be loved of My Father, and I will love him, and will manifest Myself to him" (Jn 14:21). It is certain that His nature, shared with the Father, is equally invisible as it is equally incorruptible (1 Tm 1:17), which, as previously said, the Apostle at once set forth as the divine substance, commending it to men with what words he could. But if in virtue of the changed nature of bodies at the Resurrection, bodily eyes behold it, let those who can affirm this look to it; for my part, I am more impressed by the statement of him who attributes this to clean hearts, not to bodily eyes, even at the Resurrection.

Chapter Forty-Nine

I do not refuse to keep learning more or to inquire into the problem of the spiritual body promised to those who rise again if, in this discussion, we may avoid those faults commonly stirred up by human ambitions and controversies so that "above that which is written, that one be not puffed up for another, against the other" (1 Cor 4:6), lest, while by argument we seek to learn how God can be seen, we lose that very peace and holiness "without which no man shall see God" (Heb 12:14). May He keep this far from our hearts; may He make and keep them clean so that they may contemplate Him! However, since I do not doubt that the nature of God is never seen in any place, I do not inquire into its truth.

But now, as to whether anything can be seen by our bodily eyes without being seen in a place, I am prepared to listen peacefully and charitably to those who can prove it, and with them to share my own convictions. There are some who assume that God Himself is completely corporeal, and they suppose that whatever is not corporeal is no substance at all. I think that these people are to be altogether shunned. But there are others who fully agree that God Himself is not corporeal, and they think that those who will rise again to eternal life will, therefore, even in the body see God, since they hope that the spiritual body will be such that even what before was flesh will become spirit. I think it will be easy to judge how much this opinion differs from the former, and how much more tenable it is, even if untrue: first, because it makes a great difference whether something untrue is believed about the Creator or about a creature; secondly, because we may tolerate the mind's effort to change matter into spirit, but not when it changes God into matter; finally, because what I said in my other letter (Letter 92) in regard to the eyes of our flesh, that they now can neither see God nor later will they be able to, is true even so; for this was said solely of bodily eyes which they will not be if the body itself becomes a spirit because, when He is seen, it will be a spirit, not a body that will see Him.

Chapter Fifty

Hence, the entire remaining question concerns the spiritual body: how far this corruptible and mortal one will put on incorruption and immortality, and how far it will be changed from animal to spiritual (1 Cor 15:53). This question merits careful and attentive treatment, especially because of the body of the Lord Himself "who reforms the body of our lowness, made like to the body of His glory," that he may be able "to subdue all things unto Himself" (Phil 3:21). Since, then, God the Father sees the Son, and the Son sees the Father, no doubt we should not heed those who will attribute vision only to bodies. Neither is it correct to say that the Father does not see the Son or that, if vision belongs only to bodies, He is endowed with a body in order to see. How shall we explain the fact that at the world's beginning, before the Son had taken the form of a servant (Phil 2:7), God saw the light, that it was good, and the firmament and the sea and the dry land, and every herb and every tree, the sun, the moon, the stars, all living creatures that move upon the earth, the fowls of the earth, the living soul? "And afterward God saw all the things he had made and behold they were very good" (Gn 1:4–31).

After Scripture so often repeated that about all the many creatures, I wonder how there came about the opinion that sight belongs only to bodies. But from whatever ordinary language use that opinion may have come, the Holy Scriptures are not wont to say this; they attribute vision not only to the body, but also to the spirit, and more to the spirit than to the body. Otherwise, they would not have been correct in giving the name "seers" to the Prophets who saw the future, not by bodily sight but by spiritual sight.

Chapter Fifty-One

But we must be careful not to put forward what is contrary to custom, saying that through the glory of Resurrection, the body puts off not only its mortal and corruptible state, but even the very state of being a body, and becomes a spirit. If that is so, either the substance of the spirit doubled, if the body becomes spirit, or if the spirit of man is single so that it does not receive a twin when the body is changed and turned into spirit, it is to be feared that, if it is not increased at all, then we are only saying that bodies will not remain immortal after that change, but will cease to exist and will perish completely. Hence, until we carefully inquire and, with the Lord's help, discover the more probable opinion about the spiritual body, which according to the Scriptures is promised at the Resurrection, let it now suffice that the only-begotten Son who is also the "Mediator of God and men, the man, Christ Jesus" (1 Tm 2:5) sees the Father as He is seen by the Father. As for us, let us try not to carry over that concupiscence of the eyes from this world to that vision of God, promised to us at the Resurrection (1 Jn 2:16), but let us strive for it with devout affection by cleansing our hearts, and let us not think of a corporeal face when the Apostle says: "We see now through a glass, in a dark manner, but then face to face"; especially since the Apostle adds more precisely: "Now I know in part, but then I shall know even as I am known" (1 Cor 13:12).

If then we shall not know God by a corporeal face, now we are known to Him by a corporeal face, "for then I shall know," he says, "even as I am known." From this, who would not understand that in this passage he meant our face, of which he says elsewhere: "But we, beholding the glory of the Lord with open face, are transformed into the same image from glory to glory as by the spirit of the Lord" (2 Cor 3:18), that is, from the glory of faith to the glory of eternal contemplation? Doubtless, this is achieved by that transformation by which the "inward man is renewed day by day" (2 Cor 4:16). The Apostle Peter was also referring to this when, warning of a wife's adornment, he said: "whose adorning let it not be the outward plaiting of the hair, or the wearing of gold and pearls, or fine apparel, but the hidden man of the heart which is rich in the sight of God" (1 Pt 3:3). By not going over to Christ, the Jews keep a veil over that face, since, when anyone goes over to Christ, the veil will be withdrawn, and "we with open face are transformed into the same image." Moreover, very plainly he says: "The veil is upon their heart" (2 Cor 3:15). There, then, is the face that shall be opened, and though now we see through a glass in a dark manner, we shall then see face-to-face.

Chapter Fifty-Two

If you agree, consider with me the statement of the holy man Ambrose, which is based, not on his authority, but on truth itself. My reason for liking it is not because the Lord by his words freed me from error and by his ministry gave me the grace of saving baptism, as if I should be too favorable to the one who planted and watered me (1 Cor 3:7), but because in this matter he said what God who gives the increase says to the soul which meditates devoutly and understands rightly. He said then: "Even in the Resurrection itself it is not easy to see God, except for those who are clean of heart; hence: How many kinds of blessed He had enumerated, yet to none of them had He promised the ability to see God." If, then, those who are clean of heart will see God, doubtless others will not see Him; the unworthy will not see Him, nor is he who does not want to see God able to see Him. God is not seen in any place, but in the clean of heart; He is not sought by bodily eyes, nor limited by our sight, nor held by touch, nor heard by His speaking, nor perceived in His approach. When He is thought absent, He is seen; when He is present, He is not seen. Finally, not all the Apostles saw Christ. Therefore, He says: "So long a time have I been with you, and you have not known Me?" But he who knew "what is the breadth and length and height and depth, and the charity of Christ which surpasses all knowledge," saw both Christ and the Father. For we do not know Christ according to the flesh, but according to the Spirit. Then, "our breath, Christ the Lord, is taken before our face," and may He in His mercy deign to fill us unto all the fullness of God, that we may be able to see Him.

Chapter Fifty-Three

To the extent that you understand these words of the saintly man, not carnal words but spiritual, and recognize that they are true, not because he said them but because in them truth speaks without noise of words, to that extent you understand how you may cling to God, to that extent you prepare yourself inwardly as the incorporeal place of His dwelling, to hear the silence of His discourse, and to see His invisible form. Blessed are the clean of heart, for they shall see God, not when He shall appear to them as a body coming from some intervening space, but when He shall come to them and make His dwelling with them, and thus they shall be filled unto all the fullness of God—not that they will be God in His fullness, but that they shall be perfectly filled with God. But if we think of material things only and cannot even think worthily of the source of our thought about material things, let us not seek reproaches to make against ourselves; rather, let us cleanse our hearts of this carnal tendency by prayer and by turning to what lies before us. Let me repeat not only what blessed Ambrose but also what holy Jerome said: "The eyes of the flesh can no more behold the Divinity of the Father than they can that of the Son and the Holy Spirit, because there is in the Trinity one Nature, but the eyes of the mind can, and of them the Savior said: 'Blessed are the clean of heart, for they shall see God' " (*Jerome, Commentary on Isaiah* 6:1). And according to the brief and true definitions of the same Jerome: "An incorporeal thing is not seen by corporeal eyes" (*Jerome, Commentary on Job* 42:5; *Commentary on Zechariah* 24:11).

Chapter Fifty-Four

My reason for reporting these opinions of such great men on such a great topic was not to make you think that anyone's interpretation should be accepted with the authority due to the Canonical Scripture, but that those otherwise minded may try to see with their mind what is true and seek God in the simplicity of their heart (Wis 1:1), and stop finding fault so rashly with the learned interpreters of the divine words. And do not be moved by any who say, with insufficient reflection: "What then will the bodily eyes see if they will not see God? Will they be blind or useless?" Those saying this fail to realize that without bodies there will be no bodily eyes, but if there are to be bodies, there will be something for bodily eyes to see. But let this suffice, and when you consider it, after reading and rereading the entire treatise you will probably perceive with certainty that a clean heart ought to prepare you, with His help, to see God. As for the spiritual body, I shall try in another treatise to see what arguments I can discover with the Lord's help (cf. City of God, XXII).

Letter 187: On the Presence of God

Chapter One

I admit that I have been slower in answering your letter than I should have been, my dearest brother Dardanus, whom I hold in higher esteem for the charity of Christ than for your worldly position. But please do not ask what caused the delay, for I should only make you more annoyed by my detailed excuse than you have already suffered from my late answer. No matter what those reasons were, believe that none of them could have involved my holding you in low esteem. On the contrary, I should have responded immediately had I no respect for you. But my reason for responding now is not because I have composed something at least worth your perusal, something desiring to be dedicated to your name; in fact, I have decided to respond now rather than let the summer go by, leaving me still in debt for this courtesy. And it was not your high position which frightened me and made me wait, for your kindly manner attracts more than your rank repels me. Yet because I love you so much I find it accordingly difficult to measure up to the great eagerness of your religious affection.

Chapter Two

Moreover, in addition to that flame of mutual charity which brings us to love even those never seen, if they have what we love—in which you outdo me and make me freer to fall short of your opinion and expectation of me—in addition to that, you have asked me such questions in your letter that if they were put forward by another they would entail no easy task for the free time I lack. But when put forward by you, with your mind used to probing into deep truths, it would be entirely insufficient to give a brief solution. Moreover, they have been proposed to a very busy man besieged and weighed down by an army of anxieties; hence, it is for your Prudence and Benevolence to calculate how I may satisfy you either for taking so long to respond or for even now not responding as befits the intensity of your interest.

Chapter Three

You ask, then, in what way the "Mediator of God and men, the man, Christ Jesus" (1 Tm 2:5) is now believed to be in heaven when, hanging upon the Cross and at the point of death, He said to the believing thief: "This day you will be with me in paradise" (Lk 23:43). You say that from this we are to know, perhaps, that paradise is established in some part of heaven, or that, because God is everywhere, the man who is in God is also present everywhere. From this, doubtless, you want to infer that He who is everywhere could also be in paradise.

Chapter Four

Here I inquire, or, rather, notice how you understand Christ as man. Certainly not as certain heretics do who say that He is the Word of God with a body, that is, without a human soul, the Word serving as soul for His body (the Arians); or, as the Word of God, with a soul and a body but without a human mind, the Word of God serving as mind to His soul (the Apollinarists). Surely you do not understand Christ as man in this way, but, as you expressed it previously, when you said that you accepted Christ as Almighty God, with this formula of belief that you would not believe him God if you had not believed Him perfect man. Clearly, by saying perfect man you mean to say that the entire human nature is there, since a man is not perfect if either a soul is lacking to the body or a human mind to the soul.

Chapter Five

Then, if we think He said: "This day you will be with me in paradise," in the human nature which God the Word put on, from these words we cannot conclude that paradise is in heaven, for the man Christ Jesus was not to be in heaven that day, but in hell as to His soul, in the tomb concerning His body, being placed that day in the tomb (Mt 27:60; Mk 15:46; Lk 23:53; Jn 19:41); whereas apostolic teaching declares that His soul descended into hell, since from the Psalms, Blessed Peter testifies to this fact, showing that the following prophecy was made of Him: "Because you will not leave My soul in hell, nor will you give your holy one to see corruption" (Ps 15:10; Acts 2:27). The first part of this refers to His soul, since it did not remain there, but from there returned very quickly; the second part refers to His body, which by reason of its quick Resurrection could not suffer corruption. But no one thinks that paradise was in the tomb. If anyone was so foolish as to attempt to justify that opinion by saying that the tomb was a garden (paradise), he could surely discover this to be untenable inasmuch as the one to whom Christ said: "This day you will be with me in paradise" was not in the tomb with Christ on any day. Moreover, the burial of his body, unconscious alike of joy or sorrow in death, would not have been offered to him as the great reward of his faith when he had in mind that rest where his conscious being was to go.

Chapter Six

It remains, therefore, that if the words, "This day you will be with me in paradise" were spoken in a human sense, paradise would be understood to be in hell, where Christ in his human soul was to be that day. But for me it would be difficult to say whether the bosom of Abraham where the wicked rich man, from the torments of hell where he was, saw the poor man in repose is to be included under the term paradise, or seen as belonging to hell. Indeed, of the rich man we read the words: "But the rich man also died and was buried," and "when he was in the torments of hell." In respect to the death or repose of the poor man there is no mention of hell, but it asserts: "It came to pass that the beggar died and was carried by the angels into Abraham's bosom." Thereupon, Abraham says to the rich man in the flame: "Between us and you there is fixed a great chaos" (Lk 16:22–26), as though it were between hell and the dwellings of the blessed, for it is not easy to find anywhere in the Scriptures the word hell used in a good sense. Thus, the question is often asked how we can reverently believe that the soul of the Lord Christ was in hell, if the word is not used in any sense but the penal one. A good response to this is that he descended there to rescue those who were to be rescued. Therefore, Blessed Peter says that he loosed the sorrows of hell in which it was "impossible that he should be held" (Acts 2:24). Moreover, if we are to believe that there are two regions in hell, one for the suffering and one for the souls in repose, that is, both a place where the rich man was tormented and one where the poor man was comforted, who would dare to say that the Lord Jesus came to the penal parts of hell rather than only among those who rest in Abraham's bosom? If he was there, then we should understand that to be the paradise He deigned to promise the soul of the thief on that day. If this is so, the word paradise is a general term signifying a state of living in happiness. But calling paradise the place where Adam lived before the fall, with the fruit of apples, did not prevent Scripture from calling the Church paradise, also.

Chapter Seven

Christ, however, may be understood as saying "This day you will be with Me in paradise" in a much looser sense and one devoid of all these subtleties, if He said it not as man but as God. Clearly, the man Christ was to be that day in the tomb as to His body, in hell as to His soul, but as God Christ Himself is always present everywhere. For He is the light which shines in the darkness, although the darkness does not comprehend it (Jn 1:5). He is the strength and wisdom of God of which it is written that "it reaches from end to end mightily and ordereth all things sweetiy" (Wis 8:1) and that "it reaches everywhere because of its purity and nothing defiled comes to it" (Wis 7:24). Hence, wherever paradise may be, whoever is blessed is there with Him who is everywhere.

Chapter Eight

Since, therefore, Christ is God and man, God as he tells us in the words: "I and the Father are one" (Jn 10:30), man, as He says in the words: "The Father is greater than I" (Jn 14:28), but He is equally Son of God, only-begotten of the Father (Jn 1:14), and Son of man "of the seed of David according to the flesh" (Rom 1:3), we must regard both these natures in Him when He speaks or when Scripture speaks of Him, and we must notice in what sense anything is said. For, just as a single man is rational soul and body, so the single Christ is Word and man. Therefore, in respect to the Word, Christ is creator: "All things were made by Him" (Jn 1:3), but as man Christ was created, "of the seed of David according to the flesh" and "made in the likeness of man" (Phil 2:7). Likewise, because man is twofold, soul and body, He was sorrrowful unto death through the soul: He suffered death through the body (Mt 26:38; Mk 14:34).

Chapter Nine

Yet when we say that Christ is the Son of God, we do not separate from Him His humanity, nor when we say that the same Christ is the Son of man do we lose sight of His divinity. For as man He was not in heaven where He now is but on earth when He said: "No man ascends into heaven but he that descended from heaven, the Son of man who is in heaven" (Jn 3:13), although He was in heaven in His nature as Son of God, but still on earth as Son of man, not yet ascended into heaven. Likewise, although He is the Lord of glory in His nature as Son of God, He was crucified in His nature as Son of man, because the Apostle says: "For if they had known it they would never have crucified the Lord of glory" (1 Cor 2:8). Thus as God the Son of man was in heaven and as man the Son of God was crucified on earth. Since, therefore, it could correctly be stated that the Lord of glory was crucified, although His passion belonged only to His humanity, so He could correctly say: "This day you will be with me in paradise" because, although in His human lowliness He would be in the tomb as to His body, in hell as to His soul, in respect to His divine immutability He had never left paradise because He is always present everywhere.

Chapter Ten

Have no doubt, therefore, that the man Christ Jesus is now there whence He shall come again; cherish in your memory and remain faithful to the profession of your Christian faith that He rose from the dead, ascended into heaven, sits at the right hand of the Father (Mk 16:19; Lk 26:29; Col 3:1; Heb 1:3, 10:12), and will come from no other place but there to judge the living and the dead; and He will so come, as the angels have testified, as He was seen going into heaven (2 Tm 4:1; Acts 1:10), that is, in the very form and substance of flesh to which it is true, He gave immortality, but He did not destroy its nature. We are not to think that He is present everywhere in this form. We must be sure of so upholding the divinity of the man that we destroy the reality of His body. It does not follow that everything in God is in Him so that it is everywhere that God is. With complete truth, the Scripture says: "In Him we live and move and are" (Acts 17:28), yet we are not present everywhere as He is, but man is in God in one way whereas God is in man quite differently, in His own unique way. "In Him God and man are one person, and both are the one Jesus Christ who as God is everywhere, but as man He is in heaven."

Chapter Eleven

Although in speaking of Him we say that God is present everywhere, we must keep away carnal ideas and remove our mind from our bodily senses, not imagining that God is distributed through all things by a kind of extension of size, as earth or water or air or light are distributed (for in each of these the part is less extensive than the whole) but, rather, in the way in which there is great wisdom in a man whose body is small, so that, if there were two wise men of whom one is taller in stature but neither is wiser than the other, there would not be greater wisdom in the taller one and less in the smaller, nor less in one than in the two, but as much in one as in the other and as much in each one as in both; for if both are absolutely equally wise, the two together are not wiser than each one separately. Likewise, if they are equally immortal, the two do not live longer than each one individually.

Chapter Twelve

Finally, the very bodily immortality which Christ was the first to experience and which is promised to us at the end of the world is certainly a great thing, but not great in size for, although corporeally possessed, it is an incorporeal perfection. So, although the immortal body is less in one part than in the whole, its immortality is as complete in the part as in the whole, and, although some members are larger than others, it does not follow that some are more immortal than others. In this life, likewise, when we have good health in every one of our parts, according to the present well-being of our body, we do not say that because the whole hand is larger than the finger the health of the whole hand is greater than that of the finger, but in these unequal members, it is equal. Hence, it may happen that one thing may not be as large as another when smaller things are compared to larger ones, but it can be seen as healthy. If the larger part was healthier, there would be greater health in larger members; since this is not the case, but the larger and smaller are equally healthy, there is clearly a dissimilarity of size in the members' dimensions coinciding with a similarity of health in the dissimilar members.

Chapter Thirteen

Therefore, because the body is a substance, its quantity is in the greatness of its bulk, whereas its health is not its quantity but a quality. Hence, the body's quantity could not attain what its quality could. Quantity is located in the various parts which cannot be in the same place together inasmuch as each one occupies its own space, the smaller ones less, the larger ones more, and it could not be entire or even as great in the various parts; but it is larger in the larger parts and less in the smaller ones, and in no part as great as it is in the entire body. But a quality such as we say that health is, is as great in the smaller parts as in the larger ones when the entire body is healthy, and the less extensive parts are not thereby less healthy nor the larger parts more healthy. God forbid, therefore, that a quality able to be in a created body could not exist in the very substance of the Creator.

Chapter Fourteen

Therefore, God is poured forth in all things. He Himself says through the Prophet: "I fill heaven and earth," and as I quoted a short time before of His wisdom: "He reaches from end to end mightily and orders all things sweetly" (Wis 8:1). It is also written: "The Spirit of the Lord has filled the whole world" (Wis 1:7) and in one of the Psalms these words are addressed to Him: "Whither shall I go from your Spirit, or whither shall I flee from your face? If I ascend into heaven, you are there; if I descend into hell you are there" (Ps 138:7). Nevertheless, God so fills all things as to be not a quality of the world, but the very creative being of the world, governing the world without work, sustaining it without effort. Yet He is not extended through space by size so that half of Him should be in half of the world and half in the other half of it. He is wholly present in the whole of it, as to be wholly in heaven alone and wholly in the earth alone, and wholly in heaven and earth together; unconfined to any place, He is in Himself everywhere wholly.

Chapter Fifteen

Thus He is as the Father, thus as the Son, thus as the Holy Spirit, thus as the Trinity, one God. They did not divide the world among them into three parts, each one filling a separate part, as if the Son and the Holy Spirit would have no part to occupy if the Father had occupied the whole. A truly incorporeal and immutable divinity does not exist in that way. They are not bodies, so that the Three together should be larger than each one separately. They are not present in places by their extension so that they cannot be in different places at the same time. For our soul, settled in our body, not only does not feel confined but even experiences a kind of breadth, not of physical space, but of spiritual joys, when it happens as the Apostle asserts: "Know you not that your bodies are the temple of the Holy Spirit who is in you, whom you have from God?" (1 Cor 6:19). And it would be the height of folly to say that there is no room for the Holy Spirit in our body because our soul fills it all up; how much greater folly to say that there was not enough space for the Trinity to be anywhere so that the Father and the Son and the Holy Spirit could not be everywhere at the same time.

Chapter Sixteen

Something much more remarkable is this: Although God is wholly present everywhere, He does not dwell in everyone. What the Apostle says cannot be said to all or what I have just said, or even this: "Know you not that you are the temple of God and that the Spirit of God dwells in you?" (1 Cor 3:16). Therefore, of some the same Apostle says the contrary: "Now if any man have not the Spirit of Christ, he is none of his" (Rom 8:9), who, therefore, unless he were entirely unaware of the inseparability of the Trinity, would dare to think that the Father or the Son could dwell in someone in whom the Holy Spirit does not dwell, or that the Holy Spirit could be present in someone in whom the Father and the Son are not present? Therefore, it must be acknowledged that by the presence of His divinity God is everywhere, but not everywhere by the grace of His indwelling. Because of this indwelling, in which the grace of His love is recognized with certainty, we do not say: "Our Father, who is everywhere," but "Our Father who is in heaven" (Mt 6:9). So that in our prayer we recall His temple which we ourselves ought to be, and according to this is the measure of our belonging to His fellowship and His adopted family (Rom 8:15; Gal 4:5). For if the People of God, not yet made equal to the angels (Lk 20:36) and still far from the Lord (2 Cor 5:6), is called His temple, how much truer is it that His temple is in heaven where His angelic people dwell, to whom we are to be joined and made equal when, after our pilgrimage, we arrive at what has been promised.

Chapter Seventeen

Hence, He who is everywhere does not dwell within everyone, and in those in whom He dwells, He does not even dwell equally. Otherwise, what is the meaning of Eliseus's request that in Him there might be twice the spirit of God that was in Elias (4 Kgs 2:9)? And how does it happen that some saints are holier than others, unless they have a greater indwelling of God? How, then, did we speak truly when we said previously that God is wholly present everywhere if in some He is more fully present, in others, less fully? But it should be carefully noted that we said He is in Himself wholly present everywhere, not in things of which some have a greater capacity for Him, others less. He is said to be present everywhere because from no part of the universe is He absent, and He is wholly present because He does not give one part of Himself to one half of creation and another part to the other half, in equal shares, or less to a smaller part and more to a larger one; but He is not only wholly present to the whole universe, He is equally so to every part of it. Those who by sinning have become wholly unlike Him are said to be far from Him. Those who by a virtuous life receive His likeness are said to draw near to Him, just as it is correct to say that the blinder eyes are, the further they are from the light of day, for what is so far from light as blindness, although the daylight be near at hand, shining upon sightless eyes? But it is correct to say that when through improved health eyes progress to a recovery of sight, they draw near to the light.

Chapter Eighteen

I perceive, however, there is need for a more careful explanation as to why I added "in Himself" to my statement that God is wholly present everywhere, because I think this is open to ambiguity. If He is in Himself, how is He everywhere? Everywhere, of course, because He is nowhere absent; in Himself, because He is not dependent on the things in which He is present as though without them He could not exist. Remove the spatial relations of bodies and they will be nowhere, and because they are nowhere, they will not exist at all. Remove bodies from the qualities of bodies, and there will be no place for them to be and, consequently, they will not exist. For even when a body is equally healthy throughout its entire mass, or equally handsome, neither its health nor its beauty is greater in any part than in any other, nor greater in the whole than in the part, since it is clear that the whole is not any healthier or any more handsome than the part. But if it should be unequally healthy or unequally handsome, it can be the case that there might be greater health or beauty in a smaller part when the smaller members are healthier or more beautiful than the larger ones, because what we call great or small in qualities does not depend on size. However, if the size itself of the body, however great or small it may be, should be completely removed, there will be nothing in which its qualities can subsist. But in regard to God, if less is received by the one in whom He is present, He is not thereby lessened. For He in Himself is whole, and He is not present in things so as to need them, as if He could not exist except in them. Just as He is not absent from the one in whom He does not dwell, but is wholly present although this one does not possess Him, so He is wholly present in the one in whom He dwells, although this one does not receive Him wholly.

Chapter Nineteen

He does not distribute Himself among the hearts or bodies of men in order to dwell therein, giving one part of Himself to this one, another to that one, like the sunlight shining through the doors and windows of houses. He is rather to be compared to sound, although a corporeal and passing thing, which a deaf man does not receive at all, a partly deaf one does not wholly receive, and among those who are equidistant and hear it, one receives more than another according to his keener hearing, another, less, according to his weaker hearing, and yet the sound itself does not vary from more to less, but where all are present, it is equally present to all. How much more perfect than this is God, whose nature is incorporeal and unchangeably living, who cannot be extended and distributed like sound by time intervals, who needs no airy space to exist in order to be near to those present, but who in Himself remains eternally steadfast, able to be wholly present to all and to each, and although those in whom He dwells possess Him according to their diverse capacities, some more, some less, He builds up all of them by the grace of His goodness as His most beloved temple (1 Cor 3:16; 6:19; 2 Cor 6:16).

Chapter Twenty

The phrase "varieties of graces" is used as if they were parts and members of one body in which we are all one temple taken together, but individually we are individual temples, because God is not greater in all than He is in each one, and it sometimes occurs that the many receive Him less, the one more. When the Apostle said: "There are varieties of graces," he immediately added: "but the same Spirit" (1 Cor 12:4). Also, when he had listed these same varieties of graces, he said: "But in all these things one and the same Spirit works, distributing to everyone according as He will" (1 Cor 12:11); distributing, therefore, but not Himself; those varieties are spoken of as body members because the ears have not the same function as the eyes, and "distributed," because He Himself is one and the same. Thus, various duties are harmoniously allotted to the various members. When we are in good health, however, despite these members being different, they rejoice in a common equal health (1 Cor 12:26) all together, not separately, not one with more, another with less. The head of this body is Christ (Col 1:18). The body's unity is demonstrated by our sacrifice, which the Apostle briefly refers to in saying: "For we being many are one bread, one body" (1 Cor 10:17). Through our Head we are reconciled to God, because in Him the divinity of the only-begotten Son participated in our mortality, that we might be made participators in His immortality.

Chapter Twenty-One

This mystery is far away from the hearts of the wise, full of pride, but not from Christian hearts; therefore, not from the truly wise. Among those former wise ones I include those who have known God, "because when they knew God," as the Apostle says, "they have not glorified Him as God or given thanks" (Rom 1:21). But you know in what sacrifice occur the words: "Let us give thanks to the Lord our God" (Preface of Mass). The pride and presumption of such men are very unlike the humility of this sacrifice. Hence, it is remarkable how God dwells in some souls who do not know Him yet and does not dwell in those who know Him. The latter are not part of God's temple, "who knowing God have not glorified Him or given thanks," yet like children, sanctified by the Sacrament of Christ and reborn by the Holy Spirit, are part of God's temple, although that they cannot know God yet on account of their age is certain. Hence, the one group could know God but not possess Him; the other could possess Him before they know Him. But happiest are those to whom knowing God is the same as possessing Him, for that is the most adequate, true, and happy knowledge.

Chapter Twenty-Two

Now is the time to consider that question which you appended to your letter after signing it. "If infants are as yet without knowledge of God, how could John, even before his birth, leap for joy in his mother's womb, at the arrival and presence of the Lord's Mother?" After saying that you had read my book *On the Baptism of Infants*, you added these words: "I should like to know what you think about pregnant mothers inasmuch as the mother of John the Baptist answered in her son's name for the faith of his belief."

Chapter Twenty-Three

Certainly, these are the words of Elizabeth, mother of John: "Blessed are you among women and blessed is the fruit of your womb. And whence is this to me that the Mother of my Lord should come to me? For behold, as soon as the voice of your salvation sounded in my ears, the infant in my womb leaped for joy" (Lk 1:41–44). But, so that she could say this, the Evangelist forewarns us that "she was filled with the Holy Spirit" (Lk 1:41) and it is evident that by His inspiration she knew what that leaping of her infant signified, that is, the arrival of the Mother of Him whose forerunner and herald he was to be. That could be a sign of a great event knowable to mature people but not knowable by the infant. For in the opening part of this narrative in the Gospel it did not say: "The infant leaped for faith in my womb," but "he leaped for joy." We observe instances of this leaping not only in children but even in animals, although surely not for any faith or religion or rational acknowledgment of someone arriving; but this instance stands out as utterly uncommon and new, since it occurred in a womb, and at the arrival of her who was to bring forth the Savior of man. Hence, this leaping, this greeting, as it were, offered to the Lord's Mother, is miraculous. It is to be counted among the great signs. It was not humanly accomplished by the infant, but divinely accomplished in the infant as miracles are usually accomplished.

Chapter Twenty-Four

Nevertheless, even were the use of reason and will so advanced in the child that he could, from within his mother's womb, recognize, believe, and assent to what in other children has to await the appropriate age, even this should be considered among the miracles of divine power, not considered as an example of human nature. For, when God willed it, even a dumb beast spoke rationally (Nm 22:28), yet not for this reason are men well advised to invite the counsel of asses in their deliberations. Therefore, I neither deny what happened to John, nor do I establish it as a norm for what is to be thought of infants; on the contrary, I proclaim that it was miraculous in him because I do not find this happening to others. That struggle of the twins in Rebecca's womb is something similar, but this was such a prodigy that the woman consulted the divine oracle and learned that by those two infants two nations were prefigured (Gn 25:22).

Chapter Twenty-Five

If by words we wish to show, however, that infants do not know divine things—indeed, that they do not yet know human things—I fear that we may seem to injure our own senses, since we persuade by speaking whereby all the force and function of speech readily overpower the evidence of truth. Do we not see that even when infants begin to utter any syllables at all of articulate speech they still think and say such things as would make anyone but a fool not hesitate to call them fools if as they advanced in age they remained constantly in that state? Unless perhaps we were to believe that infants were wise in their infant wailing or in the womb's silence, but once they began speaking to us, they arrived, as they grew, at that degree of ignorance which we deride. You see how absurd is the very thought of that, for when children's knowledge expresses itself in words, it is almost nothing compared with what their elders know, but compared with their state at birth, it can be called intelligence. Why, when Christian grace is offered to them in that stronghold of salvation, although by voice and movement, they mightily struggle against it, are they not held responsible for it and why has all their effort no effect until in them the Sacrament is completed, whereby there is expiated the guilt derived from original damnation, unless because, insofar as they know not what they do, they are not judged for doing it? Moreover, is there any Christian who does not realize that if he had the use of reason and free will to assent to what the sanctifying act would require, what an evil it would be to resist so great a grace and how vain the act performed would be, or even what an increase of guilt it would bring?

Chapter Twenty-Six

We affirm, therefore, that the Holy Spirit dwells in baptized children although they do not know this. They are unconscious of Him although He is in them, just as they are unconscious of their own mind, and the reason in them which they are yet unable to use is like a covered spark awaiting increased age to be enkindled. Nor should this seem strange in the case of infants, because to some of their elders also the Apostle says: "Know you not that you are the temple of God, and that the Spirit of God dwells in you?" And a little previously he had said: "But the sensual man perceives not these things that are of the Spirit of God" (1 Cor 2:14). These also he calls little ones, not in carnal but in spiritual age (1 Cor 3:1). So, their understanding did not recognize the Holy Spirit dwelling in them, and they were sensual, not spiritual, despite the Holy Spirit's indwelling, because their understanding could not recognize His indwelling Spirit.

Chapter Twenty-Seven

He is said to dwell in such as these because within them He works secretly so that they may be His temple, and He perfects His work in them as they progress in virtue and persevere in their progress. "For we are saved by hope" (Rom 8:24) as the Apostle says and repeats elsewhere: "He saved us by the laver of regeneration" (Ti 3:5). Hence, when he says: "He saved us," as though salvation itself were already assured, he explains how this is to be taken by saying: "For we are saved by hope. But hope that is seen is not hope, for what a man sees why does He hope for? But if we hope for that which we see not, we wait for it with patience" (Rom 8:24). So, many things are said in the divine Scriptures as though they were completed, but we understand that they are still a matter for hope. Therefore, that other saying of the Lord speaking to the disciples: "All things whatsoever I heard of My Father I have made known to you" (Jn 15:15), which is so clearly said of what is to be hoped for that He later said to them: "I have many things to say to you but you cannot hear them now" (Jn 16:12). Hence, in those mortal ones in whom He still dwells He goes on building His dwelling which He does not complete in this life but in the afterlife when "death shall be swallowed up in victory! O death, where is your sting?"—and what is the sting of death but sin (1 Cor 15:54)?

Chapter Twenty-Eight

Although now we are reborn of water and the Spirit (Jn 3:5) and all our sins are washed away in the cleansing of that laver, both the original sin of Adam, in whom all have sinned, and our own sins of acts, words, and thoughts, we still continue in this human life, an earthly warfare (Jb 7:1), and hence we rightly say: "Forgive us our trespasses." This prayer is also said by the entire Church which the Savior cleansed "by the laver of water in the word, that he might present it to Himself glorious, having no spot or wrinkle nor any such things" (Eph 5:26)—in the future, of course, when the work which now progresses in hope shall be completed. In this life the Church is obviously not without spot or wrinkle or any such thing, either in all men belonging to it who have the use of reason and free will and who bear the burdens of mortal flesh or, at least, as our objectors must necessarily admit, in many of its members; so how can it with truth say otherwise than: "Forgive us our trespasses"?

Chapter Twenty-Nine

Inasmuch, therefore, among the mortals in whom He dwells, as He justifies more and more the proficient in goodness as they are renewed daily, cleanses them when they confess their sins, that He may present them to Himself as a pure and everlasting temple, we correctly say that He does not dwell in those who "knowing God have not glorified Him as God or given thanks." For, by worshiping and serving the "creature rather than the Creator" (Rom 1:25), they have not wanted to be a temple of the one true God, and hence, in wanting Him along with many other things, they have succeeded more in not having Him at all than in joining Him to many false gods. And we correctly say that He dwells in those whom He has called according to His purpose, and whom He has received in order to justify and glorify them even before they can know His incorporeal nature as far as it is knowable by man in this life: "in part, through a glass, in a dark manner" (1 Cor 13:12), even though great progress is made. There are some in whom He dwells, who are like those to whom the Apostle says: "I could not speak to you as unto spiritual but as unto carnal men. As unto little ones in Christ I gave you milk to drink, not meat, for you were as yet not able; but neither indeed are you now able." And to those words He added: "Know you not that you are the temple of God; that the Spirit of God dwells in you?" (1 Cor 3:1). Even if these are overtaken by death before reaching that spiritual age of mind when they will be fed solid food instead of milk, the one dwelling in them will complete what has been lacking to their understanding here, because they have not withdrawn from the unity of the body of Christ, who has become our way (Jn 14:6), nor from being part of the temple of God. So as not to withdraw from it they held fast to the role of faith common to the little and the great in the Church; they walk in Him to whom they have come, and until God reveals to them that they have an alien mentality, they do not dogmatize their carnal thoughts since they are not hardened by clinging to contentious excuses; but walking in a certain way, the way of progress, they struggle with understanding, gaining clear vision by their pious faith.

Chapter Thirty

Since this is the case, those two phenomena, birth and rebirth, occurring in a single man, belong to two men, one to the first Adam, the other to the second Adam who is called Christ. "Yet that was not first," says the Apostle, "which is spiritual, but that which is natural; later, that which is spiritual. The first man was of the earth, earthly; the second man from heaven, heavenly.

As the earth is, so also are the earthly; as heaven is, so also are they who are heavenly. As we have borne the image of the earthly, let us also bear the image of Him who is from heaven" (1 Cor 15:46). Likewise, he says: "By one man came death and by a man the resurrection of the dead. For as in Adam all die, so also in Christ all shall be made alive" (1 Cor 15:21). In both places He says "all" because no one comes to death except by the first, no one to life except by the second. In the first we see the power of man's will to cause death; in the second we see the values of God's assistance for life. To summarize: The first man was only man, but the second was God and man; sin was committed by forsaking God, justice is not obtained without God. Hence, if we had not come from his members by carnal generation, we would not have to die, nor would we live if we were not His members by spiritual incorporation. Hence, for us there was need of birth and rebirth, but for Him there was need only of birth for our sake. By rebirth we pass from sin to justice; without any sin He passed to justice. By being baptized He through His humility recommended more highly the sacrament of our rebirth, signifying our old man by His passion, our new one by His Resurrection.

Chapter Thirty-One

Rooted in mortal flesh, the rebellion of concupiscence whereby the bodily members are stirred to action ever contrary to the will's decision is so controlled that those who need rebirth are lawfully begotten by their parents' intercourse. Christ did not will that His flesh should come into existence through this kind of encounter between male and female, but in His conception of the Virgin, without any such human passion. He took on "the likeness of sinful flesh" (Rom 8:3) for us that in us the flesh of sin might be purified. "For as by the offense of one," the Apostle says, "unto all men to condemnation, so also by the justice of one unto all men to justification of life" (Rom 5:18). No one is born without the intervention of carnal concupiscence inherited from the first man, who is Adam, and no one is reborn without the intervention of spiritual grace given by the second man, who is Christ. Hence, if we belong to the former by birth, we belong to the latter by rebirth. Since no one can be born again before he is born, it is clear that Christ's birth was unique insofar as He did not need to be born again because He did not pass over from sin, to which He was never subject. In iniquity He was not conceived, nor in sin (Ps 50:7) was He nourished in His mother's womb, because the Holy Spirit came upon her and the power of the Most High overshadowed her; therefore, the Holy One born of her is called the Son of God (Lk 1:35). He does not destroy the good of marriage, but He curbs the evil of rebellious members, so that when carnal concupiscence has been controlled it may at least become conjugal chastity. But the Virgin Mary to whom was said: "And the power of the Most High shall overshadow you," under such a shadow burned with no heat of that concupiscence in conceiving her holy offspring. Consequently, except for this cornerstone (Is 28:16; 1 Pt 2:6; Eph 2:20), I do not know how men are to be built into a house of God, to contain God dwelling within (2 Cor 6:16), unless they are born again, which cannot occur before they are born.

Chapter Thirty-Two

Moreover, no matter what is our opinion about pregnant mothers, or even about men still confined within their mother's womb, with regard to whether they can be sanctified, either because of John who leaped for joy although he had not yet emerged into daylight—and who would believe that without the Holy Spirit's action this could happen?—or because of Jeremiah to whom the Lord said: "Before you came forth out of the womb I sanctified you" (Jer 1:5), it is true that the sanctification whereby individually we become temples of God and all together form one temple of God occurs only in the reborn, which men cannot be unless they are first born. No one will make a good end to the life into which he is born unless he is born again before he ends it.

Chapter Thirty-Three

But if someone were to say that a man is already born when still in his mother's womb, and gives as proof from the Gospel the words to Joseph about the Virgin Mother of the Lord, then with child: "For that which is born in her is of the Holy Spirit" (Mt 1:20), is that any reason why a second birth should follow this one? Then, it will not be the second, but the third. When the Lord spoke about this, He said: "Unless a man be born again" (Jn 3:3), counting as the first birth, of course, the one occurring when the mother gives birth, not when she conceives or becomes pregnant;

birth happens from her, not in her. We do not say that a man is re-born when his mother brings him forth, as if he were born a second time after being born once in the womb, but not consider-ing that which makes a woman pregnant to be a birth, a man is said to be born again "of water and the Holy Spirit" (Jn 3:5). The Lord is said to have been born at Bethlehem of Judah (Mt 2:1) according to the moment of His birth from His Mother. If, therefore, a man in the womb is able to be reborn by the grace of the Spirit, since he still has to be born, he is reborn before being born, which is totally impossible. Hence, not by the works of justice which they will perform are men born into the totality of Christ's body as into a living structure of God's temple, His Church, but, by being through grace born again, they are trans-ported from a ruinous mass into the foundation of the building. Outside this building raised up to be blessed as God's eternal dwelling, the entire life of man is unhappy and rather to be called death than life. Whoever, then, has God dwelling in him, that God's anger may not fall on him, will not be hostile to this body, this temple, this birth. But whoever is not reborn is hostile to it.

Chapter Thirty-Four

Moreover, our Mediator, when manifested to us, wanted the sacrament of our rebirth to be made public. But it was something hidden from the just men of old although they were also to be saved by the same faith to be revealed in due time. For we do not dare to prefer the faithful of our own day to God's friends by whom those prophecies were to be made, since God so proclaimed Himself the God of Abraham, the God of Isaac, the God of Jacob (Ex 3:15) as to give Himself that name forever. If the belief is correct that in respect to the saints of old, circumcision served instead of baptism, what shall we say of those who pleased God before this was commanded except that they pleased Him by faith, because, as it is written in Hebrews, "Without faith it is impossi-ble to please God" (Heb 11:6)? "But having the same spirit of faith: I believed, for which cause I have spoken, we also believe for which cause we speak also" (2 Cor 4:13; Ps 115:10). He would not have said "the same" unless this very spirit of faith belonged also to them. For just as, when this same mystery was hidden, they believed in the Incarnation of Christ which was to come, so we also believe that it has come. And both we and they await His future coming as Judge, for there is no other mystery of God (Apoc 10:7) except Christ in whom all who have died in Adam are to be made alive, because "as in Adam all die, so also in Christ all shall be made alive" (2 Cor 15:22), as we previously explained.

Chapter Thirty-Five

Consequently, God, who is present everywhere and wholly present everywhere, does not dwell within all men, but only in those whom he has made into His most blessed temple or temples, delivering them "from the power of darkness," and translating them "into the kingdom of the Son of His love" (Col 1:13), which began with their rebirth. But when built by the hands of men of lifeless materials like the tabernacle made of wood, tapestries, skins, and other such movables, His temple has one meaning; as also the temple built by King Solomon, of stone, wood, and metal. It has another meaning with respect to that true Temple symbolized by those metaphors. Hence the words: "Be you also as living stones, built up, a spiritual house" (1 Pt 2:5); hence it is also written: "For we are the temple of the living God, as God says: I will dwell in them and I will be their God and they shall be my people" (2 Cor 6:16; Lv 26:12).

Chapter Thirty-Six

Yet we should not be anxious because some who are not yet part of this temple, that is, within whom God does not or does not yet dwell, perform some works of power, as with him who cast out devils in the name of Christ; although he was not one of Christ's disciples (Mk 9:37), Christ commanded that he be allowed to continue because to many people this gave a useful testimony of His Name. He also said that at the last day many would say to Him: "In your name we have done many miracles," to whom He surely would not say: "I know you not" (Mt 7:22) if they were part of the temple of God which by His indwelling He makes blessed. The centurion Cornelius also saw the angel who was sent to him and heard him saying that his prayer was heard and his alms accepted even before he was incorporated into this temple by rebirth (Acts 10:1). Even when acting through His holy angels, God does these things as One present everywhere.

ON THE PRESENCE OF GOD

Chapter Thirty-Seven

In regard to Jeremiah's sanctification before emerging from the womb (Jer 1:5), some understand that he was a type of the Savior, having no need of rebirth. However, even when taken literally, it can be properly taken in the sense of rebirth inasmuch as the Gospel speaks of those not yet reborn as Sons of God, when, after Caiphas had said of the Lord: "It is expedient for you that one man should die for the people and that the whole nation perish not," the Evangelist continues, adding: "This he spoke not of himself but as the high priest of that year, he prophesied that Jesus should die for the nation, and not only for the nation, but to gather together in one the children of God that were dispersed" (Jn 11:50). He clearly calls children of God not only the Hebrew race, but men of all other races who were not yet among the faithful, not yet baptized. How can he also call them sons of God except on the view of their predestination, in which respect also the Apostle says that God chose us in Christ before the foundation of the world (Eph 1:4)? That very gathering together in one would have made them children of God. And by the phrase "in one" he would not have signified any corporeal place, since of a similar calling of the Gentiles the Prophet made this prophecy, "They shall adore Him, every man from his own place; all the islands of the Gentiles" (Sophonias 2:11), but "gathered together in one" refers to the one spirit and one body of which the head is Christ (Col 1:18; Eph 1:22). Such a gathering together is the building of the temple of God; such a gathering together is not accomplished by carnal birth, but by spiritual rebirth.

Chapter Thirty-Eight

Consequently, God dwells within each one singly as in His temples, and in all of them gathered together as in His temple. As long as this temple, like Noah's Ark, is storm-tossed in this world, there is verified the words of the Psalm: "The Lord dwells in the flood" (Ps 28:10), although, if we are thinking of the many people of the faithful of all races whom the Apocalypse describes under the term of waters (Apoc 17:15), they can also be suitably signified by "The Lord dwells in the flood." But the Psalm continues: "And the Lord shall sit King forever" (Ps 28:10), no doubt in His very

423

temple established in eternal life after this world's tempest. Hence God, who is present everywhere and wholly present everywhere, does not dwell everywhere but only in His temple, to which by His grace He is kind and gracious, but in His indwelling, he is received more fully by some, less by others.

Chapter Thirty-Nine

Speaking of Him as our Head, the Apostle says: "For in him dwells all the fullness of the Godhead corporeally" (Col 2:9). He does not say corporeally because God is corporeal, but he either uses the word derivatively as if He dwelt in a temple made by hands, not corporeally but symbolically, that is, under prefiguring signs—for using a derived word he calls all those observances shadows of things to come (Col 2:17; Heb 10:1), for the most high God, as it is written, "dwells not in temples made with hand" (Acts 17:24)—or else the word "corporeally" is used surely because God dwells, as in His temple, in the body of Christ taken from the Virgin. That is the reason, when to the Jews demanding a sign He said: "Destroy this temple and in three days I will raise it up," the Evangelist, explaining what He intended, continued: "But he spoke of the temple as his body" (Jn 2:19).

Chapter Forty

What therefore? Are we to understand that between the Head and the other members there is this difference: that divinity may dwell in any member, however outstanding like some great prophet or apostle, yet not "all the fullness of the Godhead" (Col 2:9) as in the Head which is Christ? For our body sensation is also present within the individual members but not so greatly as in the head, where it is evident that all five senses are centered; for there are located sight and hearing and smell and taste and touch, but in the other members there is only touch. But beyond the fact that "all the fullness of the Godhead" is found in that Body as in a temple, there is between that Head and the perfection of any member another difference. This is, truly, the fact that by a certain unique taking on of humanity He became one Person with the Word. Of no saint has it been said, is it said, or will it be possible to say: "The Word was made flesh" (Jn 1:14), no saint through any high gift of grace received the name of only-begotten Son, so as to be called by the name which is that of the very Word of God Himself before all ages, together with the humanity He assumed. Hence, that act of becoming man can be shared with no holy man, however renowned in wisdom and sanctity. That is evident enough and a clear proof of divine grace. Who, therefore, could be guilty of such sacrilege as to dare affirm that any soul, through the merit of the free will, could succeed in becoming another Christ? How could one single soul, by means of free will given equally to all by nature, have merited to be joined to the Person of the only-begotten Word, unless a high grace had granted this, a grace we may rightly praise but concerning which we are forbidden to judge?

Chapter Forty-One

If I have succeeded in treating of these matters, according to my strength and with the Lord's assistance, when you decide to think of God present everywhere and wholly present everywhere, not divided into different places as if by the extending of a physical mass, withdraw your mind from all corporeal images such as you usually form. That is not how we think of wisdom or justice, or, finally, of love, of which it is written: "God is love" (1 Jn 4:8). And when you think of His indwelling, think of the communion of saints, especially in heaven where He is spoken of as dwelling in a unique way because there His will is done by the perfect obedience of those in whom He dwells. Then think of Him on earth where He dwells while building His house to be dedicated at the end of time. But when you think of Christ our Lord, the only-begotten Son of God, equal to the Father, and likewise Son of man, in which respect the Father is greater than He, have no doubt that as God He is wholly present everywhere, and also as God He dwells in the very temple of God; whereas in His true Body He is in some part of heaven.

To talk with you gives me such pleasure that I am not sure whether I have kept to a due measure of speech in my desire to compensate for my long silence by a long response. Truly to you I speak as to a friend, so closely are you joined to my heart by the ties of religion and kindness, in which you have surpassed me. Thank God for me whenever you hear that any work of my pen has been fruitful, but if you notice my shortcomings, pardon them as a most dear friend, with the same sincere affection, praying for my cure, as you grant me your indulgence.

Augustine of Hippo

THE CITY OF GOD

Introductory Note. The City of God provides a theological view of history. The first five books argue against the pagan opinion that polytheism accounted for the temporal prosperity of the Roman State. The next five books argue against the pagan position that polytheism leads to eternal happiness, a position taken by some Greek Neoplatonic philosophers. The final twelve books place history within the perspective of salvation. Books XI–XIV discuss the Scriptural facts of the origin of man, the rise of two cities or societies (heavenly and earthly), and human secular history until A.D. 425. Books XV–XVIII discuss the progress of the two Cities, while books XIX–XXII describe their ends or eschatology, the four last things: death, judgment, heaven, hell. Only at the end of the world will it be evident who belongs to the City of God, the society of good men and good angels, and who belongs to the city of the devil, the society of the fallen angels and wicked men.

The pagan accusation that the Christian prohibition of polytheism removed the source of Rome's prosperity was made on the occasion of the sack of Rome by Alaric in A.D. 410. Augustine responded by proving the accusation false in the first books, but the greater part of The City of God *describes the four pillars of civilization—Roman, Greek, Hebrew, and Christian—and demonstrates the destiny of mankind: heaven or hell according to the objects of one's love: "Two loves have built two cities, self-love in contempt of God has built the earthly city; love of God in contempt of oneself has built the heavenly city."*

The struggle between these two cities is the substance of history. The two cities are also commingled in each person, where they are struggling for possession. The consummation of history will be the separation of the two cities into heaven and hell. The doctrine of the resurrection of the body is central to this view. In arguing for it from faith, Augustine clearly manifested his conviction that the body is essential to the human reality. His insistence on personal immortality, made possible by the Resurrection of Christ, separated his views from those of Plato, Aristotle, Plotinus, Porphyry.

Here we present Book XIX, on the secular and Christian notions of happiness. Augustine returns to the theme of human desire for God which he had set forth in the first book of the Confessions and in The Happy Life. He opposes the miseries and passing pleasures of temporal life to the certain happiness of eternal life for those who live by faith. This happiness is peace—peace in eternity or eternity in peace. Peace is the presence of God. His presence in the universe was manifested in the Incarnation, which restored order, the order of love. God is Love and by the gift of Himself to mankind it is now possible to make the ascent to God by Love. Happiness, therefore, does not consist in rejecting the world but in learning to love it as it should be loved, for earthly goods can indeed contribute to human peace and to eternal life. Peace with oneself is a true love of self, that is, preferring God to self; this is the model for loving the neighbor. Authorities have much to do with peace. To be themselves happy authorities are to secure the peace of those whom they serve. In this we recognize that Augustine highly valued the State and saw it able to bring peace to citizens when the rulers themselves were at peace with God. Christian families produced the best rulers and the best citizens. Each city seeks its own peace, yet the citizens of the City of God (an invisible, mystical city) can make use of the intelligent organization of the earthly State as long as the State does not forbid the worship of the One God. After all, the City of God, like the Church, is supranational. Christians are one in mind and heart, a Christian community. No Augustinian theory of the relation between Church and State is given, but Church members have two allegiances—to God and country, with the allegiance to God having priority. As citizens, Christians have responsibilities to their fellow citizens, owing positive charity to pagan neighbors and obligated to promote public concord. A Christian "must not be all for himself, but sociable in his life and actions," so that if asked to assume public office, the law and charity require this.

Augustine's famous charge that there never was a Roman

Republic was made because Cicero's definition of a State suggested a people united for justice, and since justice required that God be given due worship, the Romans who substituted for God a legion of devils were not a true Republic. This highlights the Augustinian position that all legal rules are subordinated to justice and conscience. "Put justice aside then and what are kingdoms but great piracies?" "Now to war against one's neighbors, and to proceed to the harm of those who do not harm you, for greedy desire of rule and sovereignty, what is this but flat thievery in a greater excess and quantity than usual?" (IV.6)

The thrust of Book XIX is not political but eschatological. Everyone seeks happiness and all seek it in some good that they choose. There is no evil reality in itself but only a good proudly preferred to God. Political power is not an evil, only inordinate love of power. The vestige of God in every good thing calls on us to transcend it and allow the infinite longing of the human heart to find its true happiness in the Infinite God. Unless love for God has priority in our lives the realities we seek—wealth, power, honor, pleasure—become idols. As false gods they cannot give peace to persons who are "made toward" God. All peoples seek happiness, and complete happiness is to be found only in the supreme good, which is eternal life "where God shall be all in all, where eternity shall be firm, and peace most perfect and absolute" (XIX.20).

This happiness is visible only to the eyes of faith and is to be received from God for the asking.

Book Nineteen

Chapter One

Since I see that next I have to discuss the appointed destinies of both cities, the earthly and the heavenly, I first have to explain, within the limits of this work, the arguments by which men have struggled to make themselves happy in the midst of the unhappiness of this life, so that it may become evident for the benefit of unbelievers not only by divine authority but also through the use of reason how different from this vain thinking is our hope which God has given us and that very reality, which is true happiness, which he will give us. The philosophers have held many disputes among themselves concerning the ends of good and evil, and by seriously considering the question they tried to discover what makes a human being happy. Our final good is that for the sake of which other things are to be desired, but it itself is to be desired for its own sake, and the final evil is that for the sake of which other things are to be avoided while it itself is to be avoided on its own account. So by the end of the good we presently mean not the end whereby good is exhausted so that it no longer exists, but the end state in which it is brought to total perfection; and by the end of evil we mean not that which puts an end to it but that which brings about total harm. These two ends, therefore, are the supreme good and the supreme evil. The effort to discover these and to attain in this life the supreme good while avoiding the supreme evil has been the work of those who have devoted themselves in the midst of the vanity of the world to the quest for wisdom. And although they erred in diverse ways, yet natural insight has prevented their deviating from the path of truth, so that there is none who did not place the supreme good or evil in the soul, or in the body, or in both. From this triple division in the general classification of sects, Marcus Varro in his book *De Philosophia* has by a careful and subtle analysis noted such a great variety of opinions that he arrived at 288 sects—not that these actually existed, but they could have existed.

To indicate this briefly I should begin with what he points out in this book, that there are four things sought by men naturally, without a teacher, without the help of any instruction, without effort and without the art of living which is called virtue and is certainly learned: that is, pleasure, an agreeable moment of the bodily senses; or repose, whereby one suffers no bodily discomfort; or both these, given the single name of pleasure by Epicurus; or the primary goods of nature, among which are these and others, whether bodily, such as the health and the safety and the integrity of the members, or spiritual, such as the natural qualities, great or small, which are found in human beings. Therefore, these four —pleasure, repose, both together, the primary goods of nature—so exist in us that we have to desire virtue which will be for their sake, or them for the sake of virtue, or both of them for their own sake; and from this distinction there arise twelve sects, for each by this principle of classification is tripled. Once I have demonstrated this in one case, it will not be difficult to find it in others. Insofar as bodily pleasure is subjected, preferred, or joined to virtue, there are three sects. It is subjected to virtue when it is taken into the service of virtue. Here it is a duty of virtue to live for one's country, and for the sake of one's country to beget sons, neither of which can be done without bodily pleasure; for without pleasure neither food nor drink can be taken to sustain life, nor without it can sexual intercourse occur for the sake of procreation. But when pleasure is preferred to virtue, it is desired for its own sake and virtue chosen only for its sake and it is thought that virtue should serve pleasure so that there should be no virtuous act except to attain or preserve bodily pleasure. But this is a deformed kind of life, for where virtue serves the tyrant pleasure it no longer deserves the name of virtue. Yet this horrible deformity has had some philosophers as its patrons and defenders. Then virtue is joined to pleasure when neither is desired for the sake of the other, but both for their own sakes. Therefore, just as pleasure insofar as it is subjected, preferred, or joined to virtue makes three sects, so likewise repose, and repose combined with pleasure, and the primary natural goods make three more sects. Because human opinions vary, these four things are sometimes subjected to virtue, sometimes preferred, sometimes joined with it; so we reach the number of twelve sects. But this number is again doubled by the addition of one difference, that of social life, since whoever follows one of these sects does so either for only his own sake, or for the sake of a companion, for whom he ought to wish what he desires for himself. So there are twelve sects of those who believe that a certain philosophic position should be held only for one's own sake, and twelve others of those who take the view that they should follow this or that philosophy not merely for their own sakes but for the sake of others also whose good they seek as their own. These twenty-four sects are again doubled, and become forty-eight, by adding a difference taken from the New Academy. For any man can hold and defend any one of the twelve sects as certain, as the Stoics defended their position that the good of man which makes him happy consists solely in moral excellence; or they can be held as probable, but not certain, as the New Academy did. So there are twenty-four sects of those holding their views to be certainly true, and twenty-four others of those holding their views as being probable, but not certain. Again, because each one who attaches himself to any of these sects may adopt the mode of life either of the Cynics or of the other philosophers, this difference will double the number, and it becomes ninety-six. Finally, because each of these sects may be favored and followed by men who for themselves prefer a life of leisure, as those who by choice or necessity have dedicated themselves to studies, or by men who dedicate themselves to business, as those who while philosophizing are engaged in public administration and state affairs, or by those who choose a mixed life, as did those who gave their time partly to learned leisure and partly to necessary business: by these differences the number of the sects is tripled, becoming two hundred and eighty-eight.

I have thus put in my own words, as briefly and clearly as I could, the opinions found in Varro's book. But how he refutes all the other sects, choosing one and claiming that that one is the Old Academy, begun by Plato and continuing to Polemo, the fourth teacher of that school called the Academy which held that their teaching was certain, by which he distinguished it from the New Academy which began with Arcesilaus, the successor of Polemo, and held that all things are uncertain, and how he tries to establish that the Old Academy was as free from error as from doubt: to explain all this in detail would take too long; yet it may not be wholly omitted.

Varro, therefore, removes all those differences which had led to the multiplication of sects because they are not differences about the supreme good. For he maintains that no sect of philosophy should be recognized unless it differs from others by having its own view concerning final good and evil. For man's only reason for philosophizing is to be happy, but that which makes him happy is precisely the final good. So, when a sect has no sectarian view about the final good, it should not be called a sect. When, therefore, it is questioned whether a wise man will support social life by desiring and trying to achieve for his friend as well as for himself the supreme good which makes man happy or whether he does all that he does merely for the sake of his own happiness, this is not a question concerning the supreme good itself but about sharing or not sharing the supreme good with a friend not for his own sake but for his friend's sake in whose good he delights as in his own. Likewise, where there is question concerning the New Academy, for whom all things are uncertain, whether these are true philosophic views or whether we should hold that philosophic views are certain, which was a view acceptable to other philosophers, this question is not concerned with the final good itself, but is concerned with whether or not we are to doubt of the certainty of the truth of the good which apparently should be pursued; or to speak more plainly, whether the pursuit of the final good demands that the pursuer ought to assert that his view of the final good is true, or whether he is to assert that it seems true to him, although perhaps it is false, although the one same good is pursued. Also in regard to that difference deriving from the manners and customs of the Cynics, this is not a question about the final good, but it is about whether the pursuer of that which to him seems to be the final good, whatever it is, and to be the proper object of pursuit, should live according to the manners and customs of the Cynics. There were indeed men pursuing different final goods, some virtue, others pleasure, who nevertheless followed the same manners and customs which gave the Cynics their name. So whatever differentiates the Cynics from other philosophers has nothing to do with the choice and adherence to the good which was to make them happy. For if it would make a difference, surely the same manners would imply the pursuit of the same end, and diverse manners would rule out the pursuit of the same end.

Chapter Two

And in regard to those three kinds of life, namely, the one which, though not slothful, is nevertheless a life of leisure passed in contemplating or inquiring into truth, the other life spent in the active administration of human affairs, and the third which is a combination of the two others, when it is asked which of them should be chosen, this is not a controversy about the final good; the question raised here is which of these three hinders or facilitates attaining or preserving the final good. When any one reaches the final good it immediately makes him happy, whereas a life spent in learned leisure or in public affairs or in both by turns does not make him happy immediately. Doubtless there are many who may be living any one of these lives and who go astray in their search for the final good which makes man happy.

So the question concerning the final good and the final evil which differentiates sects of philosophy is one question; and those questions concerning social life, the doubt of the Academy, the dress and food of the Cynics, or the three kinds of life, the contemplative, the active, and a combination of both, are quite other: none of these entails an argument about the final good and final evil. Hence, Marcus Varro, once he has used these four differences either from social life, from the New Academy, from the Cynics, and from that triple classification of life to reach the figure of two-hundred-and-eighty-eight sects or any larger figure reached the same kind of way, so by removing these differences as unrelated to the final good, and therefore not constituting what can properly be called sects, returns to those twelve schools which are concerned with inquiring what that good is which makes man happy, and shows that only one of them is true, the others false. By the removal of any differentiation based on the three kinds of life, two-thirds of the total number are subtracted, and ninety-six sects remain. Remove again any differentiation based on the Cynics, and the number is reduced to a half, or forty-eight. Let us also take away the difference which was gotten from the New Academy, and again only half remain, or twenty-four. Also remove the question raised about social life; twelve remain which this difference had doubled to make twenty-four.

As for these twelve, nothing can be said against their being recognized as sects. For they seek nothing other than the final good and final evil, that is, the final good, for once this is found, the contrary, evil, is also found. But to make these twelve sects, four things are multiplied three times: pleasure, repose, the combination of the two, and the primary natural goods which Varro calls *primigenia*. Indeed these four things, one by one, are sometimes subordinated to virtue so that they seem to be desired not for their own sakes but for the sake of virtue, and are sometimes preferred to it, so that virtue is thought to be needed not for its own sake but in order to attain or preserve these things, and sometimes joined with it so that both they and virtue are believed desirable for their own sakes—we must multiply the four by three, and so we get twelve sects. But from these four things Varro takes away three: pleasure, repose, and the two combined, not because he disapproves of them but because the primary natural goods include pleasure and repose. And what is the use of making three out of these two ends, pleasure and repose taken first singly and then together, since both are comprised within the primary natural goods and included also are many other things as well? It was Varro's opinion that the three remaining sects should be studied carefully to see which one is to be chosen. For true reason does not allow more than one to be true, whether it is one of these three, or another, as we shall later see. Meanwhile let us explain as briefly and clearly as possible how Varro chooses one of these three. Surely this division into three sects comes from their holding that the primary natural goods are to be sought for the sake of virtue, or virtue for their sake, or both, that is, both virtue and the primary natural goods, for their own sake.

Chapter Three

Varro tries to show which of these three sects is true and to be followed in this way. Because philosophy seeks the supreme good not of the tree, nor of a beast, nor of God, but of man, he thinks that the answer to the question of what man himself is should be sought. He feels that there are two parts in his nature, body and soul, and he does not doubt that of these two the soul is the better and the far more excellent part. But is the soul alone, the man so that the body is to him as the horse to the horseman (for the horseman is not a man and a horse but only a man, yet he is called horseman because he has a certain relation to the horse)? Or is the body alone the man, having some relation to the soul like that of the cup to the drink (for not the cup and the drink it contains are together called the cup, but the cup alone; yet it is so called because it is designed to hold the drink), or again does neither the soul alone nor the body alone but both together constitute man of whom the soul and the body are each a part whereas the whole man consists of both (as we call two horses yoked together a pair, though we do not call the left or the right horse however related to the other, a pair, but only both together)?

Of these three positions Varro chose the third, that man is neither soul alone nor body alone but soul and body together. And, therefore, he says that the supreme good of man which makes him happy consists of a combination of bodily and spiritual goods. And so he thinks that primary natural goods are to be sought for their own sake and that virtue which is the art of living well and is communicated by instruction is the most excellent of spiritual goods. For this reason virtue or the art of regulating life when it receives the primary natural goods which exist independently of virtue and prior to any instruction whatever seeks them all and itself also for its own sake. Virtue uses them as it also uses itself so that it may take delight in and have enjoyment in all of them, greater or less according as they are themselves greater or less, and while enjoying all of them it despises the less so that it may attain or retain the greater, if necessity demands it.

Of all the bodily or spiritual goods none is preferable to virtue itself. For virtue uses well both itself and those other goods that make man happy. But without virtue no matter how many goods a man has they do him no good and so should not be called good things as long as they belong to a man who uses them ill. Therefore that life of man is called happy when it enjoys virtue and the other spiritual and bodily good things without which virtue is impossible. Life is called happier if it enjoys some or many other good things not essential to virtue, and the happiest life lacks not one of the good things pertaining to soul or body.

For life is not the same thing as virtue since not every life but only the wisely led life is virtue: for there can be some kind of life without any virtue, but there cannot be virtue without life. I might say the same of memory and reason and other such human powers. For these exist prior to instruction and without these there can be no instruction and on that account no virtue since virtue is learned. But swiftness of foot, physical beauty, and contests won by unusual strength and the like can exist without virtue as virtue can exist without them; yet they are goods, and according to these philosophers virtue seeks even these goods for their own sake and uses and enjoys them appropriately.

They say that this happy life is also social and loves the good of friends as its own good and wishes for them for their own sakes what it wishes for itself, whether such friends live in the family like wife or children or domestics, or are in the same locality like citizens of the same town, or in the entire world such as nations bound in common human brotherhood, or in the universe itself, designated by the name heaven and earth such as those whom they name gods and consider as friends of the wise men, those whom we more familiarly call angels. Moreover they assert that with reference to the final good and evil, there is no room for doubt and that this distinguishes them from the New Academy and they do not care whether a philosopher pursues those ends thought to be true in the Cynic dress or manner of life, or in some other. Finally, of these three kinds of life, the contemplative, the active, and the combination, they declare in favor of the third. That the Old Academy held and taught these doctrines Varro states on the authority of Antiochus, Cicero's master and his own, although Cicero on many points describes him as more in accord with the Stoic than with the Old Academy. But what is that to us who ought to pass judgment on the things themselves rather than to know what opinion each man held about them?

Chapter Four

If, therefore, we are asked what the City of God replies when asked about these various points and, first, its opinion about the final good and evil, it will reply that the supreme good is eternal life and that the supreme evil is eternal death and to obtain the one and escape the other we must live rightly. Thus it is written: "The just man lives by faith" (Hb 2:4). Since we do not yet see our good so it is appropriate for us to seek it by believing; neither have we in ourselves power to live rightly unless He who has given us faith to believe that we must ask help from him shall help us when we believe and pray. But those who have thought that the final good and final evil are to be had in the present life, whether placing the supreme good in the body or in the soul or in both, or, more explicitly, either in pleasure or in virtue or in both, in repose or in virtue or in both, in primary natural goods or in virtue or in both, all these have sought with a marvelous vanity to be happy in this life and to achieve happiness by their own efforts. Truth ridiculed these people through the words of the Prophet: "The Lord knows the thoughts of men" (Ps 94:11) or as the Apostle Paul testified: "The Lord knows the thoughts of the wise, that they are vain" (1 Cor 3:9).

For what torrent of eloquence suffices to explain the miseries of this life? Cicero lamented them as best he could in the *Consolation* on the death of his daughter, but how inadequate was his best! For when, where, how in this life can the so-called primary natural goods be so possessed as not to be threatened by unforeseen accidents? Why, what pain is there, the contrary of pleasure, what disquiet is there, the contrary of repose, that cannot befall the body of the wise man? Certainly amputation or weakening destroys its integrity; deformity destroys its beauty; weakness, its health; lassitude, its vigor; sleepiness or sluggishness, its activity—and which of these may not attack the flesh of the wise man? Comely fitting positions and movements of the body are also numbered among the primary natural goods; but suppose some disease makes the limbs quake and tremble? Suppose a man's spine is so curved that his hands reach the ground, making of him a quadruped, so to speak? Will this not ruin all beauty and grace of bodily stance or of movement?

What of the so-called primary natural goods of the mind itself, the sense and intellect, the first of the two for perception and the other for the comprehension of truth? But what kind of perception remains where a man becomes deaf and blind, to say nothing of other defects? And where do reason and intelligence withdraw, where do they sleep when a man is crazed by some disease? When the insane say or do many absurd things that are mostly alien to their own aims and characters—and are even contrary to their good aims and characters, when we consider or see the actions and words of these insane people we can scarcely refrain from tears, or perhaps we cannot. What shall I say of those afflicted by demonic possession? Where is their own intelligence hidden or buried while the evil spirit is using their souls and bodies according to his own will? And who can be confident that this evil will not befall the wise man in this life? Then as to the perception of truth, what kind can we hope for in this flesh and how much when, as we read in the truthful book of wisdom: "The corruptible body weighs down the soul, and the earthly frame lies heavy on a mind that ponders many things" (Wis 9:15)? And eagerness or an impulse to act, if either is the correct meaning for what the Greeks call *hormē*, is also considered to be among the primary natural goods. Yet, is not impulse itself accountable for those miserable movements and actions of the insane which horrify us, when sensation is deceived and reason deranged?

Finally, as to virtue itself, which is not among the primary natural goods, since it is added later through instruction, although it claims the highest place among human goods, what does it do here but make perpetual war with vices, not external but internal, not alien but plainly our own, a war waged especially by the virtue called *sōphrosynē* in Greek and temperance in Latin which checks the lusts of the flesh lest they win the mind's consent and drag it into every kind of crime?

For we must not suppose that there is no vice in us when, as the Apostle says, "The flesh lusts against the spirit" (Gal 5:17); for there is a virtue contrary to this vice, when, as the same Apostle says: "The spirit lusts against the flesh. For these two," he says, "are opposed one to the other, so that you do not what you would" (Gal 5:17). But what do we will to do when we wish to be made perfect by the Supreme Good unless that the flesh should not lust against the spirit, and that there should be in us no vice for the spirit to lust against? And since we cannot achieve this in the present life, no matter how much we desire it, let us with God's help achieve at least this, to restrain the soul from succumbing and yielding to the flesh lusting against it and to deny our consent to the commitment of sin. Far be it from us, therefore, to believe that as long as we are engaged in this internal war that we have already attained the happiness which we seek to reach by victory. And who is there so wise that he has no battle at all to wage against his vices?

What is to be said of that virtue called prudence? Is it not totally vigilant in discerning good from evil, so that in seeking the one and avoiding the other no error or mistake may occur about good and evil? Thus it is itself a witness to the existence of evil and of evils in us. For prudence itself teaches that it is evil to consent to sin and good to refuse this consent. Yet that evil to which prudence teaches us not to consent and temperance enables us not to consent is neither by prudence nor by temperance removed from this life. What is to be said of justice, whose task is to assign to each man his due, whence there exists in man a certain just order of nature so that the soul is subject to God, and flesh to the soul, and consequently both soul and flesh to God? Does justice not thereby demonstrate that she is still laboring at her task rather than reposing at the end of her labors? For the soul is so much the less subjected to God the less it keeps mindful of God; and flesh is so much the less subjected to the spirit as it lusts more strongly against the spirit. Hence as long as we are beset by this weakness, this plague, this sickness, how shall we dare to say that we are saved, and if not saved, how dare we say that we are already blessed with final happiness? Then truly that virtue called fortitude, though present with however great widsom, testifies very clearly to human evils which it is compelled to endure with patience.

And I am amazed that the Stoic philosophers have the gall to argue that these are not evils although they admit that if they are so great that the wise man cannot endure them, he is allowed to commit suicide, and to depart this life. But such is the stupid pride of these men who suppose that the final good is to be possessed in this life and that they can achieve their own happiness that their wise man, that is, the one they describe as such with amazing vanity, whom, even when blinded, deaf, and dumb, having lost the use of his limbs, tortured with pain, and suffering every evil tongue can tell or mind conceive, whereby he is forced to commit suicide, they are not ashamed to call happy. Oh, happy life which seeks the help of death to end it! If it is happy, let the wise man remain alive. How can those things not be evil which overcome the good of fortitude, and force it not only to yield to them but so to rave that it simultaneously calls that life happy and urges that it be escaped? Who is so blind as not to see that if it were happy, it should not be escaped? But in using the word "escape" they openly admit the weakness of their argument. What reason keeps them from admitting, their stiff-necked pride shattered, that it is a miserable life? Was it, I ask, patience or rather impatience which prompted Cato to take his own life? For he would not have done it unless he lacked the patience to endure the victory of Caesar. Where then is his fortitude? It yielded, succumbed, was so thoroughly overcome that he gave up, abandoned, escaped this happy life. Or was it no longer happy? Then it was miserable. How, therefore, were those not evils which made life miserable and something to be escaped?

And therefore those who admit that these are evils, as do the Peripatetics and the Old Academy, the sect that Varro defends, speak more intelligibly, but their error is also surprising since they argue that this is a happy life in the midst of these evils even when they are so great that he who suffers them should commit suicide to escape them. "Bodily pains and torments," Varro says, "are evils, and so much the worse in proportion to their severity; and to avoid them one must escape this life." What life, pray? "This life," he says, "that is oppressed by such great evils." Then it is definitely happy in the midst of those evils which you say one ought to escape? Or do you call it happy because it is permissible to escape these evils by death? What, then, if by some divine judgment you were held among them and not permitted either to die or to be freed from them? Doubtless you would then say that such a life was miserable? So it is not nonmiserable because it is soon relinquished since if it were everlasting even you would call it miserable; and so it ought not to be seen as free from all misery because the misery is brief, or, what is more absurd, because the misery is brief should it therefore be called a state of happiness.

There is a mighty power in these evils which force a man, and force even a wise man, according to these philosophers, to deprive himself of his own human existence; although they say and truly say that the first and greatest law of nature is that a man should cherish himself and therefore naturally avoid death and that he be a friend to himself so that he is strongly determined and eager to continue existing as a living being in this union of soul and body. There is a mighty power in these evils to overcome this natural instinct by which death is by every means and with all the effort of man avoided, and to overcome it so entirely that what was avoided is desired, looked for, and if in no other way can it be obtained, is inflicted on himself by the man himself. There is a mighty power in these evils which make fortitude a homicide, if that still should be called fortitude which is so totally overcome by these evils that it not only cannot by its patience not protect and govern man but is itself forced to kill him. Certainly the wise man ought patiently to endure even death, but a death inflicted by another. But if, according to these philosophers, he is compelled to inflict it on himself, certainly it should be admitted that those things which forced him to commit this crime were not only evils but in fact intolerable evils.

The life, therefore, that is oppressed by the weight of such great and grave evils or subject to chance would in no way be called happy if the men who use that word had condescended to yield to the truth and be conquered by sound arguments when inquiring after the happy life, as they are conquered by overwhelming evils and in the act of committing suicide, yield to misfortune, by having fancied that the supreme good was to be found in this mortal life. For the very virtues of this life, which are surely the best and most useful of man's possessions, testify more faithfully to life's miseries insofar as they are helpful against its dangers, toils, and woes. For if our virtues are genuine—which is only the case in those who have true piety—they do not claim to deliver those who possess them from all miseries (for true virtues are not so fraudulent as to profess such a thing), but they assert that human life, though forced by all the great evils of this age to be unhappy, is happy in the expectation of a future life insofar as it also enjoys the expectation of salvation. For can there be a happy life where there is no salvation? So the Apostle Paul, speaking not of men who lacked prudence, patience, temperance, and justice but of those who lived according to true piety, and who therefore had genuine virtues, says: "For we are saved by hope. But hope that is seen is not hope. For how should a man hope for what he sees? But if we hope for what we do not see, then we look forward with patience" (Rom 8:24–25). Therefore, just as we are saved by hope, so by hope we are made happy; and just as we "have no hold on present salvation, so we have no hold on present happiness but look to the future, a happiness to be attained with patience." We are among evils and so we ought patiently to tolerate them until we come to the ineffable enjoyment of unmixed good; then there will be nothing to be tolerated. Such is the salvation which in the future life will itself be also final happiness. But those philosophers, unwilling to believe in a happiness they do not see, strive to fabricate for themselves a very false happiness based upon virtue as fraudulent as it is proud.

Chapter Five

But that they wish the life of the wise man to be social, we approve much more fully. For how could that City of God, about which we are already engaged in writing the nineteenth book, have a beginning or progress or reach its proper destiny if the life of the saints were not a social life? But who can enumerate the great woes abounding in human society in the midst of our mortal state? Who can assess them? Listen to one of their comic writers expressing through a character the common feelings of all men in this matter: "I am married, what misery I have seen through this. Children were born; another anxiety" (Terence, *Adelph* 5.4.13f.). What is to be said of the miseries of love which Terence also recounts—"slights, suspicions, quarrels, war today, peace tomorrow" (Terence, *Eunuch.* 1.1.14)? Are not human affairs filled with such things? Do they not often happen even when friends are united in a noble love? On all sides human history is filled with slights, suspicions, enmities, and war, all of which are certainly evil; whereas peace is only a doubtful good, since we do not know the hearts of those with whom we want to be at peace, and even if we knew them today, we could not be sure what they would be like tomorrow. Who ought to be or who are more friendly than those living in the same home? And yet who is even secure there, since from their hidden treachery great woes have often arisen, woes the more bitter as the peace was sweeter that was considered genuine when it was most cleverly feigned?

For that reason the words of Cicero so touch all hearts that we are forced to lament: "No ambushed foes are harder to detect than those who hide their aim with a counterfeit loyalty or in the name of some necessity. For you would be on guard against an open adversary and easily able to escape him; but this hidden evil, internal and domestic, not only arises but even overwhelms you before you have a chance to observe and investigate it" (Cicero, *In Verrem* 2.1.15). That is why there is the divine saying: "A man's enemies are even those of his own household" (Mt 10:36), a saying that is heard with great sorrow of heart, because even if a man is strong enough to bear it with equanimity, or vigilant enough to guard against the designs of a pretended friend, yet, if he himself is a good man, he must seriously suffer when he finds that they are wicked, whether they were always wicked and feigned goodness, or whether they changed from goodness to evil. If then the home, our common refuge from the evils of human life, is not safe, what of the city, which, as it is larger, is so much the more filled with both civil and criminal lawsuits, and is never free from the fear and sometimes from the actual bloodshed of sedition and civil wars?

Chapter Six

What is to be said of those judgments pronounced by men on their fellowmen which are necessary in cities whatever outward peace they enjoy? How sad, how lamentable we find them, since those who pronounce them cannot discern the consciences of those whom they judge, and are therefore frequently compelled to torture innocent witnesses to discover the truth concerning the crimes of other men. What is to be said of torturing the accused man himself to discover whether he is guilty? He is tortured even if he is innocent, and for a doubtful crime he suffers a punishment far from doubtful, not because he was proven to have committed it but because it is not known that he did not commit it. And thus the ignorance of the judge is a calamity for the innocent. And what is more intolerable and more to be deplored and, if possible, purged by floods of tears is that the judge in the act of torturing the accused in order to avoid the unwitting execution of an innocent man, through wretched ignorance puts to death both tortured and innocent, the very man whom he has tortured in order not to execute him if innocent.

For if he has chosen, according to the wisdom of the philosophers, to escape this life rather than endure those torments any longer, he pleads guilty to a crime he did not commit. And after he has been condemned and killed, the judge still does not know whether he has killed a guilty or an innocent man whom he tortured so that he might not unwittingly execute an innocent man; and so he has both tortured an innocent man in order to learn the truth and put him to death without learning it. If such darkness exists in social life, will a wise judge sit on the bench, or will he not dare to do so? Clearly he will. For human society which he thinks it wicked to forsake constrains him and draws him to this office.

For he does not think it to be wicked that innocent witnesses are tortured regarding other men's crimes; or that the accused are often overcome by the pain of torture and therefore confess falsely and are punished though innocent; or that, though not condemned to death, they often die under torture or as a consequence of torture, or that the accusers, perhaps moved by the desire to help society by not letting crimes go unpunished, are themselves condemned by an ignorant judge if the witnesses give false evidence and the defendant strongly resisting torture confesses no guilt so that the accusers have no way to prove their charges, although their charges are true. He does not consider these many great evils to be sins; for the wise judge does not do these things because of any will to do harm but by the necessity of his ignorance and by the necessity of judging, which human society compels him to do. This is certainly an example of the misery of man, of which we spoke, even if there is no malice in the judge. But if by ignorance and by office he is constrained to torture and to punish the innocent is it not sufficient for us to acquit him of guilt? Must he be happy as well? Would he not be more considerate and worthy as a human being if he were to recognize the misery of this necessity and shrink from his own part in it and as a wise and religious man cry to God: "From my necessities deliver me!" (Ps 25:17)?

Chapter Seven

After the state or city comes the world, to which they assign the third level of human society, beginning with the household, then progressively coming to the city, and then the world which as larger is fuller of dangers, as the greater sea is the more dangerous. In the first place, the diversity of languages separates one man from another. For if two men, each one ignorant of the other's language, meet and by some necessity must remain together, then it is easier for dumb animals, even of different species, to socialize together than for them, though both are human beings. For when they cannot communicate what they feel to each other, merely on account of the diversity of languages, their likeness of nature so little promotes their union that a man would rather have his dog for company than a foreigner. But the imperial city has struggled to impose on conquered people not only her yoke but her language as a bond of peace so that interpreters, far from being scarce, are numerous. This is true, but how many great wars, how much slaughter and bloodshed have provided this unity!

And though the wars are past, there is no end to the miseries. For although foreign foes have not been, and are not, lacking, against whom there have always been and always are wars being waged, yet the very extent of the empire has begotten wars of a worse kind—social and civil wars—by which the whole human race is more wretchedly shaken either by the actual conflict or the fear of a renewed outbreak. If I attempted adequately to describe these many disasters, these hard and harsh necessities, though I am quite unequal to the task, where would my argument end? But the wise man, they say, will wage just wars. As if he, if he remembered his humanity, would not sorrow over the necessity of just wars; because unless they were just he would not have to wage them and so a wise man would have no wars. For it is the wickedness of the opposing group which compels the wise man to wage just wars; and this wickedness, even though it led to no war, would still be lamented by a human being because human beings do it. Let everyone, then, who reflects in sorrow upon all these great evils, so horrible and so ruthless, confess his misery. But whoever endures or thinks of them without mental anguish is far more miserable insofar as he thinks himself happy because he has lost all human feeling.

Chapter Eight

If we are not subject to a kind of ignorance, akin to madness, which often overtakes men in the wretched condition of this life so that they mistake a foe for a friend or a friend for a foe, what is there to console us in this human society full of misunderstandings and calamities except the unfeigned faith and mutual affection of true and good friends? But the more friends we have, and the more widely scattered they are, the greater is our fear that they will be affected by some of the accumulated evils of this age. For we are worried not only lest they suffer from famine, war, disease, captivity, or the inconceivable horrors of slavery but by the far more painful fear that friendship may be changed into treachery, malice, and injustice. And when these possibilities do occur (the more frequently, the more numerous our friends) and we are made aware of it, who except the one experiencing them can conceive with what pangs the heart is torn? Indeed, we would prefer to hear of their death, although this also could not be heard without sorrow. For if their life has delighted us with the comfort of friendship, how could it happen that their death should bring us no sadness? Whoever would prohibit such sadness must prohibit, if he can, all friendly conversation, must forbid or extinguish all friendly affection, must break with harsh insensibility the bonds of all human relationships or else presume that they should be so entered into that no pleasure from them might fill the mind. But if this is completely impossible, how can it be that someone's death will not be bitter to us if his life is sweet to us? Thus there comes that grief affecting the tender heart like a wound or a bruise for which we use kindly consolations to heal. Nor should we presume there is nothing to be healed simply because the better the soul the more easily is healing accomplished. For although the life of mortals is afflicted, sometimes more mildly, sometimes more painfully by the death of those very dear to us, and especially of officials whose work is necessary for human society, yet we would prefer to learn of or behold their death than to learn or perceive that they have fallen from faith or from virtue—in other words, that they were spiritually dead. Of this vast material for misery the earth is full, for which it is written: "Is human life on earth anything but a trial?" (Jb 7:1). And therefore the Lord Himself says: "Woe to the world because of scandals" (Mt 17:7), and again, "Because wickedness shall abound, the love of many shall grow cold" (Mt 24:12). And so we manifest our gratitude when our good friends die; and, although their death saddens us, it more certainly consoles us because they escaped those evils in this life by which even good men are crushed or corrupted or could be.

Chapter Nine

Indeed, in the society of the holy angels which those philosophers who taught that the gods are our friends ranked as the fourth level, as it were, passing from the earth to the universe in order to embrace in some way heaven itself, we have no fears that such friends will sadden us by their death or destruction. But because they do not mingle with us as familiarly as men (which itself is one of the griefs of this life) and because, as we read (2 Cor 11:14), Satan sometimes transfigures himself as an angel of light in order to tempt those who need the discipline or deserve to be deceived, there is great need of God's mercy lest someone, thinking he is enjoying the friendship of good angels, is really enjoying the feigned friendship of evil demons and suffering from their enmity which is the more harmful, the more shrewd and deceitful they are. And for whom is the great mercy of God necessary except for human beings of great misery, so weighed down by ignorance as easily deceived by the deceptions of these demons? And indeed it is very certain that those philosophers in the godless city who claimed that the gods were their friends have fallen a prey to the malignant demons to whom that city itself is entirely subject and whose everlasting punishment will be shared by them. For the nature of these demons is shown by those beings who are worshiped by them in the sacred or rather sacrilegious rites, and by the filthy games in which their crimes are celebrated and which they themselves originated and required from their worshipers as fitting propriation.

Chapter Ten

But not even the saints and the faithful worshipers of the one true and most high God are secure against the manifold temptations and deceptions of the demons. For in this abode of weakness and in these evil days such anxiety is not useless, since it makes us seek with more fervent desire for that security where peace is fullest and most certain. There the gifts of nature given by the Creator of all nature will be not only good but everlasting, not only in respect to the spirit, which is healed through wisdom, but also in respect to the body, which will be renewed by resurrection; there the virtues, no longer struggling against any vice or evil whatsoever, will have as the reward of victory eternal peace which no adversary may disquiet. For this is the final blessedness, this the ultimate perfection, the unending end. Here, surely we are called blessed when we have peace, however small a portion can be had in a good life; but this blessedness when compared to that final blessedness is discovered to be mere misery. So when we mortals possess such peace as this mortal life can provide, virtue, if we live rightly, makes the right use of good things; but when we have no peace, virtue makes good use even of the evils a man suffers. But true virtue is to subordinate all the good things it uses and everything it does in making good use of good and evil things and itself as well, to that end where our peace will be so excellent and so great that it cannot be improved or increased.

Chapter Eleven

So we might say as we have said of eternal life that peace is the end of all our good, especially since the sacred psalmist says of the City of God, the subject of this most laborious inquiry: "Praise the Lord, Jerusalem, praise your God, O Zion; for He has strengthened the bars of your gates: He has blessed your children within you, He has made your borders peace" (Ps 147:12–14). For when the bars of her gates are strengthened, none shall enter or leave her. So we ought to understand that her borders are that peace whose finality we wish to demonstrate. For even the mystical name of the city itself, Jerusalem, as we previously said, means "vision of peace." But since the word "peace" is frequently applied in relation to earthly matters where there is no eternal life, we have chosen to call the end of this city, its supreme good, eternal life rather than peace. Of this end the Apostle says: "But now being freed from sin and having become servants to God, you have your fruit unto holiness, truly the end, everlasting life" (Rom 6:22). But again because the life of the wicked may also be considered everlasting life by those unfamiliar with the holy Scriptures, either in accord with certain philosophers or in accord with our own belief in the endless punishment of the wicked who certainly cannot be punished forever unless they live forever, it is better to say, so that all may more easily understand our meaning, that the end of this city, whereby it will possess its supreme good, may be spoken of either way, as peace in everlasting life or everlasting life in peace. For peace is such a great good that even in respect to earthly and mortal matters no other word is heard with more pleasure, nothing is desired with greater longing, and finally nothing more gratifying can be discovered. So if we linger on this topic, we shall not be, I think, tedious to our readers, who will be attentive both for the sake of knowing what is the end of this city and for the sake of the very sweetness of peace, which is dear to all.

Chapter Twelve

Whoever attends at all with me to the pattern of human affairs and our common nature recognizes that just as there is no man who does not wish joy, so there is no man who does not wish peace. For even they who choose war desire nothing but victory. Therefore, by waging war they desire to arrive at a glorious peace. For what else is victory but the conquest of the opponent? When this is accomplished, there will be peace. Therefore, with the desire for peace, wars are waged, even by those who desire to exercise their warlike prowess whether commanding or fighting. It follows that peace is the desired end of war. For every man even in the act of waging war is seeking peace, but no man seeks war by making peace. For even those who wish that peace be broken do so not because they hate peace but because they wish it changed into a better peace. Therefore they do not desire that there shall be no peace but that peace shall be as they wish it. And in the case of sedition, when they have separated themselves from the community, they cannot fulfil their purpose unless they maintain some sort of peace with their fellow-conspirators. And so even robbers are careful to maintain peace with their comrades, so that they may more safely and more effectively attack the peace of other men. And if an individual happens to be of such powerful strength and so cautious that he trusts no partner but makes his own plots, taking his booty after overpowering and killing those he can, yet he keeps up some shadow of peace with those whom he cannot kill and from whom he wishes to conceal his deeds. Moreover, in his own home he tries to be at peace with his wife and children and other members of the household, since he is certainly pleased when they are at his beck and call. For if they are not, he is angry, he rebukes and punishes, and if necessary he secures even by cruelty the peace of his home which he feels cannot exist unless all the members of the same domestic society are subject to one head, such as he himself is in his own home. And so if a city or nation offered to submit itself to him, on the same terms which he had imposed on his own household, he would no longer hide like a robber but lift his head in the daylight like a king, though the same covetousness and malice remained in him. And so all men desire to have peace with their associates whom they want to govern as they wish. For even those against whom they wage war they wish, if possible, to make their own and to impose on them when vanquished the laws of their own peace.

But let us suppose a man such as poetry and mythology depict, one so unsociable and savage as to be called a semi-man rather than a man. Although his kingdom was the solitude of a dismal cave, and he himself was so singularly bad that he was called *Kakós* (the Greek word for bad), though he had no wife with whom to converse fondly, no little children with whom to play, no sons to do his bidding, no friends with whom to enjoy the conversation, not even his father, Vulcan, than whom in one respect he was happier as not having begotten a monster like himself; although he gave to no one but took as he wished whatever he could, from whomsoever he could, whenever he could: yet in the very solitude of his cave, "the floor of which was always reeking with fresh carnage," as Vergil says, all he sought was peace unmolested by anyone, a peace untroubled by any man's violence or the fear of it. Finally, with his own body he desired to be at peace, and insofar as he had this peace, all was well with him. His limbs obeyed his commands, and to pacify his mortal nature which rebelled when in need and to allay the incitement of hunger which threatened to evict the soul from the body, he made raids, slew and devoured; and yet, cruel and savage as he was, he was providing for the peace of his life and safety. So if he had been willing to make with other men the same peace which he made with himself in his own cave, he would neither have been called bad nor a monster nor a semi-man. Or if the appearance of his body and his belching of murky flames frightened off human companions, perhaps he was being fierce not through desire to harm but through the need of remaining alive. But he may never have existed, or at least he was not the way he was described with poetic fancy: for if Kakós were not sufficiently blamed, Hercules would not be sufficiently praised. Therefore, that such a man, or rather semi-man, as I said, ever existed is not to be believed, along with other poetic fictions.

For even the most savage beasts, from whom he derived part of his savagery (for he was called half-savage), preserve their own species by a sort of peace, by begetting, bearing, suckling, and rearing their young, although very many are not gregarious but solitary; not like sheep, deer, doves, starlings, and bees, but like lions, wolves, foxes, eagles, and bats. For what tigress does not gently purr over her cubs, and, having subdued her ferocity, caress them. What kite, however solitary in circling over his prey, does not join a mate, build a nest, hatch eggs, rear the young, and preserve with the mother of his brood as peaceful a domestic society as possible? How much more is a man moved by the laws of nature, as it were, to enter into society and to maintain peace, as far as he can, with all men, since even wicked men wage war to protect the peace of their own fellows, and would make all men their own, if they could, so that all men and things might serve but one head, and might, either through love or fear, surrender themselves to peace with him? For it is thus that pride perversely imitates God. For it despises equality with other men under Him and tries to impose a rule of its own upon its equals. It despises, that is, the just peace of God, and loves its own unjust peace. But it cannot help loving peace of some kind. For there is no vice so contrary to nature that it destroys the faintest traces of nature.

He then who prefers right to wrong and the orderly to the perverse sees that the peace of the unjust when compared with that of the just does not at all deserve the name of peace. Yet even the perverted must harmonize with and depend on some part of the whole order of things in which or out of which it is established; otherwise it would not exist at all. If a man were to hang with his head downward, this position of body and of limbs is certainly perverted, for that which nature requires to be above is below, and vice-versa; this perversity disturbs the peace of the body and is therefore painful; yet the soul is at peace with its body, and works for its safety, and hence the suffering. But if it is dismissed from the body by its pains, then, as long as the bodily limbs hold together, there is still a kind of peace among them, and hence the body remains suspended. And because the earthly body tends toward the earth and rests on the bond by which it is suspended, it tends toward its natural peace and by the demand of its weight, so to speak, it seeks a place of rest; and now, though without life and sensation, it does not depart from the peace natural to its rank whether possessing it or tending toward it. For if embalming preparations are applied to prevent the bodily frame from dissolving and disintegrating, a kind of peace still unites the various parts and keeps the whole body in a suitable place on earth, that is, in a place that is at peace with the body.

But if no embalming treatment is given and nature is left to take its course, it is disturbed by conflicting exhalations offensive to the senses (for that is what is smelled in cases of putrefaction) until the body unites with the elements of the world and little by little, particle by particle, it departs to enter into peace with them. Yet in this process the laws of the most high Creator and Ruler by whom the peace of the universe is administered are strictly observed, because although tiny animals breed in the carcass of a large animal, by the same law of the Creator all these little bodies serve the animals they belong to in peace. And although the flesh of dead animals is devoured by other animals, no matter where it is carried, nor what it mingles with, no matter what it is converted and changed into, it is still ruled by the same laws that are present everywhere for the preservation of every mortal species, acting as peacemakers by matching the parts that belong together.

Chapter Thirteen

The peace of the body, therefore, is an orderly, proportioned arrangement of its parts; the peace of the irrational soul is the harmonious repose of the appetites, the peace of the rational soul is the ordered agreement of knowledge and action; the peace of body and soul is the ordered life and health of a living creature. Peace between mortal man and God is an ordered obedience in faith to eternal law; peace among men is an ordered concord; domestic peace is ordered concord among those ruling and those obeying. Civil peace is a similar concord among citizens. The peace of the Celestial City is a perfectly ordered and harmonious enjoyment of God and of one another in God. The peace of all things is the tranquillity of order. Order is the distribution of things equal and unequal, each to its own place.

And therefore the wretched—for, insofar as they are wretched, they certainly are not in peace—lack the tranquillity of order where there is no disturbance; yet, because they are deservedly and justly wretched, they are in their very wretchedness not unrelated to order. They are not indeed united with the blessed but it is by a law of order that they are separated from them. And though they are disquieted, their circumstances are not withstanding adjusted to them, and therefore they have some tranquillity of order and therefore some peace. But they are wretched because although not wholly miserable, they are not there where any degree of misery is impossible; but still more wretched are they if they are not at peace with that law by which the natural order is administered. But when they suffer, their peace is disturbed in the part that suffers; but in the part where there is no suffering and the bodily frame is not dissolved, there is peace. Just as there can be a certain life without pain, whereas there can be no pain without life, so also there may be peace without war, but no war without some kind of peace. This does not follow from the nature of war but because war implies the existence of some natural beings to wage it and these natural beings cannot exist without some kind of peace holding them together.

Therefore there is a nature in which evil does not or even cannot exist; but there cannot be a nature in which there is no good. Hence not even the nature of the devil himself is evil insofar as it is nature; but perversity makes it evil. Thus he did not abide in truth, yet did not escape the judgment of Truth (Jn 8:44); he did not remain in the tranquillity of order, yet did not flee from the power of the Orderer. The goodness of good, which is present in his nature, did not remove him from the justice of God by which in his punishment order was preserved. Nor does God thereby punish the good He has created but the evil that the devil committed. Nor does God remove all that He gave to his nature, but takes something and leaves something so that there should remain something to feel the pain of loss.

And this very pain testifies to the good that was taken and the good that was left. For if good were not left, he could not feel pain for the good lost. For he who sins is still worse if he rejoices in his loss of righteousness; but he who is in pain, although he may gain no good by it yet grieves for the loss of health. And since both righteousness and health are good, and the loss of any good is cause for grief rather than for joy (if, at least, there is no compensation, a spiritual righteousness may compensate for the loss of bodily health), certainly it is more appropriate for an unjust man to grieve in punishment than to rejoice in sin. So just as the rejoicing of a sinner because he has forsaken what is good testifies to a bad will, so his grief in punishment because of the good that he has lost testifies to a good nature. For whoever laments the peace lost by his nature is stimulated to do so by some vestiges of that peace whereby his nature is friendly to itself. Now it is right that in the final punishment the wicked and impious should weep in their torments for the loss of the good that was in their natures, perceiving that they were taken from them by a most just God whom they despised when He was the generous distributor of bounty.

God, therefore, the most wise Creator and the most just Orderer of all natures, who placed the human race upon the earth as its greatest adornment, has granted to men certain good things which befit this life; namely, temporal peace, insofar as it can be enjoyed in the short span of a mortal life in respect to health and safety and human fellowship, and everything needed to preserve or recover this peace (such as the objects accommodated to our outward senses: light, night, air to breathe and water to drink and whatever the body requires to feed and cover it, to heal and adorn it); and all under this most equitable condition, that every mortal making good use of these benefits to the peace of his mortal condition should receive greater and better things, that is, the peace of immortality, and glory and honor appropriate to it in our everlasting life passed in the enjoyment of God and of one another in God: Whereas he who uses the goods of this life perversely shall lose them and shall not receive those of everlasting life.

Chapter Fourteen

Therefore, all use of temporal things is related to the enjoyment of earthly peace in the earthly city; but in the Celestial City it is related to the enjoyment of everlasting peace. Hence if we were irrational animals, we should seek nothing beyond the ordered proportion of the parts of the body and the repose of the appetites; nothing, therefore, beyond the repose of the flesh and a good supply of pleasures, so that the peace of the body might advance the peace of the soul. For if bodily peace is lacking, the peace of the irrational soul is also impaired since it cannot achieve the gratification of its appetites. But the two together serve the mutual peace of soul and body, the peace of an ordered life and of health. For just as animals by shunning pain show that they love bodily peace, and by pursuing pleasure in order to placate the needs of their appetites show that they love peace of soul, so by shunning death they indicate sufficiently how greatly they love the peace that harmonizes soul and body.

But because man has a rational soul, he subordinates all he has in common with the beasts to the peace of the rational soul so that he may exercise his mind in contemplation and may act in accor-

dance with it in order to enjoy that ordered agreement of knowledge and action which he called the peace of the rational soul. For
this purpose he must desire to be neither molested by pain nor
disturbed by desire nor dissolved by death in order that he might
attain some useful knowledge and regulate his life and manners
according to that knowledge. But lest by his very eagerness for
knowledge he should incur some fatal infection of error, he needs
divine teaching so that he may follow with assurance and divine
help, so that he may follow it as a free man. And since, as long as
he is in this mortal body, he is on pilgrimage away from God, he
walks by faith, not by sight (2 Cor 5:6–7) and therefore he refers
all peace, of body or of soul or of both, to that peace which exists
between mortal man and the immortal God, that there may be in
him an ordered obedience in faith to the eternal law.

Now since the Master God teaches two main precepts, love of
God and love of one's neighbor, and since in them man finds three
to love: God, himself, and his neighbor (Mt 22:37–39), and he who
loves God loves himself, consequently he is concerned that his
neighbor should love God, since he is commanded to love his
neighbor as himself (such as his wife, his children, his household,
and others as far as possible), and he would wish his neighbor to
be equally concerned for him if by chance he is in need. Therefore
he will be at peace as far as possible with all men in that human
peace or ordered concord which has this order: first, harm no one;
next, help everyone you can. Primarily, then, he has the care of his
own household, inasmuch as the order of nature or of human
society provides him with a closer and easier access to them for
serving them. Wherefore, the Apostle says: "Whoever does not
provide for his own, and especially for those of his own household, he denies the faith and is worse than an infidel" (1 Tm 5:8).
So here there arises domestic peace, the ordered concord of those
in the family who rule and those who obey.

For those who are concerned for others give commands, the
husband to his wife, the parents to their children, the masters to
their servants. But those who are objects of concern obey, as
women obey their husbands; children, their parents; servants,
their masters. But in the home of the just man who lives by faith
and who is as yet a pilgrim in exile from the Celestial City, even
those who give commands serve those whom they seem to command. For they command not through desire to dominate but

through dutiful concern for others, not with pride in exercising authority but with mercy in providing for others.

Chapter Fifteen

This the natural order prescribes, and thus God created man. For, He says: "Let him have dominion over the fish of the sea, and over the birds that fly in the heavens, and over every creeping thing that creeps upon the earth" (Gn 1:26). For He did not wish a rational creature, made in His image, to have dominion except over irrational creatures; not man over man, but man over beasts. Whereupon the first just men were established as shepherds over cattle rather than as kings of men, so that God might teach what the relative position of creatures requires and what the guilt of sinners demands. For it is with justice, we believe, that the condition of slavery is the result of sin. So we do not read of a slave anywhere in the Scriptures until the just man Noah branded his son's sin with this word (Gn 9:25). So he merited this name by fault, not by nature. The origin of the Latin word for "slave" is believed to be derived from the fact that those who by the law of war might have been killed became, when preserved by their conquerors, slaves, so named from their preservation [*servare*]; but even this would not have happened except for the guilt of sin. For even when we wage a just war, the enemy must be sinning; and every victory, even when won by wicked men, humbles the conquered through a divine judgment, correcting or punishing their sins. Witness that man of God, Daniel, who in captivity confesses to God his own sins and those of his people, and in pious sorrow recognizes these sins as the cause of his captivity (Dn 9). Therefore, the prime cause of slavery is sin, so that man was subjected to man in a state of bondage; this was done only by a judgment of God in whom there is no unrighteousness and who knows how to distribute suitable punishments according to the merits of the sinners.

But as the heavenly Lord says: "Everyone who sins is the slave of his sin" (Jn 8:34), and so there are many wicked masters who have religious men as their slaves and who are nevertheless not themselves free: "For by whom a man is conquered, to him is he also bound as a slave" (2 Pt 2:19). And surely it is a happier condition to be slave to a man than to a lust; for the cruelest dominion which devastates the hearts of mortals, to mention no other, is this very lust for dominion. Moreover, in a peaceful order in which some are subjected to others, the lowly position is as helpful to servants as the proud position is harmful to masters. But no nature, in which God first created man, is the slave either of another man or of sin. Yet penal slavery is also ordained by that law which commands us to preserve the natural order and forbids us to disturb it; for if nothing had been done contrary to that law, there would have been nothing requiring penal slavery. For this reason also the Apostle admonishes slaves to be subject to their masters and to serve them heartily and with good will, so that if they cannot be freed by their masters they may themselves make their very slavery in some sense free, by serving not in crafty fear but in faithful affection until all wickedness pass away and all human worship and power be eliminated and God be all in all (Eph 6:5; 1 Cor 15:24).

Chapter Sixteen

Hence even if our righteous fathers had slaves, they so administered domestic peace as to distinguish the lot of children from the condition of slaves in respect to these temporal goods; but as to the worship of God in whom we should find our hope of everlasting goods, they considered with equal affection all the members of their households. Thus the natural order so prescribes that from it the name of *pater familias* arose and has been used so widely that even those who rule unjustly welcome being called by that name. But those who are true fathers of their households have regard for all in their households just as for their own children to see that they worship and gain God's favor, desiring and praying that they may reach the heavenly home where the duty of commanding men will be unnecessary because there will be no duty of providing for those who are already happy in that immortal state; but until they reach there, fathers have a greater responsibility in ruling than slaves have to tolerate their slavery.

But if anyone in the household by disobedience breaks the domestic peace, he is rebuked by a word or a blow or some kind of just and legitimate punishment as far as human fellowship allows, for the sake of the offender, so that he may be readjusted to the family peace from which he had broken away. For just as it is no kindness to help a man so that he loses a greater good, so it is not innocent conduct to spare a man so that he falls into a more serious sin. To be innocent we must not only not harm anyone, but must restrain him from sin or punish his sin so that either he who is punished may profit by his experience or others may be deterred by his example. Therefore, because a man's house should be the beginning or element of the city, and every beginning ministers to some end of its own kind and every part to the integrity of the whole of which it is a part, it clearly follows that domestic peace ministers to civic peace, that is, that the ordered concord concerning command and obedience among those who dwell together in a household ministers to the ordered concord concerning command and obedience among citizens. So we see that the father of a family should draw his precepts from the law of the city, and so rule his household that it shall be in harmony with civic peace.

Chapter Seventeen

But the families who do not live by faith pursue an earthly peace by means of the good things and conveniences of this temporal life, while a household of those living by faith awaits the everlasting blessings promised for the future using like pilgrims anything earthly and temporal, not letting them entrap or distract from the path that leads to God, but using them to endure more easily and not to aggravate the burden of the corruptible body which weighs down the soul (Wis 9:15). Therefore, both kinds of human groups and of households use alike whatever is needed for this mortal life, but in using them each has its own quite different end in view. So also the earthly city which lives not by faith seeks an earthly peace and its aim at the concord of citizens concerning command and obedience is limited to a kind of agreement of human wills in respect to whatever is useful for this mortal life. But the Celestial City, or rather the part of it which goes its pilgrim way in this mortal life and lives by faith, must also use this peace until that mortal state for which such peace is necessary shall pass away. Therefore as long as it leads its life in captivity, as it were, being a stranger in the earthly city although it has already received the promise of redemption, and the gift of the Spirit as pledge of it, it does not hesitate to obey the laws of the earthly city whereby whatever ministers to the support of mortal life is so administered that since this mortal life is common to both, a harmony may be preserved between both cities concerning the things belonging to it.

Because the earthly city has had certain philosophers whose doctrine is condemned by the Divine Teaching and who being deceived either by their own conjectures or by demons supposed that there are many gods to be bribed to support human concerns, and that different provinces belong to different responsibilities of theirs, so that the body is the province of one, the soul of another; and in the body, one rules the head, another the neck, and so forth with each member; likewise in the soul, one presides over natural intelligence, another over education, another over anger, yet another over lust; and so the various affairs of life were assigned; one god cares for cattle, other gods respectively for grain, wine, oil, woods, money, navigation, wars and victories, marriage, birth, fertility, and so forth; but because the Celestial City knew only one God to be worshiped and believed with faithful piety that He is to be served with that service which in Greek is called *latria* and should be rendered only to God, it happens that the Celestial City could not have common laws of religion with the earthly city, and on this point must dissent and become a wearisome burden to those who thought differently, and must endure their anger and hatred and persecutions, except that the minds of their enemies have been alarmed by the multitude of the Christians and by the divine help accorded them.

While this Celestial City, then, pursues its path as a pilgrim on earth, it calls citizens from all peoples and collects an alien society of all languages, careless as to differences in manners, laws, institutions by which earthly peace is gained or maintained, abolishing or destroying none of it, nay, rather preserving and following them, for however diverse they may be among various nations, they aim at one and the same end, earthly peace, as long as that religion which teaches the obligation to worship one most high and true God is not impeded.

Therefore even the Celestial City in its pilgrimage makes use of the earthly peace and guards and seeks the convergence of human wills concerning what is useful for man's mortal nature as far as sound piety and religion allow, and makes the earthly peace minister to the heavenly peace, which is so truly peace that it must be considered and called the only peace, at least of a rational creature, since it is the best ordered and most harmonious fellow-ship in the enjoyment of God and one another in God. And when we reach that peace, this mortal life shall give way to one that is eternal; no animal body to weigh down the soul with its corruption, but a spiritual body lacking nothing and subdued in every part to the will. In its pilgrim state the Celestial City possesses this peace by faith; and by this faith it lives justly when it makes the attainment of that peace the aim of every good action in which it engages for the service of God and one's neighbor, since the life of a city is surely a social life.

Chapter Eighteen

As to the uncertainty about everything which Varro alleges to be the differentiating characteristic of the New Academy, the City of God utterly denounces such doubt as madness. About those things which its mind and reason apprehend, it has most certain knowledge, although this knowledge is limited because of the corruptible body that weighs down the spirit (since, as the Apostle says, "we know in part" [1 Cor 13:9]; yet it trusts the evidence of the senses which the mind uses through the agency of the body, since he is miserably deceived who thinks that they should never be trusted. It believes also in the Holy Scriptures, old and new, that we call Canonical, whence comes the very faith by which the just man lives (Hb 2:4); through this faith we walk without doubting as long as we are on pilgrimage exiled from the Lord (2 Cor 5:6). As long as this faith is sound and certain we may without just reproach doubt about those matters which neither sense nor reason has perceived and which have not been revealed to us by the Canonical Scriptures, and that we have not become aware of through witnesses whom it is absurd not to trust.

Chapter Nineteen

It is unimportant in the City of God whether whoever follows the faith leading to God does so in one dress or manner of life or another as long as these are not against the divine precepts; hence, when philosophers themselves become Christians they are not forced to change their dress and manner of living, which do not hinder religion, but only their false doctrines. So the peculiarity of the Cynics which Varro emphasized is of no concern if nothing indecent or uncontrolled is done. Indeed, of those three kinds of life, the contemplative, the active, and the mixed, although anyone might lead his life in any one of them with faith preserved and attain everlasting rewards, yet there is value in what he possesses through his love of truth, and in what he expends by the claim of Christian love. No one ought to be so entirely contemplative as not to consider his neighbor's benefit, nor so active as to neglect the contemplation of God. Leisure should not mean delight in dull vacancy of mind but inquiry or discovery of truth so that each one makes progress without withholding from others what he has discovered.

And in action we should not covet the honors and power of this life, since everything under the sun is vanity (Eccl 1:23), but we should aim at using our position and influence if these have been honorably won for the benefit of those who are under us, which is according to God's law, as we have previously explained. For that reason the Apostle says: "He that desires the episcopate desires a good work" (1 Tm 3:1). He wished to show what the word Episcopate means: a task, not an honor. For it is a Greek word derived from the fact that he who is set over others oversees or cares for them; for *epi* means "over" and *skopein*, "to see," and therefore we may if we choose translate *episkopein* into Latin as "oversee." So that a bishop who loves to govern rather than to do good is no bishop. And so no one is prohibited from zeal in inquiring into truth because that pertains to a praiseworthy use of leisure; but it is inappropriate to covet high position without which a people cannot be ruled, although the position be held and administered appropriately. Therefore, love of truth seeks holy leisure; the necessity of charity undertakes righteous activity. If no burden is placed on us we are free to discern and contemplate truth; but if it is placed on us, we should accept it under the necessity of love. But neither is delight in truth to be wholly forsaken, lest when that sweetness is withdrawn, that burden might crush us.

Chapter Twenty

Since, therefore, the supreme good of the City of God is everlasting and perfect peace, not that through which mortals pass by being born and dying but that in which immortals abide, wherein no adversity at all is suffered, who would deny that this is the most blessed life, or that when compared with it the present life, however great may be the goods of soul and body and external good things with which it is filled, is judged most wretched? Yet whoever so lives this life for the sake of that other life which he most ardently loves and most confidently hopes for can even now without absurdity be called blessed, though not in reality so much as in hope. But the actual possession of the happiness of this life without the hope of what is beyond is a false happiness and great misery; for it does not use the true goods of the mind, since that is not true wisdom that does not prudently direct its judgments, courageous actions, self-control, and just dealings toward that end where God shall be all in all (1 Cor 15:28) in sure eternity and perfect peace.

Chapter Twenty-One

This, now, is the place where I should explain as briefly and clearly as possible what I promised in the second book of this work, that if we were to accept the definitions used by Scipio in Cicero's *De Republica*, there never was a Roman state. For he briefly defines a state as a commonwealth. If this definition is true, there never was a Roman state, for there never was a commonwealth, which he wished to be the definition of a state. For he defined a people as a numerous gathering united in fellowship by a common sense of right and common interests. What he means by a common sense of right he explains by arguing that a state cannot be administered without justice; therefore, where there is no true justice, there can be no right. For what is done rightly is surely done justly, whereas what is done unjustly cannot be done rightly. For the unjust human inventions are not to be called or considered as rights, since even their makers say that right is that which flows from the fountain of justice, and deny the definition commonly given by those who misunderstand the matter, that right is the interest of the strongest.

So when there is no true justice there can be no gathering of men united in fellowship by a common sense of right and, therefore, no people as defined by Scipio or Cicero; and if no people, then no commonwealth, but only some kind of mob unworthy to be called a people. Consequently, if a state is a commonwealth, and if that is not a people, that is, not united in fellowship by a common sense of right, and if there is no right where there is no justice, then it certainly follows that where there is no justice there is no state. Furthermore, justice is that virtue which distributes to everyone his due. What justice, then, is that which removes a man from the true God and subjects him to unclean demons? Is this to give everyone his due? Or is he who retains a piece of land from the purchaser and gives it to someone who has no right to it unjust, whereas he who takes himself from the Lord God who made him and serves wicked spirits is just?

Certainly this same book, *De Republica*, argues very sharply and vigorously against injustice and in favor of justice. And since when it was previously argued on behalf of injustice against justice, maintaining that a state cannot exist or be administered except through injustice, it was put forward as the most valid position that it is unjust for some men to serve other men as masters, and yet an imperial city including a mighty state cannot govern provinces without pursuing such injustice; the answer to this argument on the part of justice was that the rule over provincials is just, because servitude is useful to such men and is established for their welfare when rightly established, that is, when license to do wrong is withdrawn from wicked men, and that those subjected will be better off because, when not subjected, they were worse off.

To confirm this reasoning a remarkable example is given, as though from nature and expressed this way: "Why, therefore, does God command man, the soul command the body, the reason command the passions and the other vicious parts of the soul?" This example teaches clearly enough that servitude is useful to some men and that service to God is useful to all.

For in serving God the soul rightly commands the body, and within that very soul the reason subject to God the Lord rightly commands the passions and other vices. Therefore, when a man does not serve God, how much justice can we suppose him to possess? For when a man does not serve God, in no way can his soul justly command his body or his human reason command his vices. And if there is no justice in such a man, without doubt there is no justice in a community of such men. Here, then, there is no common sense of right which transforms a multitude of men into a people, whose wealth has been said to be a commonwealth. For why need I speak of the utility whereby also a gathering of men, according to our definition, is called a people? Although, if you carefully note, there is no utility to those who live impiously as do all who do not serve God and serve demons—demons all the more impious in demanding that sacrifices be paid to them as to Gods —yet I think that all we have said concerning a common sense of right sufficiently demonstrates that in terms of this definition a people in whom there is no justice cannot be said to be a state. For if it is said that the Romans in their state served not unclean spirits but good and holy gods, must we repeat what we have already said enough times, nay, more than enough? For can he who has read the previous books of this work and has reached this point doubt that the Romans served evil and impure demons unless he is either exceedingly stupid or shamelessly contentious? But aside from the character of the gods to whom they offered sacrifices, it is written in the Law of the true God: "He who sacrifices to any God except to the Lord only shall be utterly destroyed" (Ex 22:20). He who prescribed such a threatening commandment did not will, therefore, that sacrifices be offered either to good gods or to evil ones.

Chapter Twenty-Two

But you may reply: "Who is this God, or how is He, and no other god besides, proven worthy to receive sacrifices from the Romans?" He who still asks who this God is must be very blind. He is the very God whose Prophets foretold those things which we behold. He is the very God from whom Abraham received the declaration: "In your seed all nations shall be blessed" (Gn 22:18). This was fulfilled in Christ, who arose from that seed according to the flesh, as even those acknowledge, whether they will or not, who have remained hostile to this name. He is the very God whose divine Spirit spoke through those men whose prophecies, cited in my previous books, are fulfilled through the Church which we see spread throughout the world. He is the very God whom Varro, most learned of Romans, thought to be Jupiter, not knowing what he said; this I considered worth mentioning merely because a man of such learning could not deny that this God existed nor consider him worthless. For he believed that he was identified with the one whom he considered the Supreme God. Finally he is the very God whom Porphyry, the most learned of philosophers, though the sharpest enemy of the Christians, confesses to be a mighty God, even through the oracles of those whom he considers to be gods.

Chapter Twenty-Three

For in the book entitled *Philosophy of the Oracles*, in which he collects and comments on the responses, supposedly divine, with regard to matters pertaining to philosophy, to quote his own words as translated from Greek into Latin: "To one inquiring what god's favor he should seek in order to recall his wife from Christianity, Apollo answered in the following verses." Then the following words are given as those of Apollo: "You will probably find it easier to write in permanent characters on water, or lightly fly like a bird through the air than to recall to her senses an impious wife once she has polluted herself. Let her persist as she wishes in her empty delusions, singing false laments to her dead God who was condemned by right-minded judges and executed publicly by violent death." Then after these verses of Apollo (translated here into Latin prose), Porphyry says: "In these verses Apollo revealed the incurable corruption of the Christians, saying that the Jews recognized God rather than the Christians." See how he misrepresents Christ and prefers the Jews to the Christians in the recognition of God. For he so explained Apollo's verses as to say that Christ was put to death by right-minded judges, as if He had been deservedly punished by just judges. What the lying seer of Apollo said and Porphyry believed or that he put forward in the seer's words are their responsibility. We shall later look into Porphyry's consistency, that is, how consistent he makes his very oracles with one another.

Here, however, he says that the Jews, as the defenders of God, judged rightly when they decreed that Christ was to be tortured by the worst kind of death. He should have listened, then, to this God of the Jews to whom he bears this testimony when that God says: "He who sacrifices to any other Gods, save to the Lord alone, shall be utterly destroyed" (Ex 22:20). But let us come to clearer statements, and hear how great a God he thinks the God of the Jews is. For example, Apollo when asked which is the better, reason or law, "replied," he said, "in these verses." Then he adds these verses of Apollo from which I select the following as sufficient: "Truly in God," he says, "the Creator and the King prior to all things, before whom tremble heaven and earth and the sea and the hidden places beneath, and their deities themselves are afraid, for their law is the Father whom the holy Hebrews greatly honor." In this oracle of his own God Apollo, Porphyry has described the God of the Hebrews as being so great that the very deities tremble before Him. Since, therefore, that God said: "He who sacrifices to any gods will be utterly destroyed," I am surprised that Porphyry himself did not tremble and fear lest he be destroyed utterly for sacrificing to other gods.

This philosopher also says some good things about Christ, as if he had forgotten that abuse of which we have just spoken, or as if his gods only when asleep spoke wickedly of Christ and when awake recognized that He was good and gave Him deserved praise. For he says, as if about to announce something marvelous and incredible: "What we shall say will certainly seem surprising to some. For the gods have proclaimed that Christ is very pious and has become immortal, and they speak favorably of him; the Christians, however, are polluted, they say, and contaminated and caught up in error, and against them the gods utter many blasphemies." Then he adds examples, as he declares, of oracles of the gods blaspheming the Christians, continuing: "But to those who inquired whether Christ were God, Hecate answered: 'You know that the immortal soul goes abroad after it leaves the body; but when it is sundered from wisdom it wanders forever. This soul is that of a man preeminent in piety; because they are estranged from the truth, they worship it.' " Then after the words of this so-called oracle he adds his own explanation: "Therefore, Hecate said that this was a most pious man, and that his soul, like that of other pious men, was invested, as it deserved, with immortality, and that the Christians in their ignorance worship it. And to those inquiring why he was then condemned, the goddess in an oracle answered: 'The body, certainly, is always subject to crippling torments; but the souls of the pious have their abode in heaven. Now that soul gave to other souls the fatal gift of becoming involved in error; these were the souls to whom the fates had not granted that they should attain the gifts of the gods or gain knowledge of immortal Jupiter. Consequently, they were hated by the gods because, although by fate they did not know God, nor receive the gifts of the Gods, this man gave them the fatal gift of being involved in error. He himself, however, was pious, and like other pious people, entered into heaven. So you must not blaspheme him but pity the folly of men: Through him there is a risk of an easy and headlong fall.' "

Who is so foolish as not to understand that these oracles either were fabricated by a shrewd man, one very hostile to Christians, or were responses of impure demons with similar intent? Since they praise Christ they hope to be believed as truthful when they blame the Christians and so, if possible, to block the way to everlasting salvation whereby the individual becomes a Christian. Of course they assume that it is not contrary to their wicked and multifarious astuteness if they are believed when praising Christ, provided that their repudiation of the Christians is also accepted. They hope that anyone convinced on both counts will be led to praise Christ provided he does not wish to be a Christian and so is not freed from the domination of those demons by the Christ whom he has praised. Besides, their praise of Christ is such that anyone believing in Him on their terms is not a true Christian but a Photinian heretic who recognizes Christ only as man and not also as God and cannot, therefore, be saved by Him and cannot evade or undo the snares of those lying demons.

We, however, can approve neither Apollo's condemnation of Christ nor Hecate's praises. The one wants us to believe that Christ was unrighteous, since he says that He was put to death by right-minded judges; the other, that He was a very pious man, yet only a man. Yet both have the same intention, to prevent men from becoming Christians, because, if they are not Christians, they cannot be delivered from their power. Indeed, this philosopher, or rather those who believe such so-called oracles against the Christians, must first reconcile, if possible, Hecate and Apollo with reference to Christ Himself so that either both may condemn or both may praise Him. But even if they could do this, yet we should avoid such cheating demons whether they condemn or praise Christ. But when their god and goddess disagree about Christ, he condemning Him, she praising Him, certainly when they blaspheme the Christians, men do not believe them if they have right judgment.

When Porphyry or Hecate, praising Christ, asserts that He gave himself totally to the Christians to involve them in error, he exhibits, as he thinks, the causes of this very error. But before I quote from his words, I first ask whether it was willingly or unwillingly that Christ gave to Christians this fatal gift of involvement in error. If willingly, how could He be just? If unwillingly, how could He be blessed? But now let us hear the causes of this error. "There are," he says, "in a certain place very small earthly spirits subject to the power of evil demons. The wise men of the Hebrews (among them was also this Jesus, as you have heard from the oracles of Apollo quoted above) turned religious men away from these very evil demons and lesser spirits and forbade them to venerate them; but they were to venerate the heavenly gods, above all, God the Father. "But this," he says, "the gods also teach and we have shown above how they admonish men to turn their minds to God and command them to worship Him everywhere. But unlearned and impious natures to which fate has not granted the gifts of the gods and a notion of immortal Jupiter, not listening to the gods and to inspired men, have rejected all the gods and instead of despising the prohibited demons have revered them. Although pretending to worship God, they do not those things through which alone God is adored. For God as the Father of all lacks nothing; but it fares well with us when we adore Him by means of justice, chastity, and other virtues and so make life itself a prayer to Him through the imitation and knowledge of him. For seeking to know purifies," he says, "while imitation deifies by promoting affection for Him."

He has well proclaimed God the Father and has spoken well of the conduct by which He should be worshiped; of such precepts the prophetic books of the Hebrews are full, when they praise or blame the life of the saints. But in respect to Christians, he errs or slanders as greatly as the demons, whom he accepts as gods, desire; as if it were difficult for anyone to remember the base and shameful actions performed in the theaters and temples to please the gods, and to compare with these what is heard in our churches and what is offered to the true God, and thus conclude where character is edified and where it is ruined. Who but a diabolical spirit has told or suggested to him such a foolish and evident lie as that the Christians revered rather than despised the demons whose worship was forbidden by the Hebrews? But that God whom the wise men of the Hebrews worshiped prohibits sacrifices being offered even to the holy angels and heavenly powers, whom we venerate and love in this our mortal pilgrimage as our most blessed fellow citizens; speaking in thunderous tones He gave His Law to the Hebrew people, saying in very threatening words: "He who sacrifices to any other gods shall be utterly destroyed" (Ex 22:20).

And lest it be thought that this command prohibits sacrifice only to those very evil demons and earthly spirits that Porphyry calls least or lesser (for even these are called gods in the holy Scriptures, not of the Hebrews, but of the Gentiles, as the seventy translators expressed it clearly in the Psalm, saying: "For all the gods of the nations are demons" (Ps 96:5), but that sacrifices to some or all of the heavenly powers were permitted, He soon adds: "Save to the Lord only" (Ex 22:20), that is, save to the Lord alone. If anyone supposes that the words *Domini soli* mean "to our Lord the Sun," to whom he thinks sacrifice should be offered, an examination of the Greek Scriptures will easily show that this is not the meaning.

Therefore, the God of the Hebrews, to whom this distinguished philosopher bears this singular testimony, gave to the Hebrew people the Law, written in the Hebrew language, not obscure and unknown but now published in all nations, in which it is written: "He who sacrifices to gods, save to the Lord only, shall be utterly destroyed." What need is there to continue the inquiry into His Law and Prophets concerning this? In fact, the need is not for inquiry, for the passages are neither few nor obscure, but rather for collecting and exposing in this argument of mine the obvious and many passages in which it appears clearer than daylight that the Supreme God chose to have sacrifice offered to no being whatever save to Himself only. Here is one brief utterance, a little one or rather a great one but spoken truly by that God whom the most learned of the Gentiles so excellently extol; let it be heard, feared, and lived up to, lest the disobedient experience utter destruction. "He who sacrifices to gods," He says, "save to the Lord only, shall be utterly destroyed," not because God has need of something but because it benefits us to belong to Him. To him the psalmist sings in the sacred Scriptures of the Hebrews: "I have said to the Lord: You are my God since you need not my goods" (Ps 16:2).

But we ourselves who are His City are his most splendid and best sacrifice, and this mystery we celebrate in our offerings, which are well known to the faithful, as we have discussed in the preceding books. For that the victims which the Jews offered as a shadow of what was to come should cease, and that the peoples from the rising of the sun to its setting should offer one sacrifice, as we see happening now, was declared by divine oracles through the Hebrew prophets; and of these oracles we have selected what seemed a sufficient number and scattered them throughout this work.

Therefore where there is not that justice whereby the One and Supreme God rules an obedient city according to His grace, so that it sacrifices to none save to Him only, so that in all men belonging to this city and obeying God the soul commands the body and the reason faithfully commands the vices in a system of law, so that as one just man lives by faith (Heb 2:4; Rom 1:17; Gal 3:11), which works by love (Gal 5:6), just so, a gathering or people of just men lives by faith which works by love, the love whereby a man loves God as He should be loved, and his neighbor as himself —where there is no such justice, I say, certainly there is no gathering of men united in fellowship by a common sense of right and by a community of interest. And if this does not exist, there surely is not a people, if this definition of people is true. Therefore, neither is there a state because where there is no people there is no commonwealth.

Chapter Twenty-Four

But if a people be defined not in this but in some other way as in this way: "A people is a large gathering of rational beings united in fellowship by agreement about the objects of their love," then certainly to see the quality of each people, we must examine what it loves. Yet, whatever it loves, if it is a large gathering not of cattle but of rational beings, and is united in fellowship by common agreement about the objects of its love, then it is not absurd that it be called a people; and surely the better the objects of its united love, the better the people, and the worse the objects of its love, the worse the people. According to this definition of ours the Roman people is a people, and its wealth is without doubt a commonwealth. But what this people loved in its early and later periods, and by what moral decline it moved into bloody sedition and then into social and civil war corrupting and disrupting that concord which is, so to speak, the health of a people, history bears witness; and in the preceding books I have enlarged upon it. And yet I shall not for this reason say either that there is no people or that the people's wealth is not a commonwealth as long as there remains, however slight, a gathering of rational beings united in fellowship by a common agreement about the objects of its love. But what I have said about this people and this state let me be taken to say and to mean about the Athenians, or any other Greeks, or the Egyptians or that earlier Babylon, about the Assyrians and about every other nation great or small which had a public government. Generally speaking, a city of the ungodly, not ruled by God, since it is disobedient to the command of God that sacrifice be not offered save to Himself only, which could not give to the soul its proper rule over the body, nor to reason its just authority over the vices, lacks true justice.

Chapter Twenty-Five

For however laudable may seem to be the rule of the soul over the body and the reason over the vices, if the soul and the reason do not serve God as God has commanded that He should be served, then in no way do they rightly rule the body and vices. For what kind of mistress over the body and the vices can that mind be which is ignorant of the true God, and which instead of being subject to his authority is prostituted to the corrupting power of the most vicious demons? Hence the very virtues which it thinks it possesses, through which it rules the body and vices in order to obtain or keep what it desires, if it does not subordinate them to God, are themselves vices rather than virtues. For although some suppose that virtues are true and honorable when they are referred to themselves and not sought on account of something else, even then they are puffed up and proud and so must be judged as vices, not virtues. For just as it is not that which comes from the flesh but that which is above the flesh which makes the flesh live, so it is not that which comes from man but that which is above man that makes him live a blessed life; and this is true not only of man but of every heavenly domination and power.

Chapter Twenty-Six

Therefore, as the life of the flesh is the soul, so the blessed life of man is God, of whom the sacred Scriptures of the Hebrews declare: "Blessed is the people whose God is the Lord" (Ps 144:15). Wretched, therefore, is the people that is alienated from that God. Yet even this people has a peace of its own not to be rejected; but in the end it will not possess it because it does not make good use of it before the end. But it is to our interest that it enjoy this peace meanwhile in this life; for as long as the two cities are commingled, we also enjoy the peace of Babylon; and the people of God is by faith so freed from it as to live as a stranger in the midst of it. On this account the Apostle also admonished the Church to pray for its kings and other nobility, adding these words: "That we may live a quiet and tranquil life with all piety and love" (1 Tm 2:2). And the Prophet Jeremiah, in predicting the captivity to befall the ancient people of God, and in commanding them by divine inspiration to go obediently to Babylon, serving God by their very patience, admonished them to pray for Babylon, saying: "Because in her peace is your peace" (Jer 29:7), that is, of course, the temporal peace of the present which is common to good and wicked alike.

Chapter Twenty-Seven

But the peace that is ours we already have with God by faith, and we shall forever have it with Him by sight. But peace in this life, whether common to all or our special possession, is such that it should be called a solace of our misery rather than an enjoyment of blessedness. Also, our very justice, although it is true in relation to the true final good to which it is subordinated, is nevertheless in this life only of such a kind as to consist rather in the remission of sins than in the perfecting of virtues. Witness the prayer of the entire City of God that is exiled on earth. Through all its members it cries out to God: "Forgive us our debts as we forgive our debtors" (Mt 6:12). Nor is this prayer efficacious for those whose faith is dead without works (Jas 2:17), but only for those whose faith brings forth works through love (Gal 5:6). For because the reason, though subjected to God, in this mortal condition and in the corruptible body, which weighs down the soul (Wis 9:15), does not perfectly rule the vices, such a prayer is necessary for just men. For although the reason exercises command over the vices, certainly this is not without struggle. And even if we fight the good fight and rule as master, after such foes have been defeated and subdued, still in this realm of weakness something creeps in so that sin is found if not in some swift action, certainly in some momentary utterance or some fleeting thought. And therefore there is no complete peace as long as the vices are being ruled, because the battle against resisting vices is precarious while those conquered do not allow for a triumph of carefree ease but one held down under a command that is full of anxiety. Among all these temptations, therefore, of which it has been briefly asserted in the divine oracles: "Is man's life on earth anything but temptation?" (Jb 7:1), who will assume that his life is such that he need not say to God: "Forgive us our debts," unless it be a proud man, not truly great, but puffed up and bloated, who is justly resisted by Him who gives grace abundantly to the humble? On this account it is written: "God resists the proud, but gives grace to the humble" (Jas 4:6; 1 Pt 5:5). And so in this life, accordingly, justice for the individual means that God rules and man obeys, the soul rules over the body and reason rules over the vices even when rebellious, whether by subduing or withstanding them, and that from God Himself we seek grace to do our duty and forgiveness for our sins, and that we offer our service of thanksgiving for the blessings received. But in that final peace to which this justice should be subordinated and for the sake of having it this justice should be maintained, since our nature will be healed of its sickness by immortality and incorruption and will have no vices and since nothing either in ourselves or in another will be at war with any one of us, the reason will not need to rule the vices, since they will no longer exist; but God will rule man, and soul the body, and in obeying we shall find a pleasure and ease as great as the felicity of our living and reigning. And there, for all and for everyone, this state will be everlasting, and its everlastingness will be certain; and therefore the peace of this blessedness or the blessedness of this peace will be the highest good.

Chapter Twenty-Eight

But, on the other hand, those who do not belong to that City of God will receive everlasting misery, which is called also the second death (Rv 2:11), because neither the soul that is alienated from God's life can be said to live there, nor the body which will be subjected to everlasting torments; and this second death will be all the harder to bear in that it cannot be ended in death. But since just as misery is the opposite of blessedness, and death of life, so war is the opposite of peace, the question is properly raised: What or what kind of war can be understood to take place in the final state of the wicked to correspond to the peace that is predicted and lauded in the final state of the righteous? But let the questioner attend to what is harmful or destructive in warfare, and he will see that it is nothing but the mutual opposition and conflict of things. Therefore, what war can he imagine more grievous and bitter than one in which the will is so opposed to passion and passion to will that their hostilities can be ended by the victory of neither, and in which the power of pain so struggles with the very nature of the body that neither yields to the other? For in this life, when such a conflict arises, either pain conquers, and death takes away feeling, or nature conquers, and health removes the pain. But in the life beyond, pain remains to torment and nature stays to feel it; neither ceases to be lest the punishment should also cease.

However, since these are the extremes of good and evil of which we should seek to gain the former and escape the latter, and since through judgment good men pass to the former, bad men to the latter, I will, so far as God may grant, discuss this judgment in the following book.

Augustine of Hippo

THE RULE OF ST. AUGUSTINE

Introductory Note. There has always been controversy about the authenticity of the Rule of St. Augustine. Widely held was the opinion, passed on by Erasmus and St. Robert Bellarmine, among others, that the only Rule written by Augustine was one for nuns to be found in Letter 211. In recent years, however, Luc Verheijen, O.S.A., a competent contemporary expert on the Rule of St. Augustine, has discovered the original text as a Rule for Men and has published a careful study of it in the manuscript tradition.

The text that I have translated for this volume is the basic Latin text authored by Augustine and present in Verheijen's critical edition of the Rule for Men.

Letter 211, which is an authentic letter, contains the Rule in the feminine version but one not made by Augustine. Verheijen calls this Rule: "Regularis informatio." We do not know who made the adaptation for women, but the text is basically the same as that of the official, authentic "Rule for Men" called "Praeceptum" by Verheijen.

There is another Rule called "Regulation for a Monastery" (ordo monasterii) which Verheijen ascribes to Alypius, who was Augustine's student, friend, and fellow bishop. This has two small additions by Augustine.

There is, however, only one basic text which was authored by Augustine and this is translated here.

The evangelical foundation of the Rule is found in the Acts of the Apostles 4:32, where we read that "the whole group of believers were united, heart and soul." And so Augustine tells his brethren: "The main purpose for your having come together is to live harmoniously in your house, intent upon God in oneness of mind and heart" (I.1).

This oneness of mind and heart or interpersonal unity is to be attained through love, a mutual love that enables all to remain "intent upon God." Charity is the environment of monastic life, enabling all to remain under the yoke of the Lord and making the burden ever lighter. In a contemplative atmosphere the monks aim at union with Christ, who lived freely for others. Just as there is a natural union of minds and bodies, so is there a material aspect to the union of minds and hearts in the monastery: This is the holding in common of all material possessions to be distributed according to each one's needs.

Fidelity to regulations that often seem too minute is, however, an effort to purify the heart for the "seeing of God." And regulations concerning common life are directed ultimately toward that inner community of thoughts and affections by which God's love is expressed for each one. As God dwells in the temple of each one's heart, so He dwells within the community as in a temple, to witness to the oneness of Christ and His members. The aim of "living in freedom under grace" remains always the ideal toward which numerous specific rules are directed. Renewal of the religious life in each age requires a reexamination as to whether the inherited regulations are efficacious in achieving the aim of religious life.

To follow the Rule of St. Augustine is to make a spiritual ascent to that Beauty which is God, the Splendor of Truth. Generosity is the response to this Beauty, which is reflected in a true community of one heart and one mind in the one Christ after the model of the first Christians at Jerusalem. A fervent monastery is a microcosm of the City of God.

Augustine's Rule represents the first monastic legislation, and his first monastery at Thagaste was that of a lay monastery. Bishop Eusebius of Vercelli (371) had already established community life for the clergy. At Hippo Augustine first established a community of lay monks and as bishop he formed an episcopal community of priests who renounced personal wealth and marriage while living ascetically and contemplatively and working for the salvation of others in humility, charity, and peace.

Augustine's Rule influenced the writing of many other Rules; it was used in the Canon Movement of the eleventh and twelfth centuries and in the Mendicant Movement of the *twelfth and thirteenth centuries. This Rule guides the religious life of the Order of St. Augustine organized in its present form in 1256 by Pope Alexander IV, and originally known as the Order of the Hermits of St. Augustine (O.E.S.A.), a title that prevailed until 1968.*

First and foremost, my very dear Brothers, you are to love God, and then your neighbor, because these are the chief commandments given to us.*

I *Mutual Love: Expressed in the Community of Goods and in Humility*

1. We urge you who form a religious community to put the following precepts into practice.
2. Above all, live together in harmony (Ps 67:7), having one mind and one heart (Acts 4:32), intent on God, since that is why you have come together.
3. Do not call anything your own but share all things. Food and clothes should be distributed to each one of you by your superior, not to all equally, but to each one according to his need, since all do not enjoy equal health. For this is what you read in the Acts of the Apostles: "All things owned were held in common, and to each one was given whatever he needed" (Acts 4:32, 35).
4. Those who had personal possessions in the world should freely consent when they enter religious life that these become the property of the community.
5. Those, however, who had no personal possessions should not seek in religious life those things which they could not have before they entered. Yet they are to be given whatever is required for their infirmities even though their poverty before they entered religious life prevented their having even life's necessities. Nor should they consider themselves fortunate because they receive food and clothes which were beyond their means in their previous lives.
6. Nor should those who formerly were poor now become proud

---

*This first sentence is not contained in the critical text established by L. Verheijen, O.S.A., but it is found in many versions.

because they associate with those whom previously they dared not approach. Instead, let them raise up their hearts and avoid empty earthly vanities lest our communities be useful for the rich and not for the poor: if the rich learn humility there and the poor are puffed up with pride.

7. But, on the other hand, those who were obviously important in the world should not look down upon their brethren who have entered the religious community from a condition of poverty. They should be prouder of their life together with their poor brothers than of the social status of their rich parents. The fact that they have contributed some of their resources to the community is no reason for them to have a high opinion of themselves. Nor should they take greater pride by sharing their riches with the community than by enjoying them in the world. For whereas all vices express themselves in evil acts, pride lurks also in our good works in order to destroy even them. And what good is it to dispense gifts to the poor and even become poor oneself if giving up riches makes a person prouder than he was when he possessed a fortune?

8. Live, then, all of you, "one in mind and one in heart" (Acts 4:32), and mutually honor God in one another because each of you has become His temple (2 Cor 6:16).

II. *Community Prayer*

1. "Persevere in prayer" (Col 4:2) at the hours and times appointed.

2. In the oratory no one should do anything out of keeping with the purpose of the place. So that if some perhaps have leisure and wish to pray outside the regular hours, they should not be distracted by those wanting to use the oratory for another purpose.

3. When with Psalms and hymns you pray to God, ponder in your heart what your voice utters.

4. When you sing, keep to the text you have, and do not sing what is not intended to be sung.

III. *Community and Care of the Body*

1. Subdue your body by fasting and by abstaining from food and drink insofar as health permits. Those unable to fast the whole

day may take something to eat even apart from the main evening meal. They may do this, however, only around mid-day. But the sick may take something to eat any time of day.

2. When you come to the table, listen until you leave to the customary reading without disturbance or dispute. Not only are you to satisfy your physical hunger but also to hunger for the word of God (cf. Am 8:11).

3. And if those entering the community who were accustomed to live comfortably have extra nourishment given to them, this should not irritate others or seem unjust to those whose former style of life made them physically stronger. They should not consider their weaker brothers more favored because they receive a more generous fare; they should rather be glad that they are able to bear what the former cannot yet endure.

4. And if more food, clothing, and bedding are given to those entering the community who were accustomed to live comfortably than is provided for others who are stronger and more fortunate, the latter should be mindful of how much the rich now have to live without in comparison with their previous life even though they cannot live as simply as those who are physically stronger.

5. Nor should all the brethren desire what they see given to a few, for it is given not as a mark of honor but out of consideration for their weakness. Otherwise, there would be undesirable abuse in religious life where the rich become schooled in hardship and the poor become more luxurious. Obviously, the sick should receive special food; if not, their illness would only increase. Even if they entered from the poorest social conditions they should, when convalescing, receive that treatment most likely to renew their strength. Their illness entitles them to what the rich are entitled to because of their former style of life. But once they have made a complete recovery, they are to resume their previous mode of life when they were happier because their needs were fewer. The simpler a way of life the better is it suited to the servants of God. Once restored to health, they should not allow the desire for food, previously needed to support their weakness, now to enslave them. Those who can lead simple lives without any difficulty should consider themselves the most fortunate of people. For it is better to make do with too little than to have many things.

IV. *Community Responsibility in Good and Evil*

1. There should be nothing that attracts attention in your attire. Try to find favor by your manner of life, not by the clothes you wear.

2. When you go out, go with someone else and stay together when you have reached your destination.

3. In walking, standing, and in all your actions do nothing that might seem offensive, but do that which befits the holiness of your way of life.

4. When you see a woman, do not fix your eyes on her. For although when you go out you are not forbidden to look at women, it is sinful to desire them or to want to be desired by them (cf. Mt 5:28). For it is not only by gestures of affection that desire between men and women is awakened but also by looks. And do not say that you have pure intentions if you keep looking at a woman, because the eye is the messenger of the heart. When impure intentions are allowed to appear not by words but just by exchanging glances and finding pleasure in each other's affection, even though not in each other's arms, we cannot speak any longer of true chastity which is precisely that of the heart.

5. Let no one who fixes his eye upon a woman and delights in having her eye fixed on him suppose that he is not seen by others; he is certainly seen, and by those he does not realize are observing him. But although his act were hidden and unobserved, how can he hide anything from that Witness above us from whom nothing is hidden (Prv 24:12)? Or are we to think that He does not see because He sees with a patience as great as His Wisdom? Let the religious man therefore fear to displease God by pleasing a woman wickedly. Let him know that God looks upon all things and so be unwilling to look upon a woman lustfully. For in this respect and for this reason fear was recommended when it was written: "The covetous eye is an abomination to the Lord" (Prv 27:20).

6. When therefore you are together in church or anywhere else where women are present, you are to consider yourselves responsible for one another's chastity. Then God who dwells in you (2 Cor 6:16) will protect you through your responsibility for one another.

7. And if you should notice this wantonness of the eye I have spoken of in a brother, admonish him immediately, so that what was begun will not progress but will be promptly corrected.

8. But if after this warning you see him repeating this on another day, then whoever happens to see this should report him as he would report a wounded brother in need of healing. Yet, first of all, the fault should be pointed out to another, and perhaps to a third so that they may be convinced (Mt 18:15–17). Thus he can be convicted on the testimony of two or three witnesses and punished with suitable severity. Do not consider yourself malicious for reporting this. For surely you are not innocent if by your silence you allow your brothers whom by reporting you could have healed to perish. For if your brother had a bodily wound which he wanted to hide because of the fear of surgery, would it not be cruel for you to remain silent, and merciful for you to reveal it? How much more then should you reveal this, lest he suffer a more deadly wound in the heart?

9. But if he fails to heed the admonition, he should first be brought to the attention of the superior before his offense is made public to the others who will have to prove his guilt, if he denies the charge. Thus he may be reproved privately so that his fault may perhaps be kept from others. If, however, he denies the charge, then others should be summoned so that he may be accused in the presence of all, not only by one witness but by two or three (1 Tm 5:20), and thus stand convicted. If proven guilty, he must submit to the punishment imposed by his superior or by the higher authority under whose jurisdiction the matter falls. If he refuses to submit to the punishment and does not voluntarily depart, let him be expelled from your midst. For this is not done out of cruelty but out of mercy, lest he ruin many others by his evil influence.

10. And let what I have said about the restraint of impure looks be diligently and faithfully observed in the discovery, prevention, manifestation, proving, and punishment of all other sins. This should be done out of charity for the neighbor but out of hatred for their sins.

11. But if any of you has so seriously fallen as to have secretly accepted letters or any kinds of gifts from a woman, let him be

pardoned and prayed for if he openly confesses his fault. But if he is detected and convicted, he must be more severely punished according to the decision of the superior or higher authority.

V. *Service of One Another*

1. Your clothes should be kept in one place and looked after by one or more brothers. They will see that they are well aired and kept free of moths. And just as your food is prepared in one kitchen, so your clothes are to come from one storeroom. If possible, have no concern as to what is given you to wear at the change of seasons. It does not matter whether you get back the same clothes you handed in or something worn by another, provided no one is denied what he needs (Acts 4:35). But if among you there arise disputes and murmuring because someone complains about receiving poorer clothing than he previously had and thinks it beneath his dignity not to be as well dressed as this one or that one of his brothers, by this you prove how lacking you are in that holy and inner garment of the heart, you who quarrel over bodily garments. But if your weakness is tolerated so that you receive what you turned in, nevertheless whatever you place aside must be kept in one place under the common charge.

2. This should be done so that no one may seek merely his own convenience but that all may work for the interest of the community with greater zeal and more readiness than if he were providing for his own individual interest. For it has been written of charity that it "is not self-seeking" (1 Cor 13:5), that is to say, it puts the interests of the community before its own interests, and not the other way around. The more you are concerned for the interests of the community rather than for your own interests, the more certain is your progress in the spiritual life. Thus through all the passing needs of men's lives something sublime and permanent will be revealed, namely, charity (1 Cor 12:31; 13:13).

3. Consequently, a religious who receives clothes or other useful things from his parents or relatives may not keep these quietly for himself. He should give them to the superior so that, as the property of the community, they may be placed at the disposal of whoever needs them (Acts 4:32; 4:35).

4. When you want to wash your clothes or have them laundered do so in consultation with the superior, lest an excessive desire for clean clothes defile your souls.

5. Neither shall the body be denied the proper hygienic care according to the requirements of good health. Let the physician's advice be carried out without objections. If anyone refuses to comply he must, at the superior's command, do what is useful for his health. But if a sick brother desires something that is perhaps not helpful, his wish shall not be fulfilled. At times something is believed helpful because it is pleasant though it may be harmful.

6. Finally, in the case of an ailment which does not externally appear, whatever a servant of God says about his illness should be believed without mistrust. Nevertheless, the physician should be consulted if it is uncertain that the remedy desired is helpful.

7. No fewer than two or three of you together should go to the public baths or elsewhere on necessary business. Nor should he who must go somewhere on business go with the companions he chooses; he ought to go with those whom the superior appoints.

8. The care of the sick and convalescent or those suffering from any weakness of health even without fever should be entrusted to a special brother so that he may procure from the dispensary whatever he deems appropriate in each case.

9. Those charged with the kitchen, clothing, or books should serve their brothers without complaining.

10. Books should be requested at a fixed hour each day. Whoever makes a request outside this time should be refused.

11. But clothes and shoes must be given to those who need them without delay by those in charge.

VI. *Unanimity and Forgiveness*

1. Let there be no quarrels among you or, if they arise, end them as quickly as possible, lest your anger grow into hatred and the splinter become a beam (Mt 7:3–5) and make your heart a murderer's den. For we read in the Scriptures: "Whoever hates his brother is a murderer" (1 Jn 3:15).

2. Whoever has offended another by harshly reproaching, insulting, or calumniating him should be quick to make amends and

he who was offended should forgive without reproaches. If, however, the injury has been mutual, both must forgive each other's trespasses (Mt 6:12). And this on account of your prayers, which should be recited with greater sincerity each time you repeat them. He who is quick-tempered yet prompt to ask pardon from one he admittedly offended is better than the one who, although less inclined to anger, finds asking for forgiveness too difficult. He who is never willing to ask pardon or who from his heart does not do so (Mt 18:35) has no purpose in being in a religious community even though he is not expelled. Take care then to avoid being too harsh in your words; but if they should escape your lips, let those same lips which caused the wound not be ashamed to speak the healing word.

3. Sometimes, however, the need for discipline may require you to speak harshly when correcting young people who have not yet reached adulthood. Even if you think you have been excessive in your language, you are not required to ask forgiveness. For if your conduct toward these young people is too submissive, then your authority, which they should be ready to accept, is undermined. In such cases you should ask forgiveness of the Lord of All who knows how much you love your brothers, even those whom you have perhaps disciplined too severely. Anyway, you are to love one another with a spiritual and not a carnal love.

VII. *Love in Authority and Obedience*

1. The superior should be obeyed as a father (Heb 13:17), with the respect due him, so that in him you honor God. This is even more true in the case of the priest who bears responsibility for all of you.

2. It belongs primarily to the superior to see that these rules are all observed, and if some point has been neglected to see to it that the fault is not carelessly overlooked but corrected and punished. Whatever exceeds the limits of his authority in this matter should be referred to a higher superior.

3. Your superior, however, ought not to seek his happiness in power which enables him to lord it over you (Lk 22:25–26) but in charity whereby he can be of service to you (Gal 5:13). As a superior let him be upheld in honor before you, as a servant

let him submit himself in fear before God. Let him be an example to all of good works (Ti 2:7). "Let him restrain the unruly, console the weak, support the sick, be patient with everyone" (1 Thes 5:14). Let him readily uphold discipline while instilling fear. And he should try to be loved by you rather than feared, although both love and respect are necessary. Let him always remember that he will have to account to God for the way he has looked after you (Heb 13:17).

4. By your ready obedience, therefore, you not only show compassion to yourselves (Sir 30:24) but at the same time also to your superior because the higher is his rank among you, so much the greater is his danger.

VIII. *Observance of the Rule*

1. May the Lord grant that you joyfully observe all these rules as lovers of spiritual beauty. Send forth the good odor of Christ (2 Cor 2:15) by your good way of living, not as those enslaved under the law but as those liberated under grace (Rom 6:14–22).

2. This little book is to be read to you once a week. As in a mirror you will be able to see in it whether there is anything you are neglecting or forgetting (Jas 1:23–25). And when you find that you are doing what has been written here, give thanks to the Lord, the Giver of all good. But if anyone finds that he has failed on any point, let him repent for the past and be vigilant for the future. Let him pray: Forgive me my trespasses and lead me not into temptation (Mt 6:12–13).

Selected Bibliography

I. *Works of Augustine*
A. Collections
Patrologia Latina. Migne edition. Paris, 1841–1842.
Corpus Scriptorum Ecclesiasticorum Latinorum. Vienna, 1891–.
Corpus Christianorum. Series Latina. Turnhout, Belgium, 1953–.
Bibliothèque Augustinienne. Desclée de Brouwer, 1969.
Biblioteca de Auctores Cristianos. Madrid, 1931–.
Oeuvres de saint Augustin. Paris. 1948–.

B. English translations in Series
The Works of Aurelius Augustinus. Edinburgh, 1871–1876.
A Select Library of Nicene and Post-Nicene Fathers. New York, 1887–1902.
The Fathers of the Church. Washington, D.C.: Catholic University of America Press, 1947–.
Ancient Christian Writers. Westminster, Md., 1946–.
Library of Christian Classics. Philadelphia, Pa., 1953–.

C. Journals
Revue des Etudes Augustiniennes. Paris.
Augustinian Studies. Villanova: Augustinian Institute, 1970–.
Augustinus. Madrid.

II. *Secondary Works*
A. Books
Armstrong, A. H., ed. *The Cambridge History of Ancient and Early Medieval Philosophy.* New York: Cambridge University Press, 1967.

Bonnardière, A. M. la. *Recherches de chronologie Augustinienne.* Paris: Etudes Augustiniennes, 1965.

Bonner, G. *Saint Augustine of Hippo.* Philadelphia: Westminster, 1963.

Bourke, V. *Augustine's Quest for Wisdom.* Milwaukee: Bruce, 1945.

———. *Augustine's View of Reality.* Villanova: Villanova University Press, 1964.

Bouyer, L. *The Spirituality of the New Testament and the Fathers.* New York: Seabury Press, 1963.

Boyer, C. *L'idée de verité dans la philosophie de saint Augustin.* 2nd ed. Paris: J. Vrin, 1940.

Brown, P. *Augustine of Hippo.* Berkeley: University of California Press, 1967.

Burnaby, J. *Amor Dei: A Study of the Religion of St. Augustine.* London: Hodder and Stoughton, 1938.

Butler, C. *Western Mysticism.* 2nd ed. New York: Harper, 1966.

Cayré, F. *Dieu présent dans la vie de l'esprit.* Paris: Desclée, 1951.

———. *La contemplation Augustinienne.* Paris: Desclée de Brouwer, 1927.

Clark, M. T. *Augustine, Philosopher of Freedom.* New York: Desclée, 1959.

———. *Augustinian Personalism.* Villanova: Villanova University Press, 1970.

Cochrane, C. *Christianity and Classical Culture.* Oxford: Clarendon Press, 1944.

Combes, G. *La charité d'après saint Augustin.* Paris: Desclée, 1934.

Courcelle, P. *Recherches sur les Confessions de Saint Augustin.* Paris: E. de Boccard, 1968.

D'Arcy, M. C., ed. *A Monument to St. Augustine.* New York: Dial Press, 1930.

du Roy, O. *L'intelligence de la Foi en la Trinité selon saint Augustin.* Paris: Etudes Augustiniennes, 1966.

Gilson, E. *The Christian Philosophy of Saint Augustine.* New York: Random, 1960.

Grabowski, S. J. *The All Present God.* St. Louis: B. Herder, 1954.

Hand, T. *Saint Augustine on Prayer.* Dublin: Gill & Son, 1963.

Henry, P. *Saint Augustine on Personality.* Villanova: Villanova University Press, 1960.

———. *La Vision d'Ostie.* Paris: Vrin, 1938.

SELECTED BIBLIOGRAPHY

Hill, W. *Proper Relations to the Indwelling Divine Persons.* Washington, D. C.: Thomist Press, 1952.

Holte, R. *Béatitude et Sagesse.* Paris: Etudes Augustiniennes, 1962.

Hultigren, G. *Le Commandement d'amour chez Augustin.* Paris: Vrin, 1939.

Ladner, B. B. *The Idea of Reform: Its Impact on Christian Thought and Action in the Age of the Fathers.* New York: Harper & Row, 1967.

Legrand, L. *La Notion philosophique de la Trinité chez saint Augustin.* Paris, 1930.

MacNamara, M. *Friendship in St. Augustine.* Fribourg, 1958.

Mandouze, A. *Saint Augustin, l'aventure de la raison et de la grâce,* Paris: Etudes Augustiniennes, 1968.

Marrou, H. *The Resurrrection and Saint Augustine's Theology of Human Values.* Villanova: Villanova University Press, 1966.

———. *St. Augustine and His Influence through the Ages.* Trans. P. Hepburne-Scott. London: Longmans, 1957.

Nash, R. H. *The Light of the Mind.* Lexington: University Press of Kentucky, 1969.

O'Donovan, O. *The Problem of Self-Love in St. Augustine.* New Haven: Yale University Press, 1980.

O'Meara, J. J. *The Young Augustine.* Paris: Etudes Augustiniennes, 1954.

Pellegrino, M. *Give What You Command.* New York: Catholic Book Publishing Company, 1975.

Plotinus. *The Enneads.* Trans. S. MacKenna. London: Faber & Faber, 1956.

Pope, H. *The Teaching of St. Augustine on Prayer and the Contemplative Life.* London: Burns, Oates & Washbourne, 1935.

Portalié, E. *A Guide to the Thought of St. Augustine.* Trans. R. J. Bastian, Chicago: Regnery, 1960.

Pourrat, P. *Christian Spirituality.* 4 vols. Westminster, Md.: Newman Press, 1953.

Reno, B. *The Order of St. Augustine.* Trans. A. Ennis. Rome, 1975.

Sullivan, J. E. *The Image of God.* Dubuque: The Priory Press, 1963.

TeSelle, E. *Augustine the Theologian.* New York: Herder & Herder, 1970.

Thonnard, F. J. *Traité de la vie spirituelle à l'école de saint Augustin.* Paris: Desclée, 1952.

SELECTED BIBLIOGRAPHY

Van Bavel, T. J. *Christians in the World*. New York: Catholic Book Publishing Company, 1980.

———. *Recherches sur la Christologie de saint Augustin*. Fribourg: Editions Universitaiies, 1954.

Van der Meer, F. *Augustine the Bishop*. Trans. B. Battershaw & G. R. Lamb. New York & London: Sheed and Ward, 1961.

Verheijen, L. *Nouvelle Approche de la Règle de saint Augustin*. Begrolles en Mauges (Maine et Loire): Abbaye de Bellefontaine, 1980.

———. *La règle de Saint Augustin*. 2 vols. Paris: Etudes Augustiniennes, 1967.

———. *Saint Augustine's Monasticism in the Light of Acts*. Villanova: Villanova University Press, 1979.

———. *Saint Augustine: Monk, Priest, Bishop*. Villanova: Augustinian Historical Institute, 1978.

B. Articles

Arbesmann, R. "The Concept of 'Christus humilis' in St. Augustine." *Traditio* 10 (1954): 1–28.

Armstrong, A. H. "Salvation, Plotinian and Christian." *Downside Review* 75 (1957): 126–139.

Aubin, P. "L'image dans l'oeuvre de Plotin." *Recherches des Sciences Religieuses* 41 (1953): 348–379.

Bardy, G. "Dons du Saint-Esprit (Saint Augustin). *Dictionnaire de Spiritualité* III, fasc. 22–23, cc. 1585–1586. Paris, 1956.

Boyer, C. "Augustin," *Dictionnaire de Spiritualité* I, cc. 1101–1130.

———. "L'image de la Trinité, synthèse de la pensée Augustinienne." *Gregorianum* 27 (1946): 173–199; 333–352.

Brunet, R. "Charité et communion des saints chez saint Augustin." *Revue d'Ascétique et de Mystique* 31 (1955): 386–398.

Cayré, F. "Dieu présent au coeur." *L'Année Théologique Augustiniennes* 13 (1953): 347–365.

———. "Le Mysticisme de la sagesse dans les *Confessions* et le *De Trinitate* de saint Augustin." *L'Année Théologique Augustiniennes* 13 (1953): 347–365.

———. "La Notion de sagesse chez saint Augustin." *L'Année Théologique* 4 (1943): 433–456.

———. "L'Oraison selon l'esprit de saint Augustin." *La Vie Spirituelle* 43 (1935): 255–263.

SELECTED BIBLIOGRAPHY

————. "Saint Augustin et la spiritualité contemporaine." Supplément: *La Vie Spirituelle* 19 (1929): 214–227.

Comeau, M. "Le Christ, chemin et terme de l'ascension spirituelle d'après saint Augustin." *Recherches de Sciences Religieuses* 40 (1952): 80–89.

Graille, R. "La spiritualité de saint Augustin." *France Franciscaines* 14 (1931): 473–503.

Heijke, J. "St. Augustine's Comments on 'Imago Dei' (exclusive of *De Trinitate*) Supplement III: *Classical Folia*, 1960.

Maréchal, J. "La Vision de Dieu au sommet de la contemplation d'après saint Augustin." *Nouvelle Revue Théologique* 57 (1930): 89–109, 191–214.

Maritain, J. "Concerning Augustinian Wisdom." *Degrees of Knowledge*. New York: Scribners, 1938, pp. 358–381.

McCool, G. "The Ambrosian Origin of the Image of God in Man." *Theological Studies* 20 (1959): 62–81.

Miano, V. "L'interiorita agostiniana." *Salesianum* 4 (1942): 120–142.

Moran, P. J. "Bibliografia sobre la Espiritualidad de San Agustin" (1925–1958). *Revista Augustiniana de Espiritualidad.* Madrid: 1960.

Morel, C. "La Vie de prière de saint Augustin d'après sa correspondance." *Revue d'Ascétique et de Mystique* 23 (1947): 222–258.

Smith, A. "St. Augustine and Religious Life." *Blackfriars* 35 (1954): 471–476.

Van Bavel, T. J. "The Evangelical Inspiration of the Rule of St. Augustine." *Downside Review* 93 (1975).

C. Collected Works

Augustinus Magister. 3 vols. Congres international Augustinien. Paris: Etudes Augustiniennes, 1954.

Living in Freedom under Grace. Rome: Curia Generalizia Agostiniana, 1979.

Searching for God. Rome: Augustinian Publications, 1981.

Index to Introduction

INDEX

INDEX

Liturgy, 4
Love, 12, 17; freedom and, 32–33

Madaura, 45
Mandouza, M. André, 36, 37
Mani, 49
Manichees, 32, 46, 49
Maréchal, J., 37
Martyrs, 5
Matter, 23
Maturity, 31
Memory, 13, 17, 18–20, 32
Mens (mind), 13, 18
Metanoia. *See* Conversion
Milan, 45, 47
Mind, 13, 18, 22–24, 29–33
Monasteries, 44, 49
Monica, St., 4, 11, 30, 39, 46–48
Morals of the Catholic Faith, The, 48, 51
Mystical Body, 41
Mysticism, 5, 35–42, 51

Naturalism, 43
Natural law, 20
Neoplatonism, 4, 6, 22, 37
New Academy, 47
Nous. See Mind

Old Testament, 47
Olphé-Gaillard, 37
On Catechesis, 51
On Christian Doctrine, 51
One and Many, 21
On Fasting, 51
On Free Choice, 35
On Genesis Against the Manicheans, 34
On Lying, 51

On the Gift of Perseverance, 35
On the Goodness of Marriage, 51
On the Morals of the Catholic Church, 48, 51
On the Morals of the Manichees, 48
On the Trinity, 15, 17–18, 22, 38, 40, 42, 51
On Virginity, 51
Oratory of France, 52
Origen, 41, 47
Original sin, 50
Order of St. Augustine, 52
Order of the Hermits of St. Augustine, 52
Ostia, 39, 48

Pagans, 49
Patricius, 45–46
Paul, St., 4–8, 10, 11, 19, 28, 38, 43, 47
Paul VI (pope), 53
Pelagianism, 29, 32, 49
Pelagius, 50
Pentecost, 43
Pius XI (pope), 52
Pius XII (pope), 52
Platonism, 10, 11, 13, 24; mysticism and, 37; reality and, 47
Plotinianism, 43
Plotinus, 6, 21–26, 36, 37, 38
Ponticianus, 11, 48
Porphyry, 21
Portalié, Eugene, 34, 36
Praemonstratensians, 52
Prayer, 9
Predestination, 34–35, 50
Psalms, 19–20, 39, 51

INDEX

Index to Texts

INDEX

INDEX

INDEX

INDEX

Servants: punishment of, 254–55;
  sons or, 253–54
Sight, internal, 366–67, 390,
  398–99
Sight, sense of: memory and, 125;
  temptations of, 151–52
Simplicianus, 80, 81–82, 83, 86
Sin, 197–98; forgiveness of,
  205–6, 289–92, 356, 417, 476,
  477; indwelling of God and,
  411, 417–18; lust, *see* Lust;
  nature of, 74, 275; original,
  94, 419, 460; pride, *see* Pride;
  repentance, *see* Contrition;
  unhappiness and, 352, 457
Singing, 486
Skill-knowledge, 278–79
Slavery, 449, 460–61
Sleep, 145–46
Smell, sense of, 129, 149
Social life, 435–38, 440, 446,
  453–55, 467
Soul: awareness of, 321–22; body
  and, 87, 438–39, 441, 467,
  474, 475, 477; child's,
  337–38; dangers, 441; food
  for, 173–74; happiness and,
  185; image of God, 166,
  336–37, 353–55;
  immortality, 336, 355,
  358–59; Jesus having, 404;
  journey, *see* Ascent to God;
  Manichean view, 61; nature
  of, 173; peace of, 456
Sounds, memory and, 129
Spirits: evil, *see* Devils; Holy, *see*
  Angels; human, *see* Soul
Spiritual body, 397–99
Stephen, St., 375
Stoicism, 435, 440, 443–44

Suffering. *See* Pain
Suicide, 443–45

Tactile perception, memory and,
  129
"Take and read" episode, 98
Taste sense, memory and, 129
Temperance, 190–91, 344, 345,
  442
Temples, 234; humans as,
  422–23
Temptations, 58, 145–46, 225,
  227, 228, 293, 477
Terence, 446
Testimony, belief and, 368–70
Thagaste, 482
Thought, 132, 338–40; memory
  and, 340; soul and, 173
Torture, 447
Treachery, 449–50
Tribes of Israel, 237–38
Trinity, 311–59, 395; charity and,
  297; definition, 311; images
  of, 166, 341, 358; invisibility,
  377, 389; lesser trinities, 335,
  339, 340, 341–46;
  omnipresence, 410–11;
  persons, *see* individual
  Persons
Truth, 142, 433; certainty and,
  436, 440; God as, 74–75,
  142–43, 159–60, 165, 192,
  315, 482; joy and, 141–42;
  memory and, 132–33; search
  for, 165, 178, 465
Trygetius, 165, 171, 172, 176, 178,
  183, 188, 193
Tullius. *See* Cicero, Marcus
  Tullius
Twins, 66–67

INDEX

Understanding, 339–40
Unhappiness, 184–86
Unity. *See* Community

Vanity, 158–59, 222, 336
Varro, Marcus, 433–36, 437–38,
    439, 444, 464, 468
Verecundus, 88, 102–3
Verheijen, Luc, O.S.A., 481
Vices, 442, 475, 476, 477. *See also*
    individual vices
Victorinus, 58, 81–84, 86
Vindicianus, 65
Virtue, 379, 472, 475; awareness
    of, 393–94; good, as, 434,
    438, 439, 441; loss of, 450;
    nature of, 173; peace and,
    451; vices and, 442–43, 445

Virtues (generally), 343, 344–45,
    346
Vision, 343

War, 446, 447, 449, 453, 455, 474,
    477–78; just war, 431, 449,
    460
Will, 317–18, 334, 339, 343;
    conversion of, 93–95; God's,
    396; perverse, 86
Wisdom, 331–59, 433; Divine
    Word as, 166, 268, 278–79;
    happiness and, 165, 178,
    187–91; throne of, 242
Witnesses, torture of, 447–48
Women religious, Rule for, 481
Word of God. *See* Scripture
Worship, 331

Other Volumes in this Series